COMPUTERS
AND
MANAGEMENT
FOR
BUSINESS

COMPUTERS
AND
MANAGEMENT
FOR
BUSINESS

Douglas A. Colbert

Senior Systems Analyst
City of San Francisco
and
Instructor
Golden Gate University
College of Marin

FIRST EDITION

petrocelli
books, New York, 1974

Library of Congress Cataloging in Publication Data

Colbert, Douglas A
    Computers and management for business.

    Bibliography: p.
    1. Electronic data processing--Business. 2. Com-
puters and civilization. I. Title.
HF5548.2.C55   658'.05'4   74-8038
ISBN 0-88405-064-5

CONTENTS

Preface   xi

**Chapter 1. USES OF THE COMPUTER AND ITS
            INFLUENCE ON SOCIETY AND BUSINESS**   1

Why Data Processing?   2
The Need for Computers   2
The Need for Business Computers   2
Scientific Need for the Computer   4
Practical Uses of the Computer   6
Summary   9
Key Terms to Remember   11
Questions   11
Coordinated Readings in Chapter 15   11

Chapter 2. COMPUTERS—PAST AND PRESENT   13

Computer History—The Beginning   13
Computers Come of Age   17
Computer Generations   24
Speed Comparison Between Generations   28
STAR and ILLIAC Computers   28

Summary   29
Key Terms to Remember   30
Questions   30
Coordinated Readings in Chapter 15   30

Chapter 3. WHAT IS PROCESSING OF BUSINESS DATA?   31

What Is Data Processing?   31
Steps in Processing of Data   33
Why Managers Need to Know about Processing   41
Order Writing and Billing   42
Summary   49
Key Terms to Remember   50
Questions   50
Coordinated Readings in Chapter 15   50

Chapter 4. APPROACHES TO COMPUTER PROCESSING   51

Methods of Computer Processing   51
On-Line Real-Time Processing (OLRT)   55
Off-Line and On-Line Operations   59
Other Processing Approaches   60
PERT and CPM   61
Summary   63
Key Terms to Remember   63
Questions   64
Coordinated Readings in Chapter 15   64

**Chapter 5. RECORDING SOURCE DATA FOR COMPUTER
                    ENTRY**   65

Cost of Data Entry   65
Symbol Representation for Man-Machine Communication   67
Problems in Processing Source Data   68
Is the Punched Card Dead?   72
Organization of Data   75
Why Documentation?   79
Key-to-Tape Recording   79
Key-to-Disk Recording   82
Coding Data   83
Summary   85

Key Terms to Remember 86
Questions 86
Coordinated Readings in Chapter 15 87

Chapter 6. COMPUTER NUMBERING SYSTEMS 89

Decimal Numbering System 90
Binary Numbering System 91
Binary-Coded Decimal System 95
Hexadecimal Numbering System 97
Binary Arithmetic 99
Summary 101
Key Terms to Remember 101
Questions 101
Coordinated Readings in Chapter 15 102

Chapter 7. ARCHITECTURE OF INTERNAL MEMORY 103

Characteristics of Internal Memory 103
Fixed and Variable Word-Length Concept 105
Movement of Data 107
Magnetic Core Storage 108
Binary-Coded Decimal Representation 112
Storage and Access of Data 115
Numeric EBCDIC Representation 117
Representing Letters in EBCDIC 120
EBCDIC and Hexadecimal Relationship 120
Summary 125
Key Terms to Remember 126
Questions 126
Coordinated Readings in Chapter 15 127

Chapter 8. COMPUTER HARDWARE AND SOFTWARE 129

Why the Computer? 129
Types of Computers 132
Defining Computer Hardware 136
Software 141
The Programmer 141
Software and Hardware Interaction 142
Auxiliary Storage and Channels 144

Summary   146
Key Terms to Remember   146
Questions   147
Coordinated Readings in Chapter 15   147

**Chapter 9. COMMUNICATING WITH THE COMPUTER—
  PROGRAMMING LANGUAGES**   149

Man versus Machine Communication   149
Creating the Stored Program   150
Programming Languages   157
Source Programs   163
Assembling versus Compiling   165
Program Listings   168
Summary   171
Key Terms to Remember   172
Questions   172
Coordinated Readings in Chapter 15   172

Chapter 10. HOW PROGRAMS PROCESS DATA   173

The Stored Program   174
How the Computer Executes Object Programs   174
Loading the Program   176
How the Control Unit Handles Instructions   176
Decision Instructions   176
Data Manipulation   180
Arithmetic Operations   183
Summary   184
Key Terms to Remember   187
Questions   187
Coordinated Readings in Chapter 15   188

Chapter 11. EXTERNAL TAPE STORAGE   189

Evaluation of Magnetic Tape   189
Tape Characteristics   193
Binary Representation on Tape   194
Efficiency through Blocking   196
Tape and File Markers   199
File Protection   200

Channels Improve I/O Performance   200
Controllers Oversee I/O Devices   203
Sequential Updating of Tape   205
Summary   207
Key Terms to Remember   209
Questions   209
Coordinated Readings in Chapter 15   209

Chapter 12. SECONDARY DISK STORAGE   211

Definition of Direct-Access Storage   211
Value of Direct-Access Storage   213
How Random Processing Works   216
How Random Access Works   218
Buffer Storage Speeds Throughput   223
Summary   228
Key Terms to Remember   228
Questions   229
Coordinated Readings in Chapter 15   229

Chapter 13. STATE OF THE ART   231

Integrated Circuits   231
Virtual Storage   232
Direct-Access Storage Devices   237
Data Entry   240
Data Communications   245
Summary   254
Key Terms to Remember   255
Questions   255
Coordinated Readings in Chapter 15   255

Chapter 14. OPERATING SYSTEMS   257

What Is an Operating System?   257
What O/S Offers Management   258
Operating System Levels   260
The Heart of an Operating System   260
Multiprogramming   262
Stacked-Job Processing   268
Input/Output Control System   274

Timesharing   277
Summary   279
Key Terms to Remember   281
Questions   281
Coordinated Readings in Chapter 15   281

Chapter 15. MANAGEMENT AND THE COMPUTER   283

The Computer—Challenge to Management   285
Impact of the Computer   296
Management of the Computer   306
Management Wants to Know   316
Involvement   330
Management of Data Bases   338
Security of the Installation   350
Technology and Future Developments   363
Society and the Computer   374

Chapter 16. A COMPUTER MANAGEMENT PRIMER   383

Traits of a Successful Manager   383
Management Defined   384
Planning in Data Processing   385
Organizing Data Processing Activities   386
Delegation of Responsibility   386
Span of Control   388
Coordinating Data Processing Matters   388
Directing People and Machines   389
Bypassing the Line of Authority   390
Motivating the Professional   392
Controlling the Resources   394
Managing through Policy   394
Staff Meetings   395
Summary   395

   Glossary   397

   Bibliography   413

   Index   415

PREFACE

This book is designed to satisfy the well-founded needs of data processing as defined by the business world. Computer education has been mistakenly concentrated on how to program the over 115,000 computers in 62,000 installations. A recent survey made by the *Journal of Data Education,* comparing college curricula against industry needs, revealed that a large percentage of companies in the private sector seek business students and managers with—

1. A broad knowledge of computer concepts.
2. The know-how to use and apply computers.
3. Management philosophies oriented toward computer systems.

The first 14 chapters of this book concentrate primarily upon the study of computers and their implications. Chapters 15 and 16 expose the student to managerial concerns and coordinate them with the technical aspects affecting computer-business interaction—the computer's impact upon the company, business people, and society. Chapter 15 comprises short, stand-alone sections for easy reference. Each of chapters 1–14 cross-references pertinent material to applicable management discussions, which are intended to be worked in as the student progresses in his study of the computer. In this way he learns how the computer affects work performance and how management utilizes computer systems to achieve maximum production and cost control.

Occupations, from clerical to marketing, are influenced by new computerized ways of doing things. A basic understanding of how computers work is needed in handling input documents and the processed results. As a result, businessmen and college students are required to learn how computers can aid management in running the company. In filling this requirement, several approaches recommended in this book are different from other computer texts for beginners: The introduction to the computer and related subjects is complemented by numerous illustrations. Thus, the student easily learns through visual translation of text concepts. In other words, the presentation is similar to that of a seasoned instructor using the chalkboard for his explanations. The technique of introducing management implications as the computer is explained allows the student immediate association with his ultimate objective—learning the functions of computer systems in specific areas of management.

The student is shown what happens to the data for which he will be responsible in the business world when it is processed and stored in the computer center. The reasons for transcribing information from an invoice into a punched card or other medium for entry into the computer are explained. The data punched in the card is shown in various parts of the computer system in a step-by-step illustration as it passes through the stages of data entry, processing, and printing of the finished product.

A program of instructions telling the computer what to do is likewise shown step by step. The program is graphically presented in the different subsystems comprising a computer. This technique demonstrates how a program works and how data is manipulated to give the desired results without learning how to program. This study of the computer should not only satisfy industry's needs, but should also fill an educational need for students who may not come in contact with a computer. Although the text is mainly business oriented, the social implications and the ways in which computers affect our lives are discussed.

Terminology is reinforced throughout the book. New terms are explained and then introduced later in a different context or expanded form. Thus the student does not have to disrupt his thought by having to search through prior chapters for explanations, and he learns how to communicate in business data processing terminology. Emphasis is upon understanding the relationship between the user's data and how he expects the computer staff to process the data, the accuracy controls that can be built into the system, and more.

In conclusion, I would like to express my appreciation to Carol Carter for her patience and valuable help in proofreading.

Douglas A. Colbert

COMPUTERS
AND
MANAGEMENT
FOR
BUSINESS

Chapter 1

USES OF THE COMPUTER AND ITS INFLUENCE ON SOCIETY AND BUSINESS

Data processing as it is applied today has evolved in recent years. Computers are everywhere handling masses of data for commercial, government, and scientific work. Some are forecasting business trends, others are planning travel in space (Fig. 1–1), and still others are busy searching for cures of diseases.

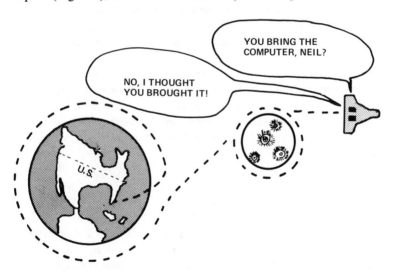

Fig. 1–1. Computers make possible achievements in space that otherwise would not be possible.

1

WHY DATA PROCESSING?

Data processing involves a group of people and machines organized to process the data requirements of a company. Its primary function is to control the use of a company's resources—people, money, materials, and facilities.

As we know, business concerns at all levels have one thing in common —competition. This compelling force, which pressures weak companies out of business, is the incentive for having a computer installed in the first place. Consequently, we can state that the decision to improve a firm's competitive position through computerization is based upon either or both of two essential reasons: to perform more work for less money; to achieve objectives through additional operations that would be impossible manually.

THE NEED FOR COMPUTERS

Americans have always faced limitless new frontiers. Some frontiers make life better, such as cheaper products everyone can afford or better transit systems to ease pollution and commuting. Today's frontiers also border on the future: for instance, the building of model communities and safer highways. The computer as a tool has made possible the crossing of these frontiers in leaps and bounds. It is being employed in new applications every day and the number of these new projects seems infinite. While the computer is being applied in a similar infinite variety of ways, the undiscovered ways in which it can be used appear boundless. Its future is really unknown.

High-speed processing by machines came into being to meet a growing need for information under increasingly complex conditions. Now computing machines are required in solving both business and scientific problems. In the beginning they were built mainly for government use in scientific and military applications, but business soon learned to employ them and now accounts for 86 percent of the market.

THE NEED FOR BUSINESS COMPUTERS

More people are engaged in handling, processing, and distributing goods and services than are engaged in their production. This means an ever-increasing volume of paperwork to handle. Processing this data usually requires performing repetitive operations, with few exceptions, on one document after another. Computers solve this problem faster than people can, and with higher reliability.

Computers installed in businesses usually act initially as superclerks. The reason is clearly accounted for by the increase in white-collar workers needed to handle the paperwork volume. Since the turn of the century, the number of estimated wage earners working in offices has steadily climbed:

1900   1 worker in 25.
1940   1 worker in 10.
1950   1 worker in 8.
1970   1 worker in 4.

Eventually, there would not be enough people in the labor force to handle clerical and professional work had this rate of growth continued.

Computers began solving the problem during the past decade or so. In addition to economic and efficient processing of paperwork, computers are used in the design of construction projects, forecasting business climates, and so forth.

Electronic Data Processing (EDP) is the input of raw data, processing inside the computer, and output of the results in meaningful form. EDP should not be justified on savings alone because in many cases, it has achieved a company's nonfinancial goals as well as its financial requirements:

Financial Needs

Financial objectives of a company include the following:

Reduce Operating Cost. Economy can be generally expected when a computer replaces other methods, since human participation in overall tasks is minimized; for example, preparing paper records and transferring them from one work station to another.

Paperwork Simplification. A company, for instance, sends a single computer-prepared check to a bank with payroll amounts to be posted to individual checking accounts by the bank's computer. Identification data and pay amounts for each employee are recorded via teletransmission between the two computers; thus a transfer of funds is effected without paper handling.

Accuracy. We know that people make mistakes in filing documents, performing arithmetic operations, and typing, but a computer does these tasks with virtually 100 percent accuracy, once it is set up properly.

Increased Revenue. Profits generally grow as a result of more sales-handling capacity and better customer relations resulting from prompt fulfillment of orders, both made possible by the computer.

Reduced Overhead. Computers update inventories of stocked items as issues and receipts take place, thereby eliminating overages and shortages. Fewer stock items in warehouses mean savings in storage cost as well as release of stock purchase money for other investments.

Nonfinancial Goals

A company's stability is often directly affected by its nonfinancial goals, which include:

Better Management Decisions. Useful reports and schedules can be designed to pinpoint areas requiring attention so that management can take action today to prevent problems tomorrow. For example, production and supply can be geared to equal demand. Because computers can measure labor efficiency, management can alter manpower requirements in order to meet varying production schedules.

Timely Information. When vital business information reaches a manager too late, something usually suffers. A customer has to wait for delivery, production may be slowed up, and decisions might have to wait. High-speed computers give prompt results and minimize the time lag between an event and its appearance in meaningful form.

Improved Quality of Information. A manager must be able to use the information given him; it cannot be too much nor can it be in the wrong form. Computers can be instructed to inform him of what is going right (blue shirts are fast sellers) as well as what is not going right (red shirts are slow sellers).

Improved Competitive Position. Computers reduce the time between receipt of an order and shipment of the merchandise. Therefore, quick handling of orders enhances customer service and satisfaction.

Helps Achieve Long-Range Goals. Decisions are made based upon information compiled and analyzed. The potential for rapid expansion is much greater when using computers because additional facts needed to accurately forecast can be taken into account in planning ahead. To illustrate: The best schedule for 15 jobs involves 1.3 trillion different combinations, which is far too costly and time consuming to compute by manual means.

SCIENTIFIC NEED FOR THE COMPUTER

We shall be studying mainly how computers help manage daily business affairs. However, since the computer has played such an important role in expanding man's ability to discover and prove challenging ideas, we shall mention some scientific progress as well.

Computers were first built to speed calculations made by scientists and mathematicians who were associated with the military complex. In fact, some computers were designed and built especially for the military; for example, computers named with acronyms such as the NORC for the Navy, ENIAC for the Army, and SAGE for the Air Force. Fortunately, attention turned toward peaceful uses of the computer.

In our exploding age of technology, the computer is irreplaceable. Two important demands on the scientific computer corroborate this:

1. Achievements are possible that might otherwise prove unconquerable. Consider whether Neil Armstrong and Edwin Aldrin could have rejoined their lunar module Eagle with the mother spacecraft Columbia without the aid of computers to tell them precisely where they were orbiting.
2. Time is of the essence in solving scientific problems. The computations required to dock the two space vehicles, Eagle and Columbia, would require several man-years if done without computers.

It is not an overstatement to say that most modern-day technological advances involve mathematical problems that are beyond the time limitations of manual computations. In many instances the actual success of scientific attempts may be directly attributed to the computer, since without it their pursuit would be impractical. Let us consider an important happening in the science of space exploration and astronomy.

Computer Helps Find a Tenth Planet

Neptune and Pluto, the last two planets found, were discovered mathematically before they were seen. An irregularity in motion or orbit of a heavenly body may be caused by some force other than that which determines its usual path. To illustrate: The orbit of planet Uranus was disturbed in 1846 and led astronomers to predict Neptune. Similarly, Neptune's orbit was observed to be disturbed in 1906 and led to discovery of Pluto by mathematical means, even though it was not seen until 1930.

A mathematician and computer scientist at the University of California Livermore Laboratory, Joseph L. Brady, has evidence that a massive Planet X may be circling the sun. Using a modern powerful computer, Brady completed in 100 hours the calculations of its orbit, mass, and distance. Computers of two decades earlier would have taken a million times longer.

The computer revealed that Planet X seems to be circling in a clockwise direction, as opposed to the other nine planets. Computer results also showed that the mystery planet is 300 times more massive than earth, six billion miles out in space, and requires 512 years to make its trip around the sun.

Computers Disprove Old Theories

Man cannot go into new areas of exploration and research unless he is certain that solutions to his problems are correct. The computer, in addition to proving new theories, has been used since its beginning to prove or disprove old theories.

For instance, the first electronic computer (called ENIAC) computed π to 2000 places in about 70 hours in 1949. William Shanks spent 20 years computing π to only 707 decimal places, and ENIAC proved that he had made an error in the 528th place.

Joseph Brady was using the computer to correct the orbit predictions of Halley's comet when he discovered the new Planet X. The passing near earth of Halley's comet has been repeatedly predicted erroneously. For example, the comet appeared four days earlier in 1759 and eight days earlier in 1682 than had been expected. The computer solved this problem for modern astrologists and has even pinpointed the precise date of Halley's comet in 87 B.C., which has been confirmed by Chinese astronomical writings.

PRACTICAL USES OF THE COMPUTER

As we have seen, computers are not confined to printing bank statements, controlling a company's inventory, and performing similar business problems. Engineers use them as powerful tools in proving and simulating their theories, just as scientists do. Computers calculate the best design for skyscrapers, bridges, and so on.

The extent that the computer can be used to help man advance civilization and technology may never be known. Before the computer, many projects could not be undertaken because of their immensity. But now its power is being harnessed to more momentous giant steps than those of the Industrial Revolution.

In some cases computers do work that seems to offer little practical use aside from learning how to use them. For example, besides playing chess by computer, what is the highest known prime number? No one really knows because of the mathematical work involved and the inconsistency of his calculations. However, a new prime number, 2^{11213}, was found in 1963 at the University of Illinois by Dr. Donald B. Gillies. The experimental ILLIAC computer was used in discovering the 3376-digit number.

In other cases the computer's solution has far-reaching implications: for example, in harnessing atomic energy for peaceful uses, sending men and satellites to other planets, and making significant strides in medical research (Fig. 1–2). Some samplings of interesting applications, of which we are often unaware, are given below.

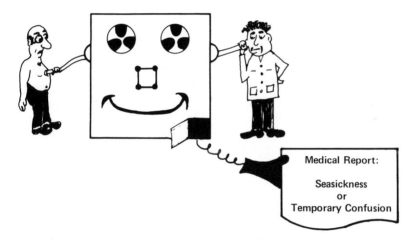

Fig. 1–2. Patient responses to medical questions, such as past diseases and ailments, are collected and evaluated by computers in order to free doctors from lengthy medical interviews, identify real problems in people who otherwise appear well, and safeguard against human error.

Computers and Safer Transit Systems

"Two Passenger Trains Collide, 85 Killed." Similar headlines appear in print several times every year. San Francisco's Bay Area Rapid Transit (BART) subway system is controlled by twin giant computers, one being a backup for the other. Only one attendant occupies the driver's seat of each passenger train. He is there in event of an emergency only and allows the centralized computer to control his train. The computer keeps dozens of the trains traveling at speeds up to 80 miles per hour, with as short as 90-second intervals between trains. In case two trains occupy the same block of track, the Westinghouse "Prodac" computer takes corrective action or automatically stops them.

Computers installed in jet airliners warn the pilot if he is on a collision course, and therefore reduce the number of mid-air collisions. By pinpointing plane speed, distance, and altitude of both planes, the computer signals the corrective direction that each pilot must take to avoid a collision. To eliminate human input, such as pilot error, computers in the future will control the vehicle during take-off, fly the jet to its destination, and land it. Computers on some planes now check out all working parts as the plane speeds down the runway. Should it discover something wrong, the computer shuts down the engines in time to stop the plane safely.

Computers Control Highway Traffic

California has some of the worst traffic jams and massive accidents in the nation, sometimes involving hundreds of cars. Now highway engineers are turning to computers to improve the changing of traffic signals at troublesome intersections. The result has been a smooth, constant speed of traffic, cutting delays and reducing accidents by 40 percent. At intersections, the $5000 minicomputers (see Section 34, Chapter 15) monitor the passing traffic 20 times a second to determine when the signal should be switched in response to changing traffic conditions.

Engineers are also using computers to design highways and overpass structures in ways that insure the greatest degree of safety.

Car Repair Problems Are Solved?

A mechanic's inspection of automobile problems has always been frustrating to owners. We have all experienced this statement: "It could be anything. Leave the vehicle all day so we can diagnose and correct the problem." Even after this inconvenience and the costly repair supposedly made, the noise will still persist. Volkswagen has pioneered an answer to this problem by installing sockets on their new models which can be connected to computers in VW dealerships. The computer checks the car and produces a printed analysis of the repairs needed, including the defective parts number.

A Plus for Data Banks

There is much controversy about computer data banks (see Section 35, Chapter 15) these days because of the far-reaching social implications. But here is one case in which most everyone will agree: Child abuse is one of the most appalling crimes in the nation. But how do we isolate valid accidents, such as a child falling down the stairs, from those cases where the child is brutally beaten? Perhaps this will never be possible, but some indicators have been found. For example, parents who bring their bruised and torn children to hospitals more than once are being investigated. As a result of pertinent information stored in a computer's data bank, many abused children are being placed in safer and happier homes. In large cities, however, a parent could take a battered child to a different hospital after each beating and never be suspected of having a history of similar child injuries. But this, too, is changing: Many hospitals are now linked to a centralized computer having an accumulated record of such cases stored in the computer's memory. Each case of possible brutality is checked with information in the computer's storage, and if a parent has been tagged previously, the police or public welfare officials are notified.

SUMMARY

We have seen that the happenings in the twentieth century have been greatly influenced by, and in many cases built around, computers. They have done for science and business what the jet plane did for air travel and the automobile did to relocate the population.

Computers came into being to meet the needs of scientific computations, but business soon learned how to apply them in profitable ways. It solved not only needs in the financial area but also nonfinancial problems that were too time consuming and costly to undertake. Once the paperwork problem was solved, computers were used to tackle business planning and the science of prediction. In addition, areas were undertaken that previously had to be ignored because of their immensity.

Other than contributing to business, computers make for more pleasant living by better schools and teaching methods, safer means of traveling, improved police protection, and recent environmental and pollution control.

As we have seen, the computer has assisted man in making great strides in space technology as well as other scientific developments. By comparing manual methods and their speed limitations with the electronic processes and speeds of computers, it is indeed within our comprehension to accept the computer as a marvelous benefit to mankind.

Up to this point the reading has been general and, in fact, similar to everyday articles found in trade journals and newspapers. The next chapter will consist of general readings also, but we should expect to find terms that will be used later. In other words, we have a vast amount to learn about using the computer in business, especially in the area of understanding data-processing terminology (Fig. 1–3). The latter involves a new world of strange talk, such as

bits and bytes	tape and disk files
buffer and virtual storage	software and hardware
tracks and cylinders	binary and hexadecimal
instructions and programs	MANIAC, Mark I, and more

Subsequent chapters will open the door and permit you to carry on a reasonably knowledgeable conversation about computer characteristics and data processing subjects. Do not be discouraged if you cannot immediately remember or understand these terms. They will be repeated often and redefined in more ways than one. For the business student and others who must eventually deal with data processing technicians and their strange dialect, this book bridges the communications gap. And as future managers, you will see that management control is the real key to the computer's importance in business.

Fig. 1–3. Data processing terminology must be understood in order to advance in companies that have computers. (Drawn by Mary Jo Pycha)

In the next chapter we shall follow computer development from its humble beginning to its present complexity.

KEY TERM TO REMEMBER

Electronic data processing (EDP)

QUESTIONS

1. How is the term *data processing* defined?
2. Without computers to process business data, what would be the impact upon today's labor market?
3. Pick the most important benefit that you feel computers contribute to management in the financial and nonfinancial areas. Defend your answer.
4. What do you think is the computer's most significant contribution toward scientific achievement?
5. The first computers were designed to solve which kinds of problems?
6. Of what significance is the fact that computers are sometimes used to disprove old theories and less sophisticated solutions to mathematical formulas?
7. Explore the ways in which data banks could be used to solve current social problems.

COORDINATED READINGS IN CHAPTER 15

"Finding Happiness in Data Banks," Sec. 35.
"The Computer's Effect Upon Management," Sec. 3.
"Depth of Management Involvement," Sec. 9.

Chapter **2**

COMPUTERS—
PAST AND PRESENT

Only a decade ago, computer professionals had a difficult time explaining what they did for a living. "A computer? What's that?" Now it is an everyday word that even small children recognize. Change has progressed so rapidly that now we can even say that we are "keypunch operators" or "programmers" and be understood.

Although the general public's awareness of the computer's existence seemed to materialize overnight, computer utilization did not. The transition from manual to computerized systems was slow in the beginning, but the pace soon accelerated. The computer has affected our lives so radically that we should devote an entire chapter to its evolution. Aside from the historical aspects discussed here, we should keep in mind the *new terminology,* which will be significant in later readings.

COMPUTER HISTORY—THE BEGINNING

The story of modern computing machines started in 1937 when a Harvard University Ph.D. candidate in physics, Howard H. Aiken, visualized and began work on a machine later called the *Mark I.* But significant milestones preceded his work.

The need to count has been recorded throughout history and early computers followed this trend of computational uses until the mid-1950s when commercial applications were introduced. The earliest man-made counting device was the abacus, invented in China about 2000 years ago. Next came the slide rule, invented around 1632 by the English mathematician William Oughtred.

The next milestone preceding the advent of modern data processing machines was the first known mechanical counting device. Around 1642, Blaise Pascal invented a gear-driven machine to count tax figures. His machine, the size of a shoe box, was used in his father's tax office at Rouen, France. In 1671, Gottfried Leibnitz improved Pascal's adding and subtracting machine by including multiplication and division. These forerunners of other mechanical devices relieved man of the labor of calculation, but their greater importance was that they demonstrated the practicability of mechanized calculation.

Automatic Punched Card Weaving Looms

In 1801 at Lyons, France, Joseph Marie Jacquard invented the first successful machine to operate automatically from information punched into paper cards. His machine was capable of weaving decorative designs into cloth according to instructions given by the punched cards. Fear of automation caused a mob to burn the weaving loom and beat Jacquard. Fortunately, this act gained the attention of Napoleon. The emperor's interest encouraged Jacquard to build other looms, and thousands were placed in French textile plants, thus gaining worldwide attention.

Babbage—The Father of Computers

Charles Babbage, an English mathematician at Cambridge University, began thinking of calculating by machine in 1812 and conceived the idea of a calculator he called the "difference engine." Due to the prestige and success of Jacquard's weaving loom in France, the British government provided Babbage with a £17,000 grant in 1823 to work on the difference engine.

Around 1830, Babbage turned his attention to a more complicated calculator, which he named the "analytical engine." It was to be steam-powered and to operate automatically from instructions fed by Jacquard's punched card. Suspending work on the difference engine in favor of the analytical engine alarmed the government and resulted in withdrawal of its financial support. As a result, the project was doomed, since in those days the expenditure of large sums of money for research was considered a waste.

Without giving up hope, Babbage continued with drawings of a machine that would store numbers, calculate them, and restore them for later use. His computer, versatile for those days, would follow instructions automatically when fed a predetermined sequence of cards. But the inventor never had a chance to construct his engine. He spent 20 years blueprinting his plans and used up most of his personal fortune. His hundreds of engineering drawings show that if his analytical engine had been developed, it would have operated similarly to present-day electronic computers with stored programs, punched card input, and printed output. The machine even had the capability of storing 1000 numbers of 50 digits each.

When Howard Aiken was well along with his work on the first large-scale Mark I computer, he learned that Babbage had covered the same ground a hundred years before. Although only Babbage's idea—not his machine—was similar to the Mark I, he is credited as the father of the computer because his work was so far ahead of his times. On the other hand, Aiken is acknowledged as the originator of the first practical computer. So, only today's techniques and technology are new, the concept having been known for more than a century.

Census Bureau Leads the Way

Mechanization was stimulated by the needs of the U.S. Census Bureau, which has pioneered better ways of processing masses of data ever since. The 1880 census was not completed until 1888. The statistics were compiled on large handwritten cards and handled or sorted countless times for different reports. It is this repetition of manual operations that lends itself ideally to computer processing.

The growing population, relocation of the population, and increasing need for more statistics pushed the demand for mechanization. Because the population had grown from 50 million to 62 million between 1880 and 1890, there was concern that the 1890 census would not be completed before the 1900 census. This delay would have prevented Congress from reallocating its seats, as required by the Constitution.

Lieutenant Colonel John S. Billings, an Army surgeon, suggested to the Census Bureau that data might be recorded on a single card by punching holes in it, and these cards might then be assorted and counted by mechanical means. His idea was associated with work he was doing in connection with the census, that is, compiling medical statistics. His suggestion was acted upon by the Bureau.

Beginning of Punched Card Data Processing

Although computers did not come into being until the 1940s, other electrical machines had been in use since 1890. Dr. Herman Hollerith, statistician for the Census Bureau, and his assistant, engineer James Powers, worked out a mechanical system using long strips of paper with holes. This was changed to punched cards, which were processed by a set of machines invented by Hollerith and Powers. The series of machines could electrically punch data into the cards, sort that data into the desired sequence, and tabulate the results.

The Hollerith tabulating machine and sorter (Fig. 2–1) counted by dropping rows of telescoping pins through card holes into mercury-filled cups, completing an electric circuit that caused a pointer to move one position on a dial. This first punched card tabulator could count 200 items per minute, and saved the Census Bureau an estimated $600,000.

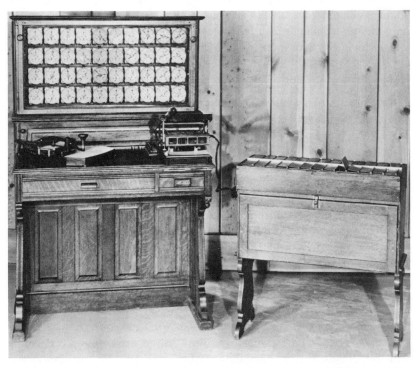

Fig. 2–1. Hollerith's tabulating machine and sorter used in the 1890 census was the forerunner of a series of faster, improved, and more sophisticated punch card machines used widely in the 1940s and 1950s. (By permission of IBM.)

Before the 1890 census was completed, Hollerith left the Census Bureau to work on the first mechanized job, a mortality rate for the city of Baltimore. He then established a tabulating service bureau and extended his mechanized methods to railroad accounting. His bureau became the forerunner of the giant corporation now known as International Business Machines (IBM).

Powers followed through with the 1890 census, completing it in 2½ years by using the Hollerith-named punched card machines. Powers also left the Bureau to form his own company, which became the forerunner of another giant corporation, Remington Rand (later, the Sperry Rand Corp.), makers of the famous UNIVAC computers.

COMPUTERS COME OF AGE

Aside from atomic energy, the twentieth century will probably be best remembered for the development of the electronic computer. Punched card equipment had faithfully served business and, to a smaller extent, scientific projects, including correction of manual calculations of the orbit of the moon. But faster calculations were needed and design of faster equipment, referred to as the computer, was imperative. Development did not happen overnight, as Table 2–1 shows. Therefore, let us trace the fast-moving life of the computer from its birth to the present.

Most computers have been electronic, meaning that the calculating portions have no moving mechanical parts. In the beginning, computers were made from electromechanical parts borrowed from the Hollerith punched card machines. An example of an electromechanical computer is the cash register, which comprises electrically driven moving wheels, gears, and other parts. Faster speed, increased reliability, and smaller components are the main reasons for using electronic components, such as the transistor, instead of the slower electromechanical devices.

Howard Aiken's electromechanical Mark I computer of the 1940s is considered to be the first successful automatic general-purpose computer, one that solved a variety of problems. However, two other computer developments were in progress at about the same time, one at Bell Telephone Laboratories and the other a private venture in Germany. Although, for unknown reasons, neither seemed to play important parts in future computer developments, they are worthy of mention.

The Bell and Zuze Computers

The first development, a special-purpose computer, was designed by George R. Stibitz at Bell Telephone Laboratories. A special-purpose computer is built to do only one job; for example, testing of antiaircraft equipment, which requires enormous amounts of computations. This model,

Table 2–1. Chronology of significant milestones in computer development.

Completed	Inventor	Development
1642	Pascal	Mechanical addition and subtraction device
1671	Leibnitz	Mechanical multiplication and division device
1801	Jacquard	Weaving loom run automatically by punched cards
1830	Babbage	Analytical engine with computer concepts designed but not built
1887	Hollerith and Powers	Beginning of punched card machines
1938	Zuze	Zuze series of relay computers appeared
1940	Stibitz	Bell telephone relay Complex Computer, first special-purpose computer
1942	Atasanoff	ABC; first small electronic computer
1944	Aiken	ASCC or Mark I; considered to be the first successful automatic general-purpose computer
1946	Eckert and Mauchly	ENIAC, first electronic computer
1948	Aiken and IBM	SSEC or Mark II, first computer where sequence of instructions could be changed
1949	Wilkes	EDSAC, first computer internally stored program in the world
1949	Eckert and Mauchly	BINAC, introduced magnetic tape as input and output instead of punched cards
1950	Bureau of Standards	SEAC, first computer internally stored program in the U.S.
1950	Forrester	WHIRLWIND, used magnetic cores for storage and cathode-ray tube similar to TV as picture output
1951	Remington Rand	UNIVAC I, first commercially produced computer; available to business in 1954
1952	Mauchly and Eckert	EDVAC, design included circuitry to check its own work and binary numbering system
1952	von Neumann, Burks, and Goldstine	IAS, widely copied computer because of its superior design concepts

called the "Complex Calculator," was constructed of mechanical relays, as were several of the early experimental computers. The Complex Calculator was finished in 1940 at a cost of only $20,000, much less than other computer projects. It used binary rather than decimal arithmetic and could do the work of 25 to 40 people. Five additional improved models were built, and the Model V could do the work of 225 people using desk calculators.

About the same time, Dr. Konrad Zuze was working in Germany on the series of Zuze computers. In 1938 he completed the mechanical Zuze Z1 with a binary floating-point arithmetic unit. But the Z1 failed to work successfully, and before he could finish the Zuze Z2, he was called into the German Army. A year later he was discharged from the army so that he could continue his computer work; the result was an improved model Z3, which was placed in use in 1941 at a leading German aeronautical research center. The Zuze Z3 would prove to be slightly faster than America's first large-scale computer, the Mark I. Although Dr. Zuze had projected an electronic computer as early as 1937, his Z22 with electron tubes did not appear until 1956. This was followed by the transistorized Zuze Z23.

As with many other research projects, neither Bell nor Zuze could gain financial support for their projects in the beginning. If they had received it, the course of history might have been altered. For example, inventor Zuze had to drop his project to engage in important military service in the German Army and was denounced for trying to gain permission to continue his work while serving his country. Ironically, an American computer (Mark I) proved later that the Nazi project for an electrically powered cannon could never have worked. Had the V2 rocket been computer-supported by the improved Zuze computers, the outcome of the war might have been different.

First Large-Scale Computer

Dr. Howard Aiken picked up where Babbage left off a hundred years earlier. Aiken, a mathematics professor at Harvard University, began work on the first large-scale automatic computer in 1939 (Fig. 2–2). He began planning the machine in 1937 and after six years of development work, with the assistance of International Business Machines (IBM), he completed the world's first large-scale computer and put it into operation in 1944. Dr. Aiken called his machine the "Automatic Sequence Controlled Calculator" (ASCC), later and more commonly referred to as Mark I.

Mark I was a large machine, 51 feet long and 8 feet high, weighed 5 tons, and had over 500 miles of wiring. This was the first successful attempt at combining all operations of input, processing, and output in a single machine. Its memory could hold 1728 decimal numbers, and adding two

Fig. 2–2. Mark I, first large-scale automatic computer, proved that an electrically powered cannon would not work for the Nazis. (By permission of IBM.)

numbers required only 300 milliseconds, a fantastic speed in those days. Mark I performed history-making work at Harvard Computation Laboratory for over 15 years. The computer was retired in July 1959, disassembled in 1962, and placed in the Smithsonian Institution.

First Electronic Computer

In spite of the fact that the electromechanical Mark I was a great improvement over other machines, scientists and mathematicians were collecting so much new data that they needed even faster calculators to handle the information. Since electronic pulses move thousands of times faster than electromechanical parts, the trend was clearly toward a more efficient electronic calculator. The first real breakthrough came in 1946 at the University of Pennsylvania when the Electronic Numerical Integrator and Automatic Computer (ENIAC) was completed (Fig. 2–3). But earlier, a professor at

Iowa State College invented the first small electronic computer, called the ABC (Atasanoff-Berry Computer).

Fig. 2–3. Mauchly's and Eckert's ENIAC, first electronic computer, became operative in 1946. Calculation time required to compute the trajectory of artillery shells was reduced to 30 seconds from the 20 minutes required by the mechanical analog computer pioneered by Vannevar Bush in 1930. (Courtesy of Sperry Rand.)

In 1942, Dr. John W. Mauchly, a physicist, and J. Presper Eckert, Jr., an electronic engineer, began formulating plans for an electronic computer that they hoped could perform calculations at fantastic speeds. The Department of the Army advanced the funds and the project got under way by mid-1943. The project to build an entirely electronic computer, except for input and output devices, was to be geared toward a general-purpose machine which was designed for more than one problem. Although it would be built mainly to calculate artillery ballistic trajectories, it was to be capable of doing other work also.

Mauchly, Eckert, 12 other scientists, and numerous technicians worked three years to develop the secret wartime machine. The first large-scale electronic computer, filled with 18,000 vacuum tubes, required 200,000 man-hours to build. The 30-ton awesome giant needed a room over 100 feet long and 15 feet wide. The tubes were linked by 500,000 hand-soldered connections, and the result was a computer a thousand times faster than the Mark I. It performed 5000 additions per second and consumed as much electricity as a large radio station. Clearly, Atasanoff was earlier in his ABC concept, but Mauchly and Eckert's ENIAC was far more important in starting the computer era.

A fast computing device had indeed been built. In 2 hours it could solve a problem that would take a hundred engineers a whole year to compute manually. But the impact was far greater than speed and accuracy because it contained advancements that would be adopted in other computers. Even though its effectiveness was somewhat restricted because of its small 200-digit memory and because it took a long time to change from one problem to another, the door was opened for still bigger and faster computers. ENIAC also has the distinction of being the first computer to forecast weather.

ENIAC was moved to the Aberdeen Proving Grounds in Maryland and operated with high efficiency and dependability until 1955. The most famous of early machines, the UNIVAC I, would be built around the concepts of the ENIAC. The UNIVAC I (*UNIV*ersal *A*utomatic *C*omputer), the first commercial computer (Fig. 2–4), was completed in 1951 by Remington Rand and introduced to business in 1954.

First Stored-Program Computer

The computer age had arrived and *one-of-a-kind* computers were being built by different inventors in rapid succession, each making a significant contribution to the next computer being designed. Work done at Cambridge University, England, produced in 1949 the first computer to operate from instructions stored within its memory, referred to as a "stored program." This model, called the "Electronic Delayed Storage Automatic Computer" (EDSAC), possessed another characteristic of modern computers, a means by which complex problems could be solved by putting together methods of solutions (computer instructions) previously used for simplier calculations. Input to EDSAC was a standard five-hole teletype tape, and output was in the form of Teletype tape or Teletype printing. Its memory was quite large, 17,406 binary digits instead of decimal digits.

Before completion of ENIAC, Mauchly and Eckert were constructing a computer that would also operate with a stored program. Although begun

Fig. 2–4. The UNIVAC I had a walk-in central processing unit and weighed about 60 tons. It was highly reliable and some models logged an impressive 600,000 hours. Average rental was $25,000 monthly. (Courtesy of Sperry Rand.)

in 1945, it did not become operational until 1952. Like the EDSAC, it employed the binary numbering system, explained in Chapter 6. This mammoth computer was named the Electronic Discrete Variable Automatic Computer (EDVAC). The EDVAC made an important contribution to modern computers in that it had duplicate circuitry for checking, known as "parity checking" (explained in Chapter 7). In general, parity checking means that any data moved within the computer's memory will be correct when it arrives at its destination.

Of these early computers, an IBM computer made the last conventional contribution to present-day computers. The Selective Sequence Electronic Calculator (SSEC), also referred to as "Mark II," was introduced in 1948. The SSEC was the first computer to employ selective sequence programming, meaning that the instructions did not have to be performed in sequence, that is, one after another. Instead, certain instructions could be bypassed. Thus, the series of steps to be taken by the computer could be altered by returning to subdivisions in the program.

Although other computers were built about this time, those mentioned here provided the most significant contributions to present-day electronic computers. The terminology used to describe these contributions will become clear as we proceed with our study of computers.

COMPUTER GENERATIONS

Prior to the computer era, the Hollerith punched card machines were used to speed up work. Each type of machine performed a separate operation such as sorting, calculating, or printing. In the modern computer these operations are tied together, whereas formerly a human had to combine them, which proved very slow.

We will speak of stored programs time and time again, but at different levels, as we progress. An internally stored program is defined as a set of instructions that tells the computer what to do. The advantage gained by inserting the instructions directly into the computer's memory is that an instruction is immediately available as soon as the preceding one has been performed.

The late 1940s were the experimentation generation of computers in that no single machine design was completely constructed before it became obsolete. A better machine would already be on the drawing board as a result of new methods discovered during the building stages of its predecessor. Many of these one-of-a-kind computers were constructed in rapid succession.

By the 1950s, all major design characteristics of these earlier computers and ideas from pioneers such as world-famous mathematician John von Neumann, A. W. Burks, H. H. Goldstine, Eckert, Mauchly, Atasanoff, and Aiken had been incorporated into a class of machines referred to as first-generation computers. Succeeding computers designed with major advances would be classified as a new generation.

First-Generation Computers

First-generation machines used vacuum tubes having a speed measured in milliseconds. A millisecond is one-thousandth of a second, or 0.001 second. Tubes were the weakest link in the computer and presented numerous problems such as excessive heat and unreliability. One can imagine the size of the air conditioning unit required to cool the ENIAC's 18,000 tubes by comparing it with a television set having 15 tubes. In addition, the bulky tubes contributed to the computer's tremendous weight.

UNIVAC I of the first-generation class was completed in the spring of 1951 by Remington Rand and delivered to the U.S. Census Bureau. The first commercial computer was also a UNIVAC I (Fig. 2–4), installed at the General Electric plant in 1954. It could tabulate at speeds of 30,000 items per minute. UNIVAC I came to the attention of millions watching the election returns of 1952 when it predicted on the first try that Eisenhower would win by 438 electoral votes. The prediction was valid, for he won by 442 votes, the largest landslide in history.

IBM's first-generation computer was the IBM 701 and delivery started at the end of 1952. Its speed was three to ten times faster (depending upon the type of operation) than UNIVAC I. In 1956, IBM had delivered 76 machines to 46 for UNIVAC. IBM has never relinquished the top place and now dominates about 75 percent of the market.

Second-Generation Computers

Transistors, rather than tubes, were the foremost innovation in second-generation computers. IBM introduced its popular transistorized 7000 medium- and large-scale computers in 1959. The even more popular 1400 series entered the market in the early 1960s. The IBM 1401 small- to medium-scale business computer, workhorse of the second generation, is still widely used. There were 8750 systems operating at an average monthly rental of $5400.

Transistors (Fig. 2–5) reduced the physical size of second-generation computers tremendously. In addition, they required less electricity and air

Third generation components
Fifty Thousand Transistors and Contacts

Second generation components
One Transistor and Contacts

Fig. 2–5. Tiny dot-sized miniaturized circuits used in third-generation computers shorten the time it takes to perform calculations because they shorten the distance an electronic impulse has to travel. (By permission of IBM.)

conditioning. But more important, they were much faster, operating in microseconds. Microseconds are one-millionth of a second, or 0.000001 second, permitting the execution of computer instructions at the rate of several hundred thousand per minute for the more powerful models. As an example, the second-generation IBM 7094 (Fig. 2–6) computed six times faster than the first-generation IBM 709 and ten times faster than the earlier IBM 704 computer. The IBM 704 was used in America's first space launching of Astronaut Allan Shepard.

Third-Generation Computers

In 1964 the revolutionary IBM System 360 was announced as a third-generation computer. The IBM System 370, enhanced by performance, hardware design, and cost, was introduced in 1970. Other computer manu-

Fig. 2–6. The large-scale IBM 7094 was the most popular of second-generation scientific computers. It was cooled by pumping chilled water through its casings. It rented for an average $80,000 monthly. Around 250 systems were operating before the third-generation IBM System 360 began replacing them. (By permission of IBM.)

facturers, such as Burroughs, UNIVAC, Honeywell, NCR, and Control Data also followed suit. Transistors had given way to miniaturized circuits, which operated in nanoseconds. A nanosecond is one-billionth of a second, or 0.000000001 second.

Engineers designed third-generation equipment (Fig. 2–7) so that new developments in circuitry technology, programming techniques, and new machine configurations could be incorporated without exchanging computers. The advancement further provided for a range of models that would satisfy performance-level requirements from small to superlarge. Thus the number of models in the IBM System 360 provides a program-compatible series of computers—a never-ending line as in a circle. All models are compatible so that a company's expanding needs can be accommodated by a more powerful model without data processing conversion troubles. In other words, a program of instructions written for a smaller configuration will also run on another larger computer in the series.

The fantastic speed in nanoseconds and virtually unlimited memory of third-generation computers owe their adoption to new circuit technologies

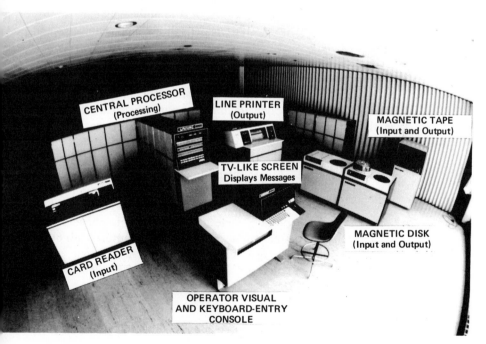

Fig. 2–7. An example of third-generation computers, the UNIVAC 9700 system.
(Courtesy of Sperry Rand.)

(see Chapter 13) known as monolithic integrated circuits and large-scale integrated circuits (LSI). The transistor has been replaced by the smaller integrated circuit, which can do the work of a transistor circuit that is hundreds of times larger. This faster speed is due to reducing the length of wiring interconnections so that electricity has less distance to travel. Although only a fraction of the size of a paper clip, the integrated circuit has the equivalent of over 150 separate electronic components.

SPEED COMPARISON BETWEEN GENERATIONS

Speeds of computers mainly determine how much work they can do. Not surprisingly, speeds have always varied between generations of computers and between models within generations (see Section 17, Chapter 15). For instance:

Speeds within second generation—The IBM 1460 could do twice the work (say, sorting 10,000 records into sequence) of the IBM 1401.

Speeds between generations—The third-generation IBM S/360 Model 30, commonly referred to as 360/30, is roughly equivalent to the second-generation IBM 1410. On the other hand, a single third-generation large-scale 360/70 can do the work of five second-generation IBM 7090 large-scale computers.

Speeds within third generation—The $7 million IBM S360/91 performs 16 million computations a second, four million more than the S360/85. It can calculate in one minute what it would take a mathematician 12,000 years or more to do. NASA's IBM S360/91 operates fifteen times faster than its predecessor, the IBM S360/75. In the IBM 370 systems, extended versions of the earlier 360 system, the medium-scale 370/145 internal performance is from three to five times that of the 360/40.

Just how far computers have come in two decades is phenomenal. Where it will end, if ever, no one can say. Control Data Corporation's 6600 was formerly the speed king, operating at 3 million instructions every second, but it was supplanted in short order by the newer CDC 7600, which operates at speeds up to 25 million instructions per second.

STAR AND ILLIAC COMPUTERS

A new generation of computers (see Section 32, Chapter 15) will likely follow with the combined architecture of two supercomputers (not planned for mass production), the $10 million CDC STAR (for *ST*ring *AR*ray) and the ILLIAC IV, built by Burroughs Corporation at the University of Illinois. Supercomputers act like thousands of smaller simple computers, all operating simultaneously. These two giants perform billions of operations a second and their mammoth storage is measured in trillions. Their applications lie in the area of weather forecasting, agriculture planning, and similar analyses requiring mass computations, but for the time being their manufacture is limited, due to cost restrictions.

SUMMARY

Modern computers had their beginning when Howard Aiken completed his Mark I in 1944 after six years of developmental work. The concept had been proved and the architecture was directed toward speed improvements. Mauchly and Eckert crossed the main threshold with their tube-filled ENIAC, the first electronic computer. A great deal of attention was being paid to the design characteristics and many brilliant pioneers were attracted. One was the world-known mathematician John von Neumann, who became acquainted with Eckert's and Mauchly's work. He joined the computer group at the University of Pennsylvania and later the Princeton University computer study group. His papers resulted in the basic philosophy of today's computer architecture, and these design features served in two of the earliest computers, the EDVAC and IAS (*I*nstitute for *A*dvanced *S*tudy).

UNIVAC I was the first commercial computer, introduced to business in 1954. Computers thereafter would be mass-produced and major advances in them would be classified as new generations. The first generation was characterized by tubes, the second generation by transistors, and the third generation by miniaturized circuits. Each generation resulted in smaller physical sized, but more powerful and less expensive, computers. The UNIVAC II weighed 60 tons and had a 9 foot high by 10 foot wide by 14 foot long central processor. Although thousands of times faster and larger in memory capacity than their predecessors, third-generation computers were much smaller in physical size.

It would be difficult to overstate the impact of computers upon business. As we saw in Chapter 1, the computer has also assisted man in making great strides in scientific progression. We shall now leave these general discussions about the computer and concentrate upon business computers and their applications use. In the next chapter, we discuss the vague term "processing of data" and the different methods of processing.

KEY TERMS TO REMEMBER

First-generation computers (tubes)
General-purpose computer
Parity checking
Selective sequence programming
Stored-program computer
Special-purpose computer
Second-generation computers (transistorized)
Third-generation computers (miniaturized circuits)

QUESTIONS

1. What significance does the study of computer history have upon modern computers?
2. Why do you think that the Bell relay computers and the Zuze computers had little, if nothing, to do with the design of early computers?
3. What is a stored program computer?
4. What does the term "selective sequence computer" mean?
5. What physical characteristic separates computers into generations?
6. Generally speaking, how is the speed of computers made faster?
7. What business requirement dictates the computer speed that a company should consider?

COORDINATED READINGS IN CHAPTER 15

"A Negative Approach to Computers by Management," Sec. 1.
"Management Sets the Pace," Sec. 4.
"When Does a Firm Need a Faster Computer?", Sec. 16.

Chapter **3**

WHAT IS PROCESSING OF BUSINESS DATA?

Just as the industrial revolution freed man from much manual labor, the computer revolution has freed him from much mental labor. In scientific and engineering work, the computer takes over the essential burden of calculating. In business, the computer takes over the repetitive tasks involved in processing of data.

This chapter clearly puts into perspective what is involved in computer processing, in order that our study about how the computer operates will be meaningful. In other words, our goal is to coordinate computer knowledge with ways of applying it in business.

WHAT IS DATA PROCESSING?

Data processing is the combined effort of people and machines organized to process the data requirements of a company. Output from the computer has unlimited uses, such as invoices for customers, inventory status for operational use by clerical staff, or management information (Fig. 3–1). Let us elaborate on the key words in this definition: data, processing, people, machines, and management information.

Data, which means fact or facts, can be thought of as elements of raw information needed in processing to produce the desired result. By way of example: A collection of raw information, unusable in its original form, may consist of:

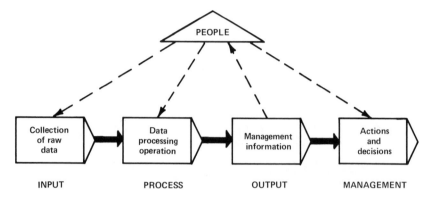

Fig. 3–1. Computer-management interrelationship.

Bank savings applications—names and addresses of customers, their account numbers, deposits and withdrawals, dates of transactions, dividends, current balances, etc.

College information systems—social security number, name and address of student and parents, sex, veteran status, date of birth, course enrollment, classroom assignment and instructor, credit hours and grades, tuition amount, degree objective, etc.

Merchandising applications—store number, cash sales, charge sales, cash refunds, charge refunds, sales and excise taxes, gross and net sales, merchandise codes and description along with on-hand balances, charge account interest, payments and ending balance, etc.

"Processing" is the term applied to reading and storing the data, handling that data by checking for accuracy and classifying it in preparation for calculation, performing decision-making operations, and summarizing the results for recording as output, such as bank statements (Fig. 3–2). Exact details of what is involved in processing a particular document are covered in the next section.

The computer must be regarded as a tool that accurately speeds up work and aids management in decision making. It does nothing without human guidance. Therefore, some people originate documents for input, other people instruct the computer how to process the data, and still others use the results. The success of a data processing operation, consequently, depends upon processing procedures and methods by which development is built around both people and machines.

The terms "data" and "information" are often used interchangeably. However, there is a difference in that data is turned into information.

CAROL CARTER	**STATEMENT**				ACCOUNT NUMBER	014-611-0	

CAROL CARTER
17 SHELLY STREET
San Francisco, Cal 94122

ACCOUNT NUMBER   014-611-0

STATEMENT DATE   02-28-74

BALANCE LAST STATEMENT	TOTAL AMOUNT CHECKS	No. Checks	No. De-posits	TOTAL AMOUNT DEPOSITS	SERVICE CHARGE	BALANCE THIS STATEMENT
703.03	770.79	15	2	745.82		678.06

Fig. 3–2. A summarized bank statement, the result of processing.

Accordingly, data consists of independent elements used for input, and information is the output results upon completion of processing, called "management" information. Management information comprises source data that has been organized into meaningful perspective to enable managers to control business activities. In order for the management information to be meaningful, it must have been needed in the first place, must reach the person using the product on time, and must be complete and accurate.

STEPS IN PROCESSING OF DATA

Chapter 1 described the processing of data as involving the input of raw data, processing inside the computer, and outputting the results in meaningful form. By way of illustration, let us discuss several major steps in processing of data, as shown in Table 3–1. In so doing, we cover typical data processing involved in an endless list of jobs performed by companies; for example, preparing billing statements based upon water, gas, and electric meter readings, and writing checks based upon invoices.

Table 3–1. Relationship of computer basic processing steps to the computer activity.

Computer Activity	Processing Step
Input	Recording and collection of input data
	Storage and retrieval of data
	Edit of input data
Process	Sort and classify data
	File maintenance
	Data manipulation
	Compute
	Summarize
Output	Report preparation and other communication means

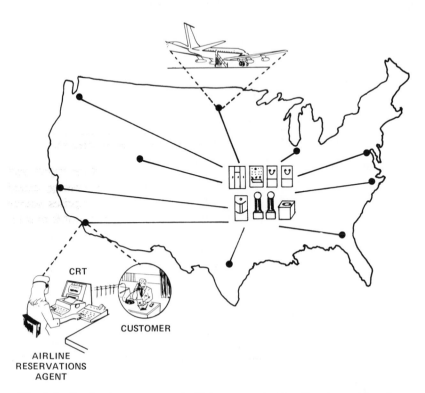

Fig. 3–3. Confirming a customer's flight reservation by directly entering data into a computer via a cathode-ray tube (CRT). The status of flights is displayed on the screen of the remote display terminal. The centralized computer handles reservations for all passengers traveling on thousands of flights.

1. *Recording and Collection of Input Data.* Ideally, the first step is to capture the raw data, such as sales at the cash register or passenger reservations counter, for direct entry into the computer (Fig. 3–3). If this is too expensive, source data recorded on documents such as invoices may be collected and recorded into one of several machine-acceptable input media such as the punched card (Fig. 3–4). Several approaches and methods on this subject are discussed in Chapter 5. For instance, data recorded in one form may be subsequently converted to another form to accommodate faster entry into the computer.

2. *Storage and Retrieval of Data.* A means of holding data in some form, such as the magnetic tape or magnetic disk (Fig. 3–5) is called "storage." Storage media have the ability to accept, remember, and transfer

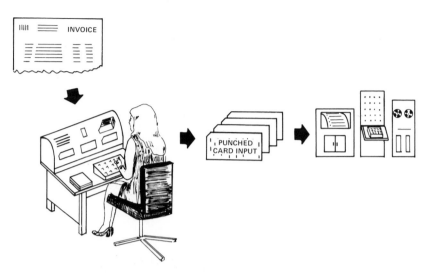

Fig. 3–4. Recording of data input. Data is read from the source document and transcribed onto the punched card in the form of holes in order to feed the raw data into the computer for processing.

data that has been stored in them. The process of obtaining the data from where it is stored is called "retrieval."

3. *Edit of Input Data.* Before processing, the input should be error-free. An important step, therefore, is to "edit" the data (Fig. 3–6), which means

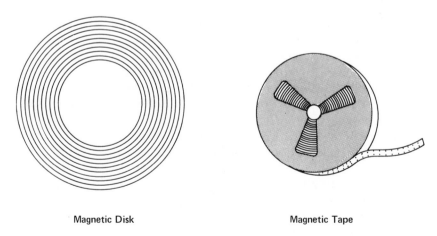

Magnetic Disk   Magnetic Tape

Fig. 3–5. Two common storage media.

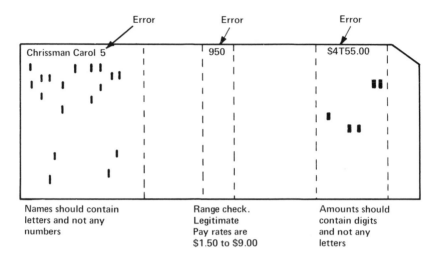

Fig. 3–6. Raw input data are edited for accuracy.

"to identify" erroneous input elements. Editing is the process of checking conformance to a particular pattern. For example, money fields may include digits, but not letters, Editing, therefore, gives added assurance that the input media has been recorded correctly, thereby reducing the possibility of having to rerun the final product because of incorrect data. In so doing, questionable data may be isolated and handled specially, returned to the originator, or subjected to other means of getting the data corrected.

4. *Sort and Classify the Data.* Sorting and classifying mean to arrange the data numerically or alphabetically into a particular sequence (Fig. 3–7), or to group similar items together or combine them with other data. For instance, insurance policy records may be in sequence by policy number, whereas automobile registrations may be in license number sequence. Of course we are familiar with codes that shorten data elements, such as the ZIP codes used to identify city and state. By using codes, identification is more exact. For example, there are no two social security numbers alike, but there are thousands of John Smiths.

5. *File Maintenance.* Up-to-date data is a vital characteristic of management information. File maintenance is the adding of new records, deleting obsolete records, and recording of transaction changes in order to update existing data before computing new balances (Fig. 3–8).

6. *Data Manipulation.* The manipulation process involves such operations as comparisons and moving data from one place to another within the computer. For example, the computer can examine arithmetic results to determine whether they are positive or negative. Two items can be com-

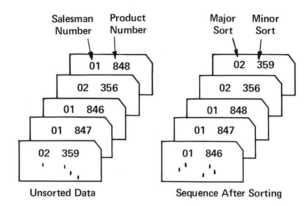

Fig. 3–7. Sort and classify data. **When two or more data elements must be
sorted, each element is referred to by its level of importance:** *major* **element
(most important),** *intermediate* **(middle importance), and** *minor* **(least
important).**

pared to determine if they are equal or unequal and which is larger. Based
upon the answer, the computer can be given courses of action to take, such
as the issuance of a purchase order when a particular item is below the
reorder level. In other cases, data is shifted to align decimal points (as in
Fig. 3–9), the results of arithmetic computations are moved to temporary

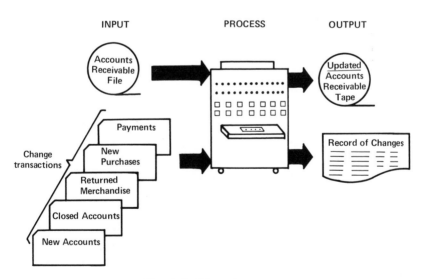

Fig. 3–8. File maintenance.

storage areas as intermediate answers, and so on.

7. *Computing.* Another form of data manipulation involves reading factors from a record such as a punched card and performing a series of calculations such as those required for social security tax contribution (Fig. 3–9), which is computed on gross earnings:

Total hours = regular hours + overtime hours
Gross pay = total hours × pay rate

Any combination of add, subtract, multiply, or divide operations can be performed. Also, a series of records belonging to identical groups can be read and their figures *accumulated;* for example, five daily time records for the same employee.

8. *Summarize.* Masses of data are often more valuable in condensed form. In order to give a manager a more usable tool, data for each group of identical categories (Fig. 3–10A) is often consolidated into single print lines (Fig. 3–10B). Information is useful at different levels. For instance, the detailed inventory transaction report is used by the warehouse and account-

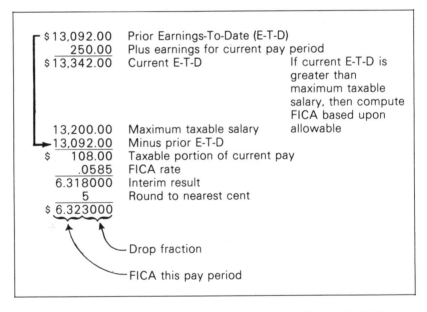

Fig. 3–9. Computing social security tax (FICA) illustrates data manipulation involving comparisons, arithmetic operations, rounding results, and decimal-point alignment. Since FICA is computed on a maximum gross earnings of $13,200, processing must take into account full taxation, partial taxation, or no taxation.

ing people and the summarized stock status report (Fig. 3–10B) is used by the manager of the ladies wear department.

9. *Report Preparation and Other Communication.* The end result of the processing steps just described is to communicate needed information to the user. This may be in the form of:

> *Report preparation* such as a Sales Report with totals allocated to proper classifications. Printing may be accomplished in many variations; for example, detail printing is printing of data from each record as it passes through the computer (Fig. 3–10A). Group printing is the function of summarizing groups of records, printing the total along with complete descriptive data to identify the totals (Fig. 3–10B).
>
> *Documents prepared for distribution,* such as payroll checks or invoice statements.
>
> *Information* that has been *updated* and *stored* for use as the need arises. For example, the cathode-ray tube (CRT), connected by telephone lines to the computer, displays the latest information about a particular flight in order that the passenger reservation clerk may confirm a seat sale.

WHY MANAGERS NEED TO KNOW ABOUT PROCESSING

The advantage of computer power is that calculations and processing which incorporate a wide range of variables can be run off accurately in a short time. The failure to find instant solutions for complex problems frustrates many managers. One reason is that many variables necessary to satisfy management requirements are omitted from processing. Consequently, the manager is not given the information needed for decision making. This situation is often due to his lack of understanding simple computer fundamentals and what is involved in processing. Because of this he does not know how to communicate his ideas of what variables are required. The result is that he makes wrong decisions, which cost a lot more money to correct.

Unless the problem is defined clearly and the data processing technicians understand exactly what information is wanted, the job will most likely be finished incorrectly and require rerunning. This is one reason why the term "electronic brain" is far from being a correct term for describing the function of data processing machines. Machines *cannot* think, will process data precisely as instructed by the human programmer, and in fact will process incorrect data as rapidly as correct data.

As an example, a report showing total sales by salesman and product

STOCK NUMBER	DESCRIPTION	UNIT COST	DOCUMENT NUMBER	TRANS CODE	TRANS DATE	OPENING BALANCE	TRANSACTION		ON HAND	PLANNING	
							RECEIPTS	ISSUES		ON ORDER	AVAILABLE
31051	DRESS 1 PC BROWN	13.75		1	15 MAY	49					
31051	DRESS 1 PC BROWN	13.75	09045	2	23 MAY		35				
31051	DRESS 1 PC BROWN	13.75	23141	3	20 MAY			49			
31051	DRESS 1 PC BROWN	13.75	71563	4	28 MAY				35	105	140
31052	DRESS 1 PC RED	13.75		1	15 MAY	93					
31052	DRESS 1 PC RED	13.75	23641	3	26 MAY			23			
31052	DRESS 1 PC RED	13.75	23750	3	30 MAY			14	56		56
31054	DRESS 1 PC BLUE	13.75		1	15 MAY	61					
31054	DRESS 1 PC BLUE	13.75	10133	2	16 MAY		15				
31054	DRESS 1 PC BLUE	13.75	09556	2	30 MAY		15				
31054	DRESS 1 PC BLUE	13.75	24100	3	21 MAY			70	21		21
31061	DRESS 2 PC GREEN	21.30		1	15 MAY	37					
31061	DRESS 2 PC GREEN	21.30	11304	2	27 MAY		25		62		62
31064	DRESS 2 PC YELLOW	21.30		1	15 MAY	55					
31064	DRESS 2 PC YELLOW	21.30	24169	3	17 MAY			15			
31064	DRESS 2 PC YELLOW	21.30	24250	3	18 MAY			40			
31064	DRESS 2 PC YELLOW	21.30	70411	4	18 MAY					40	40
31130	SUIT WOOL GRAY	37.16		1	15 MAY	26					
31130	SUIT WOOL GRAY	37.16	23190	3	21 MAY			5			
31130	SUIT WOOL GRAY	37.16	23195	3	22 MAY			7			
31130	SUIT WOOL GRAY	37.16	71355	4	22 MAY				13	15	28
31297	SLACKS TIGHT PINK	9.00		1	15 MAY	178					
31297	SLACKS TIGHT PINK	9.00	09643	2	29 MAY		80				
31297	SLACKS TIGHT PINK	9.00	24512	3	18 MAY			105			
31297	SLACKS TIGHT PINK	9.00	70480	4	19 MAY				153	30	183

Fig. 3–10. Typical reports. (A) Inventory transaction report (detail printing).
(B) Stock status summary (group printing).

STOCK NUMBER	DESCRIPTION	UNIT COST	DATE	OPENING BALANCE	TRANSACTION			PLANNING	
					RECEIPTS	ISSUES	ON HAND	ON ORDER	AVAILABLE
31051	DRESS 1 PC BROWN	13.75	1 JUN	49	35	49	35	105	140
31052	DRESS 1 PC RED	13.75	1 JUN	93		37	56		56
31054	DRESS 1 PC BLUE	13.75	1 JUN	61	30	70	21		21
31061	DRESS 2 PC GREEN	21.30	1 JUN	37	25		62		62
31064	DRESS 2 PC YELLOW	21.30	1 JUN	55		55		40	40
31130	SUIT WOOL GRAY	37.16	1 JUN	26		12	13	15	28
31297	SLACKS TIGHT PINK	9.00	1 JUN	178	80	105	153	30	183

SALES REPORT				
DATE	SALESMAN	PROD #	QTN	SALES
JAN 30	PAT COLLIER	3960	52	205.92
JAN 30	PAT COLLIER	4053	16	136.00
				$ 341.92 *
JAN 30	BILL SIMON	3960	49	195.33
JAN 30	BILL SIMON	4053	20	151.02
				$ 346.35 *
				$ 688.27 **
JAN 31	PAT COLLIER	3960	48	191.25

Fig. 3–11. Sales report showing minor totals by product, intermediate totals by salesman, and major totals by day.

for each day may be requested vaguely as "by product, by salesman, by date." In order to eliminate any confusion as to the correct sequence of data needed to produce the desired report (Fig. 3–11), each field is identified by its level of importance within the report. Major sequence is assigned to date, intermediate is assigned to salesman and minor sequence to product.

We may apply these terms to our names. Our last name would be considered major because it is the most important; our first name would be intermediate because it is next most important; our middle name would be minor because it is of least importance.

However, unlike names, classification of data can be changed by the user so that data of major importance in one report may be of minor importance in another. For instance, one report may show major totals assigned to salesmen and minor totals to product in order to compare the sales by each salesman and what he sold with sales by other salesmen.

What can or cannot be processed is one of the least understood facets of computer processing because of the instructional jargon used. We have discussed the major steps in processing, so let us continue by describing specific processing that might be employed in the preparation of invoices.

ORDER WRITING AND BILLING

Companies vary widely in their billing practices. Some summarize invoices, while others itemize purchases, computer taxes, or do other variations. Figures 3–12 and 3–13 show the billing of a typical medium-sized

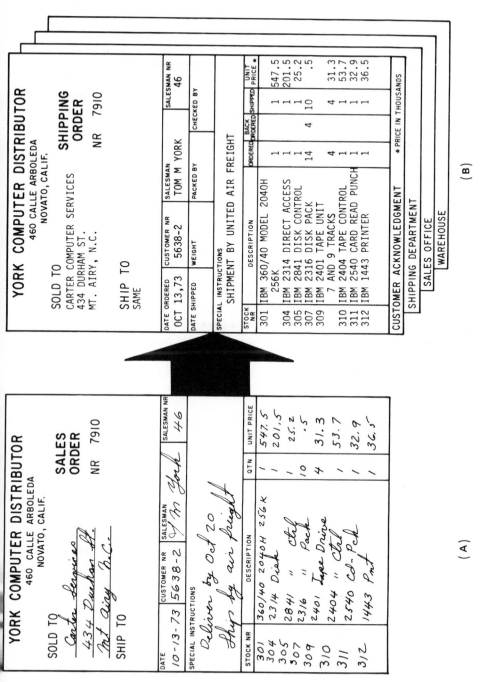

Fig. 3-12. Rewriting the order by computer assures completeness. (A) The handwritten order as processed by the computer (B) contains additional information necessary for billing and shipping.

43

computer system with equipment prices approximating those from the manufacturer. Once the seller receives an order and writes it up, the hand-written order (Fig. 3–12A) is converted by the computer into a form (Fig. 3–12B) that requests payment by the buyer. When the buyer accepts the invoice and approves it, the seller's prime objective is to deliver to the buyer the commodities or services ordered in the fastest, most economical manner and be reimbursed accordingly. Ordering is a sequence of operations, com-mencing with writing of the sales order and terminating with shipment of the goods.

There are numerous reasons for order writing. The source document, or customer sales order, originates with the vendor's salesmen or is received by mail. These orders will not be submitted in a standard form suitable for computer processing. They may be illegible, nomenclature may be wrong, and description may be incomplete. The advantages gained from rewriting the order are standardization of order forms, assured legibility, correct and complete description, and correct pricing and packing information.

Other advantages gained from order writing are confirmation to the customer that his orders have been received, notification of a shipping order (Fig. 3–12B), the packing list, shipping labels showing the name and address of the customer, a bill of lading to authorize a shipping company to move the merchandise, back-order control, notification to the customer of articles shipped, and order analysis.

Order analysis gives management an up-to-date picture of how sales are moving and gives ample warning of increased demand so that produc-tion can produce enough product to satisfy the volume of orders. Order analysis can be combined with tabulations of shipments in order to report on efficiency in filling orders.

Billing refers to operations, commencing with shipment of merchan-dise and terminating with forwarding of the completed invoice. Since over 90 percent of the information on the invoice appeared on the original order, the record created for order writing can be used for billing. Some differences between the order and the invoice are computed amounts for each item, taxes, and freight cost. The total for the invoice is added by the computer as the invoice is prepared.

Processing an Invoice

The invoice (Fig. 3–13) gives a clear picture of what is done by "pro-cessing," a vague term used to describe the selection, accumulation, and manipulating of data.

1. The billing and shipping address is copied from an accurate file of customers. Once recorded correctly, customers' names and addresses can

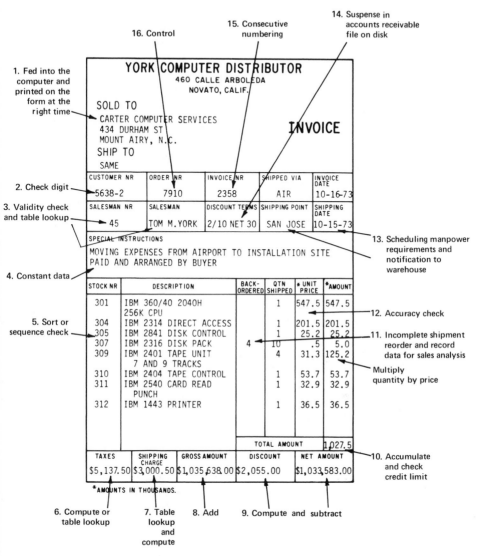

Fig. 3–13. Processing and controls involved in preparing an invoice.

be used time and time again on various documents such as purchase order, shipping list, and invoice. Processing of business data usually requires performing repetitive operations, with few variations from one document to another. Thus, a major advantage of computer processing over manual means is the elimination of retranscription of data.

2. A self-checking number is used with identification codes such as customer number or part number for the purpose of catching transmission or keypunch errors. For instance, a four-digit code has a precalculated digit appended to the basic number, making it a five-digit number. Correctness is verified by recalculating the check digit, using a special calculation technique (Fig. 3–14), and comparing the result with the digit in the record. An equal condition signals that the identification number is correct and catches over 95 percent of transposition errors.

3. Salesman number is compared against a table (Fig. 3–15) of valid numbers stored temporarily in the computer's memory during processing;

1. The units position and every alternate position of the basic code number are multiplied by 2.

2. The digits in the product and the digits in the basic code number not multiplied by 2 are crossfooted.

3. The crossfooted total is subtracted from the next-higher number ending in zero.

4. The difference is the check digit.

Example:

Basic code number:	6	1	2	4	8	
Units and every alternate position of basic code number:	6		2		8	
Multiply by 2:					x2	
Product:	1	2		5	6	
Digits not multiplied by 2:			1		4	
Cross-add:				1+2+1+5+4+6=19		
Next-higher number ending in zero:					20	
Subtract crossfooted total:					−19	
Check digit:						1
Self-checking number:	6	1	2	4	8	1

Other examples:

Basic code number	Self-checking number
45626	456269
30759	307595
73074	730747

Fig. 3–14. One technique for calculating a self-checking digit, referred to as modulus 10, is used to catch keypunch and data communications errors.

when a salesman's number corresponds with the stored number, his name is retrieved from the table stored in memory and is printed on the invoice.

4. Statements may be stored in memory as constant data during processing and printed on documents according to the agreement specifications in the contract.

5. Purchased items are sorted into numerical sequence according to the stock item number before printing. Previously sorted data can be checked to insure that data is in sequence.

6. Sales tax rates vary from state to state. The proper rate can be computed or selected from a tax rate table (see Fig. 3–15) applicable to the location of the sale in order to compute the sales tax amount.

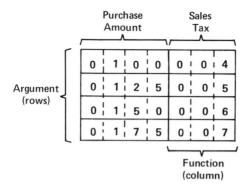

Fig. 3–15. A table is a collection of data elements stored in the form of a matrix consisting of rows (the argument) and columns (the function). A function consists of one or more data elements.

7. Shipping weights for individual pieces of equipment are stored in computer memory. In processing, each piece is identified in a weight table in order to determine the total weight of the shipment. Shipping charge is then computed, based upon the shipment mode (i.e., air freight) and rate (i.e., 50 cents per pound).

8. Gross amount is determined by adding the results of three previous computations: total amount, tax amount, and shipping charge.

9. Discount of 2 percent is computed, based upon the accumulated amounts of items shipped, and net amount is determined by subtracting the discount amount from the gross amount.

10. Individual amounts of ordered items are accumulated as they are printed and the total amount is printed after the final item has been listed. Customer credit is often set at a specified limit, and when the total order exceeds this limit, the computer writes a message to signal an overextension of credit limit.

11. Effective management control of a company's inventory involves preventing losses of sales as a result of insufficient stock while taking precautions not to overstock. Excessive stock reduces the company's profit through extra overhead and storage cost. It also ties up capital that could be invested elsewhere. Back-ordering is performed by the computer through issuance of purchase orders and monitoring incomplete orders to give management a trend of inadequate sales.

12. Unit prices are maintained, and updated as changes occur, in a table of values containing stock number, cost, and selling price of each product. As invoices are prepared, the unit price is retrieved from the table and checked to see that it falls within a range of preset values; this verifies that no price changes have been posted in error. In addition this operation serves as a cross reference to insure that the correct stock number has been used, since an error would result in an unsuccessful computer search of the table. When located, the unit price is listed and used to compute the amount by multiplying quantity times unit price.

13. As the shipping order is prepared, the computer can be used to include other shipments into the expected work load so that the warehouse can be notified via data communication means (similar to Teletype) of the schedule and pending shipments.

14. Information from the invoice is used to update the accounts receivable data (i.e., unpaid customer invoices). If payment is not received within ten days, the 2 percent discount is not allowed and the amount owed by the customer is increased in the accounts receivable ledger to the gross amount (item 8), due within 30 days.

15. Money owed to a company for merchandise sold or services rendered on a credit basis is controlled by the computer to minimize losses

from unpaid debts. A record of invoice numbers is kept in memory and a new one is created by incrementing the latest used.

16. Cross referencing, or relating two or more pieces of data to each other, is a power of the computer that far exceeds manual means. For example, consecutive numbers on the sales order make it possible to insure proper billing, and a cross reference between the sales order and invoice data gives methods to insure proper shipments.

At first glance the invoice appears to be a relatively simple document to prepare, consisting mainly of some printing and a few arithmetic operations. But there are unlimited ways to destroy customer relations and lose revenue through manual retranscription errors, mathematical errors, and failure of follow-up. As we have seen, the computer lends a strong hand in tieing together an efficient ordering and billing system, a result that is due to careful processing.

SUMMARY

Although the computer's capabilities exceed those of man in speed, accuracy, memory recall, and consistency in following instructions, people must direct these capabilities. Before doing so, we must first learn what data can be processed, after which we must master the computer mechanics that carry out our processing plans.

Data consists of facts that cannot be organized and used until processed into meaningful management information. There are several processing steps in creating management information, such as recording and editing input data, before updating and classifying it as the basis for calculation and report preparation. Detailed processing involves such things as looking up data stored in tables within the computer's memory and shifting data before arithmetic operations.

The billing process is probably the second most widely used data processing application, with payroll processing a likely first. The speed with which a businessman prepares his invoices can have a significant impact upon cash flow, and accurate invoices aid in keeping customers happy. Many businessmen realize this and attribute their increased growth to the efficiency of their data processing system. But in the final analysis, business growth is a direct reflection of management's success in solving problems, an accomplishment that would not have been possible without a knowledge of what is involved in the complex term "processing."

There are different ways in which computers process data and also different ways that computers operate to give the desired processing. In the next chapter, we shall introduce computer operational terms such as batch processing, random-access processing, real-time processing, off-line processing, and on-line processing.

KEY TERMS TO REMEMBER

Data manipulation
Detail printing
Editing of data
File maintenance
Group printing
Human Role

Management information
Processing
Storage and retrieval of data
Summarization of data
Table processing

QUESTIONS

1. Differentiate between the terms "data" and "information."
2. What is meant by the term "processing."
3. When we speak of "human guidance" in data processing, exactly what are we referring to?
4. Define the processing term "file maintenance."
5. Name several processing terms that would be classified as data manipulation.
6. What are the advantages of mechanizing sales orders?
7. Why should a check-digit code be appended to the customer number?
8. Of what value is data stored in tables?
9. What is the purpose of cross referencing?

COORDINATED READINGS IN CHAPTER 15

"Why Management Involvement," Sec. 2.
"Computer Exception Management," Sec. 10.
"Data Processing Manager in the Organizational Structure," Sec. 19.

Chapter 4

APPROACHES TO COMPUTER PROCESSING

Effective use of the computer does not necessarily mean the difference between so-many-dollars-in and so-many-dollars-out. Neither can it be measured in this manner. Benefits include new management information not available a few years ago.

Companies that do not put their computers to work in speeding information flow so that it better serves management will fall behind those competitors who do. Likewise, managers who do not upgrade their skills will find themselves trailing the field. More attention, therefore, must be put in gaining a sense of the computer's capabilities and in understanding computer jargon. Now that we have discussed what is involved in "processing," we turn to different approaches and techniques in which the computer can be employed in processing the data requirements of business.

METHODS OF COMPUTER PROCESSING

It would be ideal if data could be captured as it transpires, fed immediately into the computer for processing, and the results returned fast enough to affect ongoing business. Fortunately, this is neither necessary nor practical inasmuch as operational cost is involved for much of the data processing work. As we learn more about computer equipment, it will be clear that the cost of data processing largely depends upon the method of processing which in turn dictates the kind of equipment needed. To generalize at this point: The quicker the response, the more the cost. In other words, to get the processed results fast costs more money. For example, there is no pressing need to compute a payroll on a daily basis because pay checks are prepared only periodically. In contrast, computerized hotels must keep their room inventories current. There are three major processing approaches, each at different cost levels in processing business data:

- *Batch processing*—periodic processing of accumulated groups of similar data, such as in a payroll application.
- *On-line processing*—input for rapid processing at any time and in any sequence; for instance, inventory can be updated as transactions occur.
- *On-line real-time processing* (OLRT)—immediate processing of current data where time is critical and the results are needed while the action is still in progress, such as confirming reservations while the customer waits.

Batch Processing

The method of saving transactions for a specific time period and processing them in one computer run is called "batch" processing. Items in a batch may be processed in sequential order (i.e., 2 3 4 5 6 7) or in random order (i.e., 2 7 4 5 3 6), depending upon the size of the file. For example, it might prove beneficial to sort a large number of transactions into sequence in order to speed processing. On the other hand, it would be impractical to sort a few transactions prior to processing; therefore, random processing would probably be faster. Batch processing is often associated with sequential tape or card processing, but disks can handle data in a random or sequential sequence.

A payroll application is a typical example of batch processing. There is ordinarily no real need for maintaining current payroll information on a daily basis. Transactions such as time attendance cards, pay rate changes, additions, and deletions can be accumulated during the pay period until it is convenient to process them.

At the beginning of processing, the file is normally sorted to group together all records concerning a single employee. The computer then processes the first group of records, and the result, usually a payroll register and check, is written as output. The next record or group of records is brought into storage from the input device (for example, a tape unit) for processing. The process of computing the pay for each employee in a sequential manner continues until all records have been handled (Fig. 4–1).

From this we can surmise that storage capacity must be large enough

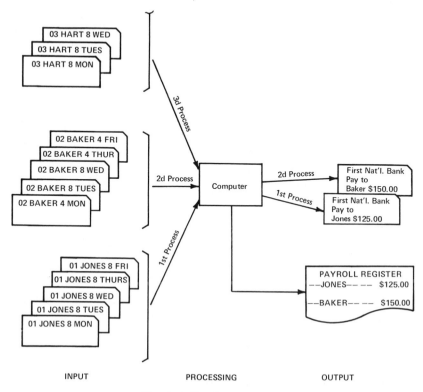

Fig. 4–1. Batch processing.

to hold the program that tells what processing is required, plus the data for one employee at a time. If all data for every employee had to be in memory at the same time, storage capacity would be greater and thus costlier.

We have described the basis of sequential processing. Each record is processed in the order in which it appears in the file; therefore, the file is normally in a particular sequence, such as employee number sequence.

Batch processing, which is the most common method, offers certain advantages. It is economical. Large volumes of data result in low cost per transaction and permit accumulation until the volume warrants processing. In addition, less expensive equipment can be used in batch processing, such as magnetic tape. On-line processing requires the more expensive magnetic disk.

The disadvantage of batch processing is the time delay caused when processing is done only if the accumulation of transactions warrants it. For example, updating the inventory file only periodically would result in over-stockage in some items and understockage in others. Consequently, this method is inadequate for inventory applications, where control demands that issues and receipts be posted soon after they occur in order to reflect the current status.

On-Line Processing

The answer to the delay caused by batch processing, such as the need to update inventory transactions often, is on-line processing. The inventory records are stored on line to the computer in large-capacity storage devices, such as disks. Disk storage is connected directly to the computer, making direct access of data possible (Fig. 4–2). Records are read from the input tape one at a time. The corresponding record is located in disk storage and brought into the computer. Then the transaction record is used to update the record from disk and the updated record is put back on the disk in the same place as the original record, thus destroying the old data. Because of this capability, disks are called "direct access" devices.

Disks can access records in random sequence, which permits random processing in any sequence, usually in the same order as transactions happen. This is the opposite of sequential processing, in which documents are accumulated, then sorted, and processed periodically in a predetermined sequence.

Random processing is somewhat like looking up a certain word in the dictionary. In order to find a word, we merely thumb to the index tab and then search for the word in the approximate location expected. This procedure is comparable to retrieving stored data randomly in that we have access to specific areas of the file without examining each individual word. In sequential processing, we would have to begin our search at the beginning of the dictionary and check sequentially through each word until the desired one was located, which requires excessive time.

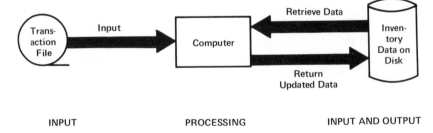

INPUT   PROCESSING   INPUT AND OUTPUT

Fig. 4–2. On-line processing.

In random processing, one record is available just about as quickly as any other, and is thus suitable for applications where data must be updated as transactions occur. For this reason it is also called "direct access" processing because any record in the file can be accessed directly. This can be contrasted to a reel of tape on which the first record in the file is available without delay, but the last record cannot be read until everything before it has been read.

In order to access any record in the file, a specially designed disk storage unit capable of holding large volumes of data is attached to the computer. The mechanics of disk storage and retrieval of data stored there are covered in Chapter 12. For the time being, we can think of a disk file as a set of disks, similar to stereo records in a juke box, stacked one upon the other with space between for an access arm. The access arm moves to the circular track on the disk where data is stored and writes or retrieves the desired data. Consequently, disks have the combined function of input (write) or output (retrieve), as conceptualized in Fig. 4–3.

The advantage of random-access processing is that it can retrieve any record directly from the disk file without searching sequentially, update the data in the computer, and return the new data to the same place on the disk. This allows updating data as transactions take place and therefore is a more current and timely operation than periodic batch processing. An important concept of direct-access processing is that any item can be fetched and displayed on a visual TV-like tube in order to determine the status, such as the on-hand balance of stock. The disadvantages are the additional cost for the disk device and the relatively slow speed in accessing records, which are usually not located adjacent to the last record randomly accessed. See Table 4–1.

ON-LINE REAL-TIME PROCESSING (OLRT)

The speed of processing for business systems varies with the particular application. Batch processing is used when the current status of the data is not critical, such as payroll applications. On-line or direct-access processing is beneficial when data must be updated rapidly, such as in inventory control. On-line real-time (or, simply, real-time) is closely related to immediate processing when response time is critical. Real-time processing systems are characterized by operations that receive input data, processing of that data while handling other inquiries, and making the results available fast enough to complete the transaction while the person waits.

By way of example, telephone confirmations of motel and plane reservations are more often made while the customer waits; thus, time is costly

Fig. 4–3. Access arms move between the stack of disks to write new data or to retrieve data stored on the tracks.

Table 4–1. General comparisons between batch and on-line processing.

Characteristic	Batch Processing	On-Line Processing
Typical application	Payroll	Inventory
Popular storage device	Tape or disk	Disk
Expense	Generally less costly	Generally most costly
When processed	Periodically	Usually as transactions occur
Sequence of data	Sequential or random	Mostly random
Terminal inquiry as to status of data	Rarely used because data is stale	Widely used, since data is as current as possible
Processing speed, few transactions	Normally slower	Normally faster
Processing speed, many transactions	Normally faster	Normally slower

to both the business and customer. Fast processing of such inquiries by the computer is directly related to the number of employees required to handle the confirmation of sales and provide information about the service. If a customer is kept waiting on the telephone because of slow computer response, he will simply hang up the phone and call another airline or motel that can furnish quick confirmations. To appreciate the speed necessary to handle real-time applications, imagine hundreds of passenger reservation clerks sharing the computer at the same time.

A real-time system is generally an on-line system, meaning that the direct-access storage device is attached by electrical cable to the computer. But on-line processing, which has a lesser time constraint, need not be in a real-time environment. For instance, although inventory control records need to be kept up to date, to what degree they are kept current depends upon the activity and size of the business. The updating of records within 10 seconds or 10 minutes is relatively unimportant in most businesses, if the stock on hand is adequate to fill present customer orders and those expected in the near future.

A real-time system can have remote terminals capable of transmitting and receiving data, connected by data communications lines (Fig. 4–4) to a centralized computer center. The terminals may vary from a few to over a thousand for huge airline reservation systems, and may be located across the hall from the computer or across the country. The 1970s will see direct communication between distant data terminals and a centralized computer (Section 5, Chapter 15) by orbiting satellites rather than by conventional telephone wires.

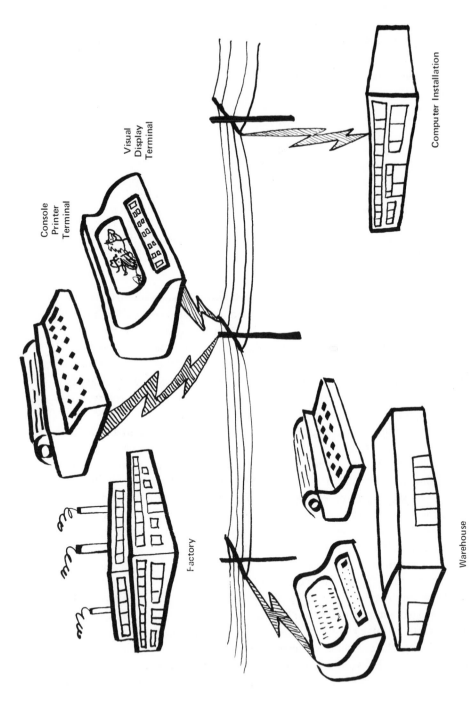

Console
Printer
Terminal

Visual
Display
Terminal

Computer Installation

Factory

Warehouse

Fig. 4-4. Example of a real-time system. (Drawn by Mary Jo Pycha)

58

OFF-LINE AND ON-LINE OPERATIONS

The terms "batch," "on-line," and "real time" involve different ways of processing data. Other terms distinguish the ways in which computers operate. "Off-line" and "on-line" operations refer to the computer equipment. Processing performed on auxiliary machines that operate independent of the computer are called off-line operations. On-line operations are defined as those operations performed by various machines, such as print and punch devices, under direct control of the computer.

Off-line operations are used mainly to relieve the computer of slow input and output operations. For example, a job requiring punched card or printed output may be handled in this manner. The computer records the data on magnetic tape, which is the fastest type of input or output media. Then the magnetic tape produced as output is converted off line to punched cards or printed documents. This process is called "conversion," a term applied to the change of one input or output medium to another by special-purpose equipment, such as a tape-to-print converter, thus releasing the computer for other work.

On-line operations are performed by input and output machines connected to the computer. This makes possible random processing and real-time processing, for instance. These operations require massive computer storage capability, which is very costly. The cost problem is alleviated by attaching a less expensive but slower storage device to the computer to hold the huge files at a reasonable cost. One such device is the magnetic disk, whose storage capacity is measured in hundreds of millions of numbers and letters.

Savings and checking accounts may be handled in real-time. Terminals at each teller's window in every branch office, for example, can be linked to the computer's on-line customer files.

We refer to the disk as being on-line to the computer because the data is accessible to the computer through electrical cables. Magnetic tape is on line if mounted on a tape device connected to the computer. Hundreds or even thousands of other reels of tape are off line, that is, stored in the tape library. Off-line storage, as a result, requires human intervention to make the data accessible to the computer.

Off-line operation does not necessarily pertain to conversion machines that perform functions which could ordinarily be part of a computer system. In many large processing installations, smaller computers are often used to support larger computers, and thus are directly off line from the main computer. Figure 4–5 shows an off-line processing system. Multiple key-display terminals located at points of data origin are connected to the off-line computer disk for entering data, which is immediately checked for

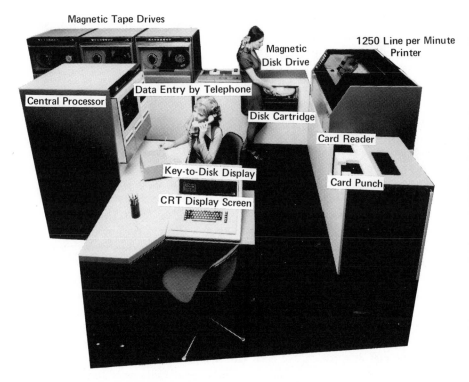

Fig. 4–5. The Mohawk Data Science 2400 system works off-line as an inexpensive slave computer in support of an expensive large-scale computer. (Courtesy of Mohawk Data Science Corporation.)

accuracy. After data-entry processing, such as sorting, the data is converted onto magnetic tape for fast entry into the costly main computer, which is reserved for computing and other processing having limited input and output operations.

OTHER PROCESSING APPROACHES

The computer allows new dimensions in processing ways that differ widely. We have seen how batch, on-line, and real-time processing can be used to economize and solve time-dependent problems in an off-line or on-line mode. Another type is "linear" programming, a technique used to optimize solutions through stating problems mathematically. This minimizes the calculations of many variables and is often used to reduce costs and increase profits. For example, a company may want to find the most economical shipping schedule or determine the optimum stockage level of merchandise. In a more unusual situation, a linear-programmed computer has been used to determine the best daily diet for cattle to improve the quality of meat while increasing profits by shortening the fattening period before marketing.

PERT and CPM

The computer programs PERT (Program Evaluation and Review Technique) and CPM (Critical Path Method) make possible the completion of complex, large construction projects on schedule; for example, the construction of New York's World Trade Center, building of jet planes, and skyscrapers. The computer analyzes the overall project into a network that shows when individual activities must begin and end. In other words, the computer shows what precedes and follows each activity as well as those occurring simultaneously (Fig. 4–6). The CPM, in essence, sequences the broken down components of a job that cannot be started until other jobs are finished.

Since a project's duration is controlled by about 15 percent of the individual activities, the critical path (longest distance between beginning and end) can be carefully planned and monitored to insure that these critical activities will not be delayed and thus prolong the project's completion. The computer calculates the earliest possible and latest allowable time for each event so that work can be expedited accordingly when trouble areas are pinpointed. In short, the known interrelationships between activities allow project engineers to plan corrective measures long before a problem situation may arise.

The PERT and CPM network diagrams are repeatedly updated in order to compare progress against original plans so that replanning can compensate for bottlenecks. Thus, PERT and CPM are used as aids in controlling both schedules and cost. For example, PERT, as developed by the Navy to accelerate its Polaris missile program, hit the target date almost three years ahead of time. Since cost may also be assigned to each activity within the circuit of a computer-generated PERT network, cost analysis is possible. Using this type of network, du Pont saved a million dollars on a plant construction project that had been estimated to cost $10 million.

Similar tools have been used to help management decide in selecting a new computer by evaluating the computer's performance. For example, such questions as these can be answered: How long will it take to program new jobs? How much memory is required for each job? How many programmers will be needed? What programming language

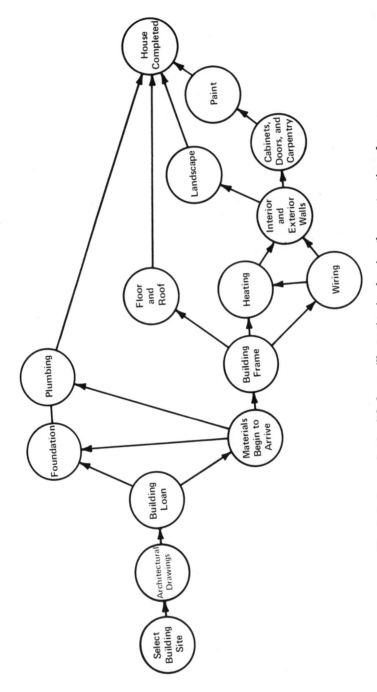

Fig. 4–6. An overly simplified CPM illustration in planning the construction of a house.

is best? Should the job be random-access or real-time processing?

Still another cost and time technique employed by the computer is "simulation." For example, the optimum stockage level for each item in a wholesale firm's warehouses can be simulated inside the computer by a trial-and-error approach to determine what happens when different quantities are received and sold. Consequently, management has many tools, such as PERT and simulator programs, that can be used in controlling manpower requirements and deadlines while minimizing cost.

SUMMARY

Computers provide management with flexible processing of data, for the usefulness of such information depends upon the speed with which it is made available to management in order to interpret and take action. However, there is always a trade-off between cost and timeliness. Information needed in order to plan for overtime will become obsolete unless it is received in time to correlate with current production volume. Management must choose, therefore, from among several alternative types of computer operations, each offering different speeds in processing at different cost.

There are three major approaches to processing of data: batch, on line, and real time. Batch processing has a time delay, but is the least expensive. On-line processing allows data to be updated on a current basis, but is more expensive. Real-time processing is the fastest of the three processing techniques, but the most costly.

In processing data, the computer operates in an off-line or on-line mode. The speed of processing varies widely with the type of business and application; therefore, each kind of processing is usually found in all data processing installations. In the next chapter, we shall elaborate on the first data processing function—that of recording and collecting data for entry into the computer.

KEY TERMS TO REMEMBER

Batch processing	Magnetic tape
Off-line computers	Response time
Off-line processing	Random processing
On-line processing	Real-time processing
Magnetic disk	Sequential processing

QUESTIONS

1. Why is it not practical to employ random processing for all applications?
2. Would a governmental income-tax system be a likely candidate for random or sequential processing? Why?
3. Which of the major processing approaches would be most suitable for a hotel reservations system?
4. The question, "How to meet a construction project deadline?", would be best answered by which advanced programming method?
5. What is the cost relationship between batch and on-line processing?
6. Remote terminals are of what value to a business with which environment?
7. If a smaller computer were a slave for a larger computer, would we refer to the slave computer as on-line or off-line?
8. What makes data either off-line or on-line?

COORDINATED READINGS IN CHAPTER 15

"EDP—Centralized or Decentralized?", Sec. 5.
"Why the Rising Computer Budget?", Sec. 13.
"Computers—Aid or Hindrance?", Sec. 6.

Chapter 5

RECORDING SOURCE DATA FOR COMPUTER ENTRY

In previous chapters we defined some of the functions performed by data processing. We also related the term "processing" to the computer's capability. In this chapter, we introduce a means of communicating with the computer in order to feed into it the data needed to accomplish the functions involved in processing.

COST OF DATA ENTRY

It is increasingly important for businessmen to know how much money they are making on a periodic basis rather than at the end of the year. This is possible only by costing their sales frequently, which means capturing every transaction and transcribing it into machine-readable language before processing.

Data entry, therefore, is an important and costly part of data processing, involving thousands or millions of transactions every month. Consider mountains of paper resulting from 50 million Americans using walletsful of credit cards. Preparing data for computer entry costs American businesses over $1 billion and involves about a third to a half of all data processing expense, or around 4 to 6 cents per record.

There was a time when the keypunch was the only way to convert source documents into a form acceptable to the computer. Today, there are hundreds of different recording devices, ranging from inexpensive portable card punches, to badge readers, to expensive machines which accept original source data such as that in Fig. 5–1. The problem warrants serious consideration by management because there can be considerable savings in data entry cost and because humans are the major cause of errors in recording and preparing data for computer entry. Management has a choice of several types of data recorders.

There are two basic categories of data entry devices, each group offering certain advantages and disadvantages:

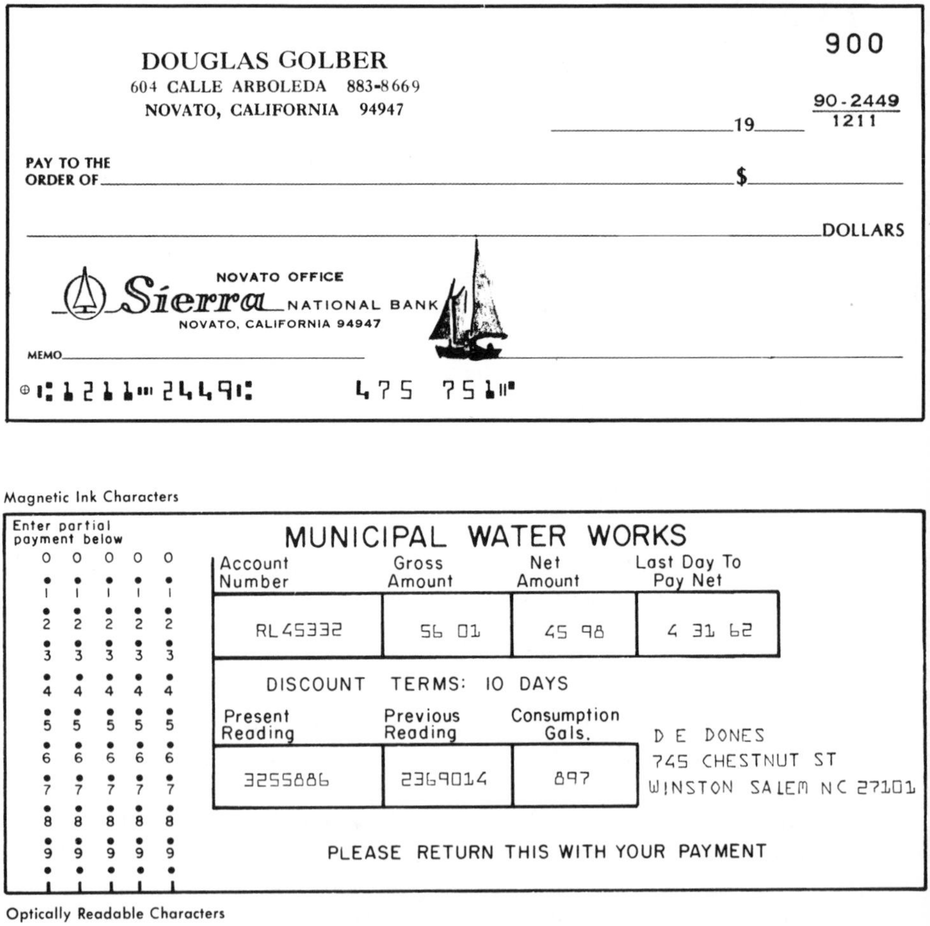

Magnetic Ink Characters

Optically Readable Characters

Fig. 5–1. Two types of direct-input source documents that are machine-readable by custom-built equipment.

- *Keying* data manually from source documents (see Fig. 5–6), such as sales orders, onto punched cards or magnetic tape, or directly onto magnetic disk for immediate processing.
- Machines that digest raw data, such as MICR (magnetic ink character recognition) readers (Fig. 5–4), developed to handle a mountain of checks estimated at over 60 million every day.

In this chapter, we shall mainly cover those of the first category, leaving the subject of capturing data by direct entry and at the point of sale until Chapter 13.

SYMBOL REPRESENTATION FOR MAN-MACHINE COMMUNICATION

Symbols convey information, but the symbol itself is not the information. It merely represents the data. The characters $ and % are symbols and, when understood, convey the writer's meaning. The dollar sign, when used with numbers, tells us that the representation is of monetary value and not the number of occurrences of an event. The percent sign, likewise, indicates a fractional part and not money.

Presenting data to a data processing machine is similar in many ways to communicating with another person by letter. That is, the symbols, which are letters, numbers, and punctuation (Fig. 5–2), are recorded on paper in a prescribed sequence and transported to another person who reads and interprets them.

Similarly, communication with a data processing machine requires that data be reduced to a set of symbols that can be read, interpreted, and acted upon by a certain machine. Some machines do not accept the same "language" as other machines, but there are data processing techniques and machines to convert the symbols to a compatible language. The important fact is that data can be represented by symbols, which become a language of communication between people and machines.

Information to be used as input to data processing machines may be in the form of punched cards, paper tape, or magnetic tape (see Fig. 5–3), and forms of direct input described in later chapters. Data is represented on the card by the presence or absence of small, rectangular holes in specific locations. In a similar manner, circular holes along a paper tape represent data. On magnetic tape, the symbols are invisible magnetized areas, called "bits," arranged in specific patterns.

In the processing machines, data is stored by many electrical and electronic components: magnetic cores, transistors, magnetic disks, and

Fig. 5–2. Symbols for communication.

drums. The storage and flow of data through these devices are represented as electronic signals. The presence or absence of these signals is the method of representing data. The representation and physical makeup are covered in detail in subsequent chapters.

PROBLEMS IN PROCESSING SOURCE DATA

Converting source documents into a language the machines will accept has long been recognized as the bottleneck of data processing. Although machines can process data at seemingly impossible speeds, most original input data has been recorded previously by manual means.

The solution would be to use all source data in its original state, thus eliminating retranscription or coding to facilitate machine processing. However, the problems confronting engineers in developing machines to digest raw data are staggering. Some of the reasons are: different document sizes, handwritten data, numerous methods for recording data, and multiple or dissimilar transactions on a single document. Some industries have solved the bottleneck with custom-built machines (Fig. 5–4).

In 1958, an estimated 10 billion checks circulated in the United States. Each check required handling six or more times. The rate had risen to 13

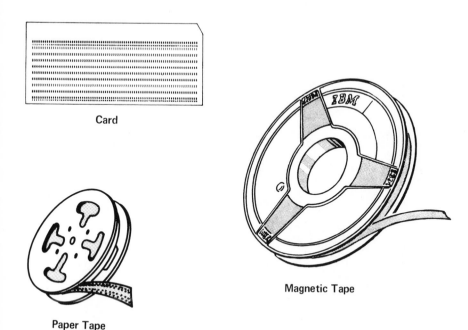

Card

Magnetic Tape

Paper Tape

Fig. 5–3. Forms of input.

billion by 1961, over 18 billion in 1967, and is estimated at 45 billion by 1980. To cope with this uncontrollable mountain of paper, computer manufacturers, in cooperation with the American Bankers Association, developed magnetic character sensing. Specific data, such as the bank of origin, depositor's account number, and other essential data, is preprinted at the bottom of the check by magnetic recording. The amount of the check is recorded with magnetic ink when it is presented at the bank for payment. Then the check can be processed as many times as necessary at computer speed, eliminating manual handling at banks and clearinghouses.

The advantages gained have been the limitation of keypunching and verifying, and the ability of both man and machine to directly read the recorded data. From an ultimate recording-solution standpoint, disadvantages exist. *Magnetic ink character recognition* (MICR) machines will read only certain kinds of type and will not read handwriting. Moreover, production cost is high, since the machines are custom-built for specific applications.

The oil industry has solved its input bottleneck by issuing to its customers plastic credit cards embossed with their names and account numbers. Briefly, the recording necessary to bill a customer occurs as follows: After

Fig. 5–4. The IBM magnetic character reader reads checks directly into the computer without transcribing data manually on punched cards or other input medium. (By permission of IBM.)

filling the gas tank, the service station attendant inserts the customer's credit card and a billing form in a data recorder (Fig. 5–5). He moves variable keys to the numeric position corresponding to the gas purchase. When he actuates the impression lever, the customer's account number and the purchase amount are imprinted onto the hard copy of the billing form. The imprinted card is processed at the oil company's data processing center. Optical character recognition equipment scans the imprinted data and transfers it onto magnetic tape or magnetic disk in order to process the billing operation. Again, the end results are elimination of manual punching and increased accuracy.

While progress is being made in the document-recording area, the keypunch is the machine most used for transcribing written data into punches in a card. Although it is not the intent of this chapter to teach card

Fig. 5–5. Gasoline purchases are imprinted on a preprinted billing form. (Courtesy of Addressograph-Multigraph Corp.).

punching, the essentials should be known to anyone studying data processing.

IS THE PUNCHED CARD DEAD?

"Obsolesence," more than any other data processing term, is the word associated more often with the punched card. In fact, its demise was predicted over a decade ago. Yet, over 300,000 keypunches and verifiers are now in use in the United States alone, and IBM continues to ship 5000 keypunches every month.

Card punches, also called "keypunches" (Fig. 5–6), offer the simplest method of converting data for computer input. Consequently, the punched card leads other data entry media. The most visible advantage of the punched card is its readability, "handability," and its ease of correction. For these reasons, it is the most effective solution in some cases. Thus, the punched card is not easily written off and will probably never die, although steady inroads are being made by replacement systems, explained later in this chapter.

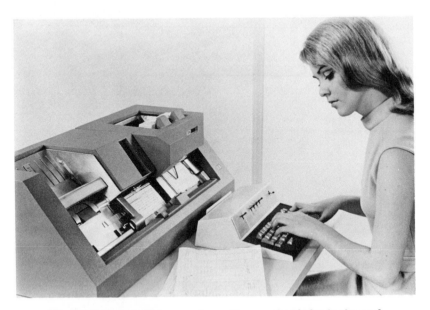

Fig. 5–6. The IBM 29 keypunch machine punches holes in the card corresponding to fields read from the transaction document.

How to Read a Punched Card

The punched card is often called "unit record." According to the unit-record principle, all data concerning a single transaction is recorded in one punched card and the punched data remains the same for each use of the card. Once the data is punched onto the card, it becomes a permanent record that may be repeatedly processed at computer speeds. Various reports may be prepared by using the same cards over and over, thus eliminating the need to recopy the data.

The Hollerith punched card, named after its innovator, Herman Hollerith of the U.S. Census Bureau machines fame, stored data represented on the card in the form of punched holes. The horizontal face of the card is divided into rows (Fig. 5–7), and each row is subdivided into columns. Each column of the card is designed to accommodate one of the digits 0 to 9, the letters A to Z, or certain special characters such as the dollar sign. We shall concern ourselves primarily with the numbers and letters.

The Hollerith card is composed of 80 vertical columns, numbered from left to right. There are 12 vertical punching positions in each column, designated from the top to the bottom of the card by 12, 11, 0, 1, 2, 3, 4, 5, 6, 7, 8, and 9. The punching positions 0 to 9 are preprinted on the card and represent the value associated with it.

The top edge of the card is known as the "12 edge" and the bottom of the card is known as the "9 edge." These designations are made because

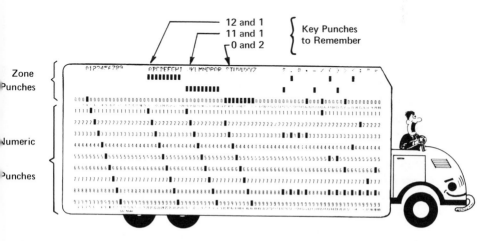

Fig. 5–7. The punched card, a vehicle to carry and store data.

cards are fed through machines that require either 9-edge first or 12 edge first.

Numeric Requires One Punch. One numeric digit is recorded on the card by punching a single hole in a given column. Since each column consists of ten numerical rows ranging in value from 0 to 9, the position punched represents that digit. For example, a hole in the 7 row has the decimal value of 7. To illustrate a multiple-digit field in columns 1 and 2, employee number 65 would be recorded by a hole punched in the 6 position of column 1 and another hole punched in the 5 position of column 2.

Alphabetic Requires Two Punches. Alphabetic data is represented by a combination of two punches, a numeric punch and a zone punch. The three zone punches are:

    12 zone, associated with the letters A to I
    11 zone, associated with the letters J to R
     0 zone, associated with the letters S to Z

The 0-zone position is the same as the numerical 0. It is not important to memorize the letters, but it is wise to remember the 12 and A, 11 and J, 0 and S relationship. That is, the A is 12 and 1, the B is 12 and 2, the J is 11 and 1, the K is 11 and 2, the S is 0 and 2, the T is 0 and 3, and so forth.

If an unprinted column is punched with the 11 and 5, it is easy to count five letters from the J inclusive and interpret the representation as an N.

Identification Characteristics

Some cards have a distinguishing color or have one of the corners cut. These features are provided as means of recognition by the personnel handling the cards and have no meaning to the machines. For example, a corrected card in a file may be a different color in order to easily locate the card at a later time.

When it is necessary for a machine to be able to distinguish between different types of cards, the distinguishing data must be punched in the card. This may be done in many ways. One of the most frequently used "control" punches is the 11-zone punch, which is usually referred to as an "X" punch. For instance, master address cards will contain an X punch (11 zone) in some column in order to distinguish them from current-purchase cards during processing (Fig. 5–9).

ORGANIZATION OF DATA

This brings us to one of the most fundamental concepts in data processing, the arrangement of data, which has a most significant effect on how processing is done. Data processing involves a variety of business operations. These operations are called "applications"; for example, demand deposits (checking accounts) for the banking industry. A family of applications is referred to as a "system" (Fig. 5–8). Individual applications are also called "subsystems." Source data is the input data extracted from transactions for processing applications. Applications are made up of files.

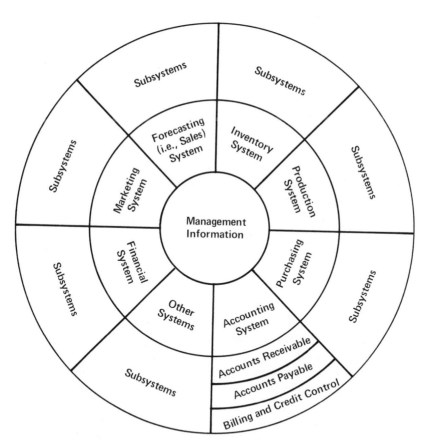

Fig. 5–8. A family of subsystems, such as replenishment of inventory application and stock demand application, make up a system.

Files

A file is a collection of records containing data about a group of related accounts, people, inventory items, etc. There are two types of files: master and detail (or transaction) files.

The master file contains semipermanent data that is used time after time in preparation of reports, checks, invoices, and so forth. In a payroll file, the master file includes a record for each employee, containing such stable data as name, employee number, department, sex, social security number, and withholding exemptions.

A detail file, on the other hand, contains data to be used in the current processing and then filed as history. The payroll transaction card representing time attendance records might include a minimum of data such as employee number, regular hours, and overtime hours. The card would be matched with the master card by employee number to obtain the pay rate necessary for computations, the authorized deductions, tax, and so forth.

Examples of files are Hospital Patient file, Inventory file, Unfilled Orders file, Accounts Receivable file, and Savings Accounts file. A file is made up of records.

Records

A group of fields related to a specific type of data that is processed as a unit is a "record." An accounts receivable file contains a master record for each customer, showing the account number, name, address, amount owed (and for which items), and other data. Two types of detail records—credit or debit records—will be processed against corresponding master records to update the file (Fig. 5–9). Records are made up of fields.

Fields

A predetermined number of columns set aside for specific data is known as a "field." Student number or social security number, amounts due, and amounts owed are examples of fields. Fields consist of one or more digits or letters called "characters." Each unit of data occupies the same positions on all cards representing any given transaction. If customer number occupies columns 12 to 17, then it must always contain that data field (Fig. 5–10).

In other words, we cannot punch characters in random columns and expect the machine to know where the needed data is punched. If we reserve columns 7 to 11 for invoice number, then we can instruct the machine to process the invoice number in the desired manner. If the field contains fewer digits than the number of columns in the field, the normal rule is to precede

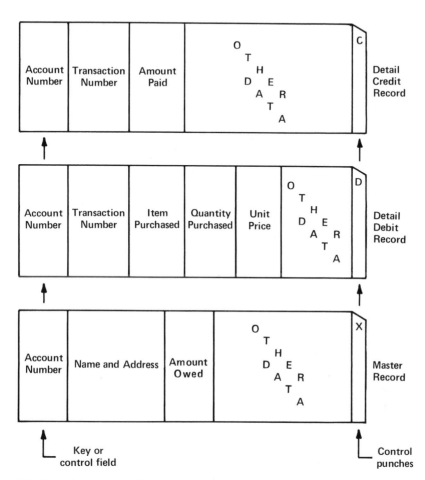

Fig. 5–9. A group of fields make up a record. A file consists of a collection of related records.

the number with zeros. For example, invoice number 479 would be punched 00479 in columns 7 to 11.

Key Fields. One or more of the fields are usually established as key or control fields (Fig. 5–9). The key distinguishes each record from all others. For instance, the master payroll card is joined with the detail time attendance card in order to compute the pay. Employee number is the controlling field, from which comes the term "key," or "control," field. Other examples are customer account number in an accounts receivable application, salesman number in a sales analysis application, and so on.

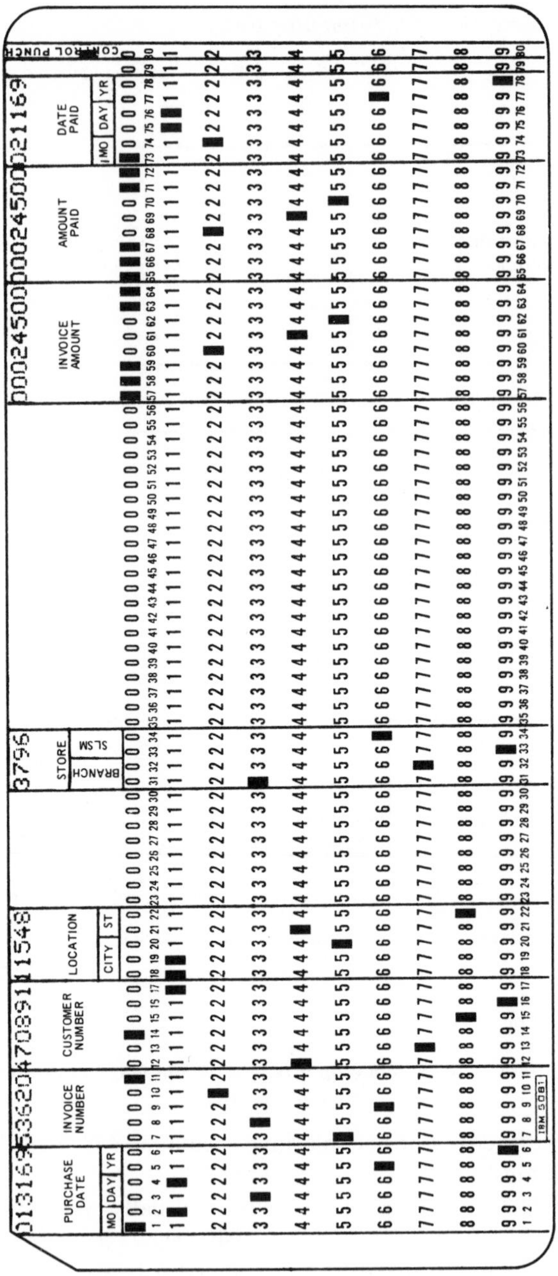

Fig. 5–10. Fields in an accounts receivable record.

WHY DOCUMENTATION?

The design of fields on a card provides us with the first important control in data processing. Suppose that four columns of a card contain the punches 0591. Does this mean customer number 0591, a quantity of 591, $5.91, or something else? We have no way of knowing what the numbers mean without knowing what they are intended to mean.

It is the responsibility of the person who is planning the application to identify the meaning of data fields in the documentation. Documentation, the paperwork that describes how a job is processed, is usually provided in separate binders for each job. This gives the keypunch operator instructions about how to punch the fields. The documentation also provides instructions that tell which columns are to be sorted, how other data is to be handled in order to process in the intended way, and so on. The computer can be instructed so that the desired processing will be achieved, if the documentation is complete and accurate. The success or failure of a data processing operation depends largely upon the enforcement of documentation standards; for additional information, see Section 8 in Chapter 15.

KEY-TO-TAPE RECORDING

The bottleneck that can occur in data processing is the input operation. Transcription of data on source documents to punched cards is no faster than the manual keying operation. Reading cards into the computer is typically done at 1000 cards per minute, but some reader speeds range up to 2000 cards a minute, still a relatively slow process. Up to 300,000 cards can be stored on 2400 feet of magnetic tape, and this single reel can be read in a matter of minutes, depending on several factors discussed in Chapter 11.

While cards can be entered into the computer at speeds up to 2600 characters per second, the transfer rate from tape is much faster—up to 350,000 characters per second. Taking advantage of the tape's faster speeds requires converting the cards to tape, using the computer or other card-to-tape converters. Then the tape can be used thousands of times on various jobs at the faster speed, a tape-to-card ratio of well over 100:1.

Another technique to speed computer throughput (the elapsed time of input, processing, and output) is to key directly to the tape (Fig. 5–11), rather than to cards. Both operations work in principle similar to typing. Instead of typing onto paper, one is typing onto cards or tape. Keying errors are easily corrected by backspacing the tape and rekeying the correct data over the old.

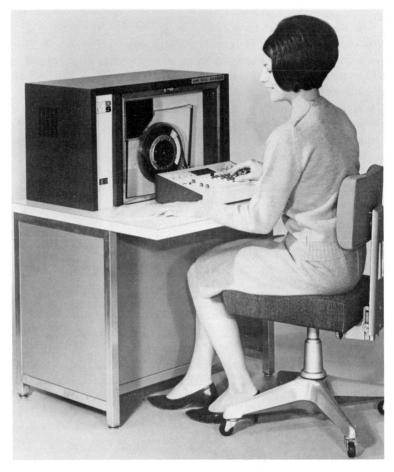

Fig. 5–11. The Mohawk Data Science 6401 data recorder is a key-to-tape operation. (Courtesy of Mohawk Data Science Corporation.)

The family of key-to-tape data recorders performs a variety of tasks besides data entry. For example, card readers are attached to some models to perform off-line conversion of punched cards to magnetic tape. Other models have typewriters or printers that print a line at a time.

Advantages of Key-to-Tape

First to consider in choosing a system is that the data processing installation must have a computer that uses magnetic tape instead of cards.

It may not be feasible to acquire a tape system merely to benefit from monetary advantages offered by key-to-tape machines. Although users report cost savings when this is done, the savings are somewhat offset because key-to-tape machines rent from $140 to $220, plus maintenance. In comparison, a keypunch rents for approximately $60 and up per month. However, if costs are subordinated by other objectives, certain advantages may be attractive.

Faster Recording. Three key-to-tape data recorders may do the work of five keypunches and verifiers. Keying is slightly faster because of the recorder's electronic structure, and new features perform faster and more automatic operations than can key-to-card devices.

Cost Savings. About 10,000 records are recorded on tape 1200 feet long, which can be erased and used over and over indefinitely. Punched cards are eliminated at appreciable savings ($1.00 per thousand) resulting from a reduction in number of card cabinets needed, decreased card handling, and less floor space for storage. The largest saving, and main objective, is the reduction of input time to the computer by using magnetic tape instead of cards.

Record Size. A tape record may be any size, 40 characters or 240 characters. A card record requiring 90 columns takes 2 cards, leaving 70 columns unused. Also, the operation of keeping both card records together is not always successful. Losing part of a tape record is improbable.

Versatility. Both recording and verifying can be done on the same unit, whereas in the punched card method the keypunch does the punching and another machine, called the "verifier," is designed to check the accuracy of the original punching.

Higher Productivity. Savings in labor result because key-to-tape machines skip over unused fields faster and duplication of repetitive data in all records is faster. Correction of tape records during the recording process is the simple operation of backspacing one character and keying the new data over the old, as opposed to having to repunch a card.

Disadvantages of Key-to-Tape

Correction of Errors. Correcting one column in a punched card after completing the job means locating the card manually, repunching it, and returning it to its place in the file. To correct a tape record requires searching the tape until the record is found, and then easily keying the desired data over the erroneous data. Either method may be faster, depending upon circumstances; for example, a card at hand could be corrected faster than searching a reel of tape.

Job Merging. Periodically, the tapes from several operators working on the same job must be merged, an operation not necessary with punched cards. In fact, data for different jobs may be recorded on the same tape, requiring separation.

Manually Used Files. The manual means of easily locating a punched card, visually reading it, and being able to write new data upon it for punching later must be considered in certain applications, an operation not allowed by the key-to-tape method.

KEY-TO-DISK RECORDING

Each new group of recording devices offers an improvement over its predecessors. In some situations, users of key-to-disk machines report up to 20 percent increase in throughput over key-to-tape machines. But the savings in these cases are not so clear-cut as with the keypunch because several key-to-disk machines must share the same storage area under the control of the computer, thus making the system more complex. Of significance is the key-to-disk rental cost, which is roughly ten times that of key-to-tape. A system with eight key-to-disk stations rents from $1500 a month upward.

The key-to-disk operation works this way: Up to 64 *keyboard terminals* (Fig. 5–12) are connected to small computers (Fig. 4–5) where data is keyed directly into disk storage. After formatting and organizing, the data is transferred from disk to magnetic tape. From a hardware standpoint, the need for buffer storage at each key-to-tape machine is thus eliminated. Buffer storage, explained in Chapter 12, refers to a small storage unit that holds several records during the keying operation.

By the keypunch and key-to-tape method, data fields must be recorded in a particular order to meet the design of the fields on the card or tape record. This is usually not convenient, thereby slowing the operator's input speed. Under the key-to-disk concept, data is keyed in the order read from the source document and the computer formats the fields into the desired sequence. The differences between the three input methods are shown in Fig. 5–13.

Another time-saving feature is that the same error in a file of records can be corrected automatically, whereas other systems require that the change be made to each record, one by one. Now that we have covered the input media, we should explain the topic of coding data before recording it from source documents by means of keypunch, key-to-tape, or key-to-disk.

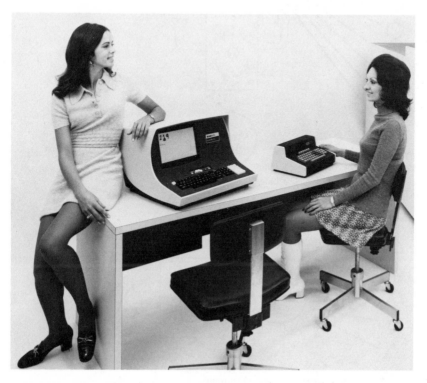

Fig. 5–12. The 2250 key-to-disk display terminal by Scan Data Corporation. Multiple key-to-disk systems provide input to the computer over telephone lines. Keyed data enters the disk and is displayed on the CRT screen. (Courtesy of Scan Data Corporation.)

CODING DATA

Coding is fundamental to all types of business systems for identifying data items. A "code" may be defined in this context as a brief title, composed of either letters or numbers and used to identify an item of data and express its relationship to other items of the same or similar nature. For instance, an employee number is used for identification purposes, is easier to control both manually and by machine than employee name, and eliminates erroneous processing resulting from duplicate or similar names. Ordering is simplified by ordering part number 456 instead of "bolt, stainless steel, 1/4 inch diameter, 1 inch long." Dates of birth, for example, are coded as 101344 rather than October 13, 1944, to shorten the data.

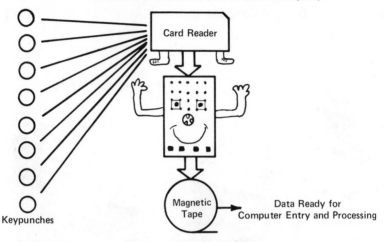

SLOWEST OPERATION (Due to Slow Card Speed)

Keypunches

Card Reader

Magnetic Tape

Data Ready for Computer Entry and Processing

Off-Line Card-to-Tape Operation

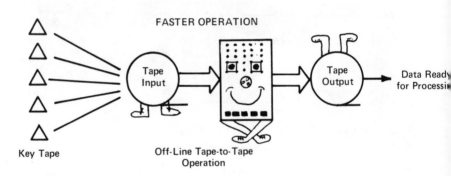

FASTER OPERATION

Key Tape

Tape Input

Tape Output

Data Ready for Processing

Off-Line Tape-to-Tape Operation

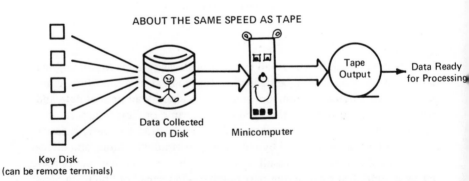

ABOUT THE SAME SPEED AS TAPE

Key Disk
(can be remote terminals)

Data Collected on Disk

Minicomputer

Tape Output

Data Ready for Processing

Fig. 5–13. Differences between three input methods: key to card, key to tape, and key to disk.

84

One purpose in assigning codes to data is to enable presentation of the data in the most meaningful and orderly fashion, as in the case of statistical reports. The ability to present related data in report form depends greatly upon the coding structure used. The complexity of the relationship between items governs the complexity in the coding structure.

The use of coding structures permits cross reference among several fields. To cite an illustration: A company is looking for an unmarried male college graduate as a skilled systems analyst who will travel extensively. Candidates may be selected from the company's personnel files if they qualify. See if you can pick the four criteria fields from Table 5–1.

Coded data is less cumbersome for manual handling and the machine acts faster on the shorter coded number than it would on the longer designation of the data. By coding, the number of positions utilized in a record is reduced, thus reducing the amount of keypunching. The user does not necessarily have to familiarize himself with the coding structure involved, since the data designation is usually reflected by both name or description and code number on printed documents.

Table 5–1. Illustrative codes used to code job-application forms

JOB POSITION	EDUCATION
1 trainee	1 high school graduate
2 skilled	2 some college
3 supervisory	3 college graduate
OCCUPATION	WILLING TO TRAVEL
461 computer operator	1 no
463 programmer	2 local
465 systems analyst	3 anywhere
467 keypunch operator	
469 document coder	
	SEX AND MARITAL STATUS
	1 male, single
	2 male, married
	3 female, single
	4 female, married

SUMMARY

The data input problem, estimated at one-third of the data processing expense, is to find a way to increase throughput without increasing cost.

There are two basic methods of capturing and recording data: manually keying the data onto cards, tapes, or disks; and entering raw data directly into the computer without conversion. The keypunch method is the simplest and most widely used of all methods.

Great steps forward in terms of efficiency were introduced by the key-to-tape and key-to-disk machines, but these techniques are neither practical nor economical for all installations. The conversion to newer systems requires extensive change, and changing the way of doing things could upset smooth input data flow. To jump from equipment costing $60 a month to machines ranging up to $2000 a month requires some study.

In the next chapter, we take up computer numbering systems in order to understand how data is represented in the computer's memory during processing.

KEY TERMS TO REMEMBER

Application

Coded data

Control punch

Character

Control or key field

Detail file

Documentation, reason for

Document conversion

Field

File

First zone-punch/numeric-punch relationship

Key-to-card machine

Key-to-disk machine

Key-to-tape machine

Master file

Record

System and subsystem

Unit record

QUESTIONS

1. Since data entry machines vary widely in cost, why would companies not take advantage of the least expensive equipment?
2. What would be the ultimate solution in the recording problem?
3. What does the phrase "capturing transactions and transcribing the data into machine-readable form" mean?
4. Relate the two terms "communicating" and "symbols" as applied to data processing machines.
5. Name three input media.
6. What is meant when one refers to machines that accept input documents in their original state?
7. What is the essential difference between the three types of keying machines?
8. Does the column or row in a punched card contain a special character?
9. How does the computer distinguish between different types of cards? How does the human distinguish?

10. What is the difference between a master file and a detail file?
11. How can we change a field, such as stock nomenclature, in order to simplify comparing one item against another?
12. Name the sequence of the hierarchy of data.
13. What would comprise the documentation of a keypunch operation?

COORDINATED READINGS IN CHAPTER 15.

"Why Program Documentation?", Sec. 8.
"How Serious Is the Threat of Computer Disasters?", Sec. 26.
"Protecting the Data Files," Sec. 30.

Chapter **6**

COMPUTER NUMBERING SYSTEMS

In this chapter we study the three main numbering systems used in computers: the "binary" numbering system, the "binary-coded decimal" (BCD) numbering system, and the "hexadecimal" numbering system.

In order to understand how data can be stored and processed inside the computer's memory, we must have a knowledge of the binary numbering system. Because we are already familiar with the decimal system, understanding binary will be easy, since all numbering systems are based upon the same principle.

The binary system, universal language of the computer, was invented by Gottfried von Leibnitz in Germany during the seventeenth century. The first computers to use the binary numbering system were the ABC (Atanasoff-Berry Computer), EDSAC (Electronic Delayed Storage Automatic Computer), completed in 1949, and the EDVAC (Electronic Discrete Variable Automatic Computer). This architectual concept was promoted by John von Neumann, one of the earlier pioneers mentioned in Chapter 2.

Previous computers had used the decimal system, thereby requiring ten "bi-stable" devices to represent one arabic numberal. This method presented numerous problems, such as excessive heat produced by the extra vacuum tubes and an area of 2000 square feet to store these early mammoth computers, not to mention the huge cost factor.

We shall see in this chapter, and in the next, that more numeric and alphabetic characters can be represented with fewer components by using the binary system than by using the decimal system.

DECIMAL NUMBERING SYSTEM

The comprehension of the true value of a number is rare. We shall therefore begin our study of numbering systems by considering the significance of the decimal system, with which we are already familiar.

An important concept in most numbering systems is that of positional notation. This means that the numerical value given to a digit is determined by its relative position in a number. Therefore, decimal symbols have varying values, depending on the columnar position. A single symbol has a fixed value, but the same symbol in a group of numbers has a different value. For example, the numeral 5 by itself has a different value than the 5 in 50 and the 5 in 501 has still another value, since the meaning of the 5 has changed with the shift in its position.

The common decimal system uses ten symbols, the arabic numerals 0, 1, 2, 3, 4, 5, 6, 7, 8, and 9. Because there are ten number symbols for counting, the base is 10.

The value of any number, regardless of its base, is determined by its base being raised to successively higher, or positive, powers, starting with the *point*; for instance, starting with the decimal point, or binary point, and working to the left increases its value. Starting with the point and working to the right decreases the base to successively lower, or negative, powers. The point shows where positive powers end and negative powers begin. Or, expressed another way, a number is made up of "coefficients" of particular powers of the base of the numbering system. Using this system, a quantity expressed with the symbols 309.75 would mean

$$(3 \times 10^2) + (0 \times 10^1) + (9 \times 10^0) + (7 \times 10^{-1}) + (5 \times 10^{-2})$$

exponent
base
coefficient

In expanded form the symbols 309.75 would be

$$(3 \times 100) + (0 \times 10) + (9 \times 1) + (7 \times 1/10) + (5 \times 1/100)$$

or	*or*	*or*	*or*	*or*
300 +	0 +	9 +	7/10 +	5/100

Although we used the powers of 10 to explain the value of a number comprising a string of digits, it is neither customary nor the best way of finding its decimal value. A better way is to commit the column value to memory:

Decimal number	3	0	9	7	5		300.00
Power of base	10^2	10^1	10^0	10^{-1}	10^{-2}		00.00
Column value	100	10	1	1/10	1/100		9.00
Value of digit	300	0	9	7/10	5/100		0.70
							0.05

309.75 *Sum*

Presence of zero in any number system simply means that the power of the base represented by that 0 digit position is not used.

When a number is multiplied by itself a given number of times, it is raised to a "power." In order to show the power that the base will be raised to, a small number (called the "exponent") is written above and to the right of the base. For example, 10×10 would be expressed as 10^2, $10 \times 10 \times 10$ as 10^3, and so forth.

Whenever a base (except 0) is raised to the "zero" power, it is always 1. This can be proved by the *division exponent law,* which is

$$\frac{a^m}{a^n} = a^{m-n}$$

Therefore, $\dfrac{10^5}{10^5}$, which is 1, equals $10^{(5-5)}$ or 10^0. Any number raised to the first power is equal to the number itself, such as $10^1 = 10$, $2^1 = 2$, $8^1 = 8$, and $16^1 = 16$.

BINARY NUMBERING SYSTEM

The binary system uses only *two* number symbols, 0 and 1. The list below shows the relationship between decimal and binary.

0 = 0000	6 = 0110	11 = 1011
1 = 0001	7 = 0111	12 = 1100
2 = 0010	8 = 1000	13 = 1101
3 = 0011	9 = 1001	14 = 1110
4 = 0100	10 = 1010	15 = 1111
5 = 0101		

Because there are two counting numbers, the base is 2. With less symbols than the decimal system, it is clear that fewer arithmetic rules must be memorized than with the decimal system, such as smaller multiplication tables. One disadvantage is that more positions are needed to represent a given quantity. For example, the value of 46 requires only two positions in decimal, whereas six positions, 101110, are needed to represent the value in binary.

It is often necessary to ascertain the equivalent of a number in a base other than the one in which it is expressed. By way of example: The contents of computer memory are printed in order to determine the cause of incorrect processing, but the numbers and letters appear in the language of the computer, such as "hexadecimal" 7E 4A 30. Consequently, we shall concern ourselves with conversion from one number system to another in order to clear up the mystery of the computer's ability to store data in forms other than decimal.

In order to convert decimal to binary, successively divide by 2 and retain the remainder. The remainder becomes the binary equivalent. For example, to find the binary equivalent of decimal 10:

		0	1
2	$\overline{\smash{)}1}$	0	
2	$\overline{\smash{)}2}$	1	Remainders are expressed as 1010.
2	$\overline{\smash{)}5}$	0	
2	$\overline{\smash{)}10}$		

To find the binary equivalent of decimal 46:

		0	1
2	$\overline{\smash{)}1}$	0	
2	$\overline{\smash{)}2}$	1	
2	$\overline{\smash{)}5}$	1	Remainders
2	$\overline{\smash{)}11}$	1	
2	$\overline{\smash{)}23}$	0	
2	$\overline{\smash{)}46}$		

The last remainder is the most significant digit; the binary equivalent of decimal 46 is read as 101110.

The binary system, and modified systems of binary, lends itself ideally to the construction of computers because electronic components operate in a "binary mode," which means that one of two tubes or transistors either conduct (representing a "1") or do not conduct (representing a "0") and magnetic cores are magnetized (representing a "1") or are not magnetized (representing a "0"). In other words, electric impulses are either present (meaning a "1") or absent (meaning a "0"). Early computers used the decimal system but von Neumann's suggestion to design computers using the binary system was quickly adapted to save cost and permit smaller machines. In Fig. 6–1, whereas the decimal configuration has 20 tubes to represent the numeral 46, the binary configuration needs only 6 tubes to represent the same value.

In order to convert binary to decimal, the binary column value is determined by each column base of 2 raised to a successively higher power from the point. For example, decimal 46 equals

$$(1 \times 2^5) + (0 \times 2^4) + (1 \times 2^3) + (1 \times 2^2) + (1 \times 2^1) + (0 \times 2^0)$$

and in expanded form equals

$$(1 \times 32) + (0 \times 16) + (1 \times 8) + (1 \times 4) + (1 \times 2) + (0 \times 1)$$

32	0	8	4	2	0
or	*or*	*or*	*or*	*or*	*or*

Similar to the decimal illustration given earlier, we can disregard the powers of 2 and memorize the column values. Whereas the value of each, decimal column is ten times the column value to its right, the binary value is double the column value to its right.

Binary number	1	0	1	1	1	0		32
Power of base	2^5	2^4	2^3	2^2	2^1	2^0		0
Column value	32	16	8	4	2	1		8
Value of digit	32	0	8	4	2	0		4
								2
								0
								46 *Sum*

We have converted decimal 46 to binary 101110 and have converted the binary symbol back to decimal. We see that the value of a binary number, like decimal, is determined by "positional" notation. That is, the value of any number, regardless of its base, is determined by its base being raised to successively higher powers, beginning at the point.

As in decimal, the zero digits in a binary number have no value. So a shorter method of determining a binary value is to add only the column values having a "1." For example, the decimal value of the binary numbers 100010 is determined by

$$2^5 = 32 \times 1 \quad \text{or } 32$$
$$2^1 = 2 \times 1 \quad \text{or } \underline{2}$$
$$34 = \text{the decimal value of 100010}$$

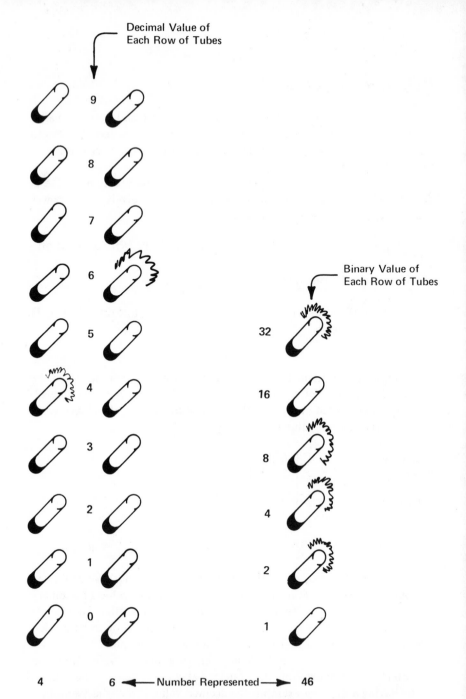

Fig. 6–1. The binary system requires less computer components than the decimal system. The digit shown in each column is determined by the "on" tube and the value of its row. The decimal system requires ten tubes for each digit stored; the binary system uses six electronic components and can store values up to 63. Here the value of 46 is determined by adding the row value of the "on" tubes, or 32 + 8 + 4 + 2.

BINARY-CODED DECIMAL SYSTEM

Some computers use "binary-coded" decimal (BCD), a form of binary that consists of the first four places of binary. This method allows the computer to communicate with the operator running the computer, and is commonly used because it is easy to understand and easy to convert.

Second-generation computers and some third-generation computers use BCD; however, the trend in most third-generation computers has been toward an extended form of BCD, called "EBCDIC." The initials EBCDIC stands for *E*xtended *B*inary *C*oded *D*ecimal *I*nterchange *C*ode, which is explained in the next chapter.

In BCD only the first four positions in the binary system and the first ten decimal numbers are used. Each position in the decimal number is represented in binary-coded decimal, as shown in Fig. 6–2. Thus, each of the ten decimal symbols has a BCD value as follows:

```
0 = 0000     5 = 0101
1 = 0001     6 = 0110
2 = 0010     7 = 0111
3 = 0011     8 = 1000
4 = 0100     9 = 1001
```

Let us assume that we are interested in a dollar amount accumulated in the computer. If the computer displayed console lights for the pure binary number

10111000000000000000001000000000100

it would take us quite some time to figure that its decimal equivalent was $61,740,195.88. However,

0110000101110100000000001100101011000100 0

has more binary digits and appears, at first glance, to be even more difficult to read. But let us take a closer look at the number if it is displayed in units of four binary symbols, that is, in BCD:

0110	0001	0111	0100	0000	0001	1001	0101	1000	1000
6	1	7	4	0	1	9	5	8	8

So the easy-to-read representation turns out to be the same $61,-740,195.88, when expressed in BCD form. Now we can see that with a little

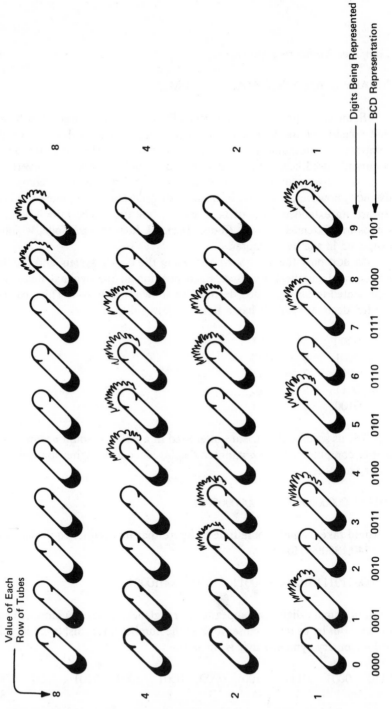

Fig. 6–2. The ten decimal digits represented in BCD. "Off" represents a zero; "on" represents 1. If two or more tubes in a row are "on," then values combine, as in the case of digit 3.

practice, the largest number can be visually translated to decimal form with little effort. Thus, BCD is an ideal means of communicating with the computer, or vice versa.

HEXADECIMAL NUMBERING SYSTEM

As mentioned earlier, third-generation computers use a different numbering system in order to store data more efficiently in memory. The IBM System 360 (Fig. 6–3), first used the hexadecimal (referred to as "hex") numbering system in 1964; most manufacturers have adopted the concept, including the newer IBM System 370 computers. Improvements in computer design have continually made it easier for man to communicate with the computer; however, a step was taken backward with hexadecimal in that BCD is simple and far easier to work with.

Hexadecimal, which means 16, uses a base of 16; thus, there are 16 symbols to represent the numbers 0 to 15. The decimal symbols 0 to 9 are used plus the single symbols A through F to represent the symbols 10 through 15. Each of the symbols, representing numbers 0 to 15, stands for four binary digits. The way in which decimal digits and letters are represented in memory is called EBCDIC (Extended Binary Coded Decimal Interchange Code), explained in the next chapter. The following list compares decimal, hexadecimal, and binary symbols.

Dec.	Hex.	Binary	Dec.	Hex.	Binary
0	0	0000	8	8	1000
1	1	0001	9	9	1001
2	2	0010	10	A	1010
3	3	0011	11	B	1011
4	4	0100	12	C	1100
5	5	0101	13	D	1101
6	6	0110	14	E	1110
7	7	0111	15	F	1111

As seen, each hexadecimal digit stands for four binary digits. Similar to BCD, we can convert binary numbers to hex by simply dividing the number into groups of four binary digits:

$$10001010111101101101_2 = 1000 \quad 1010 \quad 1111 \quad 0110 \quad 1101$$
$$= \quad 8 \quad\quad A \quad\quad F \quad\quad 6 \quad\quad D$$
$$= \quad 8AF6D_{16}$$

Fig. 6-3. The console typewriter enables the operator to type information directly into the computer. The computer then types out special instructions such as "mount the payroll input-tape on tape device 3." (By permission of IBM.)

One reason for using the hexadecimal system and storing numbers in EBCDIC rather than in BCD is that data composed of numbers is used more extensively than data composed of letters. This means that numbers can be stored more efficiently by using the hexadecimal number system instead of the BCD number system. In the next chapter, we shall see why this is true. A second reason is that large binary numbers can be converted to fewer hex digits than decimal digits.

Converting a decimal number to hexadecimal follows the same rules used previously to convert decimal numbers to binary, except that division is by 16. The division process continues until the quotient is 0 and then the remainders are retained as digits of the hex number. As shown below, the *first* remainder obtained is the *least significant* or rightmost digit and the *last* remainder obtained is the *most significant* or leftmost digit:

```
        0   1                          0   1
16 )    1   7               16 )       1   F   (15 remainder)
16 )   23   B  (11 remainder)   16 )  31   D   (13 remainder)
16 ) 379₁₀                  16 ) 509₁₀
```

$$17B_{16} \qquad\qquad 1FD_{16}$$

The hex numbers may be converted into binary by substituting the corresponding group of four binary digits for each hexadecimal symbol:

```
  1    7    B          1   F    D
0001 0111 1011        1 1111 1101
     Drop unnecessary zeroes
```

Conversion from hexadecimal to decimal is similar to the method used previously to convert other bases to decimal, the difference being the base 16. Each hex digit is converted to its decimal number and then multiplied by the power of 16 according to its digit position in the number. For example:

Hex number	A	5	E	$A \times 256 \ (10 \times 16^2) =$	2560
Power of base	16^2	16^1	16^0	$5 \times 16 \ (\ 5 \times 16^1) =$	80
Column value	256	16	1	$E \times \quad 1 \ (14 \times 16^0) =$	14
					2654_{10}

BINARY ARITHMETIC

Rather than study how to add, subtract, divide, and multiply in binary, BCD, and hexadecimal, we shall illustrate only binary addition and subtraction to show the simplicity of the computer's bi-stable components. Their two-states ("on" or "off" represents binary 1's and 0's) allow binary com putations at microsecond (one millionth of a second) speeds in second-generation computers. Third-generation computers perform operations one thousand times faster, at speeds rated in nanoseconds (one billionth of a second).

Binary arithmetic is quite simple to understand, with addition being the easiest. The rules for adding binary digits are:

$$0 + 0 = 0$$
$$1 + 0 = 1$$
$$1 + 1 = 10 \qquad \text{(0 with a 1–carry)}$$
$$1 + 1 + 1 = 11 \quad \text{(1 with a 1–carry)}$$

Of course the first two rules are no different from decimal addition, but the last two rules may seem strange. If we examine them closer, we shall see that only the base makes them appear different from the decimal system. When we go beyond the base of the decimal system, such as $9 + 1$, the result is 10 or 0 with a 1–carry. Since the binary system has only the 0 and 1 symbols, we have the same situation when we add 1 to 1; that is, 0 with a 1–carry or 10.

An explanation of the last rule makes evident the ordinary arithmetic behind all four rules:

1	1
1	1
1	10_2 (partial answer)
3_{10}	1
	11_2

Now recall from our former discussion of binary that decimal 3 is equal to binary 11. The illustrations below use the four rules of *addition*.

2 =	010	9 =	1001	7 =	111
4 =	100	12 =	1100	6 =	110
6 =	110	21 =	10101	13 =	1101

Binary *subtraction* is accomplished by the computer through binary addition. In order to understand binary subtraction, we must add four more rules to the addition rules:

Rule 1. Complement the subtrahend, which is accomplished by changing all 1's to 0 and all 0's to 1.

Rule 2. Add the complemented subtrahend to the minuend, using the rules of addition.

Rule 3. If there is no carry, complement the result. The absence of a carry indicates a negative result.

Rule 4. If there is a 1–carry, add the 1–carry to the units position of the result. The presence of a 1–carry indicates a positive result.

Examples

1.	19	=	10011	*2.*	6	=	00110
	−10	=	~~01010~~		−21	=	~~10101~~
			10101				01010
		①	01000				~~10000~~
			→1		−15	=	01111
	9	=	01001				

SUMMARY

You now have a basic understanding of number systems, especially the binary system. We have covered the decimal system in order to better understand the binary, BCD, and hexadecimal number systems. Your comprehension of number systems will provide insight for the internal operation of the computer covered in subsequent chapters.

Although other numbering systems are used in computers, we have covered the ones most widely used and will demonstrate the BCD and hexadecimal representations inside the computer in the next chapter.

At this point you may feel a little vague as to the necessity for understanding binary and coded variations of binary such as BCD. When we discover in the next chapter how the computer memory is constructed, the need for understanding it will be clear.

KEY TERMS TO REMEMBER

BCD	Hexadecimal
Binary	Number conversions
Columnar value	Remainder/conversion relation-
Complement	ship
EBCDIC	Two-state memory component

QUESTIONS

1. What is the significance of knowing numbering systems other than decimal?

2. How is any number, regardless of it's base, converted to another base?

3. Name three common number systems used by computers.

4. Of what value is positional notation?

5. Convert decimal 75 to binary.

6. Convert 1010101 to decimal.

7. Convert decimal 2761 to hexadecimal.
8. Convert hexadecimal AC9 to decimal.

COORDINATED READINGS IN CHAPTER 15

"The Changed Personnel Recruiting Scene," Sec. 18.
"The Dilemma of Promoting Good Technicians," Sec. 22.
"Controlling Computer Reruns," Sec. 11.

Chapter 7

ARCHITECTURE
OF INTERNAL MEMORY

Now that you understand binary, we shall see how data is stored inside the computer in one of three main forms: Binary Coded Decimal (BCD), Extended Binary Coded Decimal Interchange Code (EBCDIC), and binary.

Electronic data processing systems (EDPS) introduced to business a new concept in mass processing of data whereby several interconnected machines act together without human intervention. A computer system consists broadly of machines that provide data *input*, data *processing*, and data *output*. The data processing function is performed by three distinct components housed in a central processing unit (CPU). They are the *arithmetic-logic* unit, *control* unit, and internal *storage*. The latter is the subject of this chapter and the others are covered in the next chapter.

CHARACTERISTICS OF INTERNAL MEMORY

A computer has access to data stored in two types of memory, internal and external. The punched card, magnetic tape, and magnetic disk are examples of *external* storage. *Internal* memory, also called "primary" storage and "main" storage, is the fastest of all storage types; consequently, it is the most expensive. The speed of memory refers to the time it takes to access data stored within.

Access time is the elapsed time between the instant at which data is called for and the instant at which the data is available at the desired location. The speed of access has a direct bearing on the cost of the computer because, generally, the faster the memory device, the more expensive it is.

Speeds differ between manufacturers and also between models of the same computer series. Storage access time for the CDC 3100, for example, is 1.25 μs (microseconds), while the CDC 3200 is twice as fast at 0.75 μs. IBM's System 360 computer series range from 3.6 μs to 0.75 μs for the large-scale models, and other computers operate even faster. For example, the IBM 370/145 accesses eight characters from storage in 540 ns (nanoseconds).

Internal memory (Fig. 7–1) holds the program of instructions, data read from the input device (i.e., card reader or tape), data being processed, and data awaiting transfer to the output device (i.e., printer). Other data is stored on the slower and less expensive external devices serving as additional storage to augment the capacity of internal memory.

A storage device has the ability almost simultaneously to accept, remember, and transfer data that has been stored in it. In order to do this, each position of memory is numbered, permitting the computer to store data or instructions in a specific position, and then locate and use that data or instructions as needed.

All processing and data manipulations are performed by a program stored in internal memory. The program consists of a set of instructions to

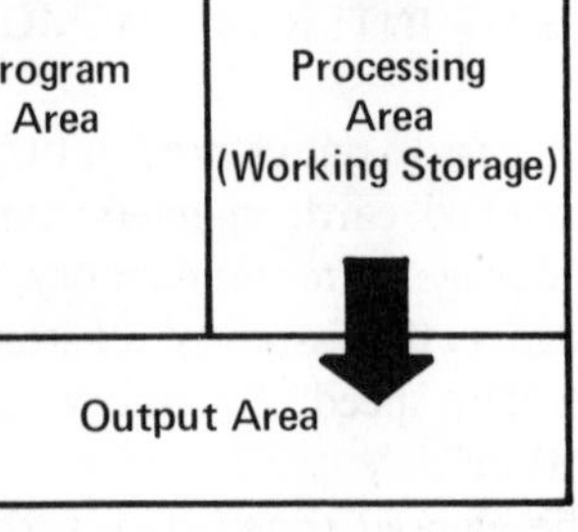

INTERNAL MEMORY

Fig. 7–1. Components of internal memory.

direct processing in sequence to produce the desired results. The amount of internal memory not used to store the program is known as "working storage." It is here that the data being processed, or awaiting processing, and intermediate results requiring further processing are stored. Working storage also holds tables and constant factors. Examples of each are tax tables and dates stored constantly for printing on documents. The input area contains data transferred from the input components that are awaiting processing. The output area stores the results of processing until the output device needs the data.

FIXED AND VARIABLE WORD-LENGTH CONCEPT

In manipulation of the data in memory, we must work with groups of characters called "words." A computer word, in many respects, is similar to a field. You will recall that earlier we set aside certain columns in a card and defined them as *fields*. These fields are necessary because they provide a means of telling the machine which data to process; for instance, customer name and money amounts.

Fields are defined by people and are handled by the computer as words. The size of a word is designed into the circuitry of the computer. There are two types of words: fixed length and variable.

Fixed and Variable Word-Length Computers. Prior to the third-generation era, computers were designed either for scientific uses or for commercial uses, but not both. For example, the IBM 7094 fixed word-length computer was the most popular for scientific computing, and the IBM 1401 variable word-length computer was the workhorse for business processing. Each type had drawbacks and advantages. Business computers made the most efficient use of memory space because of their variable word-length operation, while those designed for scientific purposes were faster because of their fixed word-length operation. Engineers designed third-generation computers, as a result, to give the flexible combination of operating as either variable or fixed word-length machines. (See Fig. 7–2).

Fixed Word-Length Concept. Data is handled in words containing a predetermined number of characters, set by the physical construction of the computer hardware. Control Data Corporation's CDC 3000 series computers are 24–bit word machines, with each word containing four BCD characters. Each word has an "address," a term referring to the numbered location in memory. If the computer memory is 16K (a term specifying the size of storage in thousands), it contains 16,000 computer words.

Variable Word-Length Concept. Data fields of any size are accom-

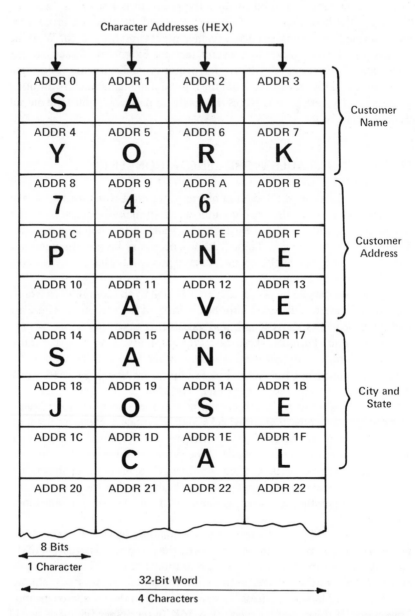

Character Addresses (HEX)

ADDR 0	ADDR 1	ADDR 2	ADDR 3	
S	A	M		Customer Name
ADDR 4	ADDR 5	ADDR 6	ADDR 7	
Y	O	R	K	
ADDR 8	ADDR 9	ADDR A	ADDR B	
7	4	6		
ADDR C	ADDR D	ADDR E	ADDR F	Customer Address
P	I	N	E	
ADDR 10	ADDR 11	ADDR 12	ADDR 13	
	A	V	E	
ADDR 14	ADDR 15	ADDR 16	ADDR 17	
S	A	N		
ADDR 18	ADDR 19	ADDR 1A	ADDR 1B	City and State
J	O	S	E	
ADDR 1C	ADDR 1D	ADDR 1E	ADDR 1F	
	C	A	L	
ADDR 20	ADDR 21	ADDR 22	ADDR 22	

8 Bits
1 Character
32-Bit Word
4 Characters

Fig. 7–2. The IBM 360 and 370 operate as either variable or fixed word length, depending on how the program is written. Note that addresses are numbered in hexadecimal.

modated because the amount of data being manipulated is specified in the instruction when the program is written. In other words, the instruction

ADD 166 (4), 170 (5)

adds the four-position field, beginning at address 166, to the five-position field, beginning at address 170. In a variable-length computer, each position rather than word has a numbered location, as shown in Fig. 7–2. Consequently, data is available by character instead of by word; thus the term "character addressable."

MOVEMENT OF DATA

Fixed word-length operations are performed on complete words (Fig. 7–3). For example, all positions of two factors in an addition operation are combined simultaneously, including carryovers. In another example, all characters of a complete word are transferred instantaneously between components. The advantage of a fixed-length machine, because of its parallel feature, is that operations are performed faster. However, this is accomplished at the expense of wasted memory.

Variable word-length operations realize more efficient use of storage space. Data is moved character by character (Fig. 7–3), added digit by digit, and so on. This method eliminates wasted memory, but the operations are slower than fixed word-length machines because data is processed *serially,* or character by character.

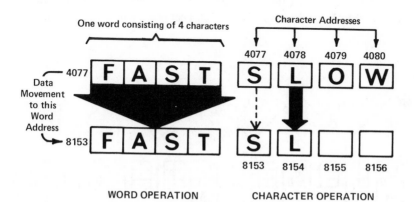

Fig. 7–3. Fixed-length operation moves all letters in a word simultaneously. Variable-length operations move in a serial fashion, character by character.

Addressing Data

We have talked about storing data within memory and moving data between internal memory and the input/output devices. To do this, we must know where the data is located. For this purpose, an address is assigned to each location. An address, therefore, is a number identifying a location in memory where data is stored.

Storage addresses can be compared to house addresses (Fig. 7–4). Storage addresses are actually numbered consecutively, beginning with zero. For example, addresses in an 8K computer are numbered from 0000 through 7999. Storage is divided into *locations,* each holding specific data and each with an assigned address. We should emphasize at this point that the *address* identifies a location and not the data stored at that address. For instance, location 500 may contain a "Z" at one time and an "8" a moment later.

MAGNETIC CORE STORAGE

In the previous chapter, we explored the way the binary numbering system can represent numbers. Further, we saw that computations can be made using numbers expressed by 1's and 0's. The following discussion of storage devices clearly points out why and how binary notation is used in computers.

Magnetic core storage is the most widely used memory in computers because it is extremely fast. Its access time is measured in microseconds or nanoseconds, depending upon the model.

The first large-scale computer to use core storage was Whirlwind I, built at the Massachusetts Institute of Technology in 1950. This dynamic

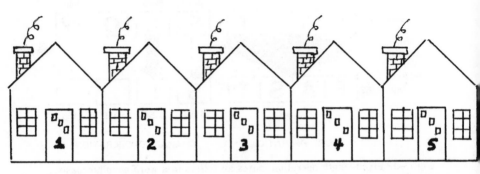

Fig. 7–4. Addresses identify a location, not the data stored at that address.

memory, developed by Jay W. Forrester of MIT, was first offered commercially in the scientific, first-generation IBM 704 computer in 1955. Soon afterward, computers using the slower vacuum tubes were retired and replaced by a new generation of computers using magnetic core storage.

How a Core Stores Binary

A magnetic core (Fig. 7–5) is a tiny (a few hundredths of an inch in diameter) doughnut-shaped device, made of ferromagnetic material. By passing a wire through the center of the core and sending electric current through it, the core becomes magnetized. This two-state device may be

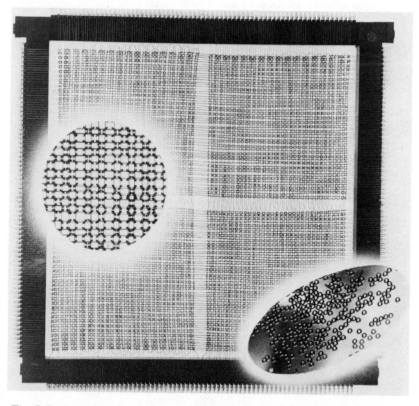

Fig. 7–5. A magnetic core plane contains thousands of small doughnut-shaped cores. A memory array is constructed of seven planes (BCD) or nine planes (EBCDIC), stacked one above the other. (By permission of IBM.)

magnetized in either a positive or negative direction; thus, it has the capability to represent a binary 1 or 0 value.

When a core is magnetized in a counterclockwise direction, the core is negative and is said to be "off." When a core is magnetized in a clockwise direction, the core is positive and is said to be "on." The core remains magnetized after the current is removed, and represents a value of 0 if "off," or a value of 1 if "on." (See Fig. 7–6.)

Magnetism of the cores is controlled in two ways. First, by controlling the polarity of the current flowing through the wires, we determine whether it is to be magnetized in the clockwise or counterclockwise direction. Once the polarity of the core is set up, the core remains magnetized in that direction until current is passed through the wire in the opposite direction. Then the core reverses its magnetic state. Second, the core to be magnetized can be selected from many cores strung on the same wire.

It is a natural question to ask how a single core can be magnetized

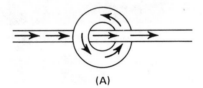

(A)

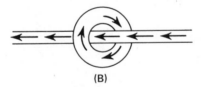

(B)

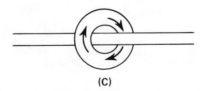

(C)

Fig. 7–6. States of core magnetization. (A) Counterclockwise magnetization represents "0"; (B) clockwise magnetization represents "1"; (C) core remains magnetized after current is removed; the "1" value stored in core remains.

when there are many cores on one wire. Selection of a certain core for magnetism is made possible by two wires that pass through each core. By simply sending through each wire only half the amount of current necessary to magnetize a core, only the core at the *intersection* of the wires with electric current is affected (Fig. 7–7). In this manner a screen of wires called a "magnetic core plane," can contain any number of cores. The 1 or 0 representation stored in a core is called a "bit," an acronym formed from "binary digit."

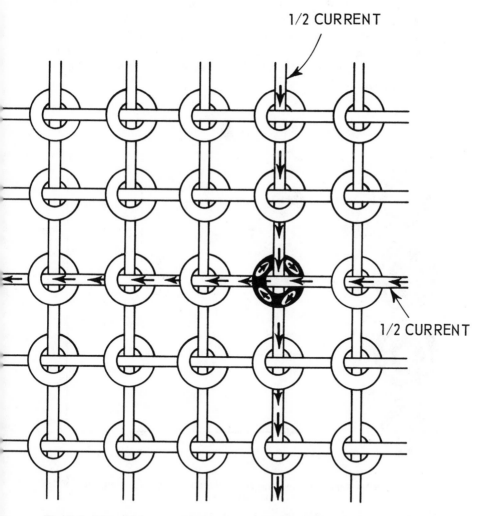

1/2 CURRENT

1/2 CURRENT

Fig. 7–7. Magnetizing a particular core by sending only half the amount of current necessary to magnetize a core through the wire. Only the core at the intersection of the wires with electric current is affected.

BINARY-CODED DECIMAL REPRESENTATION

You will recall from the last chapter that decimal information may be represented with the binary-coded decimal (BCD) number system. Using a combination of the first four places of binary, we can express any digit. Therefore, if we stack four core planes and give each a value of 1, 2, 4, or 8, as in Fig. 7–8, each column of cores will represent a number.

In other words, the cores for any storage position are located *one above the other* on each of the planes. For instance, the value of decimal 6 is represented by the binary notation 0110 in Fig. 7–8. This means that the cores in planes 1 and 8 of the same storage position are "off" (i.e., consist of "0" bits) and the cores in planes 2 and 4 of the same storage position are "on" (representing the "1" bits). Thus, the combined values of the "on" cores are equal to 6.

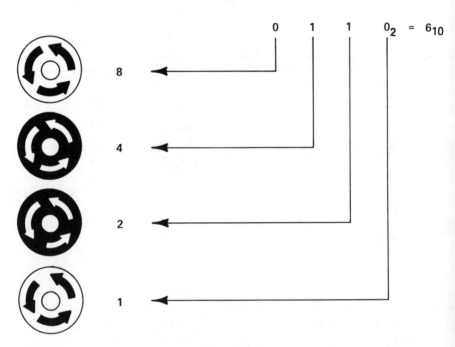

$$0 \quad 1 \quad 1 \quad 0_2 \;=\; 6_{10}$$

Fig. 7–8. **Four cores, stacked one above the other, represents any one of ten decimal digits.**

Representing Letters

By adding two more planes to the array (Fig. 7–9), we have the capability of storing alphabetic and special characters such as the % or # signs. In a punched card, zone punches are combined with numeric punches to represent letters. These two additional planes, identified as A and B, serve the same purpose:

The 12 zone (A-I) is represented by a "1" bit in the A and B plane.
The 11 zone (J-R) by a "1" bit in the B plane.
The 0 zone (S-Z) by a "1" bit in the A plane.

Although the "0" bits are necessary to represent conditions either written or illustrated, the "1" bits are usually referred to and the other bits

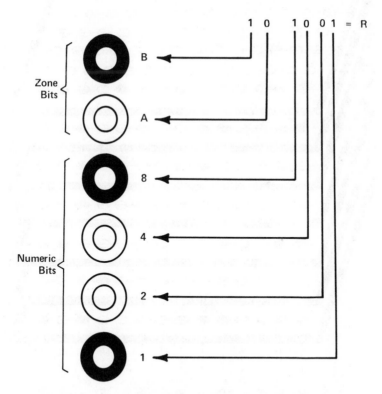

Fig. 7–9. Six cores can represent letters A–Z and 28 special characters in addition to numbers.

are assumed to be "0." BCD notation 110001, as an example, representing the letter A would be described as having a "1" bit in the A, B, and 1 planes of the storage location. Figure 7–10 illustrates how alphabetic characters as well as numbers appear in memory. The coding structures for all BCD characters except special characters are shown in Fig. 7–17.

As a final note, we should mention that the cores are magnetized automatically by the computer to represent the data read from the input device and are of no concern to the programmer. For better understanding of the computer, we shall now study how the cores work.

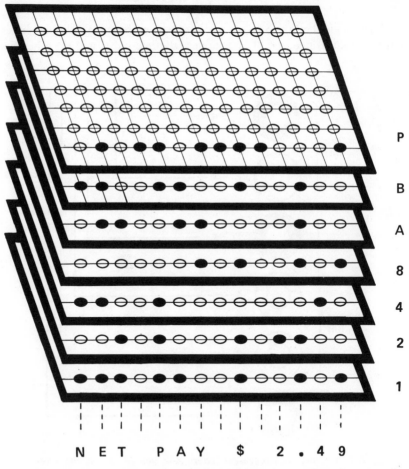

Fig. 7–10. Array of magnetic core planes representing numbers, letters, and special characters in BCD.

STORAGE AND ACCESS OF DATA

Once data is stored in memory, we must be able to recall it when needed. When data is read out of storage, only the image is transferred. The magnetism of the cores remains unaltered; thus, "read-out" is nondestructive.

This is the opposite of reading in data, where previous data in the same core position is automatically destroyed. Thus the term "read-in" implies a destructive function.

Computers Self-Check Their Work

During operations involving movement of the bits to and from each storage location, the computer automatically checks the validity of the data. This built-in method of self-checking is called "parity checking." Most computers employ odd parity, but a few are designed to use even parity.

The plane labeled "P" in Fig. 7–10 contains the parity bit. In odd parity, the bits that are turned "on" in each character position are counted. If the count is an even number, the bit in the parity plane for that position is turned "on." If the count is an odd number, the parity bit is left "off."

For the digits 0 to 9, the check bit is "on" for digits 0, 3, 5, 6, and 9 because they involve an even number of "on" bits. The check bit is "off" for digits 1, 2, 4, 7, and 8, since the total of "on" bits is an odd number. In other words, this infrequent hardware malfunction causes processing to stop and the address having erroneous data is identified on the operator console or printer whenever the total number of "1" bits encountered in a storage position is even.

In computers designed with even parity, a "1" bit is added to the parity plane for each location in memory containing an uneven number of "on" bits.

Why EBCDIC?

As we have seen, BCD uses four bits (each valued at 1, 2, 4, 8) to represent numbers plus two additional bits (A and B) to represent letters. These six bits can represent 64 (2^6) different combinations, which include the ten decimal numbers 0 to 9, the 26 upper-case letters A to Z, and 28 special characters ($ sign, for example). Most third-generation computers needed additional combinations, such as those that represent both upper- and lower-case letters.

As a result, the BCD system has been *extended* from six bits to eight bits and named the "Extended Binary Coded Decimal Interchange Code" (EBCDIC). The EBCDIC (pronounced ib-si-dick) system (Fig. 7–11) makes

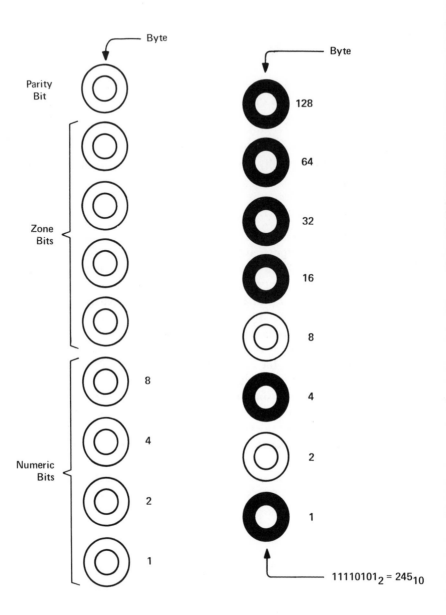

Parity
Bit

Zone
Bits

Numeric
Bits

8

4

2

1

Byte

128

64

32

16

8

4

2

1

$11110101_2 = 245_{10}$

Fig. 7–11. EBCDIC has a stack of eight cores plus the parity bit. Each column of cores can store any of the digits 0 to 9, letters A to Z, or 256 special characters.

Fig. 7–12. Larger binary numbers can be included in EBCDIC memories. A word consisting of four bytes can store up to 2,147,483,648 (2^{31}) in binary.

possible 256 (2^8) different bit combinations. The words "Interchange Code" in its name derive from this fact.

Prior to third-generation computers, manufacturers designed their equipment with no regard for standardization. This resulted in different coded forms of binary so that a program written for one computer model could not ordinarily run on a different model. Consequently, EBCDIC was adopted as a standardized code to overcome some of the problems associated with installations having two or more incompatible computers, or when installations outgrew their present equipment and upgraded to a more powerful EDPS.

Another advantage of the eight-bit code is the storage of larger binary numbers. The BCD's six bits can store a binary number equivalent to decimal 63 (0 to 63), whereas EBCDIC can handle up to 255 (0 to 255) in decimal (Fig. 7–12).

NUMERIC EBCDIC REPRESENTATION

The eight bits that comprise an EBCDIC*character make up a *byte*. The byte is broken into two halves, four bits for the zone and four bits for the BCD number. A number is represented in the same manner as BCD except that the four zone bits are *all* 1's (which have no numeric value) rather than 0's in the two zone bits, as in BCD (Fig. 7–13).

Digits Can Be Packed

Data may be operated upon in binary or EBCDIC decimal form. Binary operations, performed as fixed-length operations, are ideal for jobs needing heavy computations, such as scientific or engineering, because binary operations are faster than decimal. Decimal operations, carried out in a variable-length manner, are found in commercial operations that require few calculations.

Decimal operations permit data to be "packed," a term referring to two decimal digits placed in one byte. An advantage of EBCDIC, therefore, is that two BCD numbers can be packed into one byte comprising eight bits (Fig. 7–14). This doubles the storage capacity by using the zone bits to store as a second digit. If only one decimal digit is stored in a byte position, we say

---

*IBM devised the EBCDIC scheme for the S/360 and the IBM S/370. Other computer manufacturers also use EBCDIC. ASCII is another code used by some computers and also for transmitting data over communications lines. ASCII is also referred to as USASCII (U.S. Standard Code for Information Interchange) or ANSCII (American National Standard Code for Information Interchange).

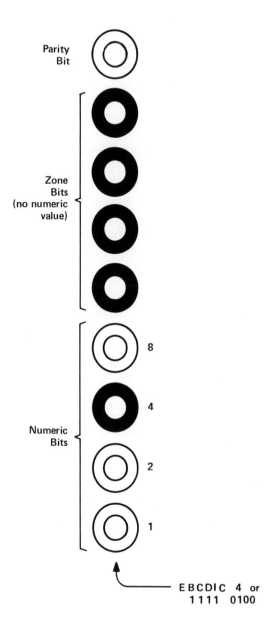

Fig. 7–13. An EBCDIC digit representation. The four-zone bits have no numerical value.

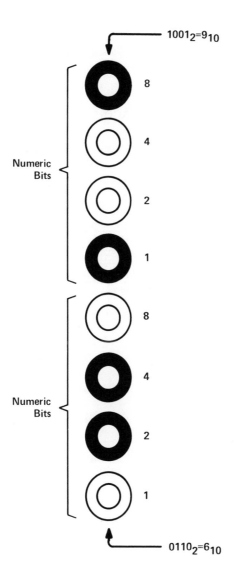

Fig. 7–14. Two BCD numbers are packed by using the zone bits, thus doubling the storage capacity.

that the byte is *unpacked.* Figure 7–15 shows two numbers in packed and unpacked form.

REPRESENTING LETTERS IN EBCDIC

As we have seen, binary-coded decimal systems are divided into two parts. The left bits in memory may be associated with letters, and thus are called "zone" bits. The right four bits are numeric bits:

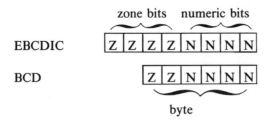

Identification is as follows:

Letters A to I are identified as 1100 in the zone portion of the byte, in combination with the BCD number in the rightmost four bits.
Letters J to R have 1101 in the zone bits in combination with the BCD number.
Letters S to Z have 1110 zone bits in combination with the BCD number.

Figure 7–16 illustrates how EBCDIC alphabetic characters appear in memory, and Fig. 7–17 shows the coding structure for other letters and numbers.

EBCDIC AND HEXADECIMAL RELATIONSHIP

Up to this point we have considered storage of numbers in BCD or EBCDIC form. In Chapter 6, we discussed several numbering systems, including hexadecimal (hex). The hexadecimal system, because of its base 16, bridges the gap between our base 10 decimal system and the computer's binary system. As such, one of the hexadecimal symbols (see Fig. 7–18) can be stored in half of a byte location. Recalling that hex F equals decimal 15, or 1111 in binary, a byte can store two hexadecimal

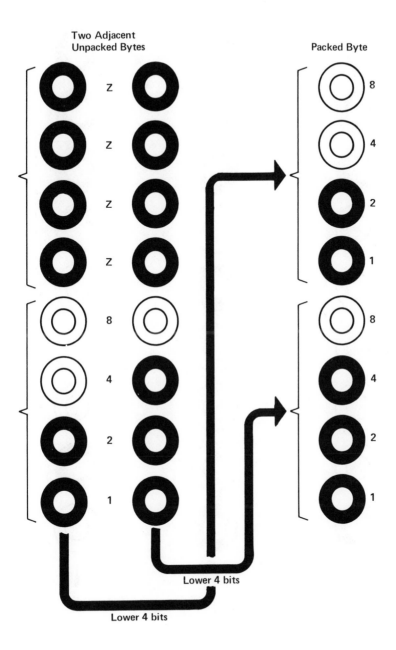

Fig. 7–15. Two unpacked bytes packed into one byte.

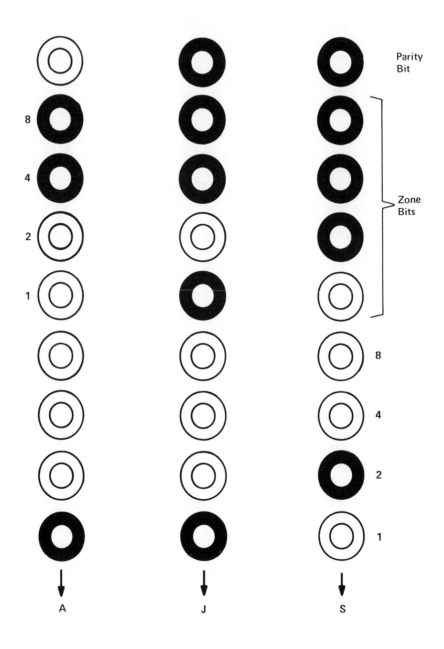

Fig. 7–16. Storage of alphabetical characters in EBCDIC.

Character	Card Code	BCD		Hexadecimal	EBCDIC	
		Zone	8421		Zone	8421
A	12-1	11	0001	C1	1100	0001
B	12-2	11	0010	C2	1100	0010
C	12-3	11	0011	C3	1100	0011
D	12-4	11	0100	C4	1100	0100
E	12-5	11	0101	C5	1100	0101
F	12-6	11	0110	C6	1100	0110
G	12-7	11	0111	C7	1100	0111
H	12-8	11	1000	C8	1100	1000
I	12-9	11	1001	C9	1100	1001
J	11-1	10	0001	D1	1101	0001
K	11-2	10	0010	D2	1101	0010
L	11-3	10	0011	D3	1101	0011
M	11-4	10	0100	D4	1101	0100
N	11-5	10	0101	D5	1101	0101
O	11-6	10	0110	D6	1101	0110
P	11-7	10	0111	D7	1101	0111
Q	11-8	10	1000	D8	1101	1000
R	11-9	10	1001	D9	1101	1001
S	0-2	01	0010	E2	1110	0010
T	0-3	01	0011	E3	1110	0011
U	0-4	01	0100	E4	1110	0100
V	0-5	01	0101	E5	1110	0101
W	0-6	01	0110	E6	1110	0110
X	0-7	01	0111	E7	1110	0111
Y	0-8	01	1000	E8	1110	1000
Z	0-9	01	1001	E9	1110	1001
0	0	00	1010	F0	1111	0000
1	1	00	0001	F1	1111	0001
2	2	00	0010	F2	1111	0010
3	3	00	0011	F3	1111	0011
4	4	00	0100	F4	1111	0100
5	5	00	0101	F5	1111	0101
6	6	00	0110	F6	1111	0110
7	7	00	0111	F7	1111	0111
8	8	00	1000	F8	1111	1000
9	9	00	1001	F9	1111	1001

Fig. 7-17. Hexadecimal, BCD, and EBCDIC characters, excluding special characters.

symbols. Consequently, the maximum that can be stored in a byte is hex FF, or binary 1111 1111.

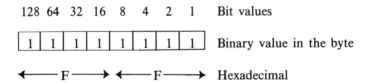

Note in Fig. 7–17 that for each EBCDIC character, there is a corresponding hexadecimal number. Recalling our hexadecimal discussion in the preceding chapter, we can see that the *left* and *right* halves of the EBCDIC representations can be identified by two hex symbols. For example, the number 6, represented as 1111 0110, has an equivalent F6 in hex:

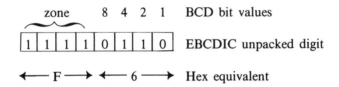

But what is the relationship between 1111 0110 and F6? As we have said, the computer operates in true binary, BCD, or EBCDIC. Therefore we need to bridge the gap between the computer's cumbersome binary language and a more easily understood language for people.

Decimal	Hexadecimal	Binary	Decimal	Hexadecimal	Binary
0	0	0000	8	8	1000
1	1	0001	9	9	1001
2	2	0010	10	A	1010
3	3	0011	11	B	1011
4	4	0100	12	C	1100
5	5	0101	13	D	1101
6	6	0110	14	E	1110
7	7	0111	15	F	1111

Fig. 7–18. *Hexadecimal* uses a base of 16, thus 16 counting symbols. Each of the symbols, representing the numbers 0 to 15, stands for four binary digits.

If we needed to see the contents of memory at a particular location, say,

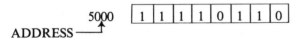

ADDRESS

we could instruct the computer to write on the printer or display on the console, and the contents of location 5000 would appear as F6. Recall that we stated that 1111 in the zone position has no numeric value if the number is unpacked—so the data at location 5000 is really decimal 6.

Had the byte been involved with an arithmetic operation, the program would have packed two digits in the byte. As a result, the computer would have printed two hexadecimal symbols. The decimal digits would be the same as hex digits; so, for example, 26 would have been printed as

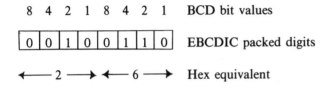

SUMMARY

There are two major classifications of digital computers, fixed word-length and variable word-length. In a fixed word-length computer, data is handled in a parallel fashion, one word at a time. A word can store several numbers or letters, depending upon the design of the computer. This is opposite to variable word-length computers, which process data in a serial manner, character by character.

Data is stored in the internal memory of most third-generation computers in two basic forms, binary or the eight-bit EBCDIC arrangement. Second-generation computers and a few third-generation computers use binary or the six-bit BCD arrangement. Internal memory is usually constructed of magnetic cores, and the data or an instruction at each location can be accessed through its word or character *address.*

Computers having six-bit BCD memory design can store one decimal digit, a binary number, or a letter at each core location. Computers designed with the eight-bit EBCDIC memory can likewise store one decimal digit, a binary number, or a letter at each core location. Greater flexibility is possible with the eight-bit code because two BCD digits can be packed into each byte location, but EBCDIC necessitates the use of hexadecimal in communicating with the computer. Unfortunately, communication with the computer is awkward because of hex's unfamiliar base 16. In addition to storage of numbers, letters, or pure binary, special characters can also be stored at each location in both BCD and EBCDIC designed computers.

In Chapters 6 and 7 we have explained how the construction of internal memory permits the storage of data in binary forms. We use this knowledge in the next three chapters as we concentrate on learning how the computer processes data according to instructions given in the program.

KEY TERMS TO REMEMBER

Access time
Address, memory
BCD
Bit
Byte
CPU
Destructive read-in
EBCDIC
Fixed-word concept
Hex or hexadecimal
Internal Storage

Magnetic core
Nondestructive read-out
Packed data
Parallel processing
Parity check
Plane, memory
Serial processing
Unpacked data
Variable-word concept
Word

QUESTIONS

1. Name the three components housed in the CPU.
2. Which of the two categories of storage has the fastest access time?
3. Name the four areas of memory needed for processing and describe the purpose of each.
4. A computer word is associated with which type of computer? A computer character?
5. What makes possible the retrieval of data from a specific location in memory?
6. Name the advantages and disadvantages of serial and parallel computers.
7. How many planes are there in a BCD computer? In an EBCDIC computer?
8. What do we mean when we say that a computer performs validity checking by odd parity?
9. Explain the two ways that the magnetism of cores is controlled.
10. What is the relationship between the zone bits in a core position and the zone punches in a card?
11. Is the programmer concerned with the terms "destructive" and "nondestructive" as relates to storage of data? Why?
12. How does hexadecimal bridge the communications gap between EBCDIC and man?
13. A stack of eight cores can represent an unpacked or packed number(s) as well as one letter. Explain.
14. Whereas a stack of six BCD cores wastes two bits in storage of numbers, a stack of eight EBCDIC cores wastes four bits in storage of unpacked numbers. Name four advantages that counterbalance the stated EBCDIC disadvantage.

15. In Fig. 7–10, what would be the bit structure for each of the numbers, letters, and special characters if the array were an EBCDIC memory?

COORDINATED READINGS IN CHAPTER 15

"Dissent in an Organization," Sec. 20.
"The Insecure Manager," Sec. 21.
"Protection of the Computer Installation," Sec. 27.

Chapter **8**

COMPUTER HARDWARE AND SOFTWARE

A computer system accepts the problem (input), solves the problem (processing), and gives the desired results (output). This process centers around the equipment, called "hardware," and the program of instructions, called "software."

WHY THE COMPUTER?

The first commercial computer, a UNIVAC I, was installed in 1954 at Louisville, Kentucky, to process General Electric's payroll. Until then, business information was handled by a series of unit-record machines, also known as punched card equipment (Fig. 8–1). Each piece of equipment performed a limited operation such as sorting, calculating, or printing. Consequently, the work flow had to progress from one machine to another during the various stages of processing. This meant also that a machine operator had to accompany the punched cards to each machine and perform certain equipment operations (Fig. 8–2).

The normal data flow was as follows:

1. *Keypunch*—sales documents converted into punched cards.

2. *Card-proving machine*—transactions cards edited for accuracy of data.

3. *Sorter*—transaction cards sorted into desired sequence, such as account number.

IBM 514 REPRODUCER

IBM 188 COLLATOR

IBM 84 SORTER

IBM 108 CARD-PROVING MACHINE

IBM 609 CALCULATOR

IBM 557 INTERPRETER

IBM 29 KEYPUNCH

IBM 407 ACCOUNTING MACHINE

Fig. 8–1. A typical punched card system composed of individual machines, each capable of performing limited functions. They are often used for economically processing low-volume jobs, thus freeing the computer for other work. (By permission of IBM.)

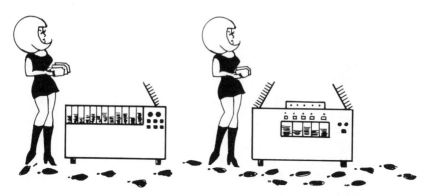

(1) She sorts the detail transaction cards.   (2) Next she merges them with master cards.

(3) Then she calculates the cards.   (4) Finally, she prints the cards.

Fig. 8–2. In a unit-record system the work flows from one machine to another accompanied by an operator.

4. *Calculator*—amount due calculated.

5. *Collator*—transaction cards merged with master address cards.

6. *Accounting machine* and *reproducer*—an accounts receivable listing produced as billing cards were punched by the electrically connected reproducer.

7. *Interpreter*—created billing cards printed with customer address for mailing.

Now the computer does all these individual machine operations at one time. The computer is composed of several components, interconnected by electrical cables. One component reads the data, another sorts and computes the data, and another does the printing. This concept makes possible the electronic control of all data processing functions with little or no *human* intervention (Fig. 8–3).

As a means of handling the ever-growing mass of business data, the computer represented a sharp departure from unit-record equipment concepts. It was faster and more accurate because electronic components replaced slower electromechanical parts. Its *larger* memory satisfied company needs to store huge quantities of information.

TYPES OF COMPUTERS

There are two major classifications of electronic computers, analog and digital. Our study will be about the general-purpose digital computer. The analog computer, after definition, will not be considered further.

Analog Computers

The analog computer was developed during a five-year period ending in 1930 by Dr. Vannevar Bush and others at the Massachusetts Institute of Technology (MIT). Two common examples illustrate the use of the analog computer: the speedometer and the gas pump. In the speedometer, tire revolutions are converted to miles per hour and translated to digits on the speedometer dial. In the gas pump, the flow of fuel is converted to gallons pumped and the dollar amount.

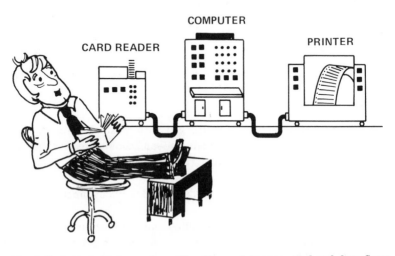

Fig. 8–3. In a computer system, all units are interconnected and data flows from one unit to another without operator guidance.

We can say that the analog computer takes a measured amount of information (such as stresses on airplane wings), calculates numbers representing these physical magnitudes, and presents the answer in measurable form or results. Analog computers, therefore, are ideal for use in engineering problems. They provide only approximate results because the quantities being measured, such as temperature or voltage, are continuously variable. The fuel pump, for example, shows $3.50 instead of $3.49 for 10 gallons at 34.9 cents per gallon.

Digital Computers

Whereas the analog computer determines the desired answer based upon physical measurement, the *digital* computer produces the desired result based upon computation of numbers. For this reason, digital computers are more accurate than analog computers. Therefore, the latter are not adaptable for processing of business data. To cite an example: The analog computer may produce accuracy to within 99.5% of the correct value, which cannot be tolerated in financial problems, where an answer to the nearest penny rather than to the nearest hundred or thousand dollars is important.

Special-Purpose Computers

Digital computers may be built for either special or general uses. A special-purpose computer is designed for the sole purpose of performing one specific task. For example, special-purpose computers made possible the landing of man on the moon.

The first docking of two space vehicles was performed on March 16, 1966. This preliminary step to the use of orbiting space stations in launching other spacecraft consisted of joining an Agena vehicle with the manned Gemini 8 capsule. With data provided by a small but highly sophisticated computer aboard Agena 8, the astronauts were able to maneuver their space capsule for docking.

This incredible docking at 17,500 miles per hour was accomplished in 30 minutes with the aid of a special-purpose computer the size of a breadbox. The computations for vital data needed to control Agena 8 during docking would have taken a mathematician about 35,000 hours, or 4 years. Thus, man does not have sufficient time in space to handle the necessary calculations by hand.

As we have seen, going to the moon is truly made possible by special-purpose computers because man cannot react fast or precisely enough. The complexities of rendezvousing in space (Fig. 8–4) boggles the mind, since everything in space is askew. In other words, the laws on earth differ from

Fig. 8–4. Docking maneuver, looking from the lunar module (LM) toward the Apollo 9 command module. A computer selects and fires thrusting rockets so that Apollo 9 will not stray from the same orbit of the LM. (Courtesy of NASA.)

those in space. For example, whenever you gain in one direction in outer space, you lose in another. To rendezvous on earth, you simple speed up to close the gap. But as soon as you speed up near the moon, you move into a higher orbit with a slower orbital velocity. By firing the spacecraft's retrorockets to slow down, you drop to a lower orbit. The problem must be solved by igniting the rocket within a split second. A small special-purpose computer, built by MIT and Raytheon Corporation, solves the tricky problem with fast and precise computations. For instance, an addition is performed in 24 millionths of a second. Although man is incapable of such performance, he can build computers that compensate for his lack of speed.

General-Purpose Computers

Business computers must be able to perform a variety of jobs, such as payroll, inventory, and sales analysis. The general-purpose computer satisfies this requirement through its ability to store different programs of instructions. This versatility means that the program to process the payroll can be carried out by the computer at one time and finished, and then be immediately replaced by the inventory control program for a new job.

We should point out at this time that third-generation general-purpose computers can handle scientific or business applications. Scientific applications are characterized by small quantities of input data (the problem), a vast amount of computations, and very little output (the solution). Table 8–1 lists differences in requirements between the two types.

In contrast, business applications involve large quantities of both numeric and alphabetic input data (i.e., employee time cards), relatively little processing, and large quantities of output (i.e., pay checks, tax data, etc.). In short, the emphasis is upon computational speed for the scientific job and speeds of input/output devices for business jobs, which comprise about 70 percent of the computer market. Figure 8–5 summarizes the applications of these computers.

We have explained the terms that distinguish different types of computers: analog, digital, general-purpose, special-purpose, and business and scientific computers. Let us now turn our attention to the general-purpose business computer, which happens to be digital.

Table 8–1. General differences between scientific and business requirements.

Processing	Common Requirements for Scientific Applications	Common Requirements for Business Applications
Input volume	Low	High
Input speed	Slow	Fast
Ratio of computations to input	High	Low
Computer speed	High	Low
Memory size	Small, but varies with type of problem	Large, but varies with type of problem
Output volume	Low	High
Output speed	Slow	Fast

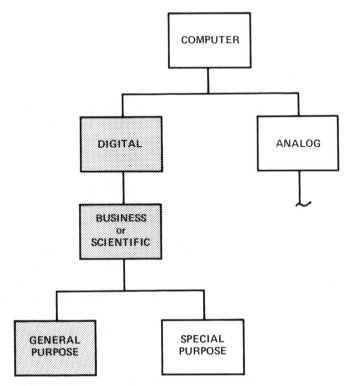

Fig. 8–5. Types of computers. The shaded blocks indicate the areas in which the bulk of computers is used.

DEFINING COMPUTER HARDWARE

Our study of how computers handle business information will begin with the simplest approach, after which we shall build up to the whole concept. A computer system (Fig. 8–6) is made up of a number of individual pieces of *"hardware"* (machines) that perform some part of the data processing operation. These different machines are interconnected by electrical cables so that they function as a single machine. Thus, one machine serves as input and reads the data, which is transferred to the processor, another piece of hardware. Similarly, after processing, the data is transferred to a third machine, which serves as output to record the result.

The term "hardware," therefore, is applicable to the physical components that perform data input, processing of the data (such as computation), and data output. Hardware consists of devices containing electrical, magnetic, mechanical, and electronic components.

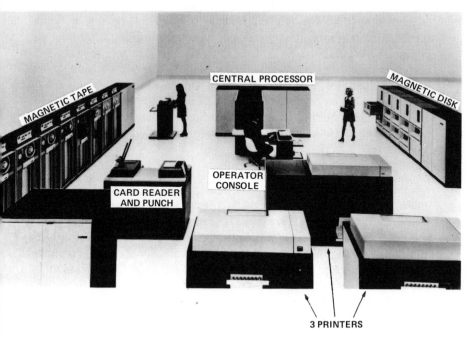

Fig. 8–6. The IBM System 370 is the outgrowth of IBM System 360, the
workhorse of third-generation computers. (By permission of IBM.)

Input, Process, and Output

The major functions of any computer system consist of *input* $\longrightarrow$
process $\longrightarrow$ *output.* A system consists of the central processor, sometimes
referred to as the computer or processor, with input and output components. Thus, we frequently interchange the terms "computer" and "central
processor," but essentially the word "system" refers to the processor *and*
its input/output (I/O) devices.

The time required to pass an input record from the input unit, through
the central processor, and have it emerge as the output unit record is called
"throughput." Throughput, therefore, depends upon the *speed* of input,
processing, and output operations.

The central processor unit (CPU) is made up of electronic parts, which
make it the fastest unit in the system. The I/O units are mechanical devices
and therefore are relatively slow in comparison to the CPU. Mechanical
parts in the I/O units consist of (for example) wheels and belts to transport
cards past reading stations or rotating print chains containing numbers and
the alphabet.

When the CPU is idle while waiting for the I/O units, the system is said to be "I/O-bound." This happens because the I/O units operate at typical speeds such as reading 1000 cards per minute or printing 1200 lines per minute. Although this seems fast, the CPU performs several thousand operations every second. Therefore, we might say that the CPU outruns the I/O units and must wait until they catch up. This idle time has been usefully shared by two or more programs occupying memory at the same time. This concept, called "multiprogramming," will receive more attention in Chapter 14.

Variety of Input and Output Units

Much versatility is given to computer processing through a number of different types of I/O devices (Fig. 8–7) that handle different kinds of data media. Certain advantages are gained by using one I/O medium rather than another. For example, small amounts of data may be economically stored in punched cards, while large volumes of data are stored on magnetic tape. The selection factors involving the I/O media are discussed in Chapter 14. For the time being, it will suffice to say that I/O media are selected on the bases of economic considerations, volume of data, frequency of processing, nature of source documents for input, and type of output required.

The CPU Consists of Three Components

We have explained in simplest terms that information is read by input units, is processed by the central processing unit (CPU), and the results of processing are recorded on output units. Next, we shall explain what happens inside the computer, as the central processing unit is often called. The CPU is considered the heart of the entire computer system (Fig. 8–8).

Data sent to the CPU must be stored until needed. Processing, such as computations and data comparisons, must also take place, and some component inside the computer must carry out processing steps and control the operation of I/O units. There are three distinct functions performed by the CPU: storage, computation, and control.

Storage. Memory inside the computer (thus, the name "internal memory") has the ability to accept, remember, and transfer information that has been stored in it. The main function of memory is to hold the program and data being processed. The size of memory may vary from a few thousand positions to several million. Each position in memory is numbered, permitting the computer to store a number or letter, and then locate and use that data as needed. More will be said about this in Chapter 10.

Arithmetic-Logic. The arithmetic-logic section of the CPU does the actual work of problem solution, which involves addition, subtraction,

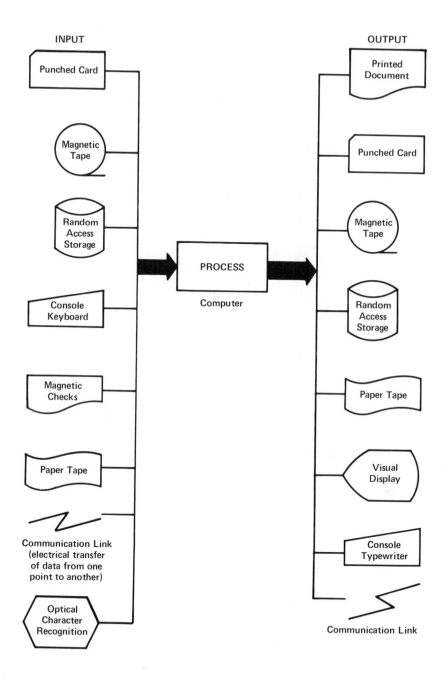

Fig. 8–7. A computer system may have a variety of input and output devices.

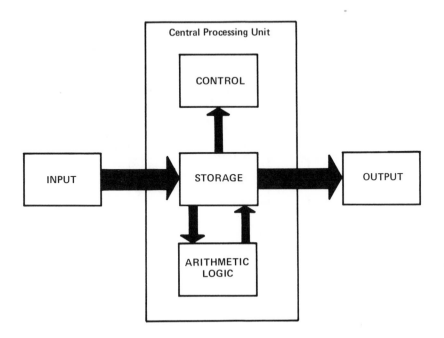

Fig. 8–8. A computer system consists of five basic components. The CPU normally houses three of these components.

multiplication, and division. The logic portion can compare two factors; based upon the decision made after the comparison, the computer carries out specific operations. From comparison of two numbers, for example, one number can be less than, equal to, or greater than the other number. When this quality has been decided, records being processed can be checked to see if they are in sequential order (Fig. 8–9). The logic portion can also distinguish positive, negative, or zero values resulting from arithmetic operations. Based upon a net pay computation, for example, the computer can be instructed to bypass writing a check for zero amounts.

Control. The nerve center of the entire computer system is the control component. Processing of data within the central processor and movement of data between components are supervised here. Also, all operations performed by the many possible I/O units are directed by the control component. Its prime function, however, is to obtain one at a time the instructions stored in memory and to execute them. By "execution" is meant the directions sent to other parts of the computer system so that they perform their specific functions. This simple description does not clearly explain just how

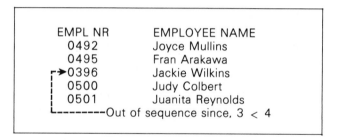

Fig. 8–9. Sequence is determined by a comparison in the arithmetic-logic unit.

instructions cause the processing of data, but Chapter 10 will clarify the procedure.

SOFTWARE

Instructions stored within the computer are called a "stored program." A program is simply a set of machine instructions that directs the computer, step by step, in the solution of a problem. These series of steps are followed by the computer in a prescribed sequence so that it will produce the desired processing.

Programs written to instruct hardware to process business data in a meaningful way are called "software." Hence, "hardware" means the physical components of the computer and "software" means the program associated with each application of the computer. Software is simply man's way of communicating to the computer what he wants done and how to do it.

According to this definition, there are two types of software: application programs and computer efficiency programs. Application programs are written by the user to solve company problems, such as payrolls. Computer efficiency programs are generally written by the manufacturer of the equipment. More commonly, the latter are called "software" in order to distinguish between company programs and manufacturer programs. For this reason, we shall refer hereafter to manufacturer programming aids as software and to user programs as application programs, or simply programs.

THE PROGRAMMER

The business computer in itself does not save time or money, improve management, deal with increased volumes of data, solve complex problems, or improve customer service. In fact, it cannot provide anything beneficial by itself. But with human guidance a computer can read input data, process it, and provide desired results in the desired format. It can compute and print the result where and when you want it, but it cannot produce management miracles. In sum, a computer is only one of many ingredients that make a successful business.

The computer's human guide is called a "programmer." A programmer essentially analyzes the problem and source data, determines the solution, and transcribes the results into a program for the computer. The programmer must know precisely how the computer works; of equal importance is his knowledge about the application or problem in order to meet the requirements expected. Although the programmer knows all about the computer and problem, the computer cannot produce the desired results unless the programmer knows how to solve the problem. Therefore, creative thinking is a "must" for effective programming.

It is too early in our study to explain how the computer hardware works with real program instructions, but some students may care to glance at the sample program given in the next chapter. We have now explained hardware and software, so let us see how they fit together.

SOFTWARE AND HARDWARE INTERACTION

Computer memory stores three basic elements: software, application programs, and data being processed (Fig. 8–10).

The manufacturer's software is called the "operating system." In general, the operating system is designed to:

1. Improve computer efficiency by reducing the amount of time that a computer is idle.
2. Aid the programmer by relieving him of complex and repetitive operations, such as input/output functions.

Without an operating system, a computer will stop at the end of every job and wait for the computer operator to set up the machine for the next job. During this time, the computer remains idle, thereby wasting money. An operating system eliminates this waste time by immediately starting a new job upon finishing another, as explained in Chapter 14.

Operating systems are relatively large programs. A typical medium-sized computer might use one with 16,000 positions, whereas an operating system for a large-scale computer could range up to 120,000 positions or more.

The program for the application being run is fed into the computer when the job is started. It remains in storage while the individual instruc-

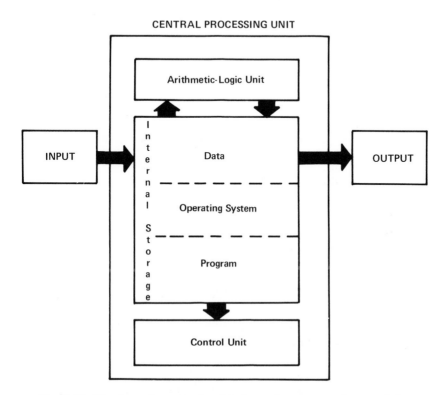

Fig. 8–10. The three elements stored in internal memory: software of the operating system (manufacturer-written); the application program software (user-written); and the data to be processed.

tions are being carried out by the control unit.

A program works something like this. The first record is read by the input device (say, a card reader) and is stored in a holding area in memory. The control unit calls the instructions one at a time from internal memory and places then in the control unit. It interprets the instructions by determining what has to be done, and then executes the instruction that tells other parts of the system what to do.

Each instruction continues to move to the control unit at the proper time until all instructions in the program have been executed. Then the second record is read into memory from the input device and the program is repeated. Instructions called by the control unit have two parts: the operation code and the address (Fig. 8–11). The operation code indicates what operation is to be performed (add, compare, etc.) while the symbolic address tells in what location the data is located in memory. A symbolic

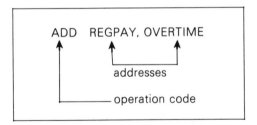

Fig. 8–11. A symbolic instruction that adds overtime pay to regular pay.

address, representative of the data at that address, identifies the location in memory rather than using its absolute address. For example, the symbolic address CUSTOMER is easier for the programmer to remember than the absolute address 4067.

In the next chapter, we shall be more specific and illustrate how a program is actually executed.

AUXILIARY STORAGE AND CHANNELS

Figure 8–12 shows the complete computer system. Note that two new devices, channels and auxiliary storage, have been added to show the whole system.

A channel is a hardware element that provides a path for the movement of data between input/output units and the central processor. Because of the differences in speed between the fast CPU and slow I/O units, the channel compensates for the variance. Once the channel has received a signal from the control unit, it operates independently to read a new record from the input device, to print a line, or to perform some other instruction. Thus, the CPU is free to continue executing more instructions in the program, which reduces idle time. This concept is referred to as overlapped input and output with processing.

Each type of I/O device has a controller (Fig. 8–12), which executes orders to one of the I/O units. The controller simply serves as an interface between the channel and one or more I/O devices. For example, Fig. 8–12 shows one controller handling three tape units. Slow I/O devices are connected to a single channel.

Storage exists in different forms. Although physically different, the functions and operations of these forms are basically the same. Auxiliary (also called "secondary") storage devices are used to hold large quantities of data. This type of storage is usually magnetic disk and costs much less

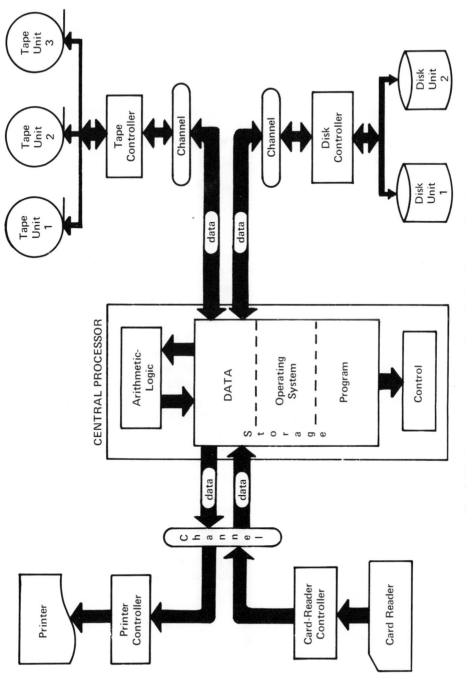

Fig. 8-12. A computer system with typical hardware and software.

145

than storage inside the central processor. The difference in cost between the two storage devices occurs because internal storage is extremely fast (thus expensive), while external secondary storage is slower (thus economical).

Large capacity files, such as an inventory of 100,000 stock records, are retained on secondary storage devices. When an item must be updated, the appropriate record is brought into main storage in a way similar to data with any other input device. The inventory on hand is perhaps increased or decreased, and the updated record is returned to its rightful place on the disk file.

SUMMARY

Management is concerned about the computer system because it involves a substantial investment. A manager must know how the individual pieces of equipment are interrelated and how much storage is available. Otherwise, how can he make a decision to increase auxiliary storage that will hold new business volumes unless he knows what auxiliary storage is?

A computer system consists of five essential components: input, storage, arithmetic-logic, control, and output. The input and output devices are numerous and perform different functions. All these pieces of hardware are interconnected by electronic circuitry and thus operate in unison. In addition, certain channels perform overlap processing and particular controllers control multiple I/O units of the same type.

Management is very interested in software because it determines the speed with which computer projects are completed. Software can reduce CPU idle time so that large savings result, or it can permit additional projects to be run that otherwise would not be possible within the time allotted. The development of hardware technology has been incredibly fast, but software has not kept the same pace. The software investment is a large slice of the computer dollar, and is rising. In 1965, hardware expenditures were $4.5 billion compared with $1 billion in software. In 1973, hardware ran approximately $9 billion and software development cost about $10.5 billion.

The next chapter discusses how programming languages are used in communicating with the computer, and how flowcharting aids in developing programs.

KEY TERMS TO REMEMBER

Address	Arithmetic-logic unit
Application program	Auxiliary storage

Central processing unit (CPU)
Channel
Controller
Control unit
Execution, program
Hardware
I/O-bound
Multiprogramming
Operation code

Overlapped processing
Programmer
Secondary storage
Software
Storage unit
Stored program
Symbolic address
Throughput

QUESTIONS

1. What is the main difference between the concept of processing data by a computer system and a unit record system?
2. How do analog computer applications differ from those of digital computers?
3. What are some uses of special-purpose computers other than in space applications?
4. How do processing requirements of scientific applications differ from those of business applications?
5. Differentiate between the terms "software" and "hardware."
6. What do we mean when we say that a computer is I/O bound?
7. Name three components that comprise the heart of a computer system.
8. What is the term applied to instructions stored inside the computer?
9. There are good and not-so-good programmers. What do you think makes the difference?
10. How does the operating system interact with application programs?
11. Instructions are interpreted and executed by which unit of the system?
12. The program instruction is made up of which parts?
13. Why does a computer have auxiliary storage instead of all-internal memory?
14. Which two parts of the system configuration would help solve the I/O problem?
15. In Fig. 8–9, would the hardware or software be responsible for detecting the out-of-sequence condition?

COORDINATED READINGS IN CHAPTER 15

"Automation, Computers, and Progress," Sec. 37.
"Security of Programs and Data Files," Sec. 28
"Protecting the Computer Operation," Sec. 31.
"The Impact of Minicomputers," Sec. 34.

Chapter 9

COMMUNICATING WITH THE COMPUTER— PROGRAMMING LANGUAGES

In the preceding chapter we saw how the components of the central processor and various input/output devices are tied together to form an electronic data processing system. We also related the software programs to the computer hardware. In this chapter we introduce a means of communicating with the computer in order to produce the desired results through processing input data.

MAN VERSUS MACHINE COMMUNICATION

There is quite a contrast between communication with people and communicating with computers. We can say to an accountant, "Give me a list of customers who have not made a purchase within the previous 90 days and show a total of their last month's activity." Any similarity between people and computers ends here. We cannot say to a computer "include anything else you think useful," or "if anything unusual comes up, do what you think best."

The computer cannot think, but when properly instructed, it can solve problems at phenomenal speeds. It can repeat the same processing on two records or thousands without making an error. This is its advantage over humans—speed and accuracy. In a sense, though, the computer is capable of decision making. It can examine data to determine whether it is positive or negative. Two items can be compared to determine which is larger and to determine if they are equal or unequal. The computer can be given alternate courses of action to take, based upon the decision. Depending on the circumstance, it can be left to decide which course of action to take.

The computer must be given explicit instructions as to what data are to be used, how to process them, and when to record the solution. These requirements are translated into machine instructions, punched into cards, and stored inside the central processor. The step-by-step instructions in the stored program are followed *sequentially* and are performed automatically by the computer to accomplish:

> Reading and storing of input data.
> Calculation and decision-making operations necessary to give the required result.
> Selection of the output device desired to record the finished product.

CREATING THE STORED PROGRAM

The stored program is created in essentially three steps: (1) *define* the problem; (2) *flowchart* the solution; and (3) *write* a program from the flowchart.

Step 1. Define the Problem

The process of communicating with the computer involves understanding the problem, gathering all pertinent facts that are necessary to break down the problem, and then finding its solution. The basic steps in arriving at a solution are: plan the desired output, determine what input data is needed, and ascertain the processing of input that will give the desired output.

Business data that serves as input can be thought of as elements of raw information needed in processing to produce the desired results. This collection of information may relate to:

- The names and addresses of employees, the number of hours worked, and the rates of pay; facts to arrive at net pay such as insurance deductions, number of exemptions to determine taxes, etc.
- Facts relative to inventory accounting, such as quantities of items received and shipped, their nomenclature, price, and terms used to describe an object, such as size and color.
- Areas of accounts receivable or accounts payable involving names

and addresses of vendors or customers, the quantity of product, and amount owed.

Once input data has been gathered, we must analyze and describe it. The description of data includes the names of each field comprising the record, the length of each, whether the data is numeric or alpha, locations of decimal points, and so on. Next, we find out what the desired result should accomplish, by talking to the department needing computerized assistance. The business solution can apply either inside or outside the company.

External. The finished product may be checks prepared in payment of money owed, invoices based upon customer orders, etc.

Internal. Solutions may apply to ledgers maintained in order to inform management of company assets and liabilities, inventory analysis reports produced to measure the effectiveness of sales objectives, or other measures to determine the profitability of business.

Step 2. Flowchart the Solution

Having defined the problem, we must determine the steps the computer must take to process the input data in order to give the desired output. This is accomplished by drawing a *systems flowchart,* showing the major processing steps, and the inputs and the outputs resulting from each computer run (Fig. 9–1). Then a detailed flowchart that depicts the processing solution, called a *program flowchart,* will be drawn. The actual program will be developed from the program flowchart as explained in the next section. Both types of *flowcharts* consisting of symbols* connected by lines assist in solution of data processing problems and selection of the computer method by which the requirements of processing are met (Fig. 9–2).

Most computer applications involve many alternatives and exceptions, making them difficult to state verbally or in written form. The data available for input and the desired output is known. Therefore, the program flowchart consists of that processing which bridges the gaps between *input* and *output* to give the necessary final product. The creation of the flowchart is based on:

---

*Programmers tend to use a variety of symbol shapes in flowcharting; thus different meanings evolve for the same symbol. To reduce confusion, a set of uniform symbols was designed by the American National Standards Institute (ANSI).

1. Known facts about the data being processed.
2. Aims of the project.
3. Programmer's knowledge of the computer and the art of programming.
4. A combination of logical thinking and common sense.

Let us consider some operations that figure in flowcharting. We must know the type of *input documents* involved, such as master files or detail files. We must also know the type of filing medium; say, the master pay records on disk and the detail time attendance records on tape. As you will recall, *master* files contain semipermanent information that is used time after time in preparation of reports, checks, etc. In a payroll file, the master file includes a record for each employee, containing such data as employee number, name, address, social security number, withholding exemptions, rate of pay, deductions, and so forth.

On the other hand, a *detail* file contains transactions of the data to be used in the current processing and then filed as history. The transaction record representing time-attendance records includes a minimum of information, such as employee number, regular hours, and overtime hours worked. The transaction record is matched with the master record by employee number to obtain the pay rate necessary for computing gross pay, for example.

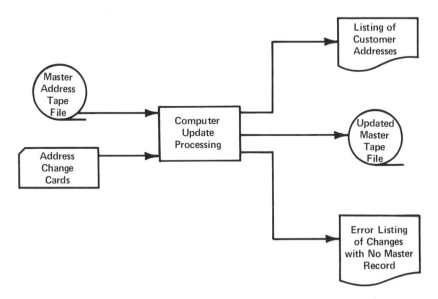

Fig. 9–1. A systems flowchart.

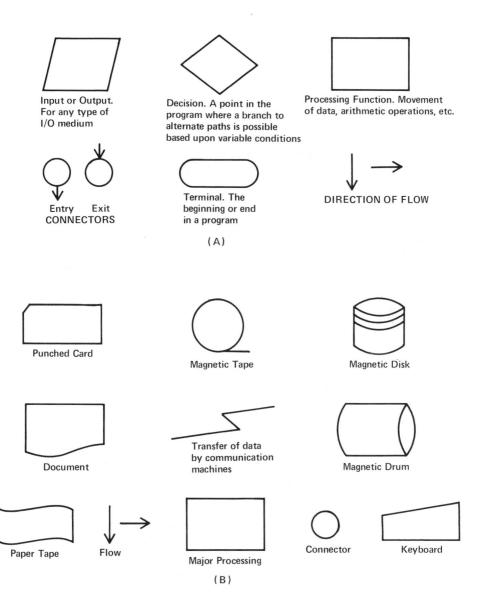

Fig. 9–2. Flowchart symbols. (A) Program flowchart symbols show step-by-step operations and processing within the computer. (B) Systems flowchart symbols show major processing operations in terms of input and output data flow.

153

Developing a Flowchart. Let us continue by developing a program flowchart to compute gross pay. To keep the problem simple, we shall assume that all information is on a single record rather than some on the master record and some on one or more detail records. Further we shall forego any overtime consideration. Nevertheless, it would be a rewarding experience for you to modify the flowchart that we develop in order to include this additional processing (see end-of-chapter questions). In a complete payroll application, a lengthy solution would be necessary to handle deductions, tax computations, etc.

Keep in mind that this flowchart will result in a *program,* which we intend to use in the next chapter in order to understand how program execution is carried out within the computer.

What information is available for input, what processing is needed, and what output is required? The input information is shown in Fig. 9–3. To sum up the processing that must be done, we compare the data on hand to be used as input with what is required for output, as shown in Fig. 9–3. Processing, therefore, consists of moving available data from the input device to the output device for printing, and the hours worked are multiplied by the pay rate, giving gross pay as the output.

The flowchart to accomplish this processing is shown in Fig. 9–4A. The first symbol ⊐ represents reading a *tape* record. Processing continues to the diamond-shaped symbol ◇ , which is a *decision* to halt the program if the last record has been read; otherwise, processing continues. The rectangle symbol □ represents *processing* of data, which involves moving the identification data elements from the input area of memory to the output area of memory. Another processing symbol performs the gross pay computation.

The processing desired has been completed, so a line of information for the record just processed is printed, represented by the symbol ⊐. The *connector* symbol ◯ represents a break in the flow of direction by indicating an *entry* ◯——▶ or an *exit* ——▶◯ point to some other part of the flowchart. The program then repeats itself in order to handle the remaining records. Without the ability for a program to repeat itself, called "looping," a separate program would be necessary for every record in the file; thus, memory locations are saved.

Step 3. Writing a Program from the Flowchart

The flowchart has made it easy for us to visualize the sequence in which operations are to be executed within the computer. In other words, the flowchart describes what takes place within a stored program. Since the flowchart represents a logical sequence in which the computer would take

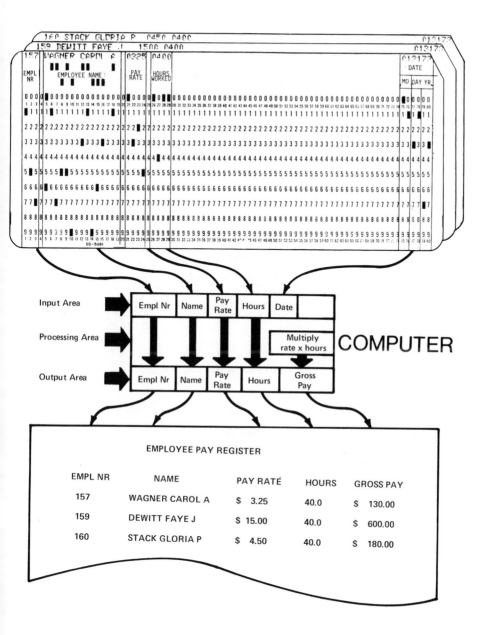

Fig. 9–3. To solve a problem, we plan the output and determine the input. "Processing" is what lies between input and output, designed to give the desired results.

155

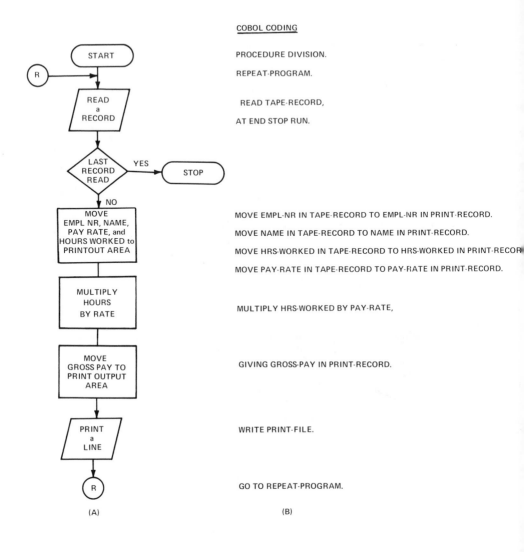

COBOL CODING

PROCEDURE DIVISION.
REPEAT-PROGRAM.

READ TAPE-RECORD,
AT END STOP RUN.

MOVE EMPL-NR IN TAPE-RECORD TO EMPL-NR IN PRINT-RECORD.
MOVE NAME IN TAPE-RECORD TO NAME IN PRINT-RECORD.
MOVE HRS-WORKED IN TAPE-RECORD TO HRS-WORKED IN PRINT-RECORD
MOVE PAY-RATE IN TAPE-RECORD TO PAY-RATE IN PRINT-RECORD.

MULTIPLY HRS-WORKED BY PAY-RATE,

GIVING GROSS-PAY IN PRINT-RECORD.

WRITE PRINT-FILE.

GO TO REPEAT-PROGRAM.

(A)   (B)

Fig. 9–4. Flowchart and program. (A) A flowchart to compute gross pay. (B) Segment of a COBOL program that produces an employee pay register.

156

in processing data, we can code the program by converting the processing that takes place within each symbol into step-by-step machine instructions.

A segment of a typical program coded from our flowchart is shown in Fig. 9–4B. Recall that we make no attempt to teach programming in a beginning text. However, we need examples of a simple program to illustrate two subjects coming up: programming languages and how the program works inside a computer.

As seen from the program in Fig. 9–4B, which is written in the COBOL (pronounced as co-ball) programming language, it is so easy to read that no explanation is needed. COBOL *(COmmon Business Oriented Language)* is the most widely used computer language written by programmers. One reason for its popularity is its *readability.*

PROGRAMMING LANGUAGES

There are three levels of programming languages: *machine* language, *assembly* language, and *high-level* languages (Fig. 9–5). In order to get a concept understanding of programming (also see Sec. 15, Chapter 15), one must be able to distinguish between the three. This understanding is also required in translating programs into machine language, a subject to be discussed shortly.

Machine-Language Programming

Programming is the means of communication between man and computer. Without this communication and without a skillful programmer to structure it, the computer could not function. The computer accepts only instructions that the engineers have designed as its vocabulary, which is an actual machine-language program. Earlier computers could accept only machine-language programs. For this reason, only the best of experts could program them. Several difficulties are encountered when writing in machine language:

1. Instructions and addresses must be coded in machine language, made up of numbers, letters, and special characters.
2. Storage locations for instructions as well as data must be kept track of by the programmer.
3. Instructions must be written in the sequence in which they are to be executed. Therefore, if an instruction is added or deleted, all succeeding instructions must be relocated and given new memory addresses.

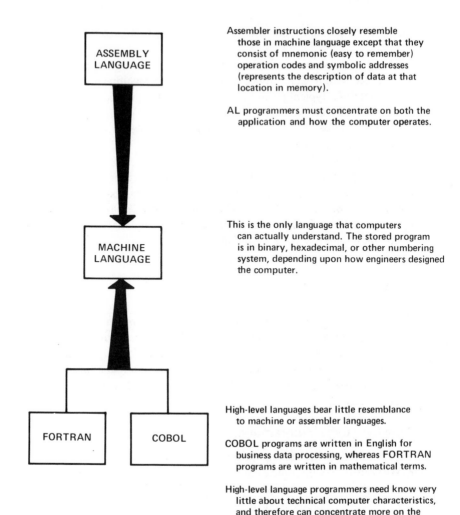

Assembler instructions closely resemble
those in machine language except that they
consist of mnemonic (easy to remember)
operation codes and symbolic addresses
(represents the description of data at that
location in memory).

AL programmers must concentrate on both the
application and how the computer operates.

This is the only language that computers
can actually understand. The stored program
is in binary, hexadecimal, or other numbering
system, depending upon how engineers designed
the computer.

High-level languages bear little resemblance
to machine or assembler languages.

COBOL programs are written in English for
business data processing, whereas FORTRAN
programs are written in mathematical terms.

High-level language programmers need know very
little about technical computer characteristics,
and therefore can concentrate more on the
problem and less on the computer.

Fig. 9–5. Three levels of programming languages.

To relieve the programmer of the difficulties of writing machine-language programs, a number of programming languages have been developed. These are easier to use and understand than machine language.

Assembly Programming

The computer must work with actual machine operation codes and addresses. However, programming in machine language burdens the programmer in that he has to look up or memorize every operation code and remember all addresses. Not only does this increase the chance of programming error, but it also intensifies debugging (correction of errors). Symbolic (assembly) programming was developed to relieve the programmer of this labor.

In assembly language, the programmer uses mnemonic operation codes and symbolic addresses. *Mnemonic* operation codes are much easier to remember than actual operation codes. For example, "D" is the operation code for "divide," which is easier to remember than the machine-language equivalent of 50. Symbolic names can be referred to instead of specifying an absolute address. The computer is given the task of assigning storage addresses to these symbolic names. As an example, the address of a storage area containing an invoice number could be referred to as INVNO. Acting under the control of a special conversion program provided by the manufacturer, the computer would then translate INVNO into an equivalent machine-language address such as 001FA0 or 000C99. Figure 9–6 shows an example of a "sort" operation programmed in assembly language.

High-Level Languages

The easiest programs to write are the so-called high-level languages such as COBOL or FORTRAN (FORmula TRANslation). High-level programming requires less effort than lower-level programming because the programmer does not need to know all the mechanics of how the computer operates, whereas the assembly-language programmer *must* know. The COBOL and FORTRAN languages are *problem-oriented* because the programming language and the method of using it are similar to the problem being solved. Thus, COBOL (Fig. 9–7) is used for business problems and FORTRAN (Fig. 9–8) is used for mathematical problems.

High-level languages were developed for two main reasons:

1. To allow programmers to express their problems in a language more easily comprehensible than assembly language. In other words, the program is written in terms more readily understood by the programmer. As a result, experts in fields other than data

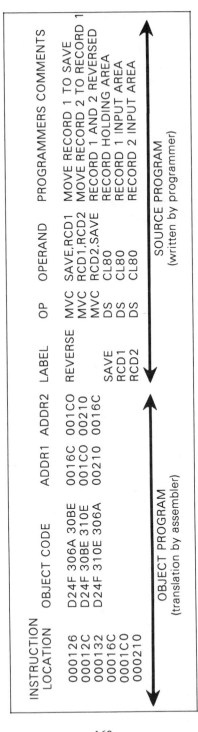

Fig. 9–6. Example of IBM assembly language, called ALC. The assembler translates each source instruction into program instructions (machine language) on a one-to-one relationship. This program segment is a SORT operation to reverse two out-of-sequence records.

160

```
B                              COBOL
12   16   20   24   28   32   36   40   44   48   52   56   60   64

OCEDURE DIVISION.
  OPEN INPUT DISK-FILE
ADI-DISK-RECORD.
  READ DISK-FILE AT END CLOSE DISK-FILE STOP RUN.
  IF EMPL-NR < LAST-EMPL-NR GO TO OUT-OF-SEQ.
MPUTE-PAY-ROUTINE.
  MULTIPLY REG-HOURS BY PAY-RATE GIVING REG-PAY ROUNDED.
  MULTIPLY OVERTIME-HOURS BY PAY-RATE GIVING INTERUM.
  MULTIPLY INTERUM BY 1.5 GIVING OVERTIME-PAY ROUNDED.
  ADD REG-PAY OVERTIME-PAY GIVING GROSS-PAY.
  ADD GROSS-PAY TO PAY-TO-DATE GIVING PAY-TO-DATE.
  SUBTRACT DEDUCTIONS FROM GROSS-PAY GIVING NET-PAY.
  ADD NET-PAY TO TOTAL-NET-PAY.
  ADD GROSS-PAY TO TOTAL-GROSS-PAY.
  MOVE EMPL-NR           TO   PNT-1
  MOVE EMPL-NAME         TO   PNT-2
  MOVE PAY-RATE          TO   PNT-3
  MOVE REG-HOURS         TO   PNT-4
  MOVE REG-PAY           TO   PNT-5
  MOVE OVERTIME-HOURS    TO   PNT-6
  MOVE OVERTIME-PAY      TO   PNT-7
  MOVE GROSS-PAY         TO   PNT-8
  MOVE DEDUCTIONS        TO   PNT-9
  MOVE NET-PAY           TO   PNT-10
  MOVE PAY-TO-DATE       TO   PNT-11
```

Fig. 9-7. Example of a COBOL program.

161

T Y P E	STATE-MENT NO.	C O N T.	FORTRAN STATEMENT
			0 = ZERO 0 = ALPHA O 1 = ONE I = ALPHA I

```
C     THIS PROGRAM COMPUTES THE AVERAGE OF DAILY
C     TEMPERATURES FOR 31 SEPARATE DAYS.
C     THIRTY ONE CARDS ARE READ, EACH OF WHICH
C     CONTAINS THREE TEMPERATURES FOR A DAY.

      DIMENSION TEMP(31,3), AVG(31)
      I=0
2     I=I+1
      READ (60,44) TEMP(I,1),TEMP(I,2),TEMP(I,3)
44    FORMAT (3F3.0)
      IF (I-31) 2,3,3
3     I=1
4     AVG(I)=(TEMP(I,1)+TEMP(I,2)+TEMP(I,3))/3.0
      I=I+1
      IF (I-31) 4,4,5
5     WRITE (61,77) AVG
77    FORMAT (20X,F31.0)
      STOP
      END
```

Fig. 9–8. Example of a FORTRAN program.

processing can be taught the art of programming with little concern about the characteristics of the computer.

2. To overcome the problem associated with installations having two or more different computers, or to compensate whenever one computer system is replaced with a different brand or model.

Let us elaborate somewhat on the latter. Since computers differ, a program written for one type will not necessarily run on another type. Two programs would therefore have to be written if a problem were to be processed on two or more *incompatible* computers. Each data processing installation is unique to some extent. For example, a manager might have more than one computer system to operate. This means he may have to write programs in as many quite different languages as he has computers. However, writing the programs in COBOL (Fig. 9–7) or FORTRAN (Fig. 9–8) eliminates the time and cost of rewriting when a job must be run on a computer for which the original program was not written.

To sum up: High-level languages—COBOL business instructions and FORTRAN mathematical instructions—merely say in effect *what* is to be done logically by the program, not *how* the function is to be performed. This latter aspect is left to our next subject, the compiler of the particular machine that will solve the problem.

SOURCE PROGRAMS

The programmer writes instructions for the computer to solve a problem. These instructions are keypunched into punched cards, one instruction per card. The resulting deck of cards is called a "source" program. But recall that the computer can execute only machine language programs, as shown in Fig. 9–5. Consequently, the source program must be *translated* into a language that the computer can understand.

Object Programs

The computer, acting under the control of a special conversion program, translates the source program, written in terms understandable by people, into machine language. These new machine-language instructions are called the "object" program. The translation process is shown in Fig. 9–9. Each manufacturer of computers (such as Burroughs, CDC, Honeywell, IBM, NCR, UNIVAC) provides a translation program that has been written especially for his make and model of equipment.

Basically, the process of translating the programmer's instructions into

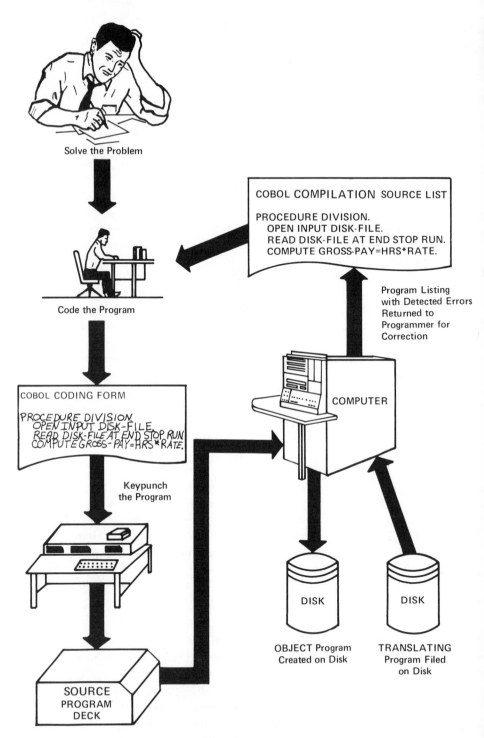

Solve the Problem

Code the Program

COBOL COMPILATION SOURCE LIST

PROCEDURE DIVISION.
    OPEN INPUT DISK-FILE.
    READ DISK-FILE AT END STOP RUN.
    COMPUTE GROSS-PAY=HRS*RATE.

Program Listing
with Detected Errors
Returned to
Programmer for
Correction

COBOL CODING FORM

PROCEDURE DIVISION.
    OPEN INPUT DISK-FILE
    READ DISK-FILE AT END STOP RUN
    COMPUTE GROSS-PAY=HRS*RATE.

COMPUTER

Keypunch
the Program

DISK

DISK

OBJECT Program
Created on Disk

TRANSLATING
Program Filed
on Disk

SOURCE
PROGRAM
DECK

Fig. 9–9. Translating a source program into a machine-language object program.

164

computer-usable form works in this manner. The translation program is stored, usually on magnetic disk but may be on magnetic tape or punched cards. The translator is called into main memory from disk. In turn this program reads into memory the source program written by the programmer, one instruction at a time. The translation program converts each instruction into machine language and records instruction by instruction onto the desired output medium, which is usually disk.

Executing Object Programs

Data cannot be processed while a source program is being translated into an object program. Once the translation is complete, however, the object program can be brought immediately into main memory from its residence on disk and tested against data to see if the program performs as expected. This separate operation of executing the object program—which means carrying out computer operations to process data, record by record —is illustrated in Fig. 9–10.

ASSEMBLING VERSUS COMPILING

The actual translation process by the computer is called "assembling" or "compiling," depending upon whether the source program is a low-level language (assembly language) or high-level language (COBOL or FORTRAN). Accordingly, the translator *programs* are called "assembler" or "compiler."

The assembler translation program usually produces one machine-language instruction* for each source-language instruction written by the programmer (Fig. 9–11). A compiler, on the other hand, is a one-to-many translator program. This means that several machine-language instructions are generated by the compiler for each single source-language instruction written by the programmer.

We are talking here of essentially technical characteristics that are of no concern to the programmer from a source-to-object program translation standpoint. In other words, the translation process converts source programs into object programs whether they be assembler or compiler. We mention this here for two reasons:

1. To define the terms, since management personnel will be exposed to them in conversations involving data processing. Too, they are used inter-

---

*Macro instructions are commonly used in assembler programs that generate more than one machine-language instruction for each macro statement used.

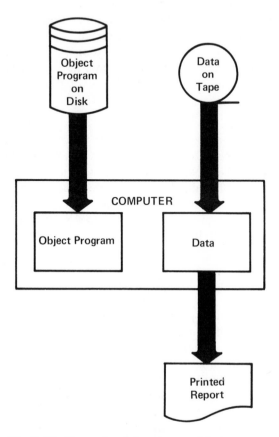

Fig. 9–10. Processing data using an object program.

changeably because either produces an object program from a source deck. But they are *technically* different.

2. A manager should be aware of the differences because the efficiency in assembler programming depends upon the programmer, whereas efficiency in high-level programming depends to a great degree upon the compiler itself. Management must be aware that expectations depend not only upon the computer hardware but also on the supporting software that the manufacturer writes. In other words, the computer may perform ideally while the software works poorly.

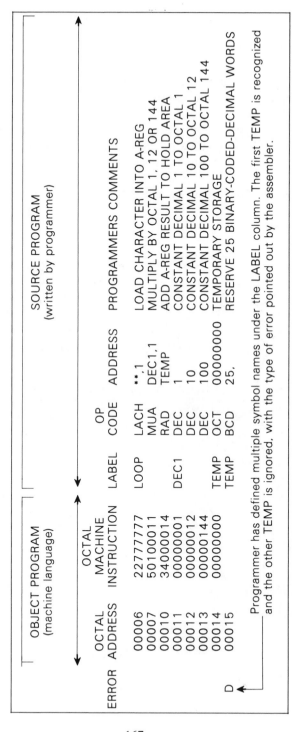

OBJECT PROGRAM (machine language)

SOURCE PROGRAM (written by programmer)

ERROR	OCTAL ADDRESS	OCTAL MACHINE INSTRUCTION	LABEL	OP CODE	ADDRESS	PROGRAMMERS COMMENTS
	00006	22777777	LOOP	LACH	**,1	LOAD CHARACTER INTO A-REG
	00007	50100011		MUA	DEC1,1	MULTIPLY BY OCTAL 1, 12 OR 144
	00010	34000014		RAD	TEMP	ADD A-REG RESULT TO HOLD AREA
	00011	00000001	DEC1	DEC	1	CONSTANT DECIMAL 1 TO OCTAL 1
	00012	00000012		DEC	10	CONSTANT DECIMAL 10 TO OCTAL 12
	00013	00000144		DEC	100	CONSTANT DECIMAL 100 TO OCTAL 144
	00014	00000000	TEMP	OCT	00000000	TEMPORARY STORAGE
D	00015	00000000	TEMP	BCD	25.	RESERVE 25 BINARY-CODED-DECIMAL WORDS

Programmer has defined multiple symbol names under the LABEL column. The first TEMP is recognized and the other TEMP is ignored, with the type of error pointed out by the assembler.

Fig. 9–11. Example of CDC assembly language, called COMPASS. The COMPASS assembler translates each source instruction into machine language instructions on a one-to-one relationship.

167

PROGRAM LISTINGS

In addition to translating the source program into an object program which the computer can execute, a program listing is printed. The listings are called "compile" or "assembly" listings accordingly. The program listing shows both the source program as the programmer wrote it and the machine-language object-program produced from it. The purpose of this printout is to detect the programmer's coding errors, commonly referred to as "bugs."

In other words, programmers make errors when writing the program

There's a bug in it! (Drawn by Mary Jo Pycha)

and the computer points out certain errors so that the programmer may correct them. For example, the programmer may have defined an area in memory for accumulating gross pay as TOTAL-PAY. He must refer to this area as TOTAL-PAY, and if he calls it something else, say TOT-PAY, the translating program will print an error next to the instruction in error.

ADD GROSS-PAY TO TOTAL-PAY   acceptable
ADD GROSS-PAY TO TOT-PAY   error
MOVE TOTAL-PAY TO PRINT-LINE   acceptable
MOVE TOT-PAY TO PRINT-LINE   error

The programmer corrects the mistakes pointed out by the computer and rekeypunches the erroneous cards in his source program. Now the source deck must be run through the computer again for a new translation. If there are no errors in the second run, the program can be tested, using data selected for this purpose (see Secs. 12 and 25, Chapter 15).

Programmer Logic Errors

Although the compiler detects many of the programmer's errors during the translation process, a compiler listing does not mean that the program will give correct results. For instance, consider a flowchart for totaling the salary of all employees earning less than $100 per week. Study the flowchart of the solution in Fig. 9–12 and try to find an error that may cause incorrect results. If you detected the error, you are ahead of the game.

The program gives the desired final total only if the last card contains a salary of less than $100. If the last card contains a salary of more than $100, the program branches to read another card, based upon the logic in the program. Since there are no more cards to be read, the accumulated total will not be printed.

If you are having trouble reading and understanding flowcharts, here is the logic: The first card is read and the salary is compared against a stored constant of 10000. If the answer to the decision symbol is NO, the program branches to read another card and no further processing for that card takes place. If YES, the program continues with the next sequential instruction, adding salary to a counter. The last-card decision is made, and the program repeats the loop if there are cards left in the card reader. If the answer is YES, the contents of the counter are moved to the print area, the accumulated total is printed, and the computer halts.

As you can see, all *paths* that the program may take must be *tested*.

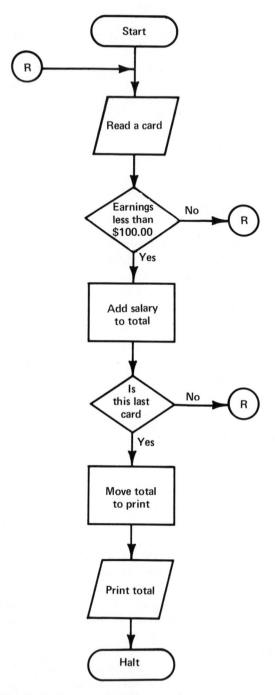

Fig. 9–12. Program flowchart to tabulate gross pay.

SUMMARY

The first language developed to permit the programmer to concentrate more on the problem and less on machine characteristics was symbolic, or assembly, language. This was an improvement over early machine-language programming where the programmer had to remember machine operation codes and actual addresses of memory. The assembly translator allowed the programmer to use easy-to-remember operation codes and to select descriptive names for data stored in memory. This use of symbolic names meant using equivalent addresses in lieu of actual machine addresses. Today, assembly programming is used primarily for software programs such as the operating system.

Coding in assembly language is the most efficient kind of programming (less storage, faster execution, etc.), but is time consuming. Also, assembly languages are designed for a specific make and model of computer. This means that programmers must know how that computer works. To speed up coding of programs and to develop a program that could be run on different computers models with little change, higher-level languages such as COBOL were developed. Another advantage is that higher-level languages are easier to learn than symbolic languages; COBOL was written to serve the business world and FORTRAN was designed to serve mathematical fields. There are many others, such as BASIC, PL/1, RPG, ALGOL, JOVIAL, and SNOBOL.

Programs written in assembly language, COBOL, or FORTRAN are called "source" programs. They are easily understood by the programmer but cannot be executed by the computer, since the instructions are not in machine language. Special programs provided by the computer manufacturers solve this problem by converting the source program into machine language, called "object" programs. The translator programs are referred to as compilers or assemblers.

Source programs are created in three steps. First, the problem is analyzed and defined. Second, the problem is solved by drawing a flowchart that shows the steps the computer must take to process the data. Third, the program is created by converting the processing that takes place within each symbol of the flowchart into machine instructions.

In the next chapter we shall see how the computer uses a program to solve business problems.

KEY TERMS TO REMEMBER

Assembler software

Assembly language

Bug

Compiler software

Debugging

Execution

Flowchart

High-level language

Logic errors

Looping

Machine Language

Mnemonic OP code

Object program

Problem definition

Problem-oriented language

Program listing

Source program

Symbolic address

Symbolic program

Testing, program

Translation

QUESTIONS

1. How does the programmer communicate his desires to the system?
2. What is meant by step-by-step execution?
3. Name the three steps involved in computer problem solving.
4. What is the difference between a high-level and low-level language?
5. Why were translation programs developed?
6. Why is COBOL referred to as a "problem-oriented" language?
7. How can high-level programs aid a multiple-computer center manager?
8. Differentiate between an object and source program.
9. Which type of program can be executed?
10. Why should management be concerned with the characteristics of compilers and assemblers?
11. Of what value is the program listing?
12. Once a programmer assigns a symbolic name to an address, what must he remember in subsequent usage in that program?
13. Can an error-free program listing still contain programming errors? Explain.

COORDINATED READINGS IN CHAPTER 15

"Testing the Program—Will It Quit on New Year's Eve?", Sec. 12.
"Why Should Management Know Systems and Programming Fundamentals?", Sec. 14.
"Why Should Management Learn COBOL and Assembly Language Concepts?", Sec. 15.
"The Importance of Creating Test Data," Sec. 25.

Chapter 10

HOW PROGRAMS PROCESS DATA

Management knows that the computer is a useful business tool, but the data processing department may be the most undertaxed resource at management's disposal. The only way to determine if the computer is dragging or pushing the company is for management to set and participate in data processing goals.

A driver may know little about the technical design of his automobile, yet feel he is an excellent driver. But if he had a knowledge of how the vehicle operates, a catastrophe might be prevented; for example, knowing how to turn the steering wheel to bring the car out of a skid on rain-slicked highways.

Similarly, companies benefit more from the computer when management knows how to use it to obtain improved managerial control. Machines cannot exercise judgment unless they have been given explicit instructions for making a decision. In the same manner, people who work with the computer must be given explicit directions. In order for a manager to give direction, he must gain insight into the way the computer is used. The simplest way of doing this is to examine the computer's internal processes during actual operation.

We learned in Chapter 9 how programmers communicate with the computer by writing a program in understandable business language. The program, which is developed from a flowchart, is converted into machine language by a translator program. This chapter is about how a program is executed, instruction by instruction, and how data is processed step by step.

173

THE STORED PROGRAM

As you will recall, the solution of a problem is drawn in flowchart form in order to show the operations visually, step by step. The program is coded by converting the processing shown within each symbol of the flowchart. Special conversion programs, called compilers or assemblers, translate the source program written by the programmer into machine language.

At this point you may be surely convinced that reading machine language (Figs. 9–6 and 9–11) is no easy task. Although the program is stored in computer memory as binary, we shall illustrate our demonstration program in easy-to-understand operation codes and symbolic addresses. Recall that programmers are allowed to use names like PAY and HOURS, leaving the conversion to actual address locations to the compiler or assembler during translation. The symbolic instructions used to illustrate how the computer executes programs in the processing of data are shown in Fig. 10–1. How the processing proceeds is explained below and illustrated in Figs. 10–2 through 10–6.

HOW THE COMPUTER EXECUTES OBJECT PROGRAMS

In Chapter 9 we studied computer hardware and software. Let us briefly recap the relationship between the program and computer. A computer system consists of the central processor and a number of special-purpose machines that serve as input and output (Fig. 8–10). The heart of the system is the central processing unit, which houses the circuitry for three components: the control unit, internal storage, and the arithmetic-logic unit.

Storage inside the computer holds the program as well as the data being processed. The control unit's function is to retrieve the instructions from memory, one at a time, interpret them, and carry out their execution. Interpreting instructions means to decode the operation code to determine what is to be done; executing them means telling other parts of the system what to do.

The latter is the substance of this entire chapter, that is, learning how the control unit executes instructions in order to process data. We shall bring each type of instruction used in our payroll program into the control unit and watch the computer in action just as it actually performs.

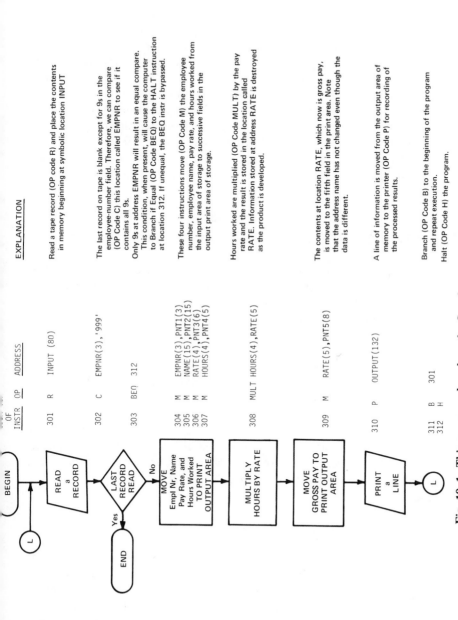

OF INSTR	OP	ADDRESS	EXPLANATION
301	R	INPUT (80)	Read a tape record (OP code R) and place the contents in memory beginning at symbolic location INPUT
302	C	EMPNR(3),'999'	The last record on tape is blank except for 9s in the employee-number field. Therefore, we can compare (OP Code C) this location called EMPNR to see if it contains all 9s.
303	BEQ	312	Only 9s at address EMPNR will result in an equal compare. This condition, when present, will cause the computer to Branch if Equal (OP Code BEQ) to the HALT instruction at location 312. If unequal, the BEQ instr is bypassed.
304 305 306 307	M M M M	EMPNR(3),PNT1(3) NAME(15),PNT2(15) RATE(4),PNT3(6) HOURS(4),PNT4(5)	These four instructions move (OP Code M) the employee number, employee name, pay rate, and hours worked from the input area of storage to successive fields in the output print area of storage.
308	MULT	HOURS(4),RATE(5)	Hours worked are multiplied (OP Code MULT) by the pay rate and the result is stored in the location called RATE. Information stored at address RATE is destroyed as the product is developed.
309	M	RATE(5),PNT5(8)	The contents at location RATE, which now is gross pay, is moved to the fifth field in the print area. Note that the address name has not changed even though the data is different.
310	P	OUTPUT(132)	A line of information is moved from the output area of memory to the printer (OP Code P) for recording of the processed results.
311 312	B H	301	Branch (OP Code B) to the beginning of the program and repeat execution. Halt (OP Code H) the program.

Fig. 10–1. This program, based on the flowchart to compute gross pay, is used in Figs. 10–2 through 10–6, which show how data is processed, instruction by instruction.

175

LOADING THE PROGRAM

When a program is placed in storage, the series of instructions is available to the control unit to direct and complete operations as dictated by the instruction being worked on. We shall assume that the source program written by the programmer has been previously assembled or compiled, as the case may be, and now resides on disk as an object program.

The operating system, part of which stays in memory at all times, takes the necessary action to bring the payroll program from disk into main memory. Whatever was left in memory from the preceding job is destroyed when the new program is loaded, or "read in" (Fig. 10–2).

Once the program has been transferred entirely into memory, the operating system turns control over to the first instruction in the application program.

HOW THE CONTROL UNIT HANDLES INSTRUCTIONS

Instructions are carried out in two phases, called the "instruction phase" (I-phase) and the "execution phase" (E-phase). During the I-phase, the instruction is brought into the control unit in order to see what has to be done. Next, the data is acted upon during the E-phase.

Instructions consist of two parts, an operation code (OP code) and one or more addresses. The OP code designates the operation to be performed, such as READ, MOVE, ADD, and so forth. The *address*(s) designates the location of the data for that specific instruction. Each address has a length factor that tells the computer how many positions in storage to work with.

The first instruction (a READ command at location 301) is brought into the control unit during the I-phase (Fig. 10–3). Next, a record is read from the input device during the E-phase and placed in the input area of storage (Fig. 10–4). For clarity and speed we shall hereafter show the I-phase and E-phase in a single operation rather than separately.

DECISION INSTRUCTIONS

Previously we discussed the decision-making powers of the computer. Certain instructions enable the arithmetic-logic unit to make decisions based upon comparison of two fields of data or from arithmetic operations. For example, if one field of data is compared with another, the result will show that it is higher than, equal to, or lower than the other field. Depending upon the decision, we can cause the computer to select a

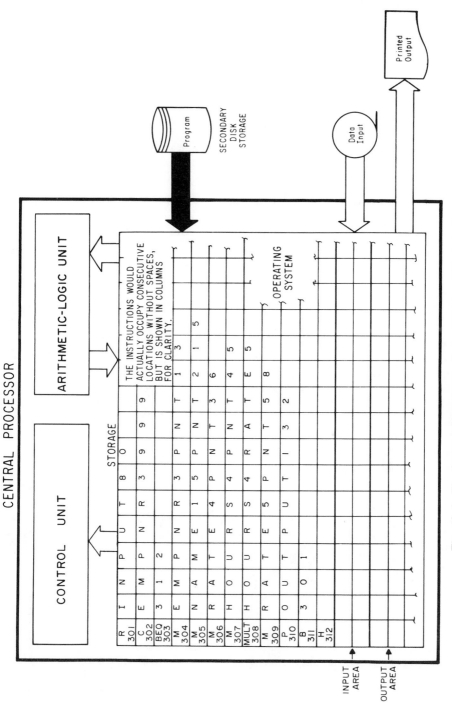

Fig. 10–2. The first process of executing a program: The operating system
directs loading of the instructions from disk into main memory of the computer.

177

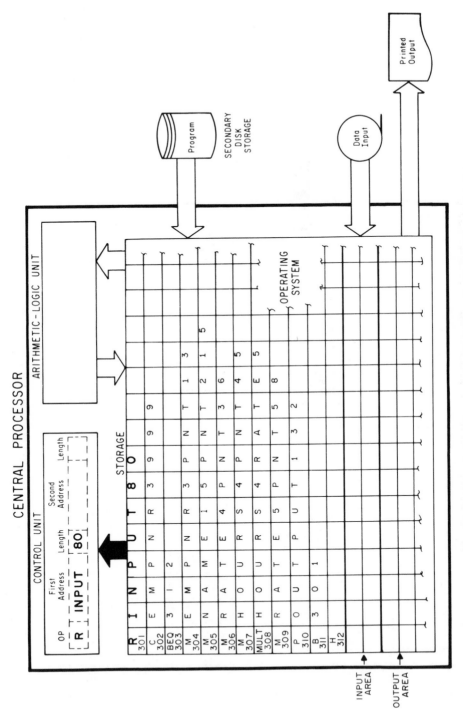

Fig. 10-3. Second step: The control unit fetches the instruction during the I-phase. No processing takes place at this time.

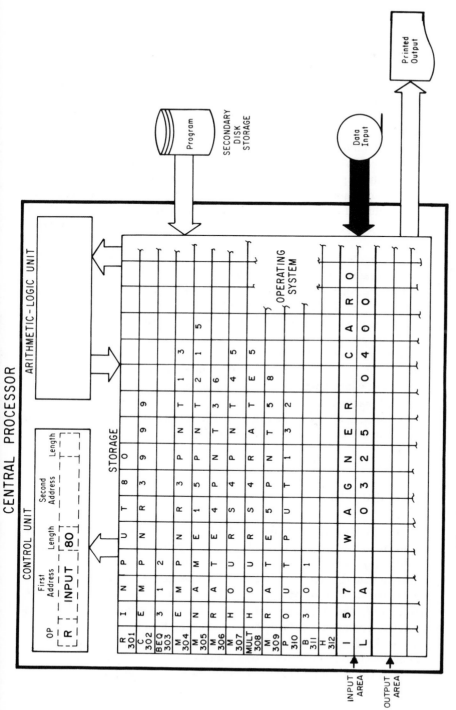

Fig. 10–4. Third step: During the E-phase the control unit executes the instruction, causing a record to be transferred from the input device into the input area. See Fig. 9–3 for format.

179

proper course of action through program control.

One such decision operation is illustrated in our demonstration program (Fig. 10–5). When the last record on the tape file has been processed, the program must be terminated. If there are additional records remaining to be processed, the program continues. This is accomplished by detecting the last record, which is different from all others in that the key field (employee number) contains all nines.

We recognize this special record at the end of the file by comparing 9's—which the program has stored as a *constant*—to each and every record to see if it contains the characters we are looking for. A constant is simply a fixed value set up by the program and never changes during execution of data. The comparison, of course, is done in the arithmetic-logic unit (Fig. 10–5).

A *branch* instruction, in our case "Branch Equal" (BEQ, Fig. 10–5), is used to cause a break in execution of the sequential instructions; that is, one after the other. An "equal compare" condition results in the arithmetic-logic unit when the last record having all 9's in the employee number field is matched to the constant of three 9's set up in memory.

Therefore, the BEQ instruction causes the program to go to the address specified in the address, which happens to be a HALT instruction that stops program execution. Notice that we used an absolute address in the branch instruction, which points out that a programmer can choose either symbolic or actual machine addresses.

Consequently, we can say that a decision to continue or not to continue processing has been made by testing for the special record at the end of the tape file.

DATA MANIPULATION

The movement of data from one place to another within the computer or the alteration of data (say, change 032575 to March 25, 75) is called "data manipulation." The next four instructions involve movement of identification data that requires no special processing other than getting it into the output area ready for printing. Figure 10–6 shows the information developed in the output area after the second MOVE instruction has been executed. To show the data after execution of each individual MOVE instruction, as the computer would really do, would be merely repetitious and so the demonstration indicates a single move.

You will recall that data moved to new locations will destroy the data that was stored there previously. However, the information that was read out for processing will remain. Consequently, these characters are in two

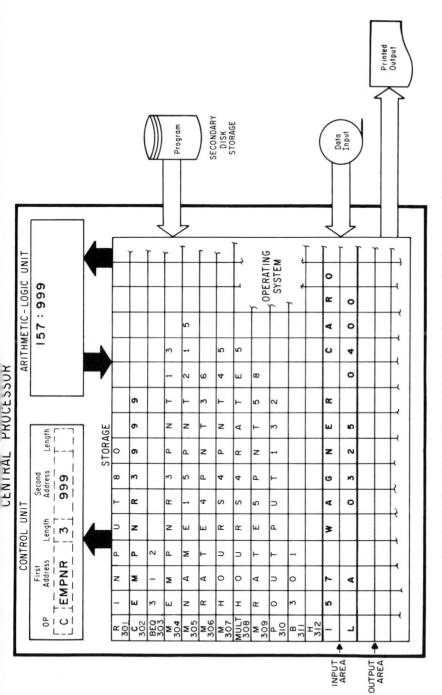

Fig. 10–5. Fourth step: The contents of employee number is compared with a constant 999 in the arithmetic-logic unit. The last-record test is found unequal, indicating that all records have not been processed. Since the following instruction (BEQ) is executed only if the comparison is equal, the instruction is bypassed and control passes to next instruction.

181

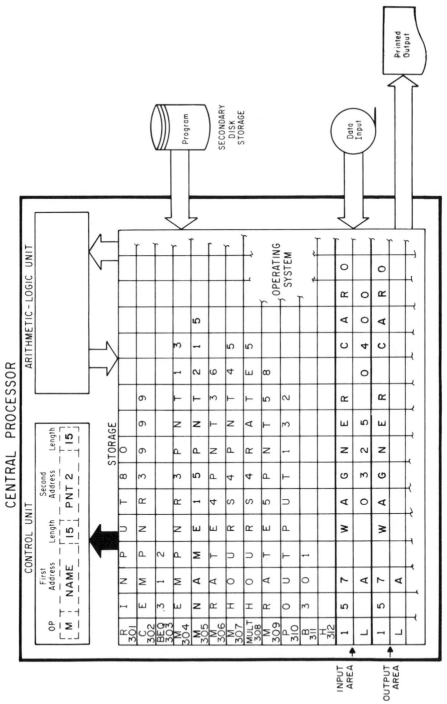

Fig. 10–6. **Fifth step: The first instruction transfers the employee number into the output area; the second instruction moves the employee name to another specified location in the output area, and so on.**

182

locations, the place read from and the place read into. In other words, read-out is nondestructive and read-in is destructive.

ARITHMETIC OPERATIONS

Most computers utilize a technique called *memory-to-memory* (Sec. 17, Chapter 15) calculation when carrying out arithmetic operations. This means that the actions taken in executing a single add, subtract, multiply, or divide instruction involve movement of two fields to the arithmetic-logic unit for the specified calculation and the result returned to one of the addresses in memory (Fig. 10–7).

The original contents of that location in memory are destroyed as the new result is read in. Consequently, the programmer must move the original field that would be destroyed to another location if he needs the information for later processing. The memory-to-memory feature saves the programmer from having to move the data to the arithmetic-logic unit, compute the data, and return the result to memory. In other words, some computers require three instructions to perform the same operation.

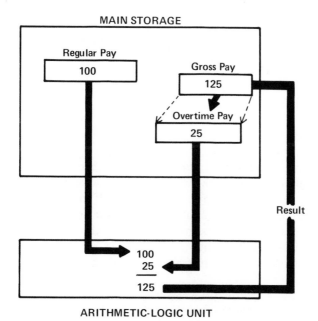

Fig. 10–7. Memory-to-memory calculation.

After executing one instruction, the computer automatically continues to the next instruction, which in our program happens to be an instruction to compute gross pay. In Fig. 10–8 we see that the hours worked are multiplied by the pay rate, and the result (gross pay) replaces the contents at symbolic address RATE. In the next instruction, the contents of location RATE, now containing gross pay, is moved to the fifth field in the print area.

This step in the processing points out that the computer simply works with addresses and data located at that address, regardless of what it is. Consequently, the computer does not attempt to determine if the data actually stored at that location represents what the symbolic address implies. For example, gross pay ended up at the symbolic location called RATE because of the way the computer works. The programmer must therefore remember the data that he puts in symbolic locations which do not describe the kind of data.

The next instruction, a move (M) at location 309 (Fig. 10–9), is executed; this results in moving gross pay to the appropriate place in the output area. Now that we have built the desired line of print in the output area, the print (P) instruction is executed. The contents of the print area are transferred to the printer, where an entire line is printed (Fig. 10–9).

When the last instruction in the program is executed, we cause the computer to branch to the beginning of the instructions and to repeat them. The process of causing the program, or a portion of the program, to repeat itself is called a "loop."* The looping in this program continues for each record until all have been processed.

SUMMARY

We write a source program, punch it into cards, translate it into an object program, and load the instructions into storage. By the time execution begins, people are no longer in the picture. If something comes up that we failed to consider, the computer does what the program says to do, even though the results may be meaningless. Hence, the data processing jargon GIGO, garbage-in garbage-out.

By understanding how instructions and data are handled as they pass

---

*A loop operation is also called "iteration," the process of repeating a sequence of instructions until some condition is satisfied. Often, modifications are made to instructions within the loop between successive repetitions.

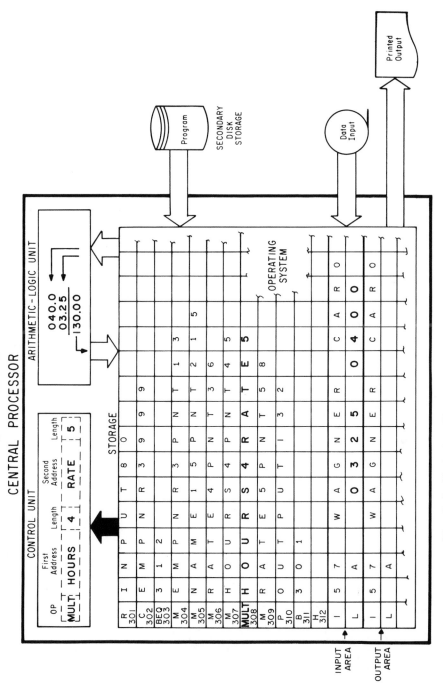

Fig. 10-8. Sixth step: Hours worked are multiplied by the pay rate and the result (gross pay) is returned to the area occupied by rate, thus destroying the original contents.

185

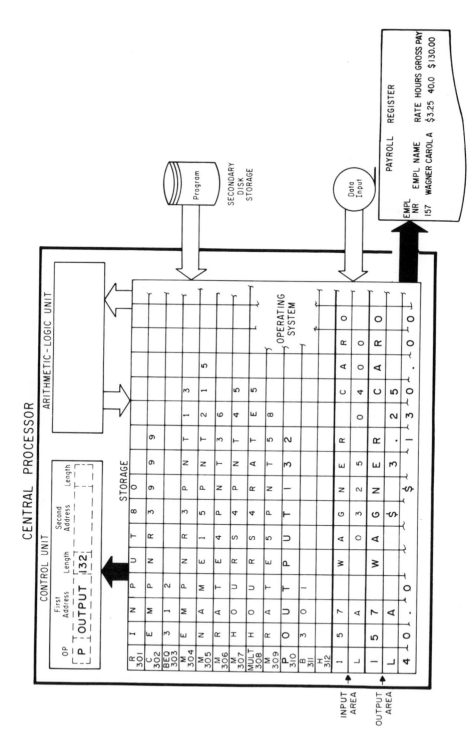

Fig. 10-9. Seventh step: The output area, filled with the desired information as a result of the program's being executed in its entirety, is moved from the output area to the printer device and written.

through various stages of processing, managers can expect to gain knowledge as to why

- Deadlines are met or not met.
- A program that operates correctly for 100 times can fail the next time.
- Programming expectations are often disappointing.

We have graphically illustrated how data is processed step by step and how programs are executed, instruction by instruction. By so doing, we learned that instructions consist of an operation code and addresses that are interpreted and executed by the control unit, the nerve center of the central processor.

As future managers, we have gained an understanding and appreciation of what the programmer goes through in order to get large programs to satisfy management wishes. Also, we find that the programmer is given great discretion in determining what goes into a program unless management becomes deeply involved in overall design and controls to insure that the contents of a program contain only actions beneficial to the firm. In the next two chapters, we gain an in-depth understanding of two important I/O devices, tape and disk.

KEY TERMS TO REMEMBER

Absolute address	Object program
Address	OP code
Arithmetic-logic unit	Program coding
Constant data	Program execution
Control unit	Read-in
Data manipulation	Read-out
Decode an instruction	Source program
Internal storage	Sequential execution
Loop (iteration)	Symbolic address
Memory-to-memory concept	

QUESTIONS

1. What direction must management provide in order to insure that the computer pays its way and aids in the company's decision making?
2. By knowing how instructions and data are handled inside the computer, management gains an appreciation for program development. How could this affect expectations from management and its outlook for instant computer solutions?

3. Explain the two phases of instruction execution.
4. What relationship do absolute addresses have with symbolic addresses?
5. How does the program get loaded?
6. Is the program in Fig. 10–9 a source or object program? Explain.
7. Why is the control unit considered the heart of the computer?
8. What makes possible the detection of the last record? Which illustration depicts this decision?
9. All instructions in the illustrations use symbolic addresses, except two. Explain the functions of these two instructions.
10. What is the advantage of a computer having a memory-to-memory calculation step as opposed to a computer not having this feature?
11. Is the data at a specific location always the same as described by the address name? Defend your answer.
12. Explain how the loop process works and how lack of it would affect the computer hardware and programmer.
13. In relation to question 12, would throughput be faster if two records were processed without the looping technique?

COORDINATED READINGS IN CHAPTER 15

"Protecting the Programs," Sec. 29.
"Future Trends in Computer Architecture," Sec. 32.
"Testing the Program—Will It Quit on New Year's Eve?", Sec. 12.

Chapter 11

EXTERNAL TAPE STORAGE

You will recall from Chapter 5 that the bottleneck of data processing is the recording of data suitable for computer input. Another time loss occurs because internal processing speeds are faster than data can be read for entry into memory and the results of processing can be recorded for output. In other words, the computer is usually input/output-*bound,* a term referring to the central processor's being idle while waiting for the slower input and output operations.

A partial answer to the problem is to use an input/output (I/O) medium that is faster than punched cards or punched paper tape, such as magnetic tape. Magnetic tape storage is the most popular form of input and output because it is more compatible with the computer's electronic speeds. In addition, magnetic tape is a widely used storage medium because of its ability to compact vast amounts of data into a small area. Figure 11–1 shows a magnetic tape setup in which the tape drives write and read data at 800 to 1600 bytes per second on nine tracks. Tape speeds vary from 75 to 200 inches per second while transferring data at 120,000 to 320,000 bytes per second. Rewind speed is 700 inches per second.

EVALUATION OF MAGNETIC TAPE

There are advantages and limitations of magnetic tape in comparison to its punched card and punched paper tape ancestors. Management ought

READ-WRITE
HEADS

TAPE CONTROLLER

TAPE DRIVE #2

TAPE DRIVE #1

VACUUM COLUMNS
TO PREVENT TAPE
BREAKAGE DURING
HIGH SPEED
START AND STOP

Fig. 11–1. Mohawk Data Science 8420 tape units. The less powerful MDS 2007 drive is compatible with IBM Systems 360 and 370 computers. (Courtesy of Mohawk Data Science Corporation.)

to be aware of the general characteristics, such as density and transfer rates of data, because many models are available at varying prices. These operating characteristics, supplied by each manufacturer, must be evaluated critically in order to select tape equipment that will give maximum throughput at the best price. The payoff can significantly affect the data processing operational budget by stepping up performance of the EDP system so that the cost of processing each transaction goes down as throughput goes up.

Advantages of Tape

Speed. Theoretical speeds of any I/O device can be misleading because processing speed must be based upon throughput; that is, how long it takes to do the job. Transfer rates (the amount of data written onto or read from tape) range from 20,000 to 320,000 bytes (characters) per second, depending upon the model of the tape drive. This speed can be compared with a typical card transfer rate of 1600 characters per second. Although recording or reading of tape is slower, we can appreciate the speed at which tape drives operate by visualizing a 2400-foot reel of tape being rewound on the IBM System 370 in 45 seconds at speeds up to 640 inches per second.

Compactness. The second important advantage of tape is its storage capacity. Since 800 to 1600 characters can typically be stored on 1 inch of tape, its capacity is equivalent to that of 288,000 to 576,000 punched cards. However, a more realistic figure would be 480,000 punched cards for the maximum capacity because data is recorded on tape in blocks and each block of data is separated by blank areas of tape.

Eraseability. Unlike punched cards, magnetic tape provides permanent storage until the data is no longer needed, in which case the old data is automatically erased as new data is being recorded. In other words, tape can be used over and over almost indefinitely.

Flexibility. A tape record can be any length, such as 40 or 400 characters, whereas punched cards have a fixed length of 80 characters.

Cost. Another reason for the extensive use of tape in data processing installations is its low cost per transaction processed. Of course a certain volume is assumed, since a computer tape system is more expensive than a card system. Savings result from the tape reusability characteristic, from the number of punched cards it can replace through greater storage capacity, and from less floor space needed for card files. Figure 11–2 shows a tape library. Tape libraries store hundreds, even thousands, of reels of tape, and each reel is equivalent to eight cabinets of punched cards. Most small businesses have less than a hundred tapes, but larger firms may have hundreds or thousands.

Disadvantages of Tape

Readability. The obvious drawback of any storage medium other than punched cards is that, unlike cards, it cannot be visually read and handled individually. Since magnetic recording is invisible to the naked eye, it must be read electronically.

Accidental Destruction. Although individual punched cards may be lost or misplaced, entire reels of magnetic tape can be mistakenly destroyed by simply writing new data over the file meant to be retained (see Section 30, Chapter 15).

Updating. A single punched card can be manually located by a sequenced key field (such as customer name), the card can be keypunched again to change some of the data, and then refiled. Also, new cards can be added and obsolete cards removed. Changing tape records is not so simple, since they cannot be physically inserted or removed, as can punched cards.

Fig. 11–2. Magnetic tape libraries vary in size according to the volume of business. For example, the Internal Revenue Service has 160 million reels of tape. (By permission of IBM.)

In order to change, add, or delete records on a tape file, the entire file must be recopied. Thus, records that require no action are handled needlessly.

Accessibility. To find a given record in a tape file, the computer must search along the length of the tape until it is located. Finding a particular punched card can be compared to thumbing manually through the dictionary to the approximate location, and then searching among the words to locate the desired one.

Programming Difficulties. Tape systems (computers that use tape as input or output) present complications that are not present in programming card systems. A block of data containing several records are read into storage at the same time. Consequently, each record must be kept track of to determine which record is next to be processed (see Chapter 14 for a solution).

Error Recovery. Handling unchanged records during updating presents some difficulty since the newly written tape may be in error. For example, records meant to be included on the new tape may have been omitted due to programming error, and the disaster may not be realized for weeks. Next, an error occurring during a READ operation presents serious difficulties in recovering the unreadable record. For example, a flake of dust on the tape can prevent the computer from reading the data in the vicinity of the dust particle.

TAPE CHARACTERISTICS

The half-inch wide magnetic tape, coated with a material that can be magnetized, is wound on individual 10½-inch reels holding 2400 feet of tape. Like stereo tapes in the home, computer tape can be reused. This is possible because data that is no longer useful can be erased by recording new data over it. Again recall that read-in is destructive and read-out is nondestructive.

The tape is read and written in a tape unit called a "tape drive" (Fig. 11–1); several tape drives can be attached to the computer. The tape is in motion (called "tape speed") during read and write operations, and moves at speeds up to 200 inches per second (ips), depending on the tape drive model. The number of bytes (characters) that can be recorded per inch (abbreviated bpi) is called the *density* (Fig. 11–3). Density can be set at 200, 556, 800, or 1600 bpi.

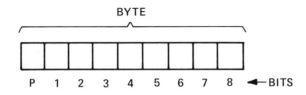

Fig. 11–3. A byte is made up of bits. The number of bytes recorded per inch is called "tape density."

BINARY REPRESENTATION ON TAPE

Data is represented on magnetic tape in one of three forms of binary: binary coded decimal (BCD), extended binary coded decimal interchange code (EBCDIC), or real binary. Accordingly, there are seven parallel rows for BCD (called "channels" or "tracks") or nine parallel channels for EBCDIC to accommodate the two different construction designs of computer memories, discussed in Chapter 7. Both seven-channel and nine-channel tape drives operate essentially the same. We shall discuss the simple differences shortly.

The tape drive, under direction of the program stored in the computer memory, moves the tape across read-write heads (Fig. 11–1) and accomplishes the actual reading and writing of data. Characters are recorded in BCD, EBCDIC, or binary in the form of small magnetized spots called "bits." Data becomes a series of columns, each containing a character, recorded in seven or nine parallel channels along the length of the tape. In other words, bits across the width of the tape produce a column of bits (Fig. 11–4) and represent a character. In binary form, this same column is part of a computer word; therefore, it is not considered a character.

As you can recognize immediately, the bit pattern is the familiar *numeric* and *zone* bits with an added *parity* bit, discussed in Chapter 7. Like other magnetic storage devices, the data can be retained indefinitely or erased by recording new data on the tape.

Error Detection

A spot of dust on the tape can cause a bad reading or writing. To detect this condition, as well as other equipment malfunctions, reading and writing are subject to several built-in checks, such as the usual parity check of each character. As each character is written, the bits are added and a parity bit is recorded whenever necessary to make *even* parity (Fig. 11–4). Tapes are always *even* parity, as contrasted to the central processor's memory, which has odd parity. A parity bit is never transmitted when moving data and is strictly a hardware characteristic of no vital human concern.

To further insure the validity of data written on or read from tape, another parity check is provided by counting the number of bits in each channel. This check, called "longitudinal" or "horizontal" check character, is recorded at the end of each block as the block of data is written, to make the count of bits in each channel even. A block may comprise one record or a group of records.

While there are other checks, those we have mentioned serve to illustrate our point that computers process data accurately and that human

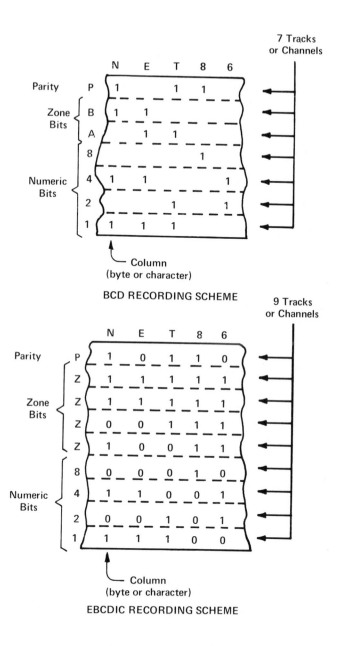

Fig. 11–4. Comparison of BCD seven-channel and EBCDIC nine-channel recording schemes. Data becomes a series of binary "1" and "0" spots along the length of the tape. Only "1" bits are recorded on seven-channel tape, whereas both "0" and "1" bits are recorded on nine-channel tape.

fallacy is the main concern in providing processing instructions.

The parity checks are made only when the tape is read. A two-gap head is used to insure that data is correctly written. There is one head for *writing* and one for *reading*. The writing head is located immediately before the reading head. During a WRITE operation, previously written data are erased, and the character is recorded and read immediately by the read head to determine if the data is readable and if parity counts are correct. If a read or write error is detected, a tape error routine in the input/output control system (IOCS; see Chapter 14) program of the operating system attempts to correct the difficulty by rereading the data several times; if unsuccessful, the job is terminated.

BCD Recording on Tape

Data BCD is recorded on *seven-channel* tape, on which only "1" bits are recorded as magnetized spots; "0" bits are not recorded. Figure 11–4 shows the familiar BCD coding; each column of bits consists of "1" bits that make up each character.

EBCDIC Recording on Tape

Most third-generation computers record data on tape in EBCDIC, which operates on nine channels. This recording scheme is also shown in Fig. 11–4. Data recording is slightly different from seven-channel tapes in that both "0" and "1" bits ("0" and "1" bits being opposite in polarity) are recorded as magnetized spots. The main advantage is that reading errors are handled automatically by regenerating *unreadable* bits in that channel rather than backspacing and rereading the tape for correction of single channel defects.

EFFICIENCY THROUGH BLOCKING

A means of coping with expanding business problems is to speed data throughput by using magnetic tape. Still another way of increasing throughput is to group several records together. The technique, called "blocking," permits reading or writing a block of records at the same time, thus reducing the amount of start-and-stop time by the mechanical movement of the tape drive.

In order to understand how time is saved, we must discuss the inter-block gap (Fig. 11–5). An interblock gap (IBG) is a blank area on tape created automatically before and after each block of records as the tape is written. The ¾-inch IBG (0.6 inch for nine-channel tape) is created by the

FIELDS IN LOGICAL RECORD 3

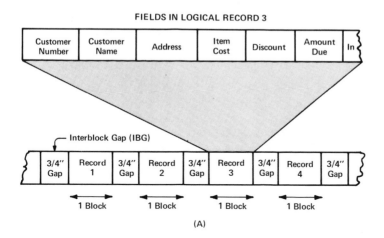

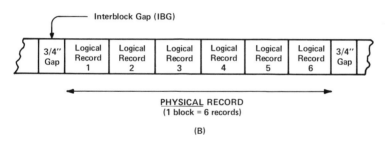

(A)

(B)

Fig. 11–5. Blocked and unblocked tape.

distance the tape moves in coasting to a stop (⅜ inch), plus the distance to accelerate to reading or writing speed (⅜ inch). The IBG also serves as a way for the computer to know where a block of data starts and what its length is. In other words, the computer starts reading data at the end of one IBG and stops reading at the beginning of the next IBG.

Clearly, a great deal of tape will be wasted by blank areas if an IBG is created after each and every record is entered on it. If a block contains only one record, it is referred to as "unblocked" (Fig. 11–5A). Because the computer's central processor operates electronically in nanoseconds, much time would be wasted waiting for the slower mechanical tape drives.

To solve this problem, a group of records is written in each block (Fig. 11–5B); this technique is called "blocking" records. Individual records *within* the block are called "logic" records, whereas the entire block is referred to as a "physical" record.

The term "physical record," therefore, derives from the fact that all records within a block are read or written in one I/O operation. This means that I/O areas in main memory must be large enough to hold the maximum number of records that a block can contain. For instance, a record length of 155 characters with a blocking factor of 10 requires in memory an area of 1550 bytes in length. As a result, the blocking factor of physical records on tape is limited by the capacity of the computer's memory minus other storage requirements, such as the program and operating system (Fig. 11–6). An I/O area of memory that is set aside to compensate for a difference in data handling rates when transmitting from electronic memory to mechanical devices is called a "buffer," and is explained in Chapter 14.

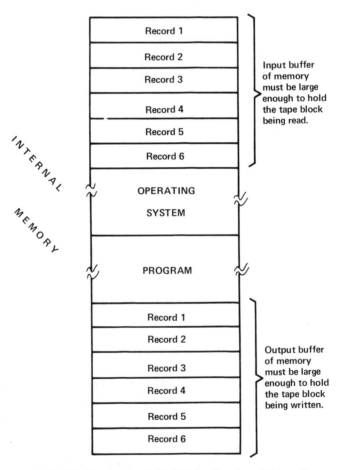

Fig. 11–6. The blocking factor is limited by the size of internal memory.

The *advantages* of blocking are:

1. That more records can be stored on tape because fewer blank IBGs are necessary.
2. A saving in I/O time, since the READ instruction brings into core storage at the same time an entire block of records and data is handled at electronic speeds. Thus the tape unit accelerates and decelerates less frequently than reading unblocked records into core storage one at a time.

TAPE AND FILE MARKERS

The beginning and end of the tape are each detected when the read-write head recognizes a reflective spot, which consists of an aluminum strip. The reflective strip is located 10 feet from the beginning of the tape, called the "load point," and is positioned when the operator pushes the load key on the tape unit in order to determine where reading or writing begins (Fig. 11–7). Detection of the end-of-reel is by another reflective strip, called the end-of-reel marker,* located 14 feet from the physical end of the tape (Fig. 11–7).

Since a collection of similar data frequently does not fill an entire reel, the end of the file is recognized by a special character, called the "tape

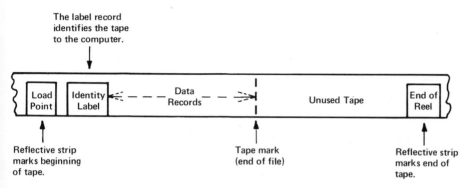

Fig. 11–7. The tape label contains all identifying information used by the program, to insure that the right tape is being processed. (See Fig. 15–14 for information contained in label.) The tape mark (end of file) indicates the end of a group of data.

mark."* The tape mark, or "end of file," is recorded by an instruction in the program when the file is written on tape. The purpose of the tape mark is to signal termination of record on a partial reel of data so that the computer will stop at the end of the file and will not run the remaining blank tape. This tape mark also permits putting several small files of data on a single reel of tape, or putting overflow of a full tape on another.

FILE PROTECTION

Like other storage devices, writing onto tape is destructive, whereas reading from tape is nondestructive. When data is read from tape, an exact copy of the contents is transferred to internal core storage and the data on tape remains unaffected. When writing onto tape, the new data is recorded over the old data, thus destroying it.

To prevent writing accidentally on tape containing valuable and permanent files and thus inadvertently destroying them, a file protection ring is provided. This removable plastic ring must be inserted on the back of the reel in order to write on tape. After writing the tape, the computer operator removes the ring immediately to lessen the possibility of destroying files by accident.

Another technique to prevent the destruction of tape records is provided by an external label stuck on the tape reel for visual identification and an internal label written as the first record on tape by the program. The labels contain information such as file name and the date on which the file was created. The information on the internal label (Fig. 11–7) is checked by the program before processing begins, thus making sure that the right tape is mounted on the right tape drive. If the information provided by the program agrees with the information written on the tape label, the computer continues by processing the first record. If not, the program notifies the computer operator by writing a message on the console typewriter, and the job is terminated.

CHANNELS IMPROVE I/O PERFORMANCE

From your knowledge of computer systems learned thus far, you realize the importance of computer performance. The performance is obtained by the:

---

*The tape mark or the end-of-reel marker is identified by IOCS, explained in Chapter 14, and the programmer determines what is to be done next through programmed instructions.

1. Speed of the computer circuits.
2. Speed of storage.
3. Speed of the I/O devices.
4. Number of events that can take place at the same time.

Input and output hardware, *peripheral* devices as they are called, greatly affect the overall performance of the EDPS because they are comparatively slower than the electronic speed of the central processing unit (CPU). Two additional devices, channels and controllers (Fig. 11–8), were designed to enhance the performance by acting as intermediaries between the physical peripheral devices and main storage in the CPU, making possible concurrent data input, internal processing, and data output.

A channel serves as a small computer to relieve the CPU of the burden of having to stop processing in order to execute I/O operations, such as tape. As such, channels provide a pathway for the movement of data between I/O devices and the CPU. The main role of a data channel is to compensate for differences in speed between I/O and the CPU speeds. In so doing, the channel collects input data into a special small storage area from the I/O device, and when enough data has been stored to justify interrupting the CPU from other processing, the channel transfers the input data into CPU main memory. For an output operation, the procedure reverses.

Types of Channels

There are three types* of channels: selector, multiplexer, and block multiplexer. All perform the same function (control of data bytes) but each employs a different method to accomplish transmission of data.

Selector Channels. A selector channel can be attached to a maximum of eight controllers, but is capable of handling only one I/O device at a time. Because selector channels can transmit or receive up to 1.85 million bytes per second, they are ideal for high-speed devices such as tape and disk units, since they transmit or receive all bytes in a record one byte at a time.

Multiplexer Channels. The advantage of multiplexer channels over selectors (Fig. 11–9) is that they are designed to handle up to 256 slow-speed I/O devices, all operating simultaneously. In other words, multiplexer channels can transfer or receive one byte at a time from 256 I/O devices at the same time. Figure 11–10 shows several slow-speed devices transmitting data one byte at a time.

Block Multiplexer Channel. This type has the advantages of both selector and multiplexer channels in that it can concurrently operate many

---

*These are IBM-oriented terms and may be called by other names by different computer manufacturers.

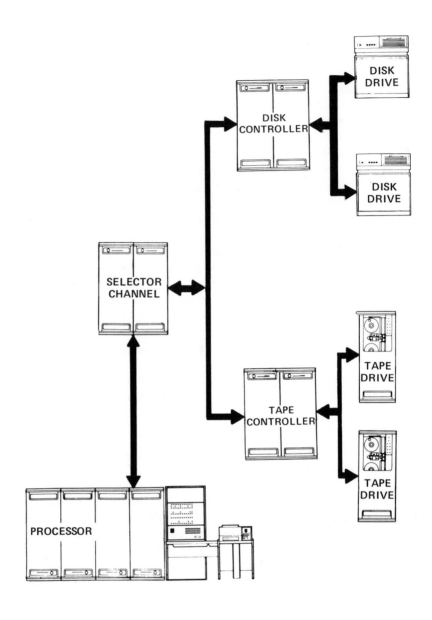

Fig. 11–8. Selector channels serve high-speed I/O devices. The controller oversees reading and writing by I/O devices.

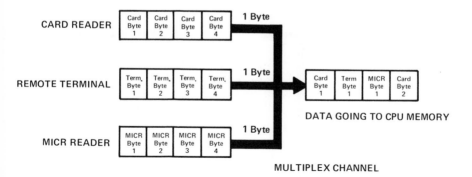

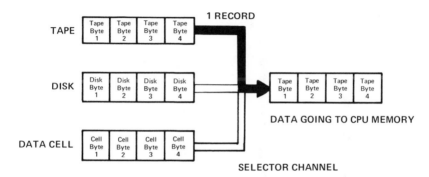

Fig. 11–9. A comparison of selector channel operation versus multiplex channel.

high-speed I/O peripheral devices. Data transfer rate is much higher than with the other types of channels, ranging from 1.2 to 3.0 million bytes per second on the IBM System 370.

In summary: Channels increase throughput by handling I/O operations while the computer does other processing. This ability to input, process, and output data concurrently is referred to as "overlapped processing." The multiplexer channel is designed for low-speed peripheral devices, such as terminal visual display tubes, and serves more than one controller at a time, whereas the selector channel can serve only one controller at a time because it handles high-speed devices, such as tape drives.

CONTROLLERS OVERSEE I/O DEVICES

Having the central processor or CPU work with many different I/O devices would slow the overall computer performance, as we have seen. The

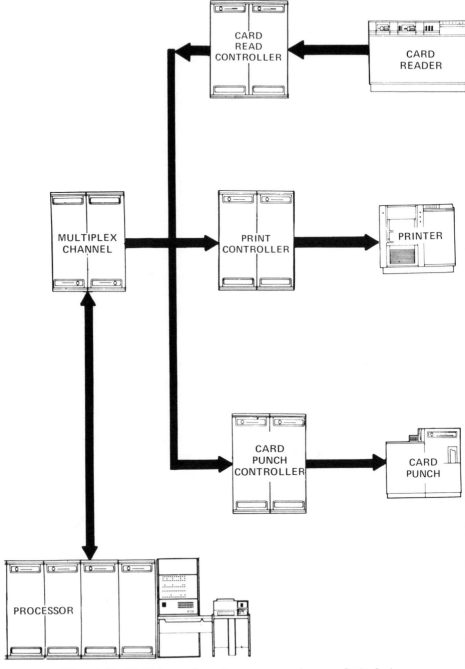

Fig. 11–10. **Multiplexer channels serve many slow-speed I/O devices.**

design departure of third-generation computers, as a result, lies in overlapping I/O operations with internal computer processing, such as computing. In order to overlap processing with I/O, the computer notifies a channel when an I/O operation should be executed, and the appropriate controller (Fig. 11–10) responds by monitoring the physical I/O device itself, and oversees reading and writing by the individual I/O peripheral devices. In other words, the channel controls the flow of data to and from I/O devices, while the controller controls one or more physical devices in the reading or writing process.

Now that we have learned the characteristics of tape devices and how they are interfaced with the computer by the channel and controller, let us conclude this chapter by illustrating a typical, but simple, tape operation.

SEQUENTIAL UPDATING OF TAPE

Magnetic tape is a sequential-file storage medium, which means that the tape file is processed sequentially, one record after another. The records are in some key sequence, such as customer account number, and each record is located by the computer's searching along the length of the tape until the desired record is found. Usually, another file is processed against the tape file, in which case both files must be in the same sequence.

Sequential processing of tape is therefore an ideal storage medium for businesses in which most records require updating. This means that it is beneficial to accumulate transactions until a large batch of transactions warrants processing, since the entire tape file must be read even though some records are unaffected. You will recall that accumulating transactions for processing is called "batch" processing.

We shall now illustrate a simple application involving both reading and writing onto magnetic tape. There are two input files (card transactions and original master tape), and one output file, the updated tape file (Fig. 11–11). The master customer account file on tape is to be updated by adding new accounts, making changes to accounts (i.e., new addresses), and retaining records that require no changing. The change transactions on cards are compared to the master tape file by customer account number, and if a transaction account number agrees with the master account number, the record is updated in memory by the program and written onto the new master tape (Fig. 11–11). An unmatched transaction card, indicated by an account number being less than the master account number, is copied onto the new master tape. Records on the master tape requiring no change are simply copied onto the new master tape.

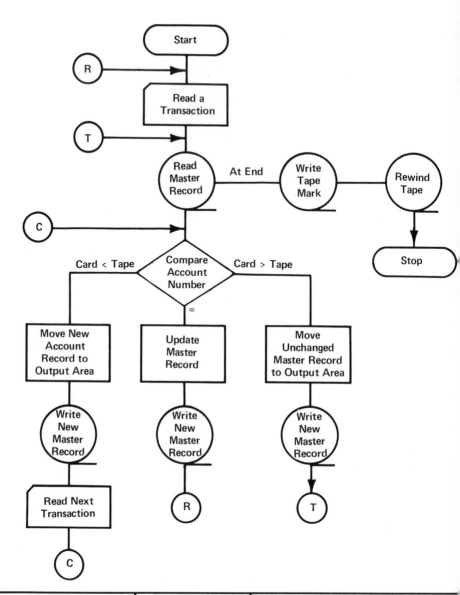

Customer Account Nr		Condition	Action
Card	Tape		
315	315	Card = Tape	Update OLD record and read next card and next tape record.
317	319	Card < Tape	Write NEW record and read next card.
321	320	Card > Tape	Write old record and read next tape record.

Fig. 11–11. Conditions and actions to be taken to update tape file of customer's account.

On-Line and Off-Line Computers

In a multiple computer installation, a large computer system may use magnetic tape exclusively as input and output, thus leaving slower I/O operations involving card reading, printing, card punching and sorting to the smaller and less expensive computer (Fig. 11–12).

For example, the cards in our customer-account update illustration (Fig. 11–11) could have been converted off line to tape and sorted by the slave computer, the customer account file updated by the master computer, and then the newly created customer-account tape printed off line by the smaller computer. In so doing, the expensive computer would be released for other processing while the supporting computer performed the slow processes of input and output, called "conversion."

SUMMARY

The advantages of magnetic tape far outweigh its disadvantages because it allows fast I/O speed and large storage capacity. Data is written on the tape in one of three forms: real binary, BCD, or EBCDIC characters. Characters that comprise one or more records are written on the tape in blocks. A block may contain 80 characters from a card or any number of characters on a tape.

Blocks are separated from each other by a blank ¾-inch gap (0.6 inch for nine-channel tape), called an "interblock" gap. This IBG is created by the distance the tape moves in coasting to a stop, plus the distance to accelerate to reading speed again. A group of data on tape is therefore defined by an interblock gap before and after the block. The interblock gap, which tells the computer when to start and stop reading data, is created automatically when the tape is written.

The beginning of tape is recognized by the load-point reflective marker and the end of tape by the end-of-reel marker. A tape mark is used to signal the computer that a file does not fill the entire reel of tape. Two essential means protect tapes from accidental destruction: (1) A file protection ring must be inserted on the reel before writing can take place; and (2) *labels* are recorded at the beginning of tape so that the computer can check to see if the right tape is being processed.

Input and output operations are turned over to a channel and controller by the central processor in order that the CPU can return to other processing, thus increasing throughput and overall processing efficiency. The selector channel (designed to handle high-speed I/O devices) and multiplexer channel (designed to operate many slow-speed I/O devices at the

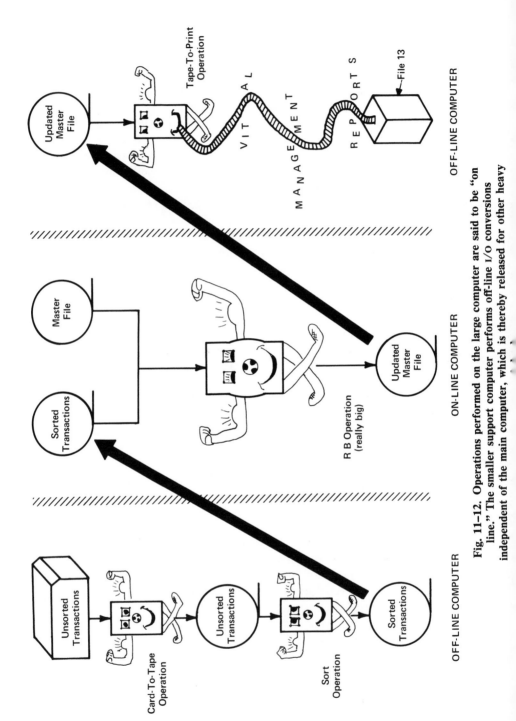

Fig. 11–12. Operations performed on the large computer are said to be "on line." The smaller support computer performs off-line I/O conversions independent of the main computer, which is thereby released for other heavy

208

same time) control the flow of data between the CPU main memory and the I/O device. The controller monitors the reading and writing performed by the actual I/O unit under the direction of the channel.

KEY TERMS TO REMEMBER

Batch processing	Off line and on line
Blocking concept	Parity checking
Channels	Read-write heads
Controller unit	Selector channel
Density	Sequential processing
I/O-bound	Slave computer
Labels	Tape advantages
Multiplexer channel	Throughput
Nine-channel tape	

QUESTIONS

1. The number of records that can be blocked is determined by what factor?
2. In the statement, "unreadable bits are regenerated rather than backspacing and rereading the tape," what is the advantage, and how is it made possible?
3. What is the necessity of having both a tape mark and end-of-reel marker to signal the end of recorded data?
4. In Fig. 11–11, which result after comparing account number signifies a new record to be written on tape?
5. In Fig. 11–11, what actions are necessary when a record requiring no change is identified?
6. Draw a systems flowchart for the processing shown in Fig. 11–12.
7. Explain the three methods that prevent accidental destruction of data on tape files.
8. Name two things that control the speed of data transfer between memory and the tape drive.
9. What purpose does the IBG serve?
10. What is the relationship between the two terms "buffer" and "blocking"?
11. Peripheral devices are connected directly to which part of the system?
12. How is throughput increased as a result of blocking records?
13. What is the purpose of a slave computer?
14. Is the following statement true: "The parity bit along with other bits making up a character are transferred from core storage and written on tape." Why?

COORDINATED READINGS IN CHAPTER 15

"Which Computer Speed Will Do?", Sec. 17.
"Computer Maintenance Problems," Sec. 7.
"Protecting the Data Files," Sec. 30.

Chapter 12

SECONDARY DISK STORAGE

Perishable commodities prevail in businesses other than those dealing in fresh vegetables and fruits. For example, empty seats in a departing plane are lost revenue that can never be recovered; in retail or wholesale businesses, revenue is lost whenever a customer takes his trade elsewhere because what he needs is out of stock.

To deal with problems such as these, competitive businesses of the 1970s need information that presents a picture of activities at any given time. Quick access to up-to-date files is the solution for prompt response tied to customer service and inventory control. Direct-access storage devices, such as magnetic disk (Fig. 12–1), offer quick access.

DEFINITION OF DIRECT-ACCESS STORAGE

Direct-access storage devices (DASD) hold huge files in such a way that any record can be retrieved from external storage and brought into the computer's internal memory without examining each individual record. In other words, DASD permits access to every location with about the same speed as to any other location.

You will recall that files stored on magnetic tape must be searched sequentially, beginning with the first record and continuing until the desired record is found; therefore it does not provide random accessibility. In contrast, DASD can find a record in the middle of the file, or anywhere else,

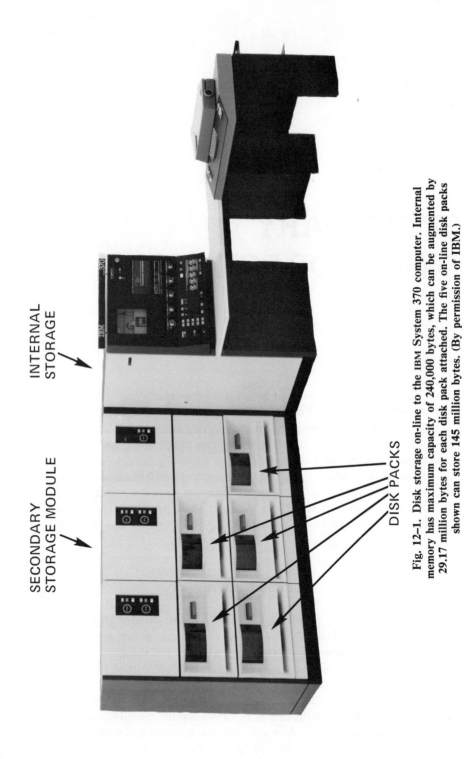

INTERNAL STORAGE

SECONDARY STORAGE MODULE

DISK PACKS

Fig. 12–1. Disk storage on-line to the IBM System 370 computer. Internal memory has maximum capacity of 240,000 bytes, which can be augmented by 29.17 million bytes for each disk pack attached. The five on-line disk packs shown can store 145 million bytes. (By permission of IBM.)

without reading the preceding records in the file. The technique, referred to as "random-access" processing, means proceeding directly to the desired memory location on disk to process records in random order. This is opposite to sequential processing, which requires that the records be in sequential order of input.

Direct-access devices provide auxiliary storage that augments the central processor's internal memory. Why have this secondary or auxiliary storage? The answer is that the DASD storage medium provides *mass storage* at *less cost* than internal core storage, although it is relatively slower. The reason for secondary storage, therefore, is that it provides random-access processing for large quantities of data at a reasonable price.

Why not use tape storage, which is even less expensive? Table 12–1 lists the advantages and disadvantages of tape and disk. Tape storage is retained in the tape library; thus it is off line and not immediately available to the computer. Direct-access storage devices, on the other hand, are attached to the computer, and data flows between the computer and the DASD through electrical cables (Fig. 12–2); thus, frequently needed data is kept on line. As we shall see, infrequently accessed data can be removed from the DASD and stored off line, the same as tape.

VALUE OF DIRECT-ACCESS STORAGE

There are two types of processing: batch and on-line processing. Batch processing involves collecting transactions for a given period of time and processing them in one group. Obviously this would not be practicable for perishable commodities such as plane seats, car tires, and the like, since the on-hand inventory might be sold out before the batch of sales transactions was processed, thereby revealing shortages. On-line processing is a way of processing individual transactions immediately as they are reported; thus,

Table 12–1. General comparisons between tape and disk storage.

Characteristic	Tape	Disk
Cost	Less expensive	More expensive
Processing method	Batch	Batch or on line
Update method	Write new tape	Write in place
Old data destroyed?	No	Yes
Access method	Sequential	Random or sequential
Data usually current	No	Yes
Programming difficulty	Simple	Complex
Location of medium when not in use	Off line	Usually on line

the commodity on hand is always up to date. On-line processing requires on-line DASD storage to make possible the locating and updating of transactions as they are concluded.

Take the situation of the airlines, which need to keep track of available seat space at all times. If a passenger cancels his reservation or unexpectedly stops over somewhere, these facts must be recorded so that the space can be sold to someone else. The status of every seat on every flight is recorded on disk, and reservation agents have access to the data via remote display terminals (Fig. 3–3) at the ticket counter. To illustrate: An airline agent schedules a customer's reservation, departure from San Francisco to New York, to include a two-day stopover in Chicago. An instant later, a request for the space from Chicago to New York can be confirmed at another terminal, possibly in another city.

The airline procedure (see Fig. 12–3) of (1) *inquiry* into the computer, (2) *response* from the computer, and (3) *reply* from the airlines agent is an example of real-time processing. It is called "real-time processing" because all three steps take place while the ticket agent waits on line for the computer results and the customer waits on the telephone. Real-time processing, therefore, combines many remote visual or typewriter terminals linked to a central computer via telephone communications lines. This very fast response time is not essential to all applications. For example, inventory control is processed by on-line processing, but keeping inventory files updated to the exact time of sale is not absolutely necessary.

To a distributor or wholesaler, inventory is the body of salable stocked

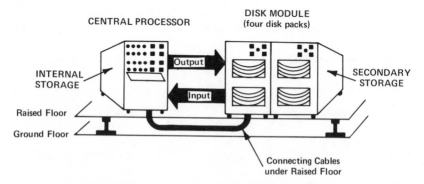

Fig. 12–2. Main core memory is augmented by removable disk packs, providing additional random-access storage of hundreds of millions or billions of characters.

items needed to promptly fill customer orders. The on-hand stockage acts as a buffer between factory shipments and an adequate supply to fill customer orders. However, excessive inventory ties up capital that could be put to other uses; inadequate inventory might mean loss of sales. The solution, therefore, is to determine the optimum stockage and have the computer reorder when materials stock is depleted to the reorder point. In order to do this, sales are fed into the computer as they occur; that is, in random order.

A typical inventory application works something like this: The sales

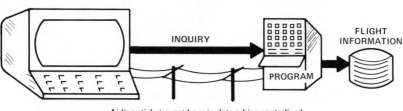

Airlines ticket agent keys in data asking centralized computer the status of available seats on a particular flight.

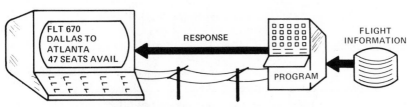

Computer responds and displays information requested.

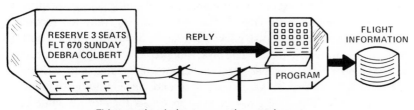

Ticket agent keys in data to reserve three seats in name of Debra Colbert. Program in internal memory updates the disk accordingly.

Fig. 12–3. Real-time processing permits terminal-to-computer communication while the ticket agent waits on line.

orders are forwarded to a pool of operators who enter transactions into the computer via key-to-card, key-to-tape, or key-to-disk methods as discussed in Chapter 5. Minutes later the inventory is updated according to the sales transactions. The difference between real-time processing and on-line processing is minimal and is distinguished by the greater speed of real-time.

HOW RANDOM PROCESSING WORKS

Unlike tape, a magnetic disk file is constructed so that it permits *bypassing* unwanted records and proceeding directly to the area on the disk concerned. This is similar to locating the word "disk" in the dictionary by thumbing to the tab labeled "D" and then searching for the correct word rather than beginning the search from letter A. In simplest terms, random processing works this way (Fig. 12–4) in keeping files current:

1. A program *locates* the desired record on secondary disk storage.
2. The program *fetches* the data from disk and transfers it into the computer's internal memory.
3. The program *adjusts* the data accordingly.
4. The program *returns* the updated record back to the same location on disk, thus destroying the original data.

The Disk Pack

Random-access storage is made possible by a stack of six disks (some stacks contain twelve or more) enclosed in a disk pack (Fig. 12–5). The magnetic-coated disks are stacked one above the other and slightly separated from each other. This ½-inch space provides for the movement between disks of five retractable arms, each having two read-write heads for reading and writing data (Fig. 12–6). One read-write head is for the top of the disk face and the other is for the bottom of the disk face; consequently, data is recorded on both sides of the disk. However, only ten recording surfaces are used on most disk packs because the outermost top and bottom surfaces are protective plates. The disk, mounted on a vertical shaft, rotates at 40 or 60 revolutions per second, permitting reading and writing at 156,000, 312,000, or 806,000 bytes per second, depending on the model.

Each disk (Fig. 12–7) has concentric tracks for storing data. Each surface of the disk contains 200 tracks for storing magnetized bits (Fig. 12–8) in the form of BCD, EBCDIC, or binary. Although the tracks get smaller as they get closer to the center of the disk, each track holds the same amount of data. This means that the bits are recorded closer together on

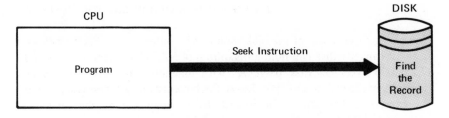

Step 1. The program executes an instruction that locates the desired record on the auxiliary direct access storage device (DASD).

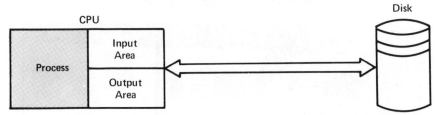

Step 2. The desired record is transferred from DASD to the input area of internal memory.

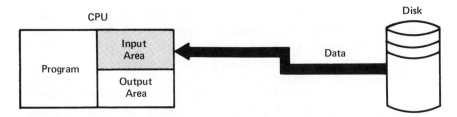

Step 3. The program updates the data temporarily stored in internal memory.

Step 4. The program returns the updated record to its rightful place on the DASD.

Fig. 12–4. How random processing works.

217

tracks near the center of the disk than on the outer tracks. Each track on a small-capacity disk can hold a maximum of 3625 characters or bytes and 7,250,000 bytes per disk pack. As with magnetic tape, records can be blocked on the disk tracks (Fig. 12–9). Each record and address is separated by gaps, thus "blocking" the record. By reducing the number of gaps, additional storage capacity is made available.

HOW RANDOM ACCESS WORKS

A disk pack may be removed and stored off line while another pack is mounted in its place. When activated, the pack of disks begins to rotate at 2400 revolutions per minute and is ready to read or write. Because there are ten read-write heads, data on ten tracks can be accessed without movement of the heads. These ten tracks are referred to as a "cylinder" (Fig. 12–10), which contains all the data that can be accessed from ten tracks. Finding a particular record involves a seek instruction in the program, which moves all ten read-write heads at the same time to some cylinder

Fig. 12–5. Loading a removable disk pack on a Burroughs 7700 large-scale computer. Up to 112 billion bytes of random-access, on-line storage augment the main memory of 6 million bytes. (Courtesy of Burroughs Corporation.)

address; say, cylinder 143. Now, one of the ten heads can read or write the data as soon as the specified record on the track has rotated under the read-write heads. For instance, if a record on track nine of cylinder 143 is to be read, the ninth head is activated at the speed of electricity as the record to be retrieved into the computer's main memory passes under the ten heads.

If the disk address of the next record to be accessed is also cylinder 143, no movement of the read-write heads is involved even though the record may be read by a different read-write head. However, accessing the required record would involve rotational delay. "Rotational delay" is the wait time while the disk spins under the stationary heads. If the record needed had

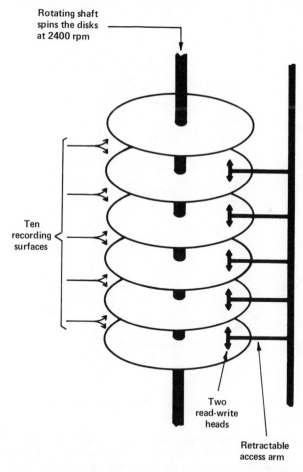

Rotating shaft spins the disks at 2400 rpm

Ten recording surfaces

Two read-write heads

Retractable access arm

Fig. 12–6. The disk pack consists of six or more disks.

already passed the read-write heads, a full rotation of the disk would be necessary to bring the record under the heads again for accessing. If the record were on the opposite side of the heads, only a half rotation would be necessary.

When a record or block of records has been accessed and transferred

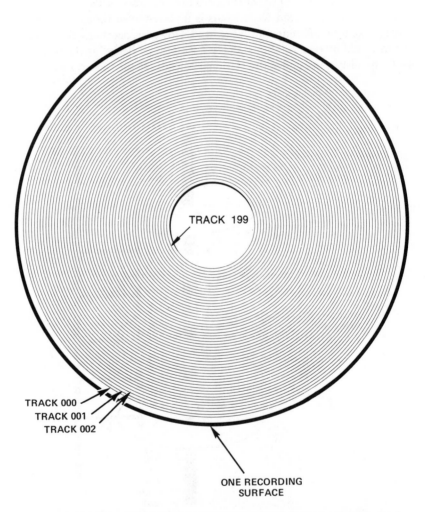

Fig. 12–7. Disks look like stereo records, but the disk has concentric tracks instead of spiral tracks. Each of the 200 tracks stores binary bits and can hold a maximum 3625 characters on small-capacity models or 14,660 on large-capacity models.

into the CPU memory for processing, the disk is free to access other records. In practice, however, the program would probably be designed so as to update the record and return it to the same place on the disk to be rewritten rather than relocate the heads to another cylinder for reading the next record in line for processing. Why, you ask? Because the fast internal processing would be completed before the read-write arms could be moved to the next cylinder, since the speeds of input and output mechanical devices are slow in comparison with the computer's electronic speeds. So, the rule is: *read, process,* and *write.* Although the random-access process appears slow, consider the read-write head movement, rotational delay times, and data transfer rates shown in Table 12–2, which indicates that throughput cannot be determined by rated speeds alone.

Faster Throughput

Applications other than accessing of data and programs stored on disks rely heavily on random-access techniques for their effectiveness. For instance, shipping cost may be extracted from a table (see Fig. 3–15) stored on a disk and which is based on different weights and mileages. In another example, sorting records on a disk is faster than by tape.

To bring disk speeds even closer to main memory speeds, thus increasing computer efficiency, additional read-write heads are attached to each access arm (Fig. 12–11). This technique reduces or eliminates access arm movement between cylinder tracks. Burroughs and IBM have built disk

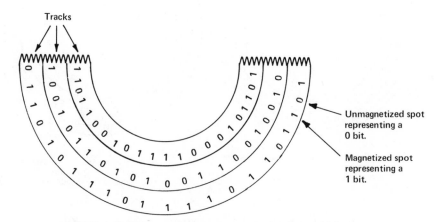

Fig. 12–8. Binary "1" and "0" bits are stored serially around the tracks. Thus, characters are stored in a row in the tracks.

models with a head for each track in every cylinder. With this design, "seek" time (head movement) is equal to the time required to revolve the requested portion of the disk under the proper read-write heads.

NCR manufactures a disk model with 12 read-write heads per disk surface, making ½ million characters available without any head movement. The UNIVAC 8414 disk-drive features 20 read-write heads mounted on each access arm mechanism; thus the 20 heads move in unison back and forth across the tracks. This means the maximum seek time is equivalent to the time needed for moving a head over ten cylinder tracks; this results in an average seek time of one-half the maximum, or five tracks.

The gain in efficiency is obvious. Access time is required to seek an individual track address, which consists of cylinder number (000 to 199) and read-write head number (0 to 9). Access time is cut if additional heads are mounted on the access arm and head movement is eliminated altogether in the head-per-track design. Still other optimization reduces access time even more by queuing several disk access requests according to their position on the disks. That is, whichever record request in the queue is nearest, its read-write head is accessed first; thus, accessing is the most efficient sequence as the disk rotates. Faster throughput is also made possible by buffer storage.

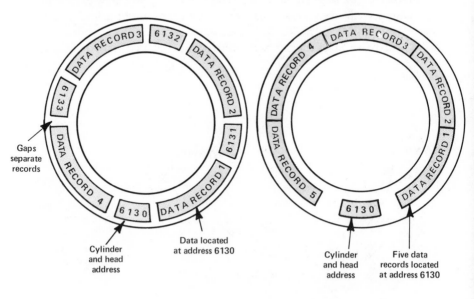

UNBLOCKED RECORDS   BLOCKED RECORDS

Fig. 12–9. (A) Unblocked disk records. (B) Blocked disk records.

BUFFER STORAGE SPEEDS THROUGHPUT

The most efficient usage made of a computer is determined by the utilization of the central processor. As previously mentioned, data throughput is increased if input and output operations can be overlapped with processing operations. "Buffering" is another term to describe the ability to input, process, and output data concurrently. Buffering refers to additional core storage—more accurately called "buffered storage"—which functions so as to compensate for differences between mechanical I/O speeds and electronic processing speeds.

Buffer storage capable of holding two or more records is a small

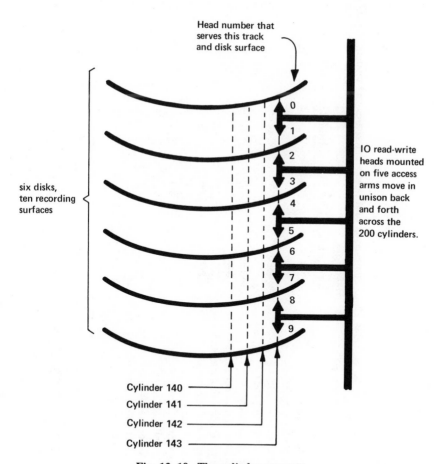

Fig. 12–10. The cylinder concept.

Table 12–2. Comparison of disk characteristics and models varying in cost performance.

Characteristic	IBM 2305, heads per track	IBM 3330	IBM 2314	IBM 2311	UNIVAC 8414	NCR 200	Mohawk 2900
Module capacity[1] (million bytes)	22.4	800	233.4	58	233.4	33.5	466
Disk pack capacity (million bytes)	5.4	100	29.4	7.25	29.1	8.4	29.1 or 58.2
Track capacity	14,660	13,030	7,294	3,625	7,294	3,500	7,294
Number tracks per surface	64	404	200	200	200	200	200 or 400
Number recording surfaces	12	19	20	10	20	12	20
Revolutions per minute	6,000	3,600	2,400	2,400	2,400	2,400	2,400
Access facts							
Average latency[2] (milliseconds)	10	8.4	12.5	12.5	12.5	12.5	12.5
Average seek/access time[3] (milliseconds)	0	30	60	75	60	43.7	30
Data transfer rate (bytes per second)	3,000,000	806,000	312,000	156,000	312,000	180,000	312,000

[1] Number of disk packs per unit.
[2] Disk rotational delay.
[3] Movement or read/write heads.

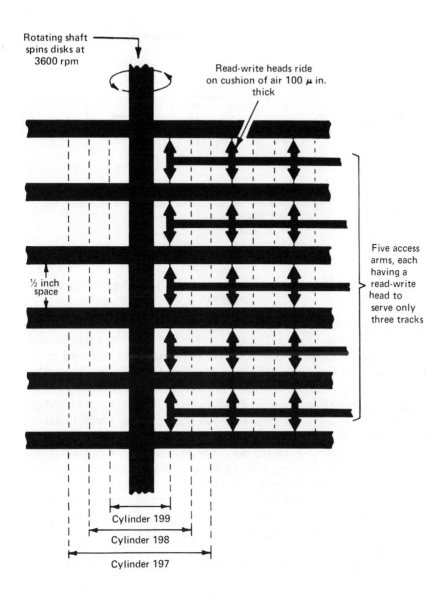

Fig. 12–11. Access time: The time required to position the read-write heads to the desired cylinder is reduced by mounting additional heads on each access arm. The head-per-track concept eliminates access or seek time altogether so that total access time consists only of time to rotate the disk under the heads.

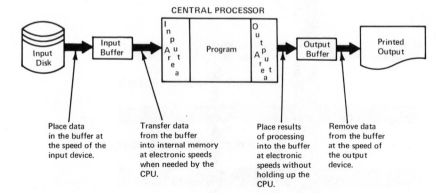

Fig. 12–12. Buffer storage allows processing to be overlapped with I/O operations.

memory device located between all input units and the CPU, and between the CPU and all output units (Fig. 12–12). The buffer may be a separate unit or may be physically built into the CPU or I/O units. Buffer storage is of two types: one set up and controlled by programming (described in Chapter 14), and one designed into the hardware. Let us examine the hardware concept to find why the CPU is kept from doing useful work if the system is unbuffered (Fig. 12–13): The record is read and transferred to internal memory while the CPU and output operations are suspended. Then, when the computer process takes place, all I/O devices become inactive. When computing is complete, the output device writes the results while the input unit and the processor wait for the next record to be read. In other words, the CPU is "I/O-bound" because of the slow I/O and is "process-bound" if the I/O units are idle because of excessive program execution. The ideal overlapping of I/O operations with the CPU takes place when processing time is approximately equal to I/O time.

With electronic buffer storage, data is collected in the buffer or dis-

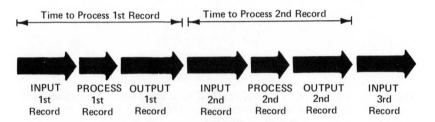

Fig. 12–13. Unbuffered processing.

posed of at the same time the CPU is busy doing other work (Fig. 12–14). When called by the program, the contents of the core buffer are transferred at electronic speeds with almost no delay; thus, the transfer rate is unaffected by slow I/O speeds. While the data is being processed by the CPU, another record is being read into the input buffer from, say, a tape drive, and the output buffer is being emptied, say, onto a printer. After each processing cycle, therefore, results of each processing are moved from main storage to the output buffer instantaneously, and the CPU summons the contents of the input buffer without having to pause for the I/O device to read the next record.

In effect, the buffer provides temporary storage between I/O units and the CPU. This enables the program to continue computations at the same time other records are being prepared for reading and writing. In fact, computers can be buffered to the extent that more than one program can be processed during the same run, resulting in maximum efficiency of the central processor. This technique, called "multiprogramming," is discussed further in Chapter 14.

Buffering is tied into the subject of channels, discussed in Chapter 11. That is, the channel and controller must have a small buffer to store data temporarily during input and output operations. Thus, buffering adds to the

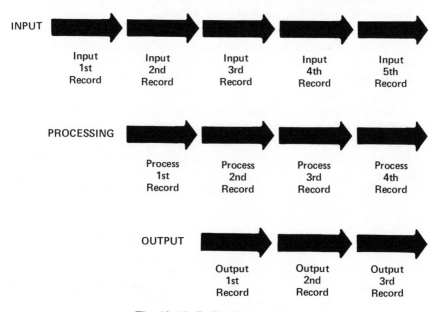

Fig. 12–14. Buffered processing.

list of other methods previously discussed in relation to maximum efficiency of the computer; for example, blocking records, which permits several records to be read at the same time.

SUMMARY

Random processing, made possible by disk storage, provides a means of processing unsequenced records. On-line processing means updating records as they become available rather than processing them in batches. Too, disk permits the storage of masses of data, all on line to the computer. Storage capacities range from a few million characters to 112 billion characters, the latter provided by Burroughs' data memory bank devices.

Magnetic disk packs contain six or more disks having ten recording surfaces. This construction design permits any record to be called from auxiliary storage and brought into internal memory without searching sequentially through the file. In this manner, a "seek" command in the program positions the ten read-write heads, mounted on five retractable access arms, on one of the 200 cylinders. Recall that a cylinder contains ten vertical tracks. The second part of the access operation is to activate the read-write head that corresponds to the track containing the desired record. To facilitate locating records, each has an address consisting of the cylinder number (000 to 199) and head number (0 to 9).

Extending our knowledge on throughput efficiency, we discussed buffer storage. Channels and controllers, covered in the preceding chapter, use buffers to store two or more records destined for input or output at the same time the CPU is processing other records. We shall read more on buffering in Chapter 14.

Up to this point, we have covered the primary media and system components that a computer uses to accomplish input, processing, and output of data. The media are card, tape, disk, and core storage, and computer operational components include those devices that process these media. In the next chapter, we expand this knowledge by presenting other forms of input and output devices, and different internal memory media.

KEY TERMS TO REMEMBER

Batch, on-line, and real-time processing
Blocked records
Buffer storage

Cylinder
Direct-access storage device (DASD)
Disk advantages

Disk pack

Disk surface

Latency, or rotational delay

Random-access processing

Secondary storage

Seek time

Track

QUESTIONS

1. Figure 12–11 has more than one read-write head per access arm. What is the relationship to the statement, "There is always a trade-off between speed and cost."
2. What factors determine the total access time for a head-per-track disk pack?
3. How does on-line processing differ from batch processing?
4. Since both real-time and on-line processing use random accessing, what is the difference?
5. Name the four steps involved in random processing.
6. How does the data on disk tracks differ from data stored on tape tracks?
7. What factors govern the length of the access time?
8. Why would the disk normally be left in an idle state while the CPU processes a data record just retrieved instead of accessing the next disk record to be processed?
9. Of what value would the cylinder concept be if a file were organized sequentially on the disk and processed in a batch mode?
10. Name uses of the disk file other than for mass storage.
11. What purpose does buffering serve?
12. What is meant when we say that there are two buffering concepts?
13. What does multiprogramming permit?

COORDINATED READINGS IN CHAPTER 15

"Data Base—What Is It?", Sec. 23.

"Data Base—Concern of Management," Sec. 24.

"What Management Should Know About Virtual Storage," Sec. 33.

Chapter 13

STATE OF THE ART

In this chapter we discuss new designs in computer architecture and the numerous input and output media that can be attached to the computer for data storage, data entry, data collection, data communication, and recording of results.

Each topic discussed here could have been covered in appropriate places elsewhere, but because each new chapter introduced enough terminology to grasp at one time, we included only the most popular subjects. This allowed the business student to develop the best conceptual understanding and avoided overtaxing him with everything there is to know about every subject. Instead, we covered the basic, popular core storage media, for example, and left alternate types, such as "MOSFET" memories, until now.

INTEGRATED CIRCUITS

Reducing the distance that electronic impulses have to flow is the main way in which computers achieve higher internal speeds. Therefore, progress in electronic components for computers has moved toward smaller circuits than those used in the first experimental computers over two decades ago. Circuit components began with the array of vacuum tubes used in first-generation computers. Next, transistors mounted on printed circuit cards, called "solid state," were used in second-generation computers. Third-generation computers have integrated circuits, which are made up of microscopic transistors and other miniaturized electronic components. More than 1000 so-called chip transistors and diodes, about the size of the period at the end of this sentence (28 thousandths of an inch square), are integrated into a single thin wafer (1/7000 inch thick), about the size of a half-dollar. This compactness allows certain circuits to function in less than 1.5 nanoseconds (billionths of a second), the time it takes light and electricity, moving at 186,000 miles per second, to travel 16 inches. The current trend is toward the LSI (large-scale integrated) circuit, a still smaller and more reliable component.

Mosfet Memory

A new memory design, called "MOSFET" (metal oxide semiconductor field effect transistor), offers more compact storage than other memory types. The MOSFET modules contain two transistor chips, each having 1024 bits of data. Thus, two MOSFET modules are equivalent to a core storage array of 4096 bits (Fig. 13–1).

Two large-scale computers, the IBM 370 models 158 and 168, use MOSFET memories. Owners of the Model 370/168, with its mammoth four million bytes of internal memory, will readily benefit from the reduction in space for the large main storage. The central processor of the 370/168 occupies 40 percent less floor space than the earlier large-scale IBM 360/165. Rent on the giant computer ranges from $93,000 to $170,000 per month; purchase price is as low as $4.2 million or may be as high as $7.3 million for a full-blown IBM 370/168.

VIRTUAL STORAGE

Core storage has always been expensive; therefore, the memory capacity largely determines the cost of the computer. Although price for performance and core storage has steadily decreased ($0.50 per bit in 1967 versus less than $0.10 now), core storage is still a major factor. As a result, extensive storage requirements have been a major constraint in putting many applications on the computer. For example, on-line data bases require large amounts of storage in order to tie together a company's operation through data terminals (see Section 33, Chapter 15). Because they were too impractical or too costly in many cases, applications were handled on a once-a-day batch basis rather than on a real-time basis.

Virtual storage is not new, but it was formerly available only on certain computers such as the Burroughs 5000 and the IBM 360/67. "Virtual stor-

Fig. 13–1. Four MOSFET chips provide the same **4K bits of memory as the core plane in the background. They provide twice the speed at half the price.** (Courtesy of © *Datamation*®.)

age" is the term applied to a technique whereby internal memory is made to appear virtually unlimited. As such, the directly addressable storage in IBM's System 370 virtual-storage models is nearly 17 million bytes, whereas the actual size of main memory is only a fraction of the 17 million bytes.

How Virtual Storage Works. What is virtual storage? Virtual storage allows the running of programs that are larger than the size of main memory. Although programmers have always been able to do this by using a programming technique called "overlaying," virtual storage shifts the task to the computer itself. In other words, the programmer has been relieved of still another responsibility. In virtual storage, all program instructions and data are not in main storage at one time. The parts of the program and data not in main memory are retained in direct-access storage devices (DASD), such as magnetic disks, until needed. For example, during processing, pages of instructions (Fig. 13–2) are transferred between the disk (virtual storage) and the CPU internal memory (real memory). This process, called "paging," frees the programmer from the complicated task of fitting

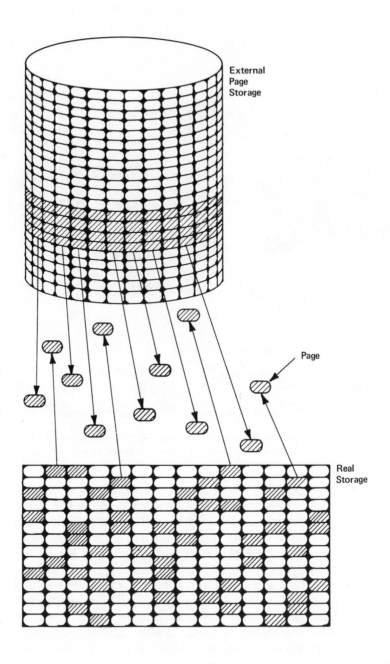

Fig. 13–2. Virtual storage extends the internal storage available to the
computer for running applications programs.

234

programs into available memory and permits program expansion.

In effect, the computer's main memory takes on a checkerboard appearance. Parts of programs and data are scattered throughout storage in blocks of 2K or 4K (actually, 2048 or 4096) bytes (Fig. 13–3). Many blocks, or "pages," can be placed into main memory at the same time by a sophisticated operating system. The number of pages that reside in main storage at any given time depends on the capacity of main storage. A program that needs 40,000 bytes of main memory when fully loaded may need only 16K during one part of the processing. During this instant of time, there is no requirement that the operating system must allocate 24K of main storage for the unused segment of the program. Thus, the computer is made more adaptive to the demands of management.

But how does the CPU execute the program without having all pages

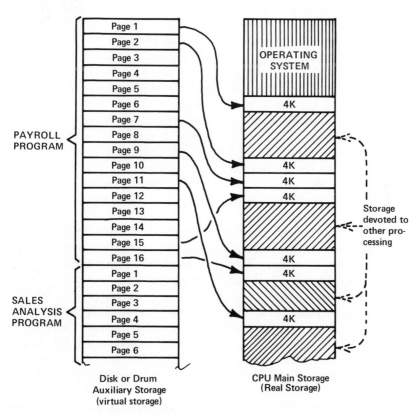

Fig. 13–3. Virtual storage consists of space in real storage plus additional space in direct-access storage devices.

in main memory at the same time? The operating system finds available memory on the disks and brings in pages and data as required. When a page is not needed at any given time, another page is brought in from the less costly disk memory and overlays the idle instructions making up the idle page. When the replaced page in main memory is needed again, the operating system (which keeps track of where each page is stored) recalls it to main memory from disk. This swapping of pages between internal and external memory operates rapidly. Such complexity would be impractical if each installation were to write into all programs the instructions needed to simulate virtual storage.

Is Virtual Storage Always the Answer? There is a saying, "So goes IBM, so goes the rest of the industry." Even though Burroughs introduced virtual storage in 1961, IBM employed virtual storage in only one of its System 360 models and did not make it available in the first models of the new System 370 line. However, virtual storage now appears inevitable and all users may be forced to shift sooner or later. Third-generation computers offer great speed and make things possible that could not be done on earlier computers, but the penalty for this flexibility has been operational complexity. Many computer users have tried to follow a trend of simple and unsophisticated programming. In order for them to retain a less costly, simple operation, they may choose to concentrate on productive work with their present computers rather than keeping abreast with industry's new technological steps, which tend to perpetuate complexity. To some, this new technology is considered a nuisance because control has become increasingly more difficult as the computers become more complex. Nevertheless, expanded application capability made possible by virtual storage computers may give new life to the simple second-generation equipment.

To illustrate virtual storage, consider the following situation in which the user usually had to structure his application programs according to the size of main memory instead of business needs. A 32K computer was installed to handle current processing needs plus some room for expansion. Some time later, a new program, or expansion of one of the older programs to meet additional requirements, needed 33K. Upgrading to a new system could not be justified because this one program required a memory bank beyond the computer's capacity. If virtual storage had been available, this problem would not have existed because parts of the program could have been stored on DASD and brought into main memory only as needed.

In addition, virtual storage also makes possible larger internal-memory buffers, which are created by the programmer. As you will recall, more buffer storage achieves greater performance because I/O devices can transfer larger blocks of data concurrently to and from main memory. In concluding our discussion of virtual storage, we should point out that it has welcome advantages, but that it costs more (see Sec. 33, Chapter 15).

DIRECT-ACCESS STORAGE DEVICES

A computer system is composed of the central processing unit (CPU) and a variety of input and output devices. The performance of the system as a whole depends to a large extent upon the efficiency of I/O units. These I/O units are designed for specific purposes: *direct entry* (such as optical readers), *sequential* input and output (such as tape), or *random-access* applications (such as disks).

Sequential processing is ideal when a large amount of records must be accessed, but if only 100 of 10,000 records are affected, then 9900 records must be read and written unnecessarily. In contrast, direct-access storage devices (Fig. 13–4) make it possible to process only the affected records with far greater efficiency because DASDs can find a record randomly and update that record in place without reading preceding records. This chapter describes DASDs other than the popular magnetic disk, such as drum and data cell storage.

Magnetic Drum

Magnetic-drum storage (Fig. 13–5) is similar in concept to that of the disk covered in Chapter 12. Whereas "0" and "1" bits are recorded *horizontally* along tracks on the disk, drum bits are recorded in parallel tracks on the outer surface of the rotating cylinder. The drum revolves under read-write heads (Fig. 13–6), one for each of the 800 tracks, which are divided into 200 addressable groups of four tracks each. Data are accessed from these four tracks a half-byte at a time rather than one byte from a single track, as in the case of disk. Thus, a high rate of data transfer is achieved, up to 1.2 million bytes per second as the cylinder rotates at 3500 revolutions per minute. Because each of the 800 tracks has its own read-write head, there is no delay in accessing tracks, and the rotational delay averages only 8.6 milliseconds. Data transfer to and from the CPU main memory varies according to model.

The magnetic drum was originally designed for use as main memory, but it now serves as an direct-access storage device when fast retrieval of data is required. Up to four IBM 2301 drum DASDs (Fig. 13–5) can be attached to each controller, providing 32 million decimal numbers (two EBCDIC digits per byte) or 16 million alpha numeric characters per each

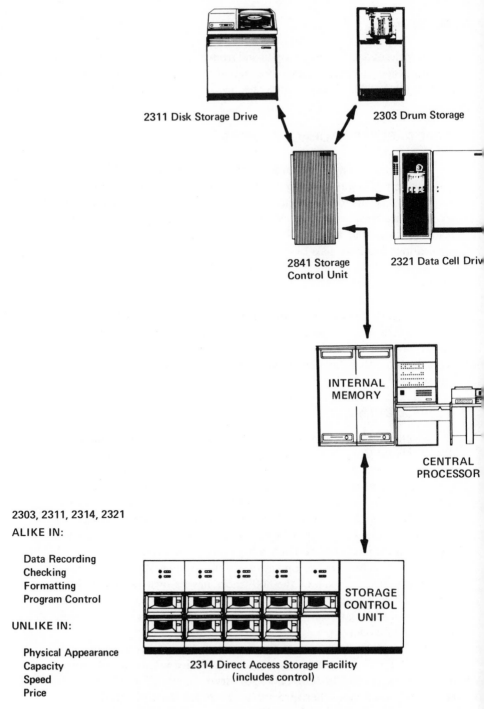

2311 Disk Storage Drive   2303 Drum Storage

2841 Storage   2321 Data Cell Driv
Control Unit

INTERNAL
MEMORY

CENTRAL
PROCESSOR

2303, 2311, 2314, 2321
ALIKE IN:

Data Recording
Checking
Formatting
Program Control

UNLIKE IN:

Physical Appearance
Capacity
Speed
Price

STORAGE
CONTROL
UNIT

2314 Direct Access Storage Facility
(includes control)

Fig. 13–4. Types of direct-access storage devices (DASD).

238

controller attached. Unlike the removable disk packs, drum storage is mounted permanently in the unit.

Data Cell Drive

The IBM data cell (Fig. 13–7) extends on-line direct-access storage capabilities beyond those of all other types of DASDs, over 150 billion characters or over 300 billion packed decimal digits. The storage media are strips of magnetic tape housed in ten data cells, each containing ten strips

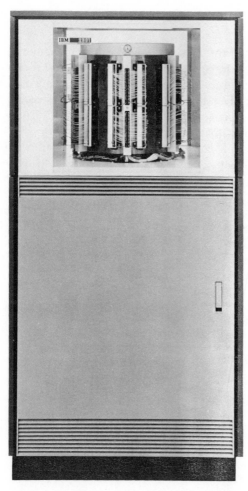

Fig. 13–5. The IBM magnetic drum storage. (By permission of IBM.)

of tape. Since each data cell is removable, unlimited bulk storage can be kept in libraries consisting of off-line data cells, which may store as many as 400 million bytes (Fig. 13–7). In the IBM 2321, eight drives can be attached to each controller and up to 48 controllers can be connected to a large-scale computer to provide a maximum 150 billion on-line characters.

Now that we have covered two popular forms of direct-access media (disk and drum) as well as the data cell drive, we turn our attention to other input and output devices designed for different purposes. Let us begin with input devices used for data collection.

DATA ENTRY

Shortening of the input cycle can be done in many ways to reduce the time lag between the conclusion of a transaction and the entry of that data into a company's business records by computers. Data can be either manually keyed directly into the computer storage, bypassing the keying of punched cards from source documents; or entered directly into the computer by machines that read source documents (Fig. 13–8).

Management is concerned with data entry methods that replace the traditional approach of employing humans to read documents and convert the data to machine-readable media. Some major considerations are:

- Studies have put the estimated cost of a manual key entry station at almost $800 a month. The cost includes salary, fringe benefits, hardware rent, and card or tape materials.
- Placement of responsibility for the correctness of input data with the department creating the data.

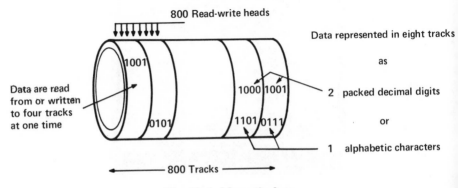

Fig. 13–6. Magnetic drum.

- Faster turnaround by providing results of processing to the user by in-line or real-time methods, since data is entered directly into the computer.
- Data accuracy is improved by capturing data at the source.
- Transcription of data into another form is eliminated.

With these time and cost factors in mind, we shall discuss a few of the input devices, such as optical readers and visual display terminals, designed to solve specific problems.

Fig. 13–7. IBM 2321 data-cell drive. (By permission of IBM.)

Optical Character Readers

Optical character recognition (OCR) machines (Fig. 13–9) were designed to enter source documents directly into the computer without retranscribing the data on punched cards or some other form suitable for computer input. Without this ability to bypass input data conversion, computerized billing for large-volume applications would be impractical and too costly. A typical application involving small purchases and massive input is gasoline credit.

An OCR machine can read documents with handwritten or machine-written data (Fig. 13–10), handle forms of different sizes, and record the data at 100 to 665 documents a minute. The speed varies according to the number of fields to be read and whether the document is handwritten or machine printed.

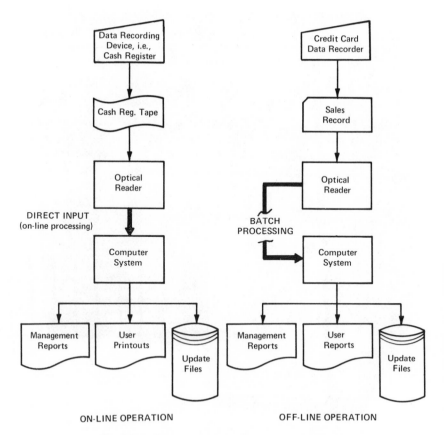

Fig. 13–8. Data entry by source-entry machines.

Optical Mark Readers

Another form of direct data entry that permits bypassing keying of data from source documents is the IBM 3881 optical mark reader, similar in appearance to the OCR machine shown in Fig. 13–9. The OMR converts pencil marks (Fig. 13–10) into binary-coded decimal and transmits that and other machine-readable data to the computer. Common applications well suited for OMR would be test scoring at colleges, inventory taking, meter reading by public utilities, and vehicle accident reporting.

Optical marks can mean anything the user wants them to mean. To illustrate, college students mark their answers by shading in the small blocks. The OMR reads the student's answer paper, or card, line-by-line and prints the number of right and wrong answers along with the computed score. In an inventory, the computer prints each item number and its description on a form designed for optical marking. The form can be used later to reorder certain items or take a physical inventory in the warehouse. Instead of writing numbers, which must be keypunched before entering the

Fig. 13–9. The IBM 3886 optical character reader (OCR) reads hand-printed numbers and alphabetic or numeric machine-printed fonts. This model operates off-line and transfers data onto magnetic tape for batch processing. (By permission of IBM.)

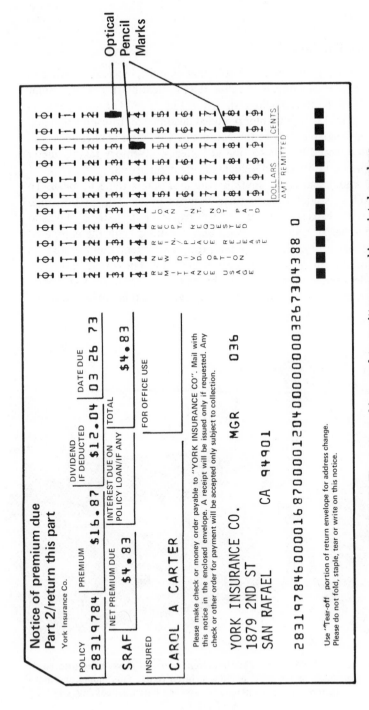

Fig. 13–10. The OCR machines read typewritten or machine-printed numbers and letters or hand-printed numbers. Optical-mark readers recognize pencil shading in the appropriate block representing numbers, such as the $4.83 shown on the card here.

computer, the numbers are coded by shading in the boxed areas the right block representing the number. Thus, recording at the source by optical marks means faster return of the results while increasing efficiency through fewer errors and lower input costs.

Optical Tape Readers

A method of eliminating hand posting of sales transactions for retail stores, banks, supermarkets, etc., is through optical tapes. Data is recorded on cash registers or adding machine tapes for a variety of applications such as savings transactions, store ordering, payment entries, and sales payments. In ringing up sales on the cash register, for instance, the account number, item number, and date are keyed along with the sales amount. This data is printed on the cash register tape in machine-readable optical-font type. Then the journal tapes are sent to the data processing center where they are read by an optical tape reader, such as the NCR optical tape reader shown in Fig. 13-11.

As with other optical equipment, the data on the cash register tape can be converted off-line onto punched cards, paper tape, or magnetic tape. The OCR machine may also be on-line to the computer, making the data immediately available to the computer as conversion takes place. The computer then uses the converted data to prepare customer statements, accounts receivable journals, sales analysis reports for management, and so forth.

Obviously, there are many "input roads" to computer processing. In Chapter 5, we covered MICR (magnetic ink character recognition) machines, which read checks, and several keying methods such as key-to-card, key-to-tape, and key-to-disk. Here, we have concentrated on the newest field of data entry, that of optical reading. The cost of optical readers is finally decreasing to within reach of most data processing installation budgets, and consequently we should see a steady increase in use of optical readers. Nevertheless, there are still applications that lend themselves better to manual keying operations.

DATA COMMUNICATIONS

Three essential steps are involved in data processing: (1) *collecting and transmitting* data to the computer center, (2) *processing* data, and (3) *communicating* the results to the user. The first and third step are the real built-in delays. Even though computers process the data at spectacular nanosecond speeds, it may require a day or more to collect, mail, and convert the data before entering it into the computer. Distribution of results

Fig. 13–11. The NCR optical tape reader converts data entries created by cash
registers or adding machines at speeds of 3120 lines per minute, in either
off-line or on-line processing. (Courtesy of the National Cash Register
Corporation.)

requires additional hours. So, it would appear that the claim of processing
the data quickly is somewhat ridiculous, since the elapsed time is in days.
In other words, we can process the data in seconds, but collection and
distribution lags.

The solution of reducing the time lag lies in data communication,
which refers to a means of transmitting data between the computer and the
point of collection or distribution. Telephone lines are used extensively to
connect these remote collection and distribution terminals to the computer.
And about half of all computer installations are using some form of data
communication devices, especially companies having their business spread
out over town or nation.

Telephone networks were designed for voice transmission. To relieve the telephone network of the data communication work load, orbiting satellites will be used more and more to relay the data between points (Fig. 13–12). The primary reason for this recourse to satellites is the tremendous growth rate of data communication. It is estimated that by 1980 the telephone network will be carrying about half *voice* and half *data* communication. This heavy work load may exceed the telephone company's capability of handling the combined demands. Therefore, satellites such as Telstar can take on the burden of data communication for operations like credit authorization and verification of bank balances preliminary to check or draft acceptance.

The subject of data communications can be a course of instruction in itself because of its huge scope. Data communication equipment varies from self-contained data collection systems that operate off line from the main

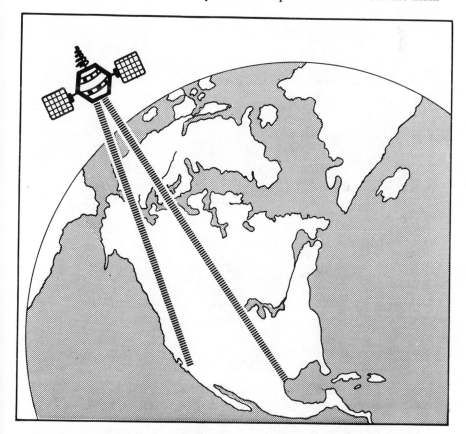

Fig. 13–12. Satellite data communication transmits input data to a centralized computer for processing and returning results to the sender.

computer to computers having a multitude of interconnected on-line I/O devices. Data-collection computer systems receive the data over telephone lines and perform input and output processing, such as data editing as the data is recorded on tape drives and printers, thus relieving the main computer of these tasks. On-line I/O devices include typewriters, telephone-to-computer hookups, visual display terminals, cash registers (Fig. 13–13), and a multitude of other subsystems.

Fig. 13–13. Retailing at the point of sale is coming to this: The salesclerk checks customer credit by touching a key on the cash register. Other keys are provided for various details of the transaction, which are printed on a receipt. All this information is transmitted to the computer for processing account records and for accumulating information required by management. (Courtesy of Singer Business Machines.)

Visual Display Communication

Cathode-ray tubes (CRT) are TV-like screens that provide a visual link to the computer by telephone cables. The kind of CRT shown in Fig. 13–14 typically displays 25 lines of data consisting of 80 characters per line. The CRT is used as both input to and output from the computer. As output, the "tube" rapidly retrieves requested data for a variety of applications. Examples of businesses that have a need for CRT displays are:

Hotels: Provides ready reference to room availability, registered guests, and other information. Connected to a centralized computer, each hotel's CRT permits checking of reservations in other hotels in the chain so that reservations can be made for each overnight stop for cross-country travelers.

Credit Bureaus: Provides instant credit background to authorize credit.

Airlines: Seat availability and flight status are provided to improve customer service.

Banks: Permits answering depositors' questions about balance, cashed checks, and so forth.

Law Enforcement: Provides retrieval and dissemination of car owners and license number inquiries, unpaid traffic citations, criminal records, etc.

Retailers: Up-to-date inventory, accounts receivable inquiries from customers, vendor data, deliveries, etc., are available.

Hospitals: Medical records and credit files are instantly available to give better patient care and service in settling their accounts.

Insurance Companies: Provides effective means for updating policy files and retrieval of premiums and claims data.

Manufacturing: Status of work in progress, inventories, and other data are available.

Input to the computer is by a typewriter keyboard. As numbers and letters are depressed on the keyboard, they enter CRT buffer storage and are displayed on the screen. When the operator finishes keying all data, a key is depressed to allow the contents in the buffer to enter the computer. To inquire about a stock quote, for instance, the stockbroker keys in certain control information as the customer waits on the telephone. The status of the stock is instantaneously displayed on the stockbroker's CRT as it is processed by the American or New York Exchange's computer. The information contains current price, buy or sell recommendation, expected price goal, and so forth. In another example of CRT usage, programmers can display portions of a program and change instructions as necessary.

Fig. 13–14. Input and display terminal lets the user display data stored in the computer or in the on-line, direct-access storage devices. Part or all of the data can be altered or replaced. (Courtesy of Burroughs Corporation.)

Another type of CRT projects graphs (i.e., sale trends), charts (i.e., sales figures), and even a chessboard (Fig. 13–15). A keyboard is a means of entry and change of computation formulas, and a *light pen* (Fig. 13–16) enables engineers to sketch drawings or pinpoint areas for changes. A light trail follows the pen much as an ink trail follows an ordinary pen.

Fig. 13–15. A NASA employee makes a chess move for the Varian Data Machine G20/i computer. This machine placed second in the First Computer Chess Championship, which was really a contest among programs.

Voice Communication

Hundreds of remote terminals can be connected to a computer for use in offices, stores, warehouses, stock exchanges, warehouses, colleges, and so on. But what about communication with the computer in a customer's place of business, in a motel while traveling, or in a prospect's home? These off-station needs are served by another data communications device that hooks into a standard telephone, making any phone a potential data terminal. Portable audio terminals (Fig. 13–17) allow businessmen and salesmen to get up-to-the-minute information or to enter data into the computer.

By attaching the telephone receiver and mouthpiece to the small, battery-operated audio terminal, contact with the computer is made. By depressing the appropriate keys, a salesman can inquire directly into his company's computer to check on availability of products as the customer waits. A voice reply returned through a speaker (or earphone) in the audio terminal tells whether the product is available. Then the salesman keys the order into the computer and receives a voice confirmation.

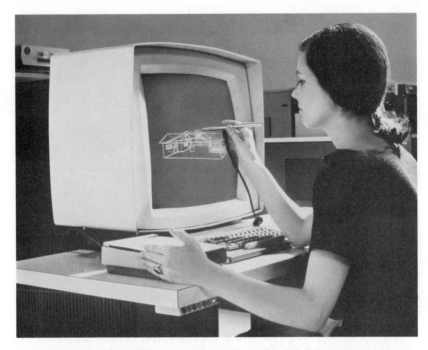

Fig. 13–16. The IBM 2250 CRT is designed for on-line display and manipulation of drawings. The screen has over a million display points, which can be individually addressed by X and Y coordinates, using a light pen. (By permission of IBM.)

One user of audio response equipment is the Playboy Club. A Bunny at the San Francisco club, for instance, dials the member's account number on a special phone connected to the home-office computer in Boston. The computer checks to see if the member's account is delinquent and sends a yes or no reply—and hopefully the member gets his drink and food.

Mystifying as it may seem, the portable audio concept is quite simple and is similar to the familiar "you have reached a disconnected number" telephone message automatically played when a caller dials incorrectly. A vocabulary needed to process all possible business inquiries is prerecorded and stored in a voice response unit attached to the computer. When an inquiry is received, the computer processes the request and transmits the appropriate words from the voice response unit to the audio terminal that has requested the information. This form of data communication is growing rapidly and may eventually be a common household device connected to your telephone.

Fig. 13–17. The IBM 2721 portable audio-terminal speeds information from a centralized computer to the place where it is needed. (By permission of IBM.)

SUMMARY

The state of the art is rapidly changing. New devices that perform different functions are being introduced so fast that it is difficult to keep abreast of all technology. More important than announcements of new equipment, however, is that the production cost is coming down for the many types of computer I/O devices, thus making their usage widespread. As a result, old ways of doing things are falling by the wayside. A classic example is the new data collection and data communication methods made possible by reasonably priced input devices that read data directly from source documents.

The long-lived core storage is slowly giving way to the new micro-miniaturized memories that cost less, work faster, and save floor space. Another innovation, referred to as "virtual" storage, has solved the age-old problem of not enough internal storage capacity. This problem may slip into the past as virtual-storage computers replace fixed-storage computers in the 1970s.

Direct access storage devices (DASD) were once reserved for those computer installations that could afford them and which had applications that required random access and rapid data retrieval. Now, DASDs are relatively inexpensive by comparison with their costs in past years and are commonplace. This is of great significance, since virtual storage requires some type of DASD such as the magnetic disk, magnetic drum, or data cell drive. Also, new ways of collecting data, such as key-to-disk, require these auxiliary storage devices to store the data until needed for processing.

Two types of DASDs covered in this chapter are the magnetic drum and the data cell drive. While both are designed to augment the internal memory of the computer, each has different advantages over the other. The drum is faster than the data cell, but the data cell offers far greater storage capacity.

Optical character recognition (OCR) equipment, once uncommon except in large data processing installations, is now widely used in applications that vary from reading handwritten zip codes to speed the mail to small-dollar-amount sales receipts in small shoe stores.

Data communication equipment is making an impact upon data processing budgets as management accepts them as solutions in closing the gap between the sales transactions and management reports. One of the fastest growing media of data communications is the cathode-ray tube (CRT), which displays an image of whatever is stored in memory. Before the CRT became available, the status of data stored at the home-office computer was unknown until printouts were received; due to the time lag, the true picture was never known because the data was ever changing. The "tube," as well as the portable audio terminal, now takes us directly inside the computer so that we can view the status of data at any given moment.

In the next chapter, we expand our knowledge of internal memory, multiprogramming, and stacked-job processing, and look into a crystal ball as we cover future computer systems in which many small computers are constructed inside a single computer main frame.

KEY TERMS TO REMEMBER

Buffer storage
Cathode-ray tube (CRT)
Data cell drive (DASD)
Data communication
Magnetic Drum Storage DASD
MOSFET Memory
Optical   character   recognition
  (OCR)

Optical mark reader (OMR)
Optical tape readers
Overlay
Pages
Portable audio terminals
Remote data terminals
Virtual Storage

QUESTIONS

1. Microminiaturized circuits were invented for third-generation computers. What three advantages were gained over the conventional transistor?
2. Referring to Question 1, what characteristic governing the flow of electronic impulses made these advantages possible?
3. Explain the terms "pages" and "virtual storage."
4. What is the advantage of virtual storage?
5. How can virtual storage increase throughput?
6. How does retrieval of data stored on drum differ from disk storage?
7. Which DASD has the greatest storage capacity?
8. What is meant by the data entry terms "OCR" and "direct input"?
9. What impact has data communication equipment had upon data collection and data entry?
10. How have remote data terminals affected customer service?

COORDINATED READINGS IN CHAPTER 15

"Why the Rising Computer Budget?", Sec. 13.
"What Management Should Know About Virtual Storage," Sec. 33.
"Future Trends in Computer Architecture," Sec. 32.

Chapter **14**

OPERATING SYSTEMS

The productivity of a data processing center depends upon how well its human resources and computer hardware do the work on hand. Man must plan all work that the computer must do, and in doing so he must plan for every contingency that might arise. How the computer hardware and program follow these orders has been discussed earlier. Now we shall see how an operating system increases the effectiveness of the computer system and makes the job easier for the programmer and operator.

WHAT IS AN OPERATING SYSTEM?

An operating system is a set of special programs that are designed to increase throughput, relieve the programmer of certain programming tasks, and aid the computer operator in keeping the system running by providing automatic transition from one job to the next. As you will recall, throughput efficiency means increasing the volume of work that can be handled by shortening the processing time between input and output operations. Operating systems support a number of different methods of processing, such as batch processing, on-line and real-time processing, and timesharing, covered later in this chapter.

Today's sophisticated operating systems, hereafter called "o/s," evolved from large-scale, second-generation systems such as IBM's scientific 7094 computer, shown in Fig. 2–6. You are already familiar with some of the characteristics of operating systems. For example, o/s reduces the amount of time that the central processor is idle, o/s monitors input and output operations, o/s resides partly in main memory and partly on external disk memory, and o/s is usually designed, programmed, and furnished by the computer manufacturer. We shall soon expand this knowledge and see advantages offered by o/s, such as multiprogramming.

WHAT O/S OFFERS MANAGEMENT

Management can better control the computer environment with the services provided by o/s. For example, o/s scheduling of jobs according to priority gives management better control of the computer's time in order to get reports that have a vital effect on the business. Another benefit is job accounting (that is, when a job started and finished) as well as the amount and cost of computer time. A record of the system's operation as pertains to program processing and operator actions is recorded for error and efficiency analysis.

Should management be concerned with what o/s can and cannot do? The answer is an emphatic yes because the capabilities of operating systems vary perhaps more than the range of computing power between the many types of computers. There is enough variety in each level of o/s and each manufacturer's o/s* to discourage a survey of all. Nevertheless, we shall cover the common attributes of most operating systems.

Desired O/S Characteristics

Multiprogramming. One or more programs occupying main memory at the same time enable the running of multiple programs simultaneously. In this way the system is kept busy, thereby increasing the amount of output.

Job Scheduling. Some jobs are urgent and must be processed immediately; others can be run at any time. To satisfy this need, several jobs entering the computer can be processed according to their importance. An o/s can monitor the flow of work so that, for instance, four jobs with priorities of 2, 1, 4, and 3 are read into the system in that order, placed on disk, and brought back into memory for processing in the order of 1, 2, 3, and 4, permitting the job with the highest priority to finish first, and so on.

Program Relocatability. Relocation of programs, or portions thereof, can be loaded or moved to any place in internal memory outside the area

---

*Burroughs, CDC, Honeywell, IBM, NCR, UNIVAC, to name a few.

occupied by o/s. This facilitates filling memory with the maximum of programs, since each program need not use the same locations (addresses) each time it is loaded.

Storage Protection. Since multiprogramming permits more than one program to reside concurrently in main memory, o/s generally prevents unauthorized or unintentional attempts by one program to access or alter another program. Passwords or keywords act as controls so that some programs are permitted to alter stored data, while other programs may read data but not change it.

Modularity. Data processing needs differ greatly from one installation to another. However, an operating system designed to satisfy such diverse needs with a single, huge o/s would end up with many EDP centers wasting memory space and computer time for unwanted facilities. Consequently, o/s normally consists of parts, called "modules," that can be assembled to meet each user's needs; thus, a tailor-made o/s consists of only those modules desired. In addition, modules can be replaced or added as business needs change. Also, modular design allows only those modules in use to reside in internal memory at any given time. Other modules are called in from disk as needed, significantly reducing the amount of main memory needed for resident o/s.

Job Recovery. A long-running job that is terminated because of program error, equipment malfunction, or power failure can be restarted near the interrupt point rather than starting the job over. The programmer initiates various stages in the production run, called "checkpoint-restart." This causes the o/s to stop executing the program and store on disk that data necessary to restart the program from the point at which the checkpoint was taken. In event of interruption, production can resume, using the checkpoint information such as restoring data in memory or positioning I/O devices.

Operator Communication with the Computer. The o/s largely takes over much control of the computer from the operator; for example, o/s handles transition from one job to the next with little operator intervention. Even so, an operator should be able to control the system so as to make changes as necessary. For instance, he must be able to cancel jobs, change the priority of jobs, and achieve proper mix between I/o-bound and process-bound jobs such as excessive I/O or processing. The o/s types messages on the console typewriter to notify the operator of what action is to be taken next, such as mount a tape; or of the status of I/O units, such as that the disk drive on which he wants to mount a disk pack is being used.

OPERATING SYSTEM LEVELS

Operating systems perform a multitude of additional tasks; for instance, handling error interruptions, reserving space in internal and external memory, and so on. The benefits derived from O/S increase as the size of the hardware increases. Consequently, the varied levels of O/S differ in range of capability.

By way of example, IBM has tape O/S, which is stored on tape; disk O/S, stored on disk; and the most powerful OS/VS for systems with virtual storage. Because each higher level of O/S provides greater capability, each type of O/S requires considerable more storage space. For instance, disk O/S requires about 16K for a medium-scale computer, whereas the space for O/S varies from 30K to over 120K.

Earlier, we said that an operating system is a set of programs written by the computer manufacturer to improve the overall performance of the computer. These sets of programs are often referred to as "software," but all programs that the computer hardware uses in processing data are also called "software." So, let us make a distinction. Programs written at the computer installation are called "application programs;" thus the term "application programmers." Those programs designed to improve the efficiency of the computer are called "systems software," and so the term "systems programmers."

Systems programmers, sometimes called "software programmers," are generally the highest qualified and thus demand more salary. This is because operating systems are complicated and written at the assembly language level rather than at the easier higher-level languages such as COBOL. But even more important is the extensive knowledge that systems programmers must have of the computer system, the hardware interaction, and the needs of computer users.

THE HEART OF AN OPERATING SYSTEM

The collection of programs comprising a multiprogramming operating system is divided into two basic parts: the control programs and the processing programs (Fig. 14–1). The important thing to remember at this point is that the control programs operate the computer hardware efficiently and supervise the execution of the processing programs. Processing programs are directly used by the applications programmer in writing programs that process company data and solve company problems. Thus, control programs are designed to make the computer hardware and service programs work together as an integrated system.

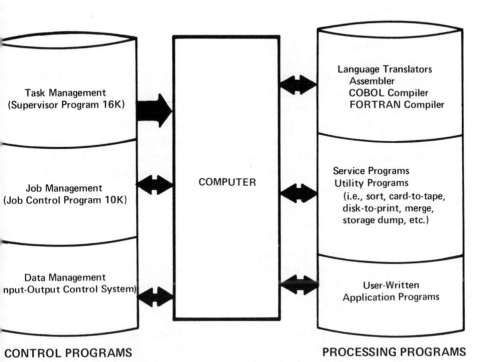

CONTROL PROGRAMS   PROCESSING PROGRAMS

Fig. 14–1. Relationship of control and processing programs. Most of the supervisor program remains in main memory and other modules of O/S remain on disk and are called into main storage as needed.

We shall concern ourselves with the heart of an operating system—the control program—which consists of three subdivisions: the task management programs, the job management programs, and the data management programs.

Task Management Programs. These programs allow the user to control the manner in which the system operates on its jobs. The programs, which mostly reside in main memory, serve as a mediary between the computer hardware and the remainder of the software programs. Task management, more commonly called the "supervisor" (and sometimes the monitor, executive, or master program), performs many tasks:

1. Brings in application programs from their residence on disk, called the "library."
2. Allocates space for them in main memory.
3. Arranges programs in main storage in their proper place.

4. Supervises multiprogramming.
5. Notifies the channel of pending I/O operations.

Job Management. Job control allows the programmer to communicate with the O/S through control cards, called JCL (job control language). Information needed by O/S in order to select a job for processing and preparing it for execution comes from the JCL cards; for example, which type of device one wants the output recorded on.

Data Management. These programs allow the programmer to move data between main storage and I/O devices with a minimum amount of programming effort, which without an input/output control system (IOCS) might require 40 percent more time. Data management provides programmer benefits such as:

1. Blocking and deblocking of records.
2. Input and output buffering.
3. Processing of identity label on files.
4. Protection of data files from unauthorized access.
5. Disk file organization and access methods, such as random or sequential.

Most of the terms mentioned above were covered previously, but some may not be remembered. Therefore, they will be explained again and in more depth in further discussion of multiprogramming O/S. Coming up is a pragmatic approach to see why the supervisor, JCL and IOCS, are important to computer efficiency, which translates into savings. Before taking up task management or the supervisor, we should spend some time expanding our knowledge of the important topic of multiprogramming and see how this is made possible through partitioned memory.

MULTIPROGRAMMING

Multiprogramming is defined as the concurrent execution of two or more programs that reside in memory (Fig. 14–2). However, only one program is actually being executed at any given instant because the control unit in the CPU is capable of executing only one instruction at a time. The idea is to keep the CPU busy by executing instructions in one program whenever another program is temporarily suspended while waiting for an input or output operation. Since multiprogramming can be easily misunderstood, we shall use an example to clarify its definition:

When program A cannot continue processing until a special event has

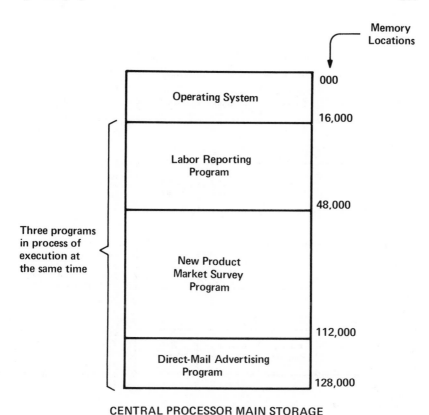

CENTRAL PROCESSOR MAIN STORAGE

Fig. 14–2. Multiprogramming permits two or more programs in memory to be executed concurrently.

occurred, such as an I/O interruption, the CPU stops executing instructions in that program and executes a few instructions from program B. This orderly transition from program to program is controlled by the operating system. After the I/O interruption caused by program A has been taken over by the channel and controller (see Fig. 8–12), the CPU resumes its work with program A and remembers the last instruction executed in program B (Fig. 14–3). In other words, the "interrupts" switch the computer from the program state to the operating system (supervisor program) state, and vice versa. Thus, the CPU alternates programs so that several programs are processed at the same time. In this manner, work is performed on a second program when the first program cannot continue because of a channel interrupt.

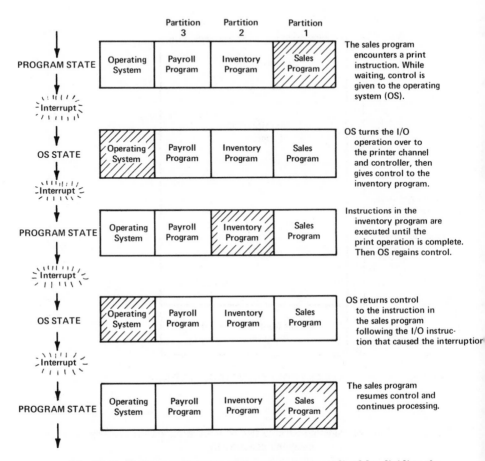

Fig. 14–3. Optimum efficiency of the computer is realized by dividing the processing time among two or more programs during "interrupts."

This process can be made clearer by reviewing in Chapter 10 the way in which a program is executed. As shown in Fig. 10–8, instructions in a program are executed sequentially, that is, one after another. Arithmetic instructions and instructions that move data from one memory location to another, or instructions that compare two sets of data, are all performed rapidly. For instance, two numbers can be added in decimal in 2.75 microseconds (μs) on the CDC 3500 computer as compared with 1.40 μs in binary. The IBM 370/155 takes 4.93 μs to add two numbers as compared with 0.99 μs in binary.

However, printing a line of data takes much longer. Moreover, the I/O operation may have to wait because the channel connected to the printer is being used to transfer data from another program. As a result, the next instruction in that program cannot be executed, so the central processor is idle because I/O time exceeds the processing time. In multiprogramming, the computer would not be I/O-bound while waiting for the controller and channel to complete the I/O operation. The computer would simply start executing instructions from another program stored in memory.

Why Memory Is Partitioned

Because more than one independent program is stored in memory at the same time, memory must be divided into areas to hold each program. These areas are called "partitions" or "regions" (IBM) or "slots" (Burroughs), both having essentially the same meaning. "Partitions" are fixed unless the operator changes their size, but "regions" and "slots" are flexible in size. In some IBM S/360 computers, there are only three fixed partitions (Fig. 14–4), depending upon the type of operating system. The IBM S/370 has 5 to 63 regions, again depending upon the type of operating system. The Burroughs operating system assigns jobs to slots according to the program size and the amount of memory space available, and therefore has no fixed partitions.

To prevent an instruction in one program from inadvertently altering or destroying a program or data in another partition, *storage protection* is provided (Fig. 14–4). Generally speaking, each partition has a lock so that a program must have the numerical key in order to operate in that partition. If a program attempts to enter another partition, that program is interrupted and terminated.

What makes it possible for the computer to distribute processing time among partitions when performing multiprogramming? In a three-partition computer (Fig. 14–5), each partition is assigned priority status. Partition 1 has the highest priority; partition 2 has second priority; and partition 3 has lowest priority. To say it another way, partition 1 takes precedence over a program in partition 2, which in turn takes precedence over a program operating in partition 3.

Figure 14–5 shows how programs in the three partitions interact. A program in partition 1 is being executed and an I/O instruction is encountered. This interruption causes the operating system to turn control over to the next highest program, which is stored in partition 2. In the event that program is also awaiting completion of an I/O operation, control is given to the partition 3 program. Therefore, whenever all three programs are I/O-bound, the computer becomes idle until one of the I/O operations is finished.

But how is control taken away from a lower-priority program when-

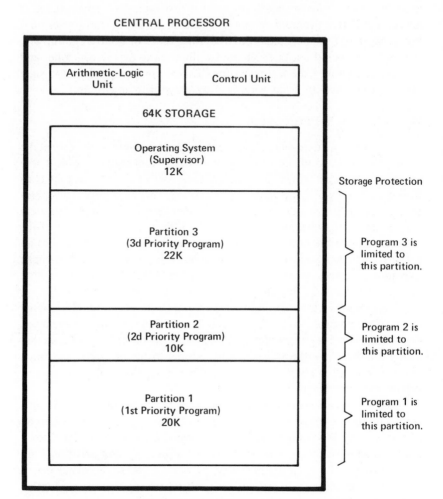

Fig. 14–4. In this illustration three partitions hold three separate programs.

ever the condition for which a high-priority program was waiting has been completed? In simplest terms, the channel, for example, signals the operating system that the I/O condition has been taken care of, and the operating system switches control back to the higher priority program.

In more complex terms we can say (referring to Fig. 14–5) that an instruction in partition 1 calls an input record from a tape unit. Control is given to the supervisor module of O/S, which notifies the channel and controller to carry out the tape READ operation, and O/S turns control over

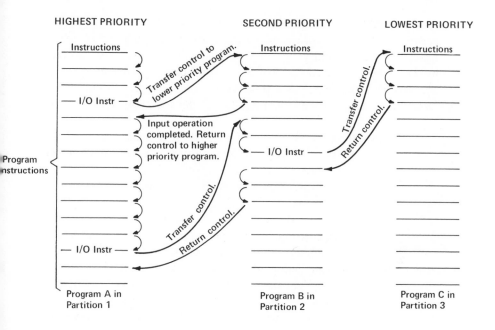

HIGHEST PRIORITY   SECOND PRIORITY   LOWEST PRIORITY

Fig. 14–5. How multiprogramming works.

to the next highest priority program. Instructions in that program are executed until the tape record has been transferred into CPU memory. Then the O/S takes control from the lower priority program and returns control to the higher priority program, for which processing is resumed at the instruction that follows the point of interruption.

To summarize multiprogramming and partitions: Programs compete with other programs for CPU processing time. Because partitions have assigned priorities, the user can schedule his jobs for completion by simply assigning rush jobs to the higher priority partitions and less important jobs to the lower priority partitions. Since operating systems play an important job in multiprogramming, let us describe some of the functions performed by individual programs within the operating system.

The Supervisor

Only part of the operating system is in main memory at any given time. The part of the operating system that remains in main memory is called the "supervisor."* Some part of the supervisor may be held in DASD until needed; that is, some program modules in the operating system may be resident in main memory, but others are called into core storage as needed by the supervisor. The supervisor is the workhorse of an operating system, and as such it acts much as a traffic officer directing cars through a busy intersection. Some of the responsibilities of the supervisor are:

- Controlling the alternating back-and-forth traffic between higher and lower priority programs in a multiprogramming environment, as described earlier.
- Notifying channels and controllers of pending input and output operations.
- Handling of interrupts that are caused by machine errors (i.e., parity errors), various kinds of programming errors, and unusual conditions such as erroneous data being processed (for example, employee name field contains unpermitted numbers).
- Job accounting logs the computer activity, such as the amount of CPU time, how long the job requires, the number of records read and printed, and computed charges. The log permits management to (1) maintain surveillance of efficiency with which his computer center is operating; (2) allocate computer time for each department; and (3) charge departments according to time used, or bill outsiders if the computer is rented.
- Scheduling "stacked jobs," which means terminating a completed program and automatically loading the next highest priority program from disk for immediate execution.

STACKED-JOB PROCESSING

The control programs—specifically the supervisor and job control— are the backbone of the operating system because these two supervaluable programs make stacked-job processing possible. The term "stacked-job processing" (Fig. 14–6) refers to the technique of recognizing the end of one job and starting the next job automatically with little or no operator intervention. Early computers stopped when a job terminated, and the operator had to set up the computer for the next scheduled job, engaging in such time-consuming tasks as changing the paper in the printer and mounting tapes on the tape drives. After this preparatory work, he loaded the program

---

*Various computer makers refer to the supervisor by other names, such as monitor, executive, or master programs.

through a card reader and pressed the start button. It is not surprising, then, that the computer sat idle during a large part of the day while excessive time was used for program setup.

In an operating system, the programs are automatically loaded from disk and executed one after another rather than going through the stop-and-

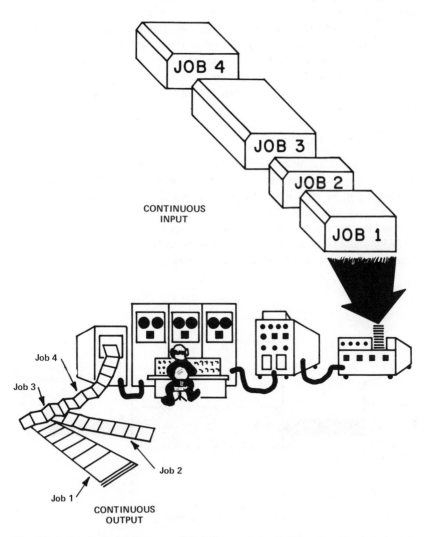

Fig. 14–6. In stacked-job processing, jobs are processed in a continuous stream, one after the other, without operator interference.

go procedure in which the computer stops at the end of each and every program. This was the case in all second-generation computers except in the medium- to large-scale systems. It was not until the third-generation era that continuous processing of independent jobs was available to all computers so that jobs could be done serially as they entered the system or read directly onto a disk and then brought into main memory according to their priority classification. We should give deserved credit to the operator for keeping the system busy. He sets the jobs up and starts the computer, rearranges scheduled programs to do rush jobs first, prepares input devices in anticipation of the next job, and other important duties.

In order to understand the concept of stacked-job processing, we must introduce a new subject, called "job control language" (JCL), then show how the operating system uses JCL to process consecutive jobs without interruption.

Job Control Language

Job control language was designed to relieve the operator as a middleman between the individual programs and the computer. In this role, JCL is acted upon by one of the programs in the operating system, called the "job control program" (Fig. 14–7). JCL consists of a set of job control statements that are normally punched on cards (but which may be on tape or disk), loaded into main storage, and then read by the job control program from the input device where they are stored.

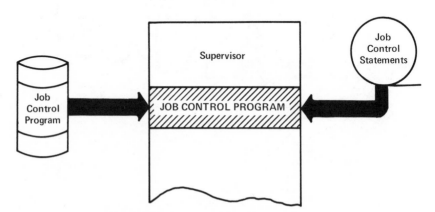

Fig. 14–7. The job control program calls into memory the JCL statements and initiates a new job based upon information in JCL.

These JCL statements mark the beginning of a job and identify by name a specific program that could be executed in processing data that follows the job control statements (Fig. 14–8). The JOB card contains the name of the job, and the EXEC card specifies the program name. Each job, having its own JCL statements, is defined as an independent unit of work. It may be:

- An application program such as a payroll program.
- A utility program that, for example, sorts the payroll input data into employee number sequence.
- A language translator program such as a compiler that, for instance, translates the programmer's COBOL source program into a COBOL object program (machine language).

A continuous stream of jobs can be processed without interruption by simply stacking individual decks of JCL statements, along with the data to be processed, into the card reader, as shown in Fig. 14–8. As soon as one job step is completed, the control programs in the operating system read the next stream of JCL statements, which initiate the next job; thus the term "stacked-job processing." Just how this is done will be explained next.

How JCL and OS Work Together

In order that we can have a better understanding of stacked-job processing, let us investigate what the operator does at the beginning of a new day. An answer to the question, "Where does the operator start?" lies in one of the control programs within the operating system.

The operator calls in the initial program loader (hereafter called "IPL") from disk by manually pushing certain buttons at the computer console shown in Fig. 6–3. Once loaded, IPL locates the supervisor on disk and loads it into main storage of the central processor. Control now passes to the supervisor, and a part of the supervisor, called the "system loader" (Fig. 14–9), loads the job control program.

The job control program in turn loads the JCL statements that identify the program to be run and provides other information needed to make the computer ready for the job. In other words, the JCL statements tell the computer what the programmer wants done. For example, one JCL statement provides the name of the program to be fetched from disk and another statement provides information as to which I/O devices contain the data that is to be processed.

When the JCL cards have been acted upon, control passes back to the supervisor. The supervisor instructs the system loader once again to locate

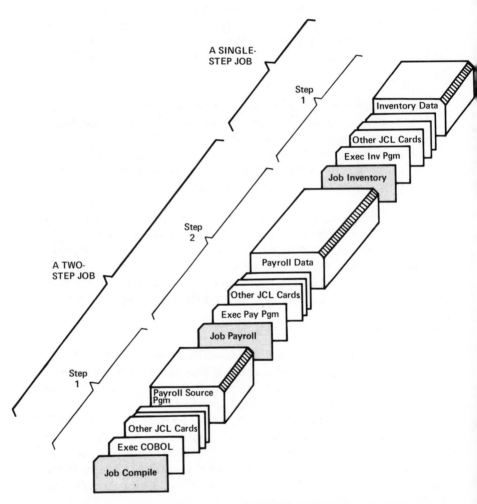

Fig. 14–8. A job stream consists of a continuous input of jobs, each having its own control cards to define the job, and is followed by the data to be processed.

and load the application program from the disk that was identified by the JCL statements. Once the application program is loaded, the supervisor transfers control to it and program instructions commence executing in a sequential manner in the processing of data. The application program remains in control until all data has been processed, with the exception of interrupts. Whenever interrupts occur (for example, in the case of I/O operations), the supervisor regains control temporarily in order to turn the

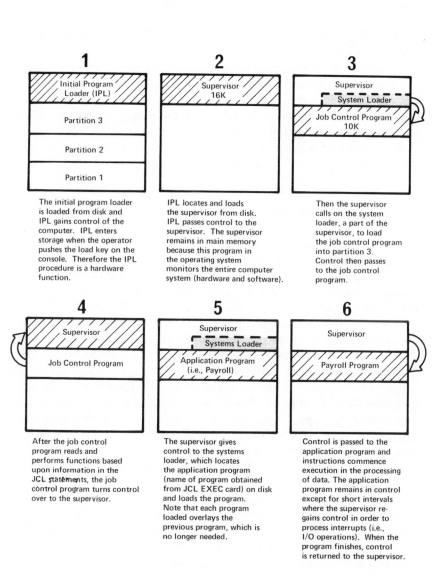

1

| Initial Program Loader (IPL) |
| Partition 3 |
| Partition 2 |
| Partition 1 |

The initial program loader is loaded from disk and IPL gains control of the computer. IPL enters storage when the operator pushes the load key on the console. Therefore the IPL procedure is a hardware function.

2

| Supervisor 16K |

IPL locates and loads the supervisor from disk. IPL passes control to the supervisor. The supervisor remains in main memory because this program in the operating system monitors the entire computer system (hardware and software).

3

| Supervisor |
| System Loader |
| Job Control Program 10K |

Then the supervisor calls on the system loader, a part of the supervisor, to load the job control program into partition 3. Control then passes to the job control program.

4

| Supervisor |
| Job Control Program |

After the job control program reads and performs functions based upon information in the JCL statements, the job control program turns control over to the supervisor.

5

| Supervisor |
| Systems Loader |
| Application Program (i.e., Payroll) |

The supervisor gives control to the systems loader, which locates the application program (name of program obtained from JCL EXEC card) on disk and loads the program. Note that each program loaded overlays the previous program, which is no longer needed.

6

| Supervisor |
| Payroll Program |

Control is passed to the application program and instructions commence execution in the processing of data. The application program remains in control except for short intervals where the supervisor regains control in order to process interrupts (i.e., I/O operations). When the program finishes, control is returned to the supervisor.

Fig. 14–9. Software interaction.

273

I/O operation over to the channel and controller for execution so that the CPU can do other useful work.

Once the application program is complete, the supervisor regains control and repeats the process that we have described, which involves reading the next set of JCL statements for a new job. While the previous job was running, the operator was busy setting up the next job, which probably included the mounting of data tapes on unused tape drives, and other tasks. In the next section we cover another responsibility of the operating system, that of IOCS, a program in data management.

INPUT/OUTPUT CONTROL SYSTEM

A significant improvement in the performance of the computer system was realized by overlapping processing with input and output operations. By this technique, much of the CPU idle time that would be wasted while waiting for the transfer of data between main storage and the I/O units was put to effective use.

Another improvement involves the method by which I/O operations are programmed. Whereas overlapping was accomplished through hardware design, this new programming improvement is related to software. Since input and output routines are similar in all programs, designers proposed that programming time and effort could be saved if all application programs were linked to a common I/O routine. To satisfy this important requirement, an input-output control system (IOCS) was designed. This system comprises a group of routines that schedules and oversees the operation of channels, performs label checking on tapes and disk files, and resolves I/O error conditions such as unreadable records.

In addition, IOCS manages the internal storage buffers set up by the programmer. These storage buffers hold physical blocks of data consisting of two or more logic records that are awaiting processing. In this role, IOCS functions as an interface between the programmer's program and the actual I/O devices, such as the printer. In the use of IOCS, the programmer needs only to define the files used in his program by specifying the names of data fields, their size, and a few other characteristics.

Whenever the programmer writes an input instruction and that instruction is executed, IOCS furnishes him a single record from the buffer storage (Fig. 14–10). Since the buffer holds two or more logic records, the area in memory that is reserved by the program for the buffer must be large enough to hold one physical record.

In general, IOCS reads a physical record and places the individual logical records into the buffer. Each READ instruction in the program that

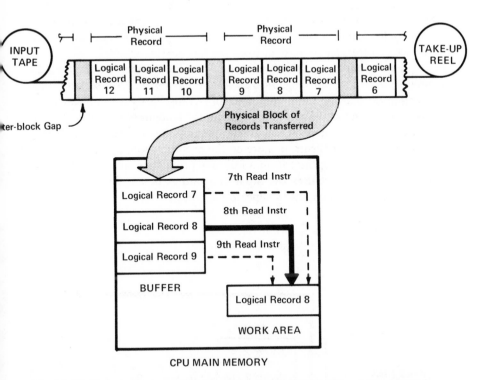

Fig. 14–10. Two or more records are read into the input buffer at the relatively slow speed of the input device. When called by the program, the next logical record in turn for processing is moved into the input work area at electronic speeds for processing.

is executed causes IOCS to move the next record that is to be processed from the buffer into the working storage area (Fig. 14–10); this record overlays the preceding one. After the buffer has been emptied, IOCS refills the buffer with new input data by reading the next physical record from the tape unit and makes each record available to the program as needed. Whenever the buffer has been emptied, all records have been moved, one by one, as needed to the input work area and processed. This one-at-a-time transfer of records from the buffer is called "deblocking."

During the time that IOCS spends in reading another physical record from input hardware to refill the buffer, the computer would enter an idle state because the program cannot process the next record until it has been made available. This problem is solved by ingeniously reserving *two* input storage buffers; the additional programming involves very little effort. As records are deblocked and made available, one at a time, to the program from one buffer, the other buffer is being refilled by IOCS (Fig. 14–11). Thus, by the time the last logic record has been processed, the next record in the other buffer is immediately available and the computer does not have to wait for IOCS to transfer more data from the I/O device.

The output processing works in a similar manner except that the procedure is reversed (Fig. 14–12). As we have seen, IOCS serves a dual function of relieving the programmer of writing his own complicated I/O instructions and at the same time reduces the amount of CPU idle time. As a result, more than one-third of the programmer's time is saved, thus allowing him to concentrate more on the problem itself, and a cost saving results from keeping the CPU in a full-time productive state. Figure 14–12 illustrates how IOCS uses the input and output buffers in order to take advantage of the computer's superspeed.

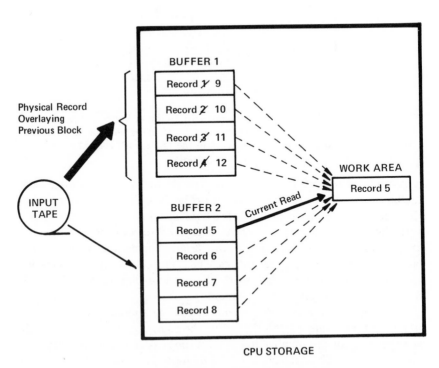

Fig. 14–11. A double input buffer speeds throughput.

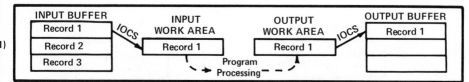

The program executes a read instruction and IOCS gets Record 1 from the buffer. The program processes Record 1 and builds the results of processing in the output area. The program executes a write instruction and IOCS puts the record into the buffer.

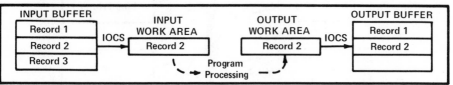

Next, the program repeats itself and reads the next record. IOCS makes the record available to the program for processing. A write instruction is executed and IOCS blocks the new record into its rightful place in the output buffer.

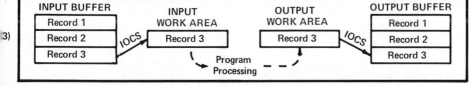

The program loops once again and processes another record. Now that the output buffer is filled, IOCS empties the contents onto the output tape or disk in the form of a physical record. What now? IOCS has been filling the alternate input buffer and the next processing is performed on records read from the alternate buffer. (not shown)

Fig. 14–12. The concept of I/O buffering. IOCS aids the programmer and reduces the amount of CPU idle time.

TIMESHARING

Timesharing began in the mid-1960s and is used extensively with medium- and large-scale computers. The concept of timesharing is based on proportioning a centralized computer's time among several users via on-line communications data terminals. As you will recall, any combination of data terminals can be connected to the computer to perform input, inquiry, or output operations (Fig. 14–13). Although any form of multiprogramming can be thought of as timesharing, the art of timesharing more appropriately refers to hundreds of independent users who share the computer at the same time via numerous remote input and output data terminals.

Each user enters his programs and data over communications lines by means of one of several types of input terminals and receives the results via output terminals such as the cathode-ray tube, Teletype, or high-speed line

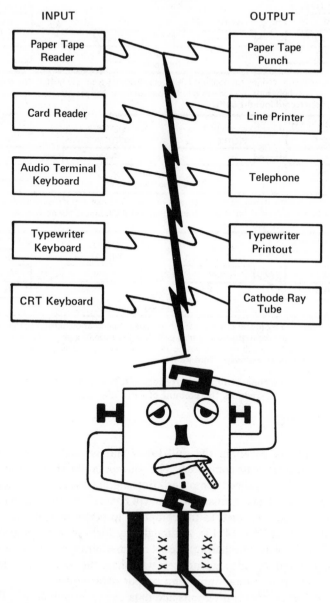

Fig. 14–13. Independent users share time via numerous types of remote input and output data terminals.

printers. Even though individual users compete for processing time, the response time is so fast that the computer appears to be working independently for each user. Timesharing systems can be divided into two general categories:

1. Those serving the users in business, such as bank tellers who use the data terminal to record a savings deposit, or programmers who use the terminal to modify their programs stored on disk.

2. Those selling available time to different firms for a profit because their computers are partly or fully idle. The rental of computer time is a fast-growing business. Revenue from timesharing has grown from $210 million in 1969 to $1 billion in 1973, up from $700 million the previous year.

Computer Time and Processing Services

Banks often sell their idle computer time, and service bureaus are devoted to processing a company's business requirements for a fee. A different breed of service, called "facilities management," involves a company that will assume all data processing problems of another company, including programming and running of the computer at the firm's location. Sometimes the last two methods work, but sometimes they don't. Comments range from "For the first time, I get what I want" to "A manager who turns over his processing to an outside company is crazy."

Perhaps you are wondering who buys computer time. To cite one case, a computer center may have peak work loads where all data cannot be processed by the time needed and acquiring another computer is not justified. The solution lies in buying time from another computer user who has it available, either in a timesharing, real-time mode or by the less expensive batch-processing mode. Another case is the small company that cannot afford to support its own data processing operation; therefore, it contracts with service bureaus that specialize in programming and processing work on the service bureau's computer. Still other companies wish that the computer and the computer people were out of their lives forever. They turn the entire computer operation over to a "facilities management" company to run. Obviously, there are various sources of computer assistance to aid management in running a business.

SUMMARY

Operating systems were created in order that the computer could be used to its fullest extent. Because operating systems offer such potential efficiency, they are constantly being revised to include new improvements. The workhorse of the operating system is the supervisor program, since it controls the interaction between the application programs and the hardware.

Operating systems make possible multiprogramming, which in turn allows different users to share computer time. In timesharing and multiprogramming, two or more programs operate in independent partitions and the computer concurrently executes all programs under the direction of the supervisor program.

Stacked-job processing operates according to instructions punched into JCL cards and are acted upon by the job control segment of the operating system. This important concept reduces the setup time between jobs by permitting the processing of a continuous stream of jobs without manual interruption.

The CPU executes long sequences of instructions at impressive speeds, but unless the input/output devices can read the data and record the results fast enough, the CPU remains idle much of the time. Another of the operating system programs is IOCS, which plays an important part in keeping the computer productive through blocking and deblocking records for the programmer. The IOCS transfers multiple records into main storage in a single READ cycle so that the program has access to each of those records at internal electronic speeds instead of the slower I/O equipment speeds.

From Chapters 1 through 14 you have acquired a working knowledge of the principles of computer science. Career-minded data processing students will find this to be a solid background that will permit them to proceed into other data processing subjects at a more rapid pace, and *business students* will be prepared to enter their chosen field with a computer knowledge that blends into modern business operations.

In the first few chapters, we explored the evolution of computers and their uses, we saw how modern computing is applied to data in order to give management the necessary working tools, and we discussed different approaches to computer processing. Next, we covered the architecture of different types of computers and related this to how the computer works with programs in solving problems. Finally, we studied how memory devices store huge volumes of business information, discussed the importance of multiprogramming, and explored new technology such as virtual memory. As we progressed in our studies, all this knowledge was related to practical applications, and we became acquainted with management implications of the computer through various management discussions presented in Chapter 15.

As managers, or future managers, we are now better prepared to challenge new ways of doing things. Those students who wish to advance to computer management will find in Chapter 16 the more important guidelines to managerial qualification. These, together with newly acquired knowledge, provide firm ground on which to build a career.

KEY TERMS TO REMEMBER

Blocked records	Operating system (os)
Buffer storage	Partition or slot
Channel	Program overlay
Control programs	Setup time
Disk operating system (DOS)	Stacked-job processing
Input/output control system (IOCS)	Storage protection
	Supervisor
Interrupts	Systems programmer
Job control language (JCL)	Systems software
Multiprogramming	Timesharing

QUESTIONS

1. Briefly describe the purpose of an operating system.
2. What is the most important program in the operating system?
3. Describe how multiprogramming increases the efficiency of the computer.
4. What is the relationship between the terms "idle time" and "I/O-bound"?
5. Why is storage protection necessary to multiprogramming?
6. What do we mean when referring to a higher priority program?
7. Differentiate between the two categories of software programs.
8. The operating system is divided into two categories of programs. To which category would a disk-to-print utility program belong?
9. Why is the supervisor sometimes in control of the computer and the problem program in control at other times?
10. The systems loader loads which two types of programs?
11. What purpose does stacked-job processing serve and what technique makes it possible?
12. Explain how IOCS blocks and deblocks records for the programmer.
13. How does timesharing differ from multiprogramming?

COORDINATED READINGS IN CHAPTER 15

"Management Sets the Pace," Sec. 4.
"The Dilemma of Promoting Good Technicians," Sec. 22.
"When Does a Firm Need a Faster Computer?", Sec. 16

Chapter **15**

MANAGEMENT
AND THE COMPUTER

The management discussions gathered in this chapter are the outgrowth of notes and rough drafts accumulated over a number of years in different jobs. They represent experience in computer work and observations made of people with whom I have had contact and with whom I have associated while gaining this experience. Consequently, the discussions present a typical picture of what may be expected in the world of business data processing.

Later, these notes and drafts, showing both positive and negative aspects of computer processing, were formalized in lecture outlines for presentation to management classes that I conducted. So that the sections cross-referenced in Chapters 1 through 14 may be readily identified and easily located by their respective titles, the content of this chapter is listed below.

THE COMPUTER—CHALLENGE TO MANAGEMENT
    1. A Negative Approach toward Computers by Management
    2. Why Management Involvement?
    3. The Computer's Effect on Management
    4. Management Sets the Pace
IMPACT OF THE COMPUTER
    5. EDP—Centralized or Decentralized?
    6. The Computer—Aid or Hindrance?

   7. Computer Maintenance Problems
   8. Why Program Documentation?
MANAGEMENT OF THE COMPUTER
   9. Depth of Management Involvement
  10. Computer Exception Management
  11. Controlling Computer Reruns
  12. Testing the Program—Will It Quit on New Year's Eve?
MANAGEMENT WANTS TO KNOW
  13. Why the Rising Computer Budget?
  14. Why Should Management Know Systems and Programming Fundamentals?
  15. Why Should Management Learn COBOL and Assembly? Language Concepts?
  16. When Does a Firm Need a Faster Computer?
  17. Which Computer Speed Will Do?
  18. The Changed Personnel Recruitment Scene
INVOLVEMENT
  19. The Data Processing Manager in Organizational Structure
  20. Dissent in an Organization
  21. The Insecure Manager
  22. The Dilemma of Promoting Good Technicians
MANAGEMENT OF DATA BASES
  23. Data Base—What Is It?
  24. Data Base—Concern of Management
  25. The Importance of Creating Test Data
SECURITY OF THE INSTALLATION
  26. How Serious Is the Threat to Computer Disasters?
  27. Protection of the Computer Installation
  28. Security of Programs and Data Files
  29. Protecting the Programs
  30. Protecting the Data Files
  31. Protecting the Computer Operation
TECHNOLOGY AND FUTURE DEVELOPMENTS
  32. Future Trends in Computer Architecture
  33. What Management Should Know about Virtual Storage
  34. Impact of Minicomputers
SOCIETY AND THE COMPUTER
  35. Finding Happiness in Data Banks
  36. A Computerized, Checkless Society
  37. Automation, Computers, and Progress

THE COMPUTER – CHALLENGE TO MANAGEMENT

1. A NEGATIVE APPROACH TOWARD COMPUTERS BY MANAGERS

"That lousy hunk of bolts causes more trouble than it is worth." Sounds like a quick burst of temper when the family buggy breaks down again, doesn't it? But this and similar statements commonly occur around anyone associated with the processed results from the computer. People who make these statements are not only bankers, salesmen, and other businessmen, but also *managers* of data processing centers.

Surprisingly enough, the anger is directed at the computer and only indirectly at the technicians involved. Yet, computers are highly reliable, make few errors as a result of malfunctions, and in fact do only what they are instructed. Given this, something besides the computer must be responsible for the bad results. *Humans* are that something—but do not prematurely point the finger at the computer people without getting the facts. Certainly, programmers and other data processing professionals make their share of blunders. But the truth of the matter is that management is to blame whenever the money and time spent on data processing is greater than the benefits derived. Remember that managers have the *power* to change things that go wrong.

What does this "computer thing" mean to management? First of all, the manager's concept of a computer might very well be that it is a showcase full of meaningless blinking lights, twirling tapes, spinning disks, and lots of other confusing things. Such a concept hardly contributes meaningful knowledge to the many managers whose work is built around the "computer thing." That "damn thing" makes possible many management tools that were impossible or impractical before the computer came along. In other words, the computer is supposed to aid professional managers in a modern business environment, not hinder them. So, to managers who have avoided and left computer operation to others: "Why not learn about the fantasy world behind those blinking lights?"

Someone must shoulder the responsibility of initiating new applications or of improving existing ones. This is often left to the business users or the programmers. This escapist attitude may be comfortable, but management cannot perform its functions efficiently unless it furnishes a guiding hand or at least an approving hand that knows what and what not to approve.

Where does a busy manager start? Could it be that he does not *want* to find the time? Obviously, his business will continue to run when he is out of town or on vacation, so lack of time is a bit of nonsense to be discarded. He begins by firmly suppressing the notion of "no time" and replacing it with a curiosity about how the computer works. His next step is to roll up his sleeves and plunge into a course that helps him understand the computer, and then observe around the installation to find out how it works. Once he has tackled the fundamentals, such as writing a few small programs and doing a simple systems study, learning will be a challenge thereafter, and perhaps even fun. Having the feeling that he is back in control (as he felt in the "good-ole" days??), he can communicate with the computer people and leave the minor decisions—not the important decisions—to the experts.

From this simple goal, he can set his own pace as to how much he should know in order to control the computer operation, rather than having it control him. His ultimate goal will likely settle somewhere between the executive who shuns the problem altogether and the vice-president who has become so proficient at programming that the auditors caught him embezzling by means of the computer. Once past the introductory stage, the manager can benefit from the flood of semitechnical management articles in numerous trade journals that deal with data processing pitfalls and experiences of other computer users.

Learning to solve computer problems at the management level will pay enormous dividends in the areas of profit, efficiency, and management know-how. After all, *the computer is here to stay and problems are definitely not solved to the best interest of the company without management help!*

2. WHY MANAGEMENT INVOLVEMENT?

Managing is the process through which organizational objectives are fulfilled. Objectives are achieved through other people, using their skills, techniques, and company equipment. The management function is typically carried out in this order:

1. *Planning.* Deciding what goals should be set to reap profits. The goals are decided by identifying a problem or opportunity, analyzing gathered facts, and selecting the best direction from several alternatives.

2. *Organizing.* Putting plans into action by selecting people to carry out the plans and grouping them into working teams.
3. *Controlling.* Checking accomplishments and progress to see if the plan is going according to schedule, and taking corrective action where indicated.

Why should management be involved in computer operations? For a lot of reasons. *Foremost,* increased profits. More work can be performed with less error and for less money.

Second, computer planning enables management to make better decisions. But managers frequently do not know all the information they need until they discover it missing when a decision has to be made. Too, a manager should know the cost of producing information. If he asks for an overtime report and it costs more than the overtime itself, then the requirement is meaningless.

Third, a manager should be aware that no one is paid to second-guess what he really needs. The hierarchy of rank dictates that he must get what he asks for. Say that a requirement for overtime spent in each department is fulfilled. But does the manager want the overtime trend in order to curtail secondary projects? Or does he want to forecast work load? Perhaps he *really* needs ratios comparing each month this year with the corresponding month last year.

Fourth, computers require a sizable investment. The most profitable firms in a recent survey allocated 1.25 percent of revenues toward the data processing operation. The firms with least profit spent only 0.75 percent of their income. That profits are linked to the portion of computer expenditures strongly drives home the importance of management involvement in the data processing environment.

Fifth, firms using their computers most successfully are those in which top management participates actively. In these cases, not surprisingly, the superior computer operations were run by professionals knowledgeable about profit goals of other departments. *Axiom:* Successful businesses have managers at all levels who are interested in general and computer operations.

Sixth, management should approve new systems with awareness of the risks involved. For example, a new job once on the air may fail to achieve the anticipated gains. Two main reasons for this failure are:

1. *Understating Costs.* The implementation estimates were too optimistic. More programming time is needed than expected, causing the deadline to slip; maintaining the programs is more costly, creating the input data files is more costly, computer run time is longer, and on and on.

2. *Overstating Savings.* Eliminating part of a clerk's effort is not a true saving. His job still requires 6 hours instead of 8. We know that the clerk's job will spread out over 8 hours. Likewise, elimination of duplicated effort is usually not a savings. What is a true saving? The situation results in one or more employees' salary being reduced from the payroll.

In the final analysis, management will be responsible for the success or failure of the data processing contribution toward a profitable company. All levels of management should balance their know-how with know-why. The balancing maneuver must begin with general management's becoming more technically minded and with EDP management's becoming more business minded.

3. THE COMPUTER'S EFFECT ON MANAGEMENT

The predictions in early 1960s that computers would replace middle managers are talked about very little these days. Instead, computers and middle managers work together in ever-increasing numbers. The talk now is directed toward making the middle manager more effective, since a vast amount of routine work is done by the computer. The computer has resulted in an increased volume of information, people must be hired to utilize this data, and these people require managing.

Middle managers are those between operating or line managers and the

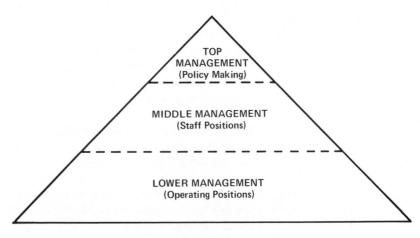

Fig. 15–1. Management pyramid.

policy makers, who are top management (Fig. 15–1). Operating, or line, managers are warehouse foremen, district sales managers, bank branch managers, and shift foremen in plants. This lowest level of management directly supervises the work of operating employees. Operating managers carry out the action plans devised by middle management.

Policy making is done by top management executives with titles such as vice-president. They determine the broad objectives that the company as a whole must follow. They make overall decisions, such as when to expand or whether to introduce a new product.

What is the middle manager? He is responsible for developing detailed operational plans to implement the broader ones handed down by top management. He directs lower or operating management in putting these plans into effect. So, a middle manager is above the rank of operating managers who direct production and below the rank of vice-president (Fig. 15–2). He is a staff manager.

Computers have rapidly and radically changed the manner in which middle managers operate. Precomputer-era managers performed their jobs to a great extent by intuition and imagination, based largely upon experience. Manually compiled facts and estimates guided their decisions, but could not be relied upon wholly because they were last weeks' or last months' facts.

Now, up-to-date and reliable data processed by computers forms the basis of decisions within the corporation structure. Too, additional facts not otherwise possible by manual means are computer-generated. For example, simulation is being used widely for problem solving. Simulation is a trial-and-error approach to determine what happens to business conditions when certain elements are provided. Ideal reorder levels based upon shipping times are determined by simulated inventory amounts and simulated consumptions.

Before the computer, middle management shuffled papers a lot more than now, taking some burden off top management so that it could directly manage company affairs. Of course this was not the way it was supposed to work. Much detailed administrative work and work planning, formerly the middle manager's duties, have been taken over by the computer. This opened up opportunities for the middle manager.

First, more top management authority has passed down to the middle manager. This allows top management more time for policy making and seeing that goals are met. Middle managers are involved with more decision making and actual management contribution toward organizational goals, the jobs they were hired for in the first place.

Second, the increased volume of computer output has to be evaluated by experienced people; thus, middle managers are needed to direct these

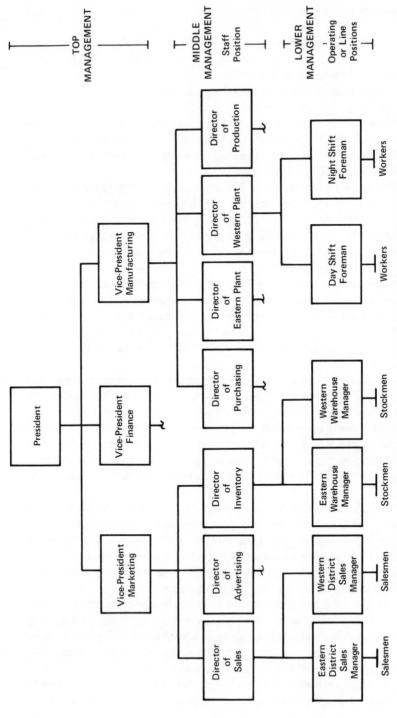

Fig. 15–2. Organizational chart showing top-management, middle-management, and lower-management levels.

Table 15–1. The computer allows a sales manager more time to manage.

Job	Before the Computer	After the Computer
1. Manage a sales force.	Too little time was spent here, the job he was hired for.	Free to spend more time actually leading the sales force. Computer keeps him informed through exception reporting (see Sec. 10) whenever the paper or warehouse operations are not functioning according to established objectives.
2. Office function	Overseeing salesmen's payroll, billing and collection, credit limitations, etc.	Computer routinely handles all paperwork in the head office, such as payroll, customer ordering, shipping, invoicing, billing, etc.
3. Overseeing warehouse function	Movement of merchandise from many warehouses to the customer on time, stock replenishments problems, etc.	Computer keeps track of a centralized inventory in the head office, yet all district sales offices and their warehouses have access to balances as well as the ability to update the file as stock is received and sold. The number of warehouses has been reduced through consolidating inventories.

people. This is the main reason the computer has not replaced middle managers, as predicted a decade ago. Those early prophets could not even imagine that today the computer would be taxed to its limits. Their prediction was based upon bookkeeping chores and the like being taken over by computers. As a result, accountants and their supervisors would be displaced. New jobs that the computer now performs were not considered. This is where their forecast failed.

The brief and over-simplified representation in Table 15–1 demonstrates how a sales manager spends his time before and after the computer. Middle managers now have more time for coordination, the sometimes missing element that makes effective managing. Coordination is more demanding because the computer crosses departmental lines; that is, data from one department is combined with data from another department, and the resulting decision affects more than one department.

More facts can be taken into account in planning ahead; thus, more accurate forecasts are possible. Before computerization, it was too costly and time consuming to analyze data collected from two or more departments. Now, a report to analyze the effectiveness of a company's training program can be generated by including data from the personnel department, payroll department, and the production department.

The computer has not displaced many middle managers. In fact, EDP has increased the number of those positions proportionately to the growth of the company through new positions needed to handle the additional information generated. The few managers who were displaced failed to adjust to the computer era or were unwilling to abandon old ways. Naturally, some of these conventional managers still hold powerful positions.

The computer has reshaped the middle manager's image, and business moves at a faster pace now. A new generation of managers fill staff positions, and they are more highly specialized in new management techniques than were their predecessors, mainly because they are familiar with computerized methods.

Managers are either directly or indirectly pressured to become adept in systems analysis and actual computer techniques. Although they are not expected to write production programs, they need to have some experience with programming. This may mean a night course in programming, with actual computer testing of his own program. Just as any programmer will do, he will make errors, search for the answers, be frustrated with his own silly mistakes, and enjoy satisfaction when his program finally runs. This is necessary in order to understand:

- How the computer produces results.
- What can and cannot be done.

- That overcommittal of the EDP staff based upon unattainable objectives is a death blow.
- The effects new program changes will have on the present system.
- What is involved in effectively using computers.
- Appreciation of time and cost involved in developing new systems.

It cannot be expressed too strongly that management must become knowledgeable in the art of data processing if it is to keep in control. It cannot simply set objectives and step aside while technicians decide what the system should do and how it will do it. If studies and design of new requirements are left to subordinates without monitoring, then management can expect the number of reports to grow, yet fail to yield information necessary to make managing easier.

This challenge falls primarily on the middle manager. To sum up the future of the middle manager: The more an organization relies upon computers, the more it must rely upon middle management.

4. MANAGEMENT SETS THE PACE

One of top management's most important contributions to the data processing operation lies in appointing a technically competent computer-center manager who is also a good businessman. Not one but both levels of management are responsible to see that the existence of the computer is justified by its enhancement of company product values, not by unnecessary and irrelevant work that is nonproductive. Although other management discussions in this chapter stress the responsibility of management in areas outside data processing, we point out here how management information should flow all ways—up, down, and across the organizational lines of authority.

The philosophy behind an interlocking organization is that the left hand must know what the right hand is doing, and vice versa. The data processing manager, for example, might be attempting to gear the management information system (including thoughts about upgrading to more expensive equipment) to meet greater company growth, while the president foresees a downhill rate because of market competition. In other words, a $2 million-a-year company can easily become a $1 million-a-year company by the time the revised management information system is on the air. Conflicting actions such as this may happen because EDP management and executive management fail to intercommunicate.

Top management can establish goals by defining problem areas for data processing management so that both can sit down and discuss how the problem might be solved. The company needs additional financing, for instance. One alternative would be to borrow money, but this could very well be avoided if some way were found to use idle funds or those tied up unnecessarily. Cash flow is one area in which to look for inefficient use of money: If a company receives $50,000 a day in checks, but spends several days in moving the revenue through a slow accounting system, then idle cash amounts to $50,000 plus interest for each day of the elapsed time between receipt of payment and deposit into the bank. Consequently, top management might establish a goal that would improve the financial position of the company by speeding accounts receivables via data entry terminals at no greater cost than the present manual method. Another source of funds might be excessive inventory, as mentioned in a previous chapter.

Just how does each level of management satisfy the expectations of the other? Starting with the data processing manager, he must know and understand the user's problems and the desires of management. He can acquire this knowledge by learning about business operations outside the computer activity. In so doing, it is evident that vital communication will result and data processing feedback will take place. Today, management is kept informed of ongoing data processing work, and in turn the data processing manager is made aware of related business happenings. As a result of this communication, the user becomes more knowledgeable and less confused about data processing, and the data processing manager learns about the nature of the business end.

Insofar as proposals are concerned, the data processing manager must not believe that all work need be channeled through the computer. He should not avoid new projects by passing them off as being unworthy of computer processing because of low volume or some other stall tactic. Neither should he commit the computer to every use that is suggested. On the other hand, top management has responsibility to determine which jobs should be computerized, but this can take place only when top management understands the nature of the computer.

Once a project is under discussion, it should not be oversold. The time to be honest is when estimating the man-hours and cost. If a project must be sold by being based on low estimates, then the thing is marginal to begin with. Again, management should be aware of the techniques used in figuring computer cost in order to detect an oversell when weighing cost versus benefits.

The statement that "management sets the pace" works both up and down the organizational chart. There is more to data processing management than being technically competent at bringing new systems into being. The manager's specialty must not be so narrow and limited that he believes business affairs belong in other departments. In a highly hypothetical case, it would be discouraging to finish that six-month-old system for improving decentralized shipping only to find that the company was considering centralizing shipments. Top management should not forget that the product of pencil and instincts might prove just as effective as the product of an expensive information system. It takes some doing in order to know, instead of feel, that the computer is paying off, but this area is overlooked in numerous installations. In addition, top management must not become so involved with company matters that the data processing facility is left entirely to technicians.

IMPACT
OF THE COMPUTER

5. EDP—CENTRALIZED OR DECENTRALIZED?

The early-computer days were characterized by decentralization. That is, the data processing activity was located in the division where the work originated. Third-generation computers had larger memories and were fast enough to handle normal processing as well as many remote terminals. The input/output terminals served distant users for data entry, inquiry to data stored inside the computer, and response in the form of visual or printed output. This made possible the trend toward centralized EDP at the head office. Centralized EDP brought hopes of:

1. Better managerial control from the top level, in order to benefit the company as a whole.
2. Economies in lower processing cost, from the belief that one large computer is cheaper to operate than two or more smaller computers.
3. Integrating scattered information processing, to give a total management information system.
4. Better communications, to make it economically feasible to exchange data between the home-office computer and remote input-/output devices by electrical impulses rather than by mail or courier.

A small beginning business is centralized. All decision making is in the hands of one or more partners. As the business grows, so does the span of control. Management cannot keep a handle on the increasing functions and bulk of data. So, the firm decentralizes. The decision-making powers, previously in the hands of a few, are delegated to lower levels. However, this brings about the difficulty of feedback to top management, often too late to mesh with other plans. A familar example of decentralization is the Ford Motor Company, which is divided into the Lincoln-Mercury and Ford-Thunderbird divisions. An insurance company, on the other hand, is a typical example of centralization.

It becomes apparent that the type of business and the size of an organization largely determines if authority is centralized or decentralized.

The computer is capable of handling one concept as well as the other. The success of either, therefore, depends more upon what is proper for the company.

For example, some firms are too big for central control. Some applications, such as a centralized inventory control, make for better decision making than can be done by regional managers. The right level of stock is easier to maintain, with less money tied up in inventory. Managerial decisions, consequently, prompt organizations to centralize. The computer has made it possible to centralize authority on a large scale, but the technical considerations of programming are also greater because of complexity.

In a decentralized organization (Fig. 15–3), computers are located at the level were the work is. Top management naturally relinquishes some decision making and control. In a centralized organization (Fig. 15–4), the computer is located at corporate headquarters, thus retaining more control at the top level.

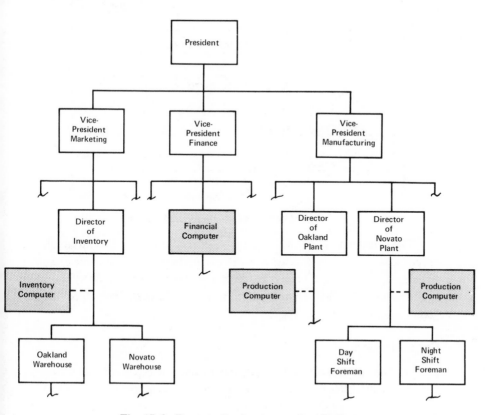

Fig. 15–3. Decentralized computer installation.

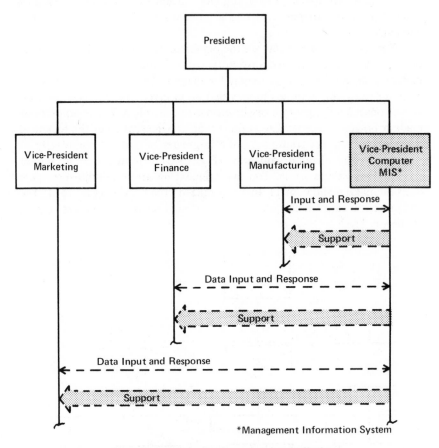

Fig. 15–4. Centralized computer installation.

The decision to have one large centralized computer or several smaller decentralized computers is to a great extent based upon organizational structure, as mentioned before. Nevertheless, there are arguments for and against each, especially from the data processing aspect. Both "pro" and "con" are listed for both types.

Centralization

1. Top management has at its disposal the ability to access information from a central data base. Thus, it does not have to wait for needed data to arrive from decentralized points.
2. Company-wide priorities can be given first attention, leaving less important (as judged by top level) requirements until later.

3. The data processing staff may be smaller than required for multicomputer installations. Greater emphasis is necessary to coordinate and approve new demands from each division and to set priorities. Additional highly qualified and technical positions, therefore, may cancel savings in staff positions.
4. Better utilization of the computer's capacity is more likely under centralized control, since some divisions otherwise may be overworked at peak periods while another is underworked.
5. Replacing two or more computers with one large system is a risky undertaking. Benefits may not be so great as expected; savings may not materialize as estimated; and complexity is likely to result in an unwanted monster that is difficult to control from a financial and operational standpoint.
6. Data communication allows divisions to furnish input and receive output from a computer across the country as easily as if the computer were in the next room.

Decentralization

1. Use of the computer should be where the work is located. The computer staff, by being near the user, is more versed in divisional applications and needs.
2. Divisions can satisfy special requirements easier than having to get approval from the central computer site.
3. Divisions must share limited people and hardware resources, since control lies at corporate headquarters.
4. Some applications affect only individual divisions, and impartial support may be a problem. Also, these requirements may end up costing more than when the division had its own computer.
5. Advancements in future technology could reverse the economies of scale. For example, many minicomputers might give more computing per dollar than a supercomputer. Competition and methods of doing business could force the firm to return to decentralized management.
6. Transactions in error can easily be accepted into the system, but getting the error out can try one's patience. Recall cases where customers are rebilled, then threatened, for purchases already paid for. Accuracy and ease of correction is more likely at the source.

For every advantage to centralization, someone can think of a disadvantage. The same applies to decentralization of computer installations. Each organization must, nevertheless, make the choice based upon its managerial goals and competitive forces. The trend is clearly in the direction of centralization for large companies, perhaps more so because everybody else is doing it. In any case, managers must keep in mind that sheer size generates complexity. Large corporations know well the law of diminishing returns: The larger the sales, the smaller the return on investment.

Caution must be exercised therefore so that management does not spend its time working to make the system work, rather than having the centralized data processing system work for it.

6. THE COMPUTER—AID OR HINDRANCE?

The computer has had a vital effect upon management and customer relations, both aiding and hindering. This is especially true for middle managers. According to one bank-branch manager, the computer has made his job more difficult overall, even though aiding him in many areas.

The status of each customer's savings, checking, and loan account is provided through printouts from a centralized computer located in nearby San Francisco. The printed status of accounts arrives by courier each morning for the previous day's business.

Savings and checking accounts are routine record keeping. This clerical function is simple arithmetic, increasing the account for deposits and decreasing the account for checks written. This burden, according to the branch manager, is happily transferred to the computer. Most customers' queries concern balances on their accounts or whether a check has been processed. This information is readily available from computer printouts and therefore is a definite aid to the middle management function.

Conversely, loan accounts are the manager's biggest problem. He needs answers to questions such as: Has a customer made a particular payment? Was the payment on time? What was the amount of the payment? A serious time lag occurs whenever computer verification is required for a loan account transaction that took place months ago. This was simple before record keeping was centralized in a computer. All the information was available on an individual account card in the branch office. In this manner, checking the status of an account was easy because every transaction from the original date of the loan to the present was recorded on a single document. Quick response is a valuable asset in customer relations and the manually maintained record kept the information at the banker's fingertips.

Now the information is centralized in the computer without a continuous record. Instead, it shows a minimum of data, such as last payment date and the latest balance. Other data about past transactions is stored off line on magnetic tape. To get a complete history of a customer's account requires a written request to the centralized computer installation. The needed information is then extracted from the daily transactions stored on numerous magnetic tapes. According to the branch manager, the delay may run as long as two months, a hindrance in carrying out day-to-day business and a frustrating experience for the customer.

In still another situation, the computer of Playboy Clubs International, Inc., is programmed to automatically bill the customer an annual fee for renewal of his club card, whether he agrees or not. The billing system is not geared to acknowledge a written explanation that renewal is unwanted. Consequently, the computer continues to generate monthly statements, treating the fictitious balance as an unpaid bill. Obviously, this improper oversight in computer billing is costly for the company and certainly has adverse effect on public relations.

Although these problems reflect the manner in which the systems were designed, the problems are still a real hindrance. Perhaps cost may have prohibited keeping all the bank's information on a central file, but it is evident that both illustrations cited are examples of inept planning. In any event, the bank and membership systems could be modified to satisfy the company's goals of keeping customers happy, but this would involve a cost penalty for poor foresight. Where was management during the planning stages? In these cases the computer becomes an irritant to customers and businesses. The bank manager's hands are tied when it comes to handling loan payment disputes, and the Playboy billing system removes the all-important human element that permits handling of written complaints from the customer.

7. COMPUTER MAINTENANCE PROBLEMS

The words "timely data" are found more often in the stated objectives of new projects than perhaps in any other. A prerequisite for timely data is a reliable computer system, and this unpredictable element can set back business activities if failure happens at the most inopportune time. The company payroll is a clear example. Whenever the computer or an adjunct unit suddenly quits, management expects quick response from the vendor and immediate repair.

Several elements affect the time that the system stays "down." Foremost is the availability of a computer repairman, called the "customer engineer" (CE) or some other name. If the CEs are out on other repair calls, then the customer must simply wait until he arrives. The next consideration is whether the CE can find the problem. If he has difficulty in isolating the trouble, and this has been known to take hours, he must call for help. Assuming that the trouble is quickly identified, the question of availability of parts must be considered. Last, we have the inevitable fact that the CE makes the repair, departs, and the system goes "down" again, either for the same problem or another created as a result of the repair.

Fortunately, third-generation computers are highly dependable insofar as the electronic central processor is concerned. When certain parts of the CPU become inoperable, many computers are designed to switch over to backup components, the trouble is diagnosed and recorded for the CE, and processing continues uninterrupted. But the input and output units are not so reliable because of their mechanical nature. In the case of a tape-drive failure, the problem may be temporarily handled by the operator's switching the reel of tape to an unused tape drive and restarting the job. Disk drives with multiple-disk packs usually have a backup drive that can be used when another is giving trouble, and once again no major setback is experienced.

Such procedures are not normally available for printers, card punches, and card readers where only one unit is available. In most cases, the inoperable I/O device does not affect the performance of the entire system. What about the many CRT (cathode-ray tube) terminals scattered among branch offices of the firm? If there is only one data terminal, then its user cannot enter or retrieve data from the computer until it is fixed.

Of significance is the inexperienced CE and those who simply cannot perform as well as others. The latter is a situation that we must tolerate, other than requesting that the vendor send a keener CE next time. The inexperienced CE is a problem that requires understanding and patience because experience comes only with time on the job beyond the classroom. The problem is somewhat compounded by the rapid growth in the number of data processing installations. The training necessary to produce experienced CEs has not kept pace. As many data processing managers can vouch from experience, a machine may remain inoperable for hours, or even days, while repairs are made on a learn-as-you-go basis. Restoring the equipment to service is the only concern of the data processing manager. All he wants is the best of CEs, and he does not care to participate in training them how to analyze problems and isolate causes since this is the vendor's responsibility.

It is difficult to recognize and verify that a CE does not know what he is looking for. Close observation over several visits may confirm his ineptness, and the fact that a particular CE calls for assistance often cinches the suspicion. But the costly time lost cannot be recovered, nor can the damage done by lateness be repaired. Granted, computer repair is a sometime mystery when everything seems to function as it should, but trouble nevertheless continues. The truth of the matter is that poor maintenance is more often at fault than not.

Major computer manufacturers offer a variety of computer models to fit every business need. Also, they are usually priced competitively. But maintaining the equipment and living up to sales contracts has indeed varied among computer manufacturers. During the process of selecting the computer that best fits the requirements, visits should be made to other installations in the area to discuss maintenance difficulties and adequacy of the service. Worthy of note is that maintenance support often varies from one locality to another, regardless of manufacturer.

Of particular importance is the interest a manufacturer places upon emergency ordering of parts. To illustrate, using a true case: One computer site had to process its payroll in a distant city because the computer manufacturer had to wait days for an unavailable part to arrive by mail from the opposite coast. Yet another manufacturer handled a similar situation by phoning the order to a major parts center, who in turn expedited transportation by sending the parts by a passenger airliner, resulting in a repaired machine within hours.

Although the maintenance and parts problems are usually handled expertly by the vendor, the computer manager and top management cannot ignore the possibility that his service may be inadequate. Consequently, quality repair is of extreme importance long after the computer is installed, putting production at the mercy of the manufacturer's support reputation. Maintenance limitations by the vendor, therefore, should be carefully considered when selecting computers. Cost may be a factor in deciding whether a particular computer is purchased or rented, but it becomes irrelevant if the inevitable failures cannot be repaired quickly.

8. WHY PROGRAM DOCUMENTATION?

Although the computer was supposed to eliminate paperwork, we find that the operation of a computer cannot survive without it. Paperwork describes how a job came into being in the first place, the specifications of a requirement, the flowchart solutions, the program listings, the work flow, the computer operation instructions, and more. It is a necessary evil in any business, but data processing seems to have more than its share. In addition, each level of user has to have documentation written at his level. For instance, the user of the computer product has documentation telling him how to use the output; the input people are instructed how to code and keypunch data; and management needs generalized flowcharts rather different from the programmer's detailed flowchart.

Why so much documentation? No business ever stands still, since it is either going forward or backward as a result of public opinion of its service or product. Consequently, a program that serves a useful purpose must be modified to meet changing business needs, which in turn necessitate documentation. Without formal documentation, therefore, continued success of the program depends upon the continued employment of programmers who designed it. But even so, no one person can remember why he changed a program after a few modifications.

To illustrate the value of documentation: One company purchased an expensive programming package from an independent software house. After using the software for some time, the company discovered that it had an almost identical piece of software, developed in-house but never used because of lack of documentation and the fact that the innovator had departed. There are similar tales in every installation. The most repeated story is about an application that had to be reprogrammed because changes had been made so often without documentation that no one really knew how the thing worked.

Documentation is usually best provided when the system is designed and programmed. When developing his program, the programmer diligently observes the written programming standards. The programming supervisor reviews the completed work and confirms it conforms to documentation standards. So, how can documentation become outdated? The greatest threat lies in the programmer's bypassing documentation standards whenever changes are made. This happens because many programmers basically hate documentation, do not recognize its importance, and find other programming requirements more challenging. Although a programming supervisor cannot personally follow up every modification at the time it is effected, there are certain ways to insure that documentation is complete.

Most programmers have the best intentions of completing the documentation after the program is changed and tested, but keep putting it off until it is forgotten. One way to avoid this is to keep program changes on a simply designed form, usually called the "program change" authorization. The control form includes such pertinent information as the change number, program number and name, description of the change, why it was made, and who modified the program. In addition, an explanatory note is placed in the program itself, using a special instruction that prints the note on the program listing but has nothing to do with program execution (see Section 29). Now anyone can tell at a glance if the documentation is complete and who did it. This gives both external and internal program substantiation. Of course the programming supervisor will spot-check as often as necessary to let each programmer know that he is interested in compliance and completeness. This also permits identifying those who follow documentation standards so that compliments or other acknowledgments can be extended on a personal basis.

Without some form of control, a disaster is in the making because the program being run on the computer will eventually bear no resemblance to the program documentation. In this case, the program will invariably have to be rewritten sometime, with all ensuing costs and embarrassing explanations necessary to cool the less-than-understanding top management. In order to become a firm believer in the necessity for documentation, one need only step into a job where the programmer or analyst has departed for greener pastures and has carried away in his mind the why's and how's of the operations.

MANAGEMENT OF THE COMPUTER

9. DEPTH OF MANAGEMENT INVOLVEMENT

Computers catapulted businesses into the new management era of the past decade. Rather than growing with new computer techniques as technology advanced, managers were often left behind. Of course this is rarely admitted, but much control of the firm's operations lies in the hands of data processing professionals. This happens because management has stepped aside after deciding what the computer should do.

Data processing professionals (or so we think) design these requirements, and thus decide the procedures by which processing will be done. Controls, or lack of controls, are left to the systems analyst and programmer. After all, they are in the best position to discover them. These technicians have become pretty good "behind the scene" managers in the firm. Heard in every firm is the advice, "Call Ed down at EDP and see if he thinks it ought to be done this way."

Nonparticipation of management in the computer operation can result in its cost becoming out of line with its contribution toward increased profits. Every manager should be keenly aware of the worth of current operations. Often overlooked are uses of computer time committed to processing data that should have been solved by manual means. Management should look for glaring cases involving jobs with very low input volume and should review reports to see if they have outlived their usefulness. If all daily output from the computer were delivered to the president's office, he would likely have a difficult time finding space to sit. Analyzing the value of report usage, therefore, should be a way of life in keeping cost down.

Managers may feel that the computer makes no unusual demands upon them personally. Answers to every imaginable problem can be had by simply defining the objective. A little far fetched but on target is: *Send a man to the moon.* Where should the rocket be launched from? Should the space capsule land? If so, exactly where? Is the man to return? How much money can be spent?

In business, the design and programming are turned over to the data processing staff. Without specific guidelines, the result could very well be a stack of useless paper or yield something less than the boss intended.

After a new application or computer system is on the air, actual costs and savings should be measured. This allows comparison with the original estimates used as the basis for "go" and "no go" decisions. Less than half of all company analysts perform a post-evaluation. Yet management feels that expectations have been met—a purely intuitive judgment. If management had realized the worth of a post-evaluation and had required it, an analysis might have been shown, for example, that future estimates should be multiplied by a factor of 2 before the next decision is made.

An impressive post-evaluation result comes from the Veterans' Administration. In this federal agency, millions of insurance policies are now handled by computers and 3000 employees. In 1950, the employee payroll listed 17,000 employees. Annual operating costs have been cut from $9.03 in 1950 to $3.88 per policy at present.

The operating cost of computers has a tendency to rise as a firm expands its use of the system. For example, initial mechanization is in the financial area: accounting, payroll, budget planning, invoicing, and billing. Mechanization usually starts here because clerical savings are greatest. Later, the company begins thinking about expanding into other areas such as:

- *Future Planning.* Capital investment evaluation and expansion through simulation (what happens if . . .?)
- *Distribution.* Processing shipment orders and warehouse operations through inventory control.
- *Marketing.* Processing sales orders, sales forecasting, and analysis.

Additional applications would likely overtax the present computer, so new equipment is installed and the cost of running the data processing operation increases. Before taking the step to acquire faster and more powerful computer systems, management could hire a firm that specializes in measuring idle time of the central processor. It is possible that input and output devices could be rearranged on less demanding channels (path of data flow) to give faster "throughput" (a term denoting the time needed to pass a transaction from the input device to the output medium). A study involving 155 computers in 89 firms revealed that only 64 percent of available time is used but that 100% utilization would be impossible because of maintenance, downtime, etc. Yet, 64 percent is a long way from straining the computer's power. Even more revealing was that only 48 percent of available time was used *productively.* For example, rerun time is not productive. These results of the study indicate that management has failed generally to establish quality controls that measure benefits derived from computer products.

One area in which management overexerts its power is in computer selection and purchasing. Too often, the contract is sealed before the data processing manager has been selected or consulted to any great extent. Nevertheless, he is responsible if the system does not live up to expectations. How does this seemingly inequitable situation come about? The answer is that too much reliance is placed on the vendor's recommendation in suggesting a particular computer configuration. He may tell management what his equipment will do best, but not how that performance compares with the product of a competitor's computer. This tendency to rely heavily on the vendor became even more puzzling when a survey revealed that many executives did not know the background of the salesman: 31 percent did not know the salesman's area of work specialization and 43 percent had no inkling of his past work experience. Consider what would happen to a company if employees were hired in this haphazard manner!

No magic formula or procedure can ascertain the degree to which management should be involved. Computer professionals need a free environment in which to create and enhance their skills. General managerial direction should be given, however, so that good teamwork will assure that the data processing installation successfully carries its own weight.

It may be that management will never understand enough about computers to exercise full control. For example, the complexity of programming and the sizes of programs continue to conceal theft of company money and supplies. Therefore, if management needs to know certain particulars of a problem before a decision is made and if computer jargon leaves the manager speechless, then he would be wise to say, "I don't understand." With some assistance from his experts, he can avoid decision pitfalls.

10. COMPUTER EXCEPTION MANAGEMENT

Executives need information that enables them to analyze and evaluate the influences of internal as well as external facts. They may interpret the proper data and fit it into a plan of action.

Impressive is the fact that computers can create massive piles of information about the company operation, sales analysis, computations, and so on, but the difficulty of total reporting is that a manager must sift through these stacks of reports to find what he is looking for, if indeed he finds it at all. After hours of reviewing, he may conclude that everything is going according to schedule, but can he be sure that he didn't miss an important sign of company weakness?

The principle of "exception management" is that the person in charge should attend to only those matters requiring his action. Since every business has a management hierarchy, the computer must produce useful information at all levels. Managers are given "exception" matters about things that require immediate corrective action (negative approach). Included also are things that are going extremely well but which continue to need guidance in the direction of profitability (positive approach). Other matters, such as collection of overdue bills, are delegated to subordinates, or in the case of historical facts, are disregarded altogether.

The computer can generate some decisions on the basis of rules established beforehand by management. To illustrate three simple examples:

1. The computer decides when to restock an item by checking after each issue to see if the balance on hand is below the reorder point. Based upon the total and frequency of all sales, the computer can produce an exception report on items losing their popularity, or which fall into the nonprofitable turnover class.

2. Large quantities of supplies are preferred by the purchasing department, to prevent shortages. For the same reason, the sales department knows that partial shipments make unhappy customers. But the vice-president of finances is concerned about having excess funds tied up and the consequent increase of storage expenses. An inventory investment value is set to keep all three departments happy. This provides a check to inform the financial executive by exception reporting when the inventory limit is exceeded.

3. Departmental spending must be kept to a minimum; therefore, each is allotted a budget. Management is notified by exception reporting whenever any department exceeds their allowed expense by a certain percentage.

Exception reporting, therefore, results in the computer taking automatic action upon routine decisions and reporting important decisions in "exception" reports for management's examination. If management by exception is effective, the executive should see a trend toward fewer and shorter exception reports.

Let us presume that an operation is constantly running into overtime. One way to isolate the problem and its cost would be to set aside the computer work that is not part of the normal routine or work that is behind schedule. This selected work is run on the overtime shift, consequently drawing attention to the exceptions needing corrective action.

Reruns would be an excellent prospect for assignment to the overtime shift. This would place strong emphasis on forethought because the extra cost would be charged to the originating department. What better management tool could one expect in handling departmental budget increases than one that pinpoints inefficiencies?

11. CONTROLLING COMPUTER RERUNS

Incomplete or inaccurate products from the computer must be reprocessed at extra cost, and reruns come when the firm can least afford them. Few things are as useless to a businessman as information that reaches him too late.

Reruns should definitely be of interest to management. They are normally a taboo mystery which is treated in various ways. Either managers shake their heads and grumble a warning or accept them as one of the evils of computer processing.

Nevertheless, reruns should be examined with the view that a *lesson* can be derived from each instance. Procedural improvements or employee retraining are possible corrective measures. Too often, the reaction to reruns is fear that "heads will roll." This may be necessary in extreme cases, but more often a sense of individual responsibility can be strengthened by demonstrating how forethought and careful work will prevent most reruns.

Computers were installed to relieve some of the pressures caused by rising costs and shrinking profits. Without control, however, the computer simply becomes part of the financial picture. How can the computer be controlled in order to make it contribute toward company profitability?

First, an answer must be found to the question, "What is the cost to operate the computer installation?" If data processing were to simply process whatever is required on an unlimited budget, the answer would never be known. But if data processing is given its own budget and each department is charged for services rendered, the price tag works silently to eliminate unnecessary work.

Before asking for some "nice-to-have" reports, otherwise known as unessential, a department chief will think twice if the cost of the computer processing is charged to him. Too often, a one-time report can be had by a simple telephone call. Many times, however, there are misunderstandings about what data is to be included, what sequence the report should have, and on and on. The solution is to rerun the job *only* after the requesting department has taken time to sit down with the data processing staff and explain precisely what it wants.

Most data processing installations have a form (Fig. 15–5) to request such one-time processing. This control forces the user to write down what he wants and have the data processing department go over it to avoid misunderstandings. Usually, this form is approved by someone knowledgeable who can determine if the information is worth the cost to generate, if the information might already be in another department, and so forth.

Surveys indicate that reruns cost American business around one-quarter billion dollars annually. These unproductive operations take 4 percent

TITLE Customer dropouts		JOB NUMBER OT 46	DATE Jan. 5, 74

☒ TYPE OF OUTPUT	☐ CREATE INPUT	☐ INPUT ON FILE	DATE NEEDED Jan. 10, 74
cards MEDIUM	——— EST VOLUME	_1500_ FILE SIZE	
_1_ NR OF COPIES	——— DATE DUE IN	_M53_ FILE ID	AS OF DATE
SALES RECIPIENT			Use latest tape

DESCRIPTION OF PROCESSING DESIRED

Request that customer's master file be searched for customers who have a last-purchase date of Nov. 15, 1973 or earlier. Punch the selected customer records onto cards and include account number, customer name, address, last purchase, amount of purchases to date, and salesman's number. Sort cards by salesman's number (major) and customer's name (minor). Interpret cards.

JUSTIFICATION

Vice-president of marketing has directed follow-up on lagging sales orders. Customers will be contacted in order to negotiate new orders.

DEPARTMENT Sales	DATE Jan. 5, 1974	SIGNATURE OF REQUESTOR Carol Chrissman

DATA PROCESSING USE

	Machine Time				Man-hours					Cost	
	Aux Equip	EDP Test	EDP Run	Total	Plan	Progm	Debug	Total	Material	Machine Time	Man-hours
Est.	10 min	5 min	5 min	20 min	0.5 hr.	1 hr.	0.5 hr.	2 hr.	$1	$15	$30
Actual											

REMARKS Change to Marketing Dept			DATE PROMISED Jan. 10, 1974
☒ APPROVED ☐ DISAPPROVED	DATE Jan. 6, 1974	CHIEF OF DATA PROCESSING C A Carter	DATE COMPLETED

Fig. 15–5. A one-time data processing project.

311

of the computer's available time. Yet, data processing operations periodically call for faster computers to catch up with the increased work load.

An important control should be to report computer reruns to higher management through exception reporting, thus calling for corrective action. Such a report might list only those products requiring a repeated treatment and might be submitted daily or weekly. Then the rerun could be charged to the originating department; for example, to the data processing department for programming error or to the customer for input error.

It is appropriate to end this discussion with some words of advice: Learn from past mistakes. Plan carefully the next time; it's easier and cheaper than reconstructing bad results.

12. TESTING THE PROGRAM—WILL IT QUIT ON NEW YEAR'S EVE?

Thorough testing of a program—to see if it works under all types of input data, and in fact to make sure that all parts of the program perform as expected—is an investment in the future. That is, testing is insurance that increases the likelihood that a program will continue to run time after time and not blow up* unexpectedly. It would appear that a program is satisfactory if specific input data is processed with predicted results. But too often the testing leaves much to be desired. The embarrassing consequences can be attributed to two main reasons.

First, the program may fail because the user of the processed results did not communicate precisely what the requirement should accomplish, or because the programmer failed to understand. Second, the programmer either did not have the experience or foresight to visualize every condition, or neglected to care enough.

Testing is the attempt to run a working program until it fails under given conditions. Since this concept conflicts with human behavioral patterns, unexpected failure places a stressful burden on the programmer. In the first place, it is discouraging to find that his masterpiece has flaws. But more important is the fact that errors found must be corrected at the expense of other projects scheduled to begin. Most program defects can be explained by understandable, but unacceptable, human failure. As a highly simplified example: Should the programmer accept the user's promises that the amount field will always contain numbers? An emphatic *no* is the answer. He should design the program to edit this field for nondigits, that is, for characters that cannot be computed. He should then test the program

---

*The term "blew" or "blowup" is used universally in referring to programs that have bugs or errors causing program failures.

to make sure that such records are rejected and recorded onto an error tape or on whatever other means are preferred.

Since the number of checks against potential errors can be practically unlimited, how many should be reasonable? This is an important consideration, for an extensive amount of testing is expensive because of time expended in preparing test data and repeatedly running the test on the computer. Consequently, management must establish guidelines to establish a cost-to-error ratio. Although the amount of testing is often left to the programmer's discretion, these guidelines can be generalized as follows:

- How important is the accuracy of the product? In monetary accounting, perhaps no error margin is tolerable, whereas inventory accounting may be 99 percent or more accurate.
- How frequent is the program run, with how much volume? Can the program be rerun without an exorbitant amount of computer time? A monthly 10-minute job may not justify the testing of improbable errors, whereas rerunning a weekly 4-hour job would certainly be expensive. Therefore, thorough testing of the latter would be appropriate.
- What suffers if the program blows? Programs are interrelated and data output from one program is usually used as input to another. Consequently, a blown program at the beginning of a series of jobs can halt further processing of the programs that rely on the crippled program.
- What is the life expectancy of the program? A program for a one-time job would be written with a minimum of testing, but a permanent program should be extensively tested.

Generally speaking, it can be said that a program should be tested to the fullest satisfaction of those creating the test data, and that testing should not be skimped in order to finish by the deadline, nor should it be curtailed because other projects are pressing. If the work load is too great to permit adequate testing, management must decide which priorities take precedence or what action must be taken to *resolve* the peak work load.

It is definitely not intended to play down the complexity of program testing or to imply that programmers are incompetent in creating programs that work successfully time and time again. There is no guarantee that a program will run forever without failure, but adequate testing can prolong its life, and ways of doing this come only with experience. How well a program performs depends on varying capabilities among the programming staff. With this in mind, let us become acquainted with the sequence of events and considerations in testing.

Programmers have high hopes of getting some form of output on the first test run which will give an indication of how well the program is put together. The initial step in achieving this desire is to exercise care in writing the program according to the flowchart, coding the *instructions* correctly, and analyzing the logic for inadequacies as they code. Many programmers detest flowcharting and defend their dislike by arguing that it is a waste of time. Nevertheless, reliable programmers flowchart their solutions while poor programmers struggle through coding of the instructions as things come to mind, getting it to work through trial and error but seldom on time.

Next, the program is keypunched and the program instruction cards are checked visually against the handwritten coding sheets for obvious errors. For example, the numbers 0, 1, 2, and 5 are easily misread and punched alphabetically as O, I, Z, and S. Also, all instructions are checked to insure that they were in fact punched, that the cards are in sequence, and that mispunched cards which were repunched were not left in the program deck. Although the computer will tag as unprocessable most keypunch errors in the program compilation stage, this is expensive and only slows the testing process. This is especially true whenever high-priority work delays testing for a day or more. No good programmer will argue that his time is more valuable than computer time.

Next, the program is compiled and tested to determine if the performance is as expected; for example, printing of fields and computations. Errors are identified, instructions in the program changed, and the source program is compiled and tested once more. Instead of debugging one error condition at a time and then resubmitting the program to see how far it executes before blowing again, the programmer desk-checks the program in order to catch as many errors as possible, to speed the testing process. In desk checking, the programmer examines the path that the computer can take for every possible condition and instruction in the program, thereby shortening the number of trial runs.

The program can be tested using either test data prepared by the programmer or actual "live" data already available. Test data is generally preferred because live data normally consists of many of the same type of transaction and may not contain all conditions that are provided for in the program. For instance, the testing of a subroutine or part of a program that arithmetically handles a particular kind of transaction differently from others is bypassed by the computer unless that condition is present in the test data. As a result, the program will blow unexpectedly as that unused path of the program is tried with live data. Unfortunately, the unique data that causes the program to halt may not appear in a processing cycle for months.

Another reason that favors the use of test data over actual data files is the unnecessary waste of computer time in processing thousands of multiple transactions of a similar nature. Moreover, bulky output is more difficult to check out than the predetermined output from test data selected by the programmer to represent all conditions included in his program.

Testing with representative test data, however, does not give the ultimate assurance that a program is complete and accurate. To the contrary, live data has always proved that many programs can fail after months or years of flawless operation. As a result of blown programs, there is a continuing need to patch the loopholes, and eventually the time spent correcting errors may justify rewriting the program entirely. This in no way implies incompetence on the part of the programmer or the source from which the test data originated. It simply points out that changing business requirements necessitate modifications to programs after their implementation and that seemingly small changes can effect other parts of the program. Thus, business data contains unknown conditions, and program changes result in unpredictable outcomes in many cases.

Some human fallacy and carelessness must be recognized by everyone working around computers. For example, the customer may not be able to identify every conceivable exception, the systems analyst and programmers have a tireless job in predicting unforeseen processing results, and the computer operator has been known to goof during the testing stage. Consequently, program corrections are always probable when the final product is run with live data. Therefore, the programmer must allow and plan for this uncertainty when estimating the completion date. Such a contingency might be the batch control cards used to separate groups of documents keypunched by different operators, which end up recorded on tape along with the actual data in the card-to-tape conversion.

Operation of the computer during testing may be performed by the programmer himself, but this practice is discouraged at most installations. There is a definite advantage to the programmer's running his own program test, in that he can make minor corrections when the program blows and can retest immediately. Conversely, programmers might play at the computer console all day long, running endless experiments. The primary reason for the policy of having computer operations run the test is to conserve computer time. It would be ideal to permit the programmer as much time as necessary to test his program, make alterations, and retest, but this practice obviously interferes with production. Consequently, testing of programs must be scheduled along with other priority processing. However, management should be aware that adequate program design and testing can prevent headaches in the future, and that the effort and time spent should be commensurate with the cost.

MANAGEMENT WANTS TO KNOW

13. WHY THE RISING COMPUTER BUDGET?

Management in all organizations is concerned about the ever-increasing dollar commitment to the computer installation. But some managers worry more than others and even question the value of computer operations. In the days of simple card-and-tape systems with limited memory, the computer budget was of minor importance. Now the point has been reached where the data processing operation is one of the more expensive departments to maintain.

As computer operations become more complex and difficult to control, management is faced with the prospect of upgrading to more expensive computers. But some companies have in fact resisted this pressure and discarded their computer operations, creating great financial loss.* The possibility of retrenchment seems impossible, however, because the business world is geared to the computer, even though attempts to correct its deficiencies have failed.

The rising computer budget was inevitable when companies ordered equipment merely to simplify paperwork or to enhance their prestige, or because they believed it to be a cure-all for company ills. Flashing lights in an expensive showcase soon grew monotonous, and management began thinking about getting returns from their investment by using the computer to improve their competitive status.

Just what does this investment run in a typical EDP operation and how is the money spent? According to an Infosystems Publishing Company survey, the average monthly investment for equipment is $11,400 in addition to over $22,000 for salaries and overhead. This closely parallels a McKinsey and Company study of 36 companies, representing 13 different industries (Table 15–2). According to a Diebold Group survey of 108 companies, the median average was $5600 for each $1 million of sales.

Trouble began when management set unclear and high objectives that

---

*The Infosystems Publishing Company sent 2000 questionnaires to independent suppliers of software, requesting verification of their lines. Of these, 5 percent (or 100) envelopes were returned, marked "Moved—Not Forwardable." Since all companies addressed had been in business the year before, a possible failure rate of 5 percent was indicated. This rate of attrition cannot be simply accounted for by incompetency, for software houses are generally thought to have the best of talent.

Table 15–2. Approximate dollar operating cost devoted to the computer installation.

Budget Item	Cost, %	Cost, dollars
Computer rental	35	11,700
Program maintenance	15	5,000
New program development	20	6,700
Salaries, supplies, and overhead	30	10,000
Total		33,400*

*Cost breakdown based upon total operating estimate, by Infosystems Publishing Company, using McKinsey and Company percentages.

could not be reached within the given time. Overnight success is simply not possible, but realistic goals can be met when properly laid out at reasonable intervals. When optimism failed, management tried again with expensive talent. In some cases, this did not work out because the talent had the wrong kind of experience. But more important, the best of talent does not require the interpretive capability of translating broad management statements into processing terms, although managers seemed to expect it. Consequently, many companies replaced their data processing manager when failures were apparent, but these switches in midstream offered no instant solution because it is difficult for a new manager to fulfill the promises of his predecessor. This is especially true when more expensive equipment has been brought in after a vendor makes the sale based upon overstatements in solving the company's problems.

Another reason for the rising computer budget was the constant change of the original requirements as programs were being developed. It points out that, to begin with, people did not know exactly what they wanted. This is a perfect example of unclear objectives. Enough thought was not given during the planning stages, when objectives should crystallize, and companies pushed too hard for impossible deadlines. In the final analysis, cost expectations could be easily exceeded when programming had to be interrupted in order to accommodate new requirements not planned for.

Since management knows so little about computers in the first days following installation, it is easy to leave problem solution and important detail to data processing technicians and the user of the computer information. If managers leave design of information systems to lower working levels, then they can expect masses of paper output that do not yield management information necessary to make managing easier. Some cases, where manual techniques were set up to verify computer results, have been known to increase the computer budget even more.

As time goes on, programmers learn better methods, the user becomes better versed in communicating in computer terminology and uses of computer products, and management looks closer at the EDP operation. But the lesson learned late in the game could have come earlier with advance planning, thereby decreasing rather than increasing the computer budget. To stem the rising computer budget, clear objectives must be established and met within the estimated cost and time planned, which by no means is a simple undertaking.

14. WHY SHOULD MANAGEMENT KNOW SYSTEMS AND PROGRAMMING FUNDAMENTALS?

Many influential managers have admitted that their computer accomplishments have fallen short of goals and that cost effectiveness has been disappointing. On the other hand, more managers boast of significant strides made by introduction of the computer. Why, then, has harnessing the computer's tremendous capability been so difficult for some companies and successful for others?

Management usually concedes that idealistic aims and glamour played an important part in acceptance of the computer at the onset. After the newness wore off, managers began to see the computer as a valuable but abstract tool. Nevertheless, computerized information was not always available when needed, nor was the information used intelligently in every case. Business profits rose and fell accordingly until businessmen began to realize the powerful control that they could exercise over the computer operation. Failure to realize this in the beginning can be largely attributed to the fact that management did not understand computer processing concepts and passed either simple or unrealistic guidelines to the data processing manager. Although some top managers gained a knowledge of the computer's ability and set fairly effective goals, they failed to follow up, or they did not know how to correct unsuccessful results.

Management has been somewhat reluctant to accept responsibility for computer failures and, to some extent, rightfully so. Should we blame the data processing manager, or are the analysts, programmers, and computer operators at fault? Certainly, all data processing technicians have at some time made some terrible misjudgments, even though they are highly talented. Some were unfortunately not suited to succeed in data processing in the first place. Others were inexperienced and learned through errors at the company's expense. Nevertheless, management was around when the groundwork for failure was being formulated and should have taken action when programs did not give expected results or when projects fell behind. In isolated cases, computer equipment was to blame for setbacks, but by far this was not the real problem, even though inadequate repairs may have caused temporary delays.

Whenever management has no appreciation for the time and effort involved in getting a system on the road, it has a tendency to push too far and too fast in crash plans. On the other hand, management has allowed project deadlines to be missed consistently and cost estimates to be shockingly exceeded. It was as if management had given its blessing to implementing a project with no deadline at all and with an unlimited budget; yet they were at a loss to explain why.

As we review this situation, we can see that noncomputer management was not geared to the changed way of doing business when the computer was initially installed because it had not taken the time to update its skills. Had managers known more about the computer, realistic goals might have been set that would have have resulted in a smooth transition from manual methods to computer methods. Instead, management kept hands off in the beginning and hired programmers to *guess* at company goals. The rest is history. We know that programmers, no matter how brilliant, cannot foresee the necessary planning that it takes top management years to prepare.

Computer courses at all management levels have been available since the mass production of computers began, and a manager's active participation in them will have a direct bearing upon the success of the overall data processing benefits. The courses vary in scope and in depth; therefore, managers need not become adept in systems studies or in programming in order to set desired goals and to follow through to see that they are met. But it is imperative that they have an appreciation of the time, know-how, and effort required by systems analysis and programming of new or revised projects.

Short courses geared to management needs offer the opportunity to study hypothetical business cases, arrive at a computer solution, and write a small program to accomplish the simple task. The rationale behind management's knowing such technical fundamentals is that they enable it to communicate with the computer staff. Computer processing offers many alternatives, and the choice from among these alternatives must be made with the long-term demands of business in mind. At the same time, benefits must be weighed against cost. Consequently, management must certainly be aware of what is involved in computerizing any job if it is to make the right decision based upon business demands and what it costs to satisfy those demands.

15. WHY SHOULD MANAGEMENT LEARN COBOL AND ASSEMBLY LANGUAGE CONCEPTS?

Ben Franklin gave us this bit of advice, "An investment in knowledge always pays the best interest." It is especially true in the computer era because managers can direct others in applying computers to solve business problems, once they have adequate knowledge of the equipment.

Computers produce problem solutions written in one of two types of programming languages, high-level or low-level. Low-level languages are referred to as "machine-oriented" because the program of instructions is similar to the actual machine language that the computer uses. High-level languages such as COBOL and FORTRAN are much more like English and mathematical notation, and so are referred to as "problem-oriented." In other words, a programmer writing a COBOL or FORTRAN program can concentrate more on what he wants to accomplish without having to worry too much about how the computer does it.

Aside from the level of programming complexity, just what advantages does each offer? (For a comparison, see Table 15–3.) Foremost is that low-level language programs can be skillfully designed to run faster and use less storage than can high-level programs. But the disadvantage is that each type of computer has its own low-level language, more often called "assembly language." Consequently, assembly programs written for one computer

Table 15–3. Comparisons of high-level and low-level languages.

Characteristic	Low-Level Language*	High-Level Language†
Type of use	Efficiency software	Business applications
Type of programming	Machine-oriented	Problem-oriented
Program size	Smaller	Larger
Programming difficulty	More	Less
Experience of the programmer	Considerable	Less
Number of machine instructions	Fewer	More
Computer speed comparison	Faster	Slower
Machine-dependent	No	Yes
Time to translate	Less	More
Self-documented	No	Yes
Debugging difficulty	More difficult	Easier
Time to code	Greater	Lesser
Amount of coding	Large	Small
Error probability	More	Less

*Example: Assembly Language.
†Example: COBOL.

may not run on another type of computer. On the other hand, COBOL and FORTRAN were designed to be machine-independent; that is, they have the ability to run on any computer. But we said that each computer model has its own language, so how is this possible? The source program is simply recompiled by the other computer's compiler by giving a new machine language program in that computer's language. In other words, each computer has its own specially designed compiler.

Each program sentence in high-level language generates a series of machine instructions depending upon the operation. Here we appreciate the importance of assembly language over the COBOL language. These same COBOL statements could likely be programmed several ways, all producing the same result. Because high-level languages generate generalized instructions so that a wide range of data processing needs can be met with a minimum of programming effort, the compiler might produce inefficient machine language. Then these additional instructions, which might not be needed for a particular solution, affect production time because they take longer to run. A skilled programmer might produce less assembler instructions to solve the same problem, thus reducing execution time. In such a situation, the assembly language permits flexibility in choosing the kind of economy required, either faster run time or more efficient storage usage, or both. Another facet that might be considered is that translation time varies. It takes longer to translate a COBOL program into machine language than to convert a assembler program. Therefore, time can be saved if the program task has a high number of changes requiring frequent recompilation, especially if the program is large.

Assembly language is more difficult to learn than COBOL; therefore it takes less time to train a higher-level language programmer. This is one reason why a systems programmer (one who writes software such as compilers) is usually more valuable than an applications programmer (one who writes business programs in COBOL). Although COBOL programs are generally easier to debug than assembler programs, a higher-level language programmer who does not understand machine language will have trouble reading and interpreting a memory dump printed in hexadecimal. A COBOL program is easier to debug for several reasons. First, the COBOL program list includes English-like sentences, such as MULTIPLY GROSS-PAY BY TAX-RATE GIVING TAX-DEDUCTION. Obviously, errors will be easier to detect in these easy-to-read statements in comparison to a long series of cumbersome assembler instructions required to give the same solution. Second, COBOL requires less material to be written; therefore the physically shorter program list should be debugged in less time.

Because COBOL sentences are meaningful even to the casual reader, documentation is built into the program to a large degree. This allows someone other than the programmer to read and understand the problem solution, even though he does not understand how to program.

The choice of programming language involves weighing the lesser cost of programming time invested in higher-level languages against the savings in machine time that could result from programs written in lower-level languages. Generally, business applications are programmed in COBOL because of considerable savings in programming time, ease of program modifications, and simplification of program testing. Software efficiency programs (such as operating systems, compilers, and data management programs designed to retrieve and update data stored on disk files) are usually written in assembly language. The efficiency of assembler programming, nonetheless, can be combined with COBOL programs. For example, parts of a COBOL program that are used extensively may be rewritten in assembly language, to increase the speed efficiency, and made a part of the higher-level language program.

Although management hires programmers to do the programming, it should know how and when high-level or low-level languages should be employed. For instance, management is better prepared to make the best decision if it can intelligently discuss tuning-up of time-consuming programs versus stepping up to faster equipment. Further, management should be aware that both types of languages are necessary tools in utilizing the computer to its fullest extent and that each type has advantages as well as drawbacks.

16. WHEN DOES A FIRM NEED A FASTER COMPUTER?

There are essentially two reasons why faster computers should be considered by management: when all the processing required in one day's business cannot be handled in a 24-hour period and when the response time must be shortened to meet competitive forces. For example, a customer calls an airline to check departure times in the morning for Los Angeles. The computer is too busy to give a prompt answer. Consequently, the impatient customer calls another airline for his reservation.

Expanding business brings increased activity, and the additional processing eventually reduces the computer's idle time to zero. What then? Hopefully, the problem was solved long before becoming that critical; otherwise, something is delayed and business suffers.

This is especially true in real-time processing* such as airlines reserva-

---

*Real-time is the rapid processing of input data so that the results can be used immediately.

tions. Since most reservations are made by phone, information necessary to make a seat sale on a particular flight must be readily available. As more and more people travel by jet, the response time becomes longer. To get an idea of the magnitude of passenger reservations systems, a typical airline's computer will handle over 100,000 calls for information every day. This means that the computer must respond to several hundred customer responses each minute. To meet increasing demands, the speed of processing has to become proportionately faster. For instance, some airlines have gone so far to improve service that special foods for customers with medical or diet restrictions are included along with reservation information in the computer.

Increased business alone is not sufficient to order a souped-up computer, however. To cite an example applicable to at least 30 percent of all installations: Firms should not rush into new equipment when applications on the present computer are not living up to expectations. If the computer is capable of getting the job done, increased power cannot wipe out poor planning, inadequate staff work, lack of guidance, or whatever has contributed to failure.

Consider next that the present system is doing the job, but business is expanding. Several alternative solutions are available before calling anxious vendors to haul out the reliable workhorse and replace it with a system that, at best, will cause some headaches.

1. When the computer is not being fully utilized, faster input and output devices should be considered: for example, a newer model tape reader, disk, or printer to replace slower models. If a computer is slowed down by input or output, a faster central processor will not solve the problem.
2. A second computer like the first one allows the installation to continue operation without interruption, and needs no conversion, no reprogramming, and no retraining. All that is required is to switch some jobs onto the second computer.

When it is clear that the present computer is inadequate to handle the anticipated workload, look for faster hardware.

17. WHICH COMPUTER SPEED WILL DO?

It is often heard that computer hardware changes so rapidly that it is obsolete before becoming operational. The speed of new models does make the older units appear as slowpokes. Nonetheless, the judgment of obsolescence is unrealistic and contributes greatly to the excessively large number of data processing installations operating unprofitably. That is, the benefits derived from the new computer cost more than they are worth, thus eating into, rather than contributing to, profits. How does this happen? A decision, for instance, is made to upgrade to a faster and more expensive computer that can handle the increased work load. This decision is often made without investigating how the efficiency of the present equipment can be improved so that it is comparable to, and yet costs less than, the new computer.

The procedure begins with systems analysis. Management looks for inefficient programming practices that degrade the capability of the computer. The experience level of programmers can be raised in several ways in order to increase throughput. One sure way is by having experienced programmers share their knowledge with ill-trained beginning programmers. Surprisingly, this is assumed to be taking place all along, but in actual practice the experienced programmer is under stress to complete one rush project after another; therefore, he has little time for training others. As a result, new programmers are left to re-invent efficient techniques that were known all along by others.

It is a common occurrence to assign individuals with little training to the less complicated programs and leave them there. Rotating programmers should not be overlooked, however. Great benefits can be derived by having each programmer read another person's programs and try to improve them. This important exchange of experience and ideas results in better and faster running programs as each operator improves the work of someone else. In other words, programmers learn from one another, and in the final analysis the improvement in programming—thus computer efficiency—is perpetuated.

Before selecting faster computers, management should ascertain whether maximum throughput is being achieved from the lower-priced system. This means that a job requiring 4 hours to run may be made to run in 3 hours by cleverly tuning up the system peripherals such as channel tie-ups, which keep the CPU idle. Channels can be upgraded by switching one of two busy disk drives using the same channel to a less used channel, thus speeding throughput. Management ought to be aware also that specialized software packages are available to schedule I/O devices more efficiently. For example, POWER (priority output writers, execution processors, and input readers) is a free IBM package that a salesman may overlook when confronted with the problem of how to get faster processing. Among other things, POWER allows the inclusion of the job control language on disk and retrieval whenever needed, instead of JCL being read by the slower card reader.

One insurance company reported a 30 percent increase in overall throughput of its computer by increasing the core capacity. It is possible to raise system performance in many cases without raising operating cost. Additional memory enables the user to extend the size of buffers so that, for instance, IOCS (input output control system) can read more input records into storage at the same time. In Chapter 12, we found that the larger the input and output buffers, the more the efficiency of the computer is improved.

Larger memories also allow users to take advantage of more powerful operating systems and compilers that cut the time required to process data or compile programs. In addition, more speed is gained by altering the operating system to keep frequently used parts of the supervisor in the added memory, rather than calling them into core from disk whenever needed.

As seen, there is no need to rush into faster and more expensive systems without taking full advantage of the lower-cost system's power. Assuming that a faster system is needed, however, the task of selection is no easy one. Different manufacturer salesmen will claim that their system is superior to others, but speeds vary, as do the capabilities of operating systems. The result is often more confusing than clear.

From Table 15–4 we can tell that a true evaluation is similar to comparing apples to oranges. For example, the CDC computers fetch four BCD characters at a time while the IBM models fetch from 2 to 16 EBCDIC characters. From our study of internal memories (Chapter 7), we know that an EBCDIC character may contain two numbers when packed. In a cost comparison, the CDC 3500 appears to be much faster than the IBM 370/145, and is available at a lower price. However, one must know a little about programming each computer in order to realize that the IBM S370 has a memory-to-memory feature as opposed to the CDC 3500, which performs arithmetic operations with a single-address instruction. In other words, in a single-address computer, one additional instruction is required to get the first number added into the arithmetic register, and another instruction is needed to return the result to where you want it in memory. This is not necessary in a memory-to-memory (see Chapter 10) arithmetic operation, so which one is really faster? Hardware characteristics differ widely among computers, thus making comparison difficult when deciding on the model to purchase or rent.

Nonetheless, let us see how today's faster computers outperform their ancestors, and then relate speed to practical business uses. The first large-scale computer, the Mark I, was electromechanical and required 300 milliseconds to add two numbers. Shortly thereafter, the ENIAC was built with tubes, and the speed to add two numbers was improved to 200 mi-

Table 15-4. Hardware characteristics of various computers.

Computer type	Approx. CPU Monthly Rental Cost, thousands of dollars	Time to Add Two Numbers in BCD, microseconds	Time to Add Two Numbers in Binary, microseconds	Storage Cycle, microseconds	Characters Fetched	CPU cycle time, nanoseconds
CDC* 3300	4.5	24.60	7.37	1.25	4	500
CDC 3500	9–12	2.75	1.40	0.90	4	–
IBM S360/40	3.7–10.6	40.00	12.00	2.50	2	625
IBM S360/50	10.3–20.7	20.00	4.00	2.00	4	500
IBM S370/145	12–14	11.90	2.14	0.54 Read 0.60 Write	8	203–315
IBM S370/155	20–23	4.93	0.99	2.07	16	115

*CDC- Control Data Corporation.

croseconds. These experimental computers were the forerunners of first-generation computers, such as the IBM 700 and UNIVAC series. The UNIVAC I performed addition in 525 milliseconds and the IBM 701 surpassed it with a faster rate of 45 milliseconds, but both were slower than the experimental ENIAC prototype. Each succeeding first-generation computer became faster, such as the IBM 704 (twice as fast as the IBM 701) and the IBM 709 (computed ten times faster than the 704 model).

Second-generation computer speeds were boosted by replacing the tube with the transistor. The second-generation IBM 7090, for example, computed six times faster than its tube-filled predecessor, the IBM 709. The IBM 709 is noted for its use in tracking Allan Shepard in America's first orbital space flight.

Just how far third-generation computers have come in cutting down processing time can be seen by the fact that the IBM S360 Model 70 is equivalent to five second-generation 7090s. An even faster speed king, the IBM 360/75, was replaced in two short years at NASA's Goddard Space Center by the 15 times faster IBM 360/91. Even so, the latter's 16 million computations a second appears turtle slow when compared to subsequent computers (see Section 32). The IBM 360/91 speed can be more easily comprehended when compared to man's slower, less reliable calculations. It would take a mathematician over 35 million hours, or 4000 years, to do the same amount of calculations that the 360/91 can do in 1 minute.

Scientific applications in space, weather forecasting, and similar fields have pushed the need for more powerful computers. But what effect does this have on business data processing, where most of the computers are used? Very little, generally speaking, because business computers for the most part do relatively few internal calculations in comparison to scientific processing. In contrast to scientific computers, business computers have a great amount of input and output processing, such as printing masses of checks and invoices. There are exceptions, however, where ultrahigh speed is needed for commercial applications. One is in real-time processing, such as the often-mentioned airline reservations system and timesharing applications, where many users at remote data terminals are trying to use the computer at the same time.

In generalizing computer speeds, commercial data processing is usually limited by input devices that feed the computer being processed and output devices that record the results. Because of their mechanical nature, construction of faster I/O equipment has not kept pace with the improved internal electronic speeds of the central processor. Consequently, management is concerned more with the efficiency of operating systems, channels, and other computer features that are designed to compensate for the differences between internal and external speeds.

In summary: There are computers designed for every job, small or large, but management need not be concerned to any great degree about one computer outdating another. However, expansion of present data processing systems to meet growing business needs is of concern, with the first order of consideration being devoted to getting maximum throughput from the present low-cost system before moving up.

18. THE CHANGED PERSONNEL RECRUITMENT SCENE

In the 1960s the problem of recruiting the quantity and quality of computer technicians was a main concern. Also, job hopping was a practice that left a cloud over personnel stability. Due to the shortage of programmers, the rule seemed to be for most firms to train potential talent at the company's expense.

The picture has now changed. Management's concern over job shortages and losing good people to higher-paying positions has faded into the past as salaries have stabilized and the supply of programmers exceeds the demand. According to a recent survey by Infosystems, EDP managers and programmers had been with the same employer for an average of almost seven and four years, respectively.

In the 1960s a company advertisement to recruit a programmer with no specific training brought little or no response. As a result, recruitment was done almost exclusively through computer placement agencies. By 1970, companies turned once again to news media ads. By then they could specify a certain number of years' experience in exact applications the company was interested in. In addition, they could call for experience in assembly language, COBOL, or JCL (job control language) for a particular computer. This response reversal, which was impossible in the mid-1960s, now brings hundreds of résumés.

Worthy of note is the fact that the changing job market came as a surprise to the data processing industry. No one seems to have made this prediction. The economic slump, which began in the late 1960s, forced many firms into bankruptcy and others to cut back their staffs. For the first time, the computer field had a significant unemployment rate. In fact, the computer professional unemployment rate was higher than the overall unemployment figures in areas hard hit with defense cutbacks.

At the same time, the flourishing business of commercial EDP education, along with college programmer turnouts, were flooding the market with trainees. So, these two factors—experienced EDP technicians forced into unemployment and an oversupply of trainees—turned the computer programmer's market into an employer's market.

This supply in excess of demand has been long overdue, even though many top-notch managers and computer professionals are unfortunately out of work for extended periods. The overall trend has been to upgrade the quality of technicians while the weak or unfit programmers were forced into new fields more adaptable to their talents.

As a result, new reliance upon computer usage to aid business has built up three sagging areas. First, the higher quality of data processing managers and their subordinates has meant more workable EDP systems. Second, completion times are closer to targets. Third, budget costs to implement new or revised systems are nearer to the original estimated costs.

A byproduct of this quality and quantity increase in EDP talent is the ability to extend the power of the computer into new and more sophisticated areas beyond record keeping: for example, planning to determine feasibility of capital investment, simulation to forecast results of expansion, and marketing analysis for predicting sales.

INVOLVEMENT

19. THE DATA PROCESSING MANAGER IN THE ORGANIZATIONAL STRUCTURE

The manager of data processing can best serve company objectives if he is on an equal level with other managers (Fig. 15–6). His increased responsibilities, of course, have boosted him up the line of authority since computer operations have been separated from the accounting department, where mechanization started. This sign of top management involvement has been rising steadily. A recent Infosystems survey reported that 81 percent of data processing managers report to the president, vice president, secretary, or treasurer level, as compared to 28 percent in 1967. Why should the data processing manager be nearer top management? There are compelling circumstances brought about by position politics and human behavior that make it necessary. In this article we discuss typical cases of each.

Equal status with other department heads allows the data processing manager the ability to give impartial service to all departments. If the computer facility is placed under the director of accounting, then it is obvious that the data processing manager will satisfy his boss first. Consequently, the work of other users of the computer must take second priority to accounting applications. When the manager is given equal positional status, the outcome is more equitable support to other areas. For example, if two departments have priority projects of similar importance, the data processing manager may decide to divide his resources between both projects rather than do one first and then the other.

Independent status gives the data processing manager more authority in resolving conflicts between departments as to who gets what processed and when. For example, assume that additional data elements not previously recorded in computer entry form are needed for a one-time job. The budget and purchasing departments have this data available in their areas, but both have pressing work loads. Consequently, each department head feels that the other should compile the new data elements. The data processing manager, by being on an equal level, might convince the purchasing department that the best approach involved keypunching the new data along with other elements to be punched from the purchase order. Accordingly, the new data could be annotated directly on the purchase order, since the forms are coded in that department. Had the head of the budget department been the superior of the data processing manager, a hassle might have

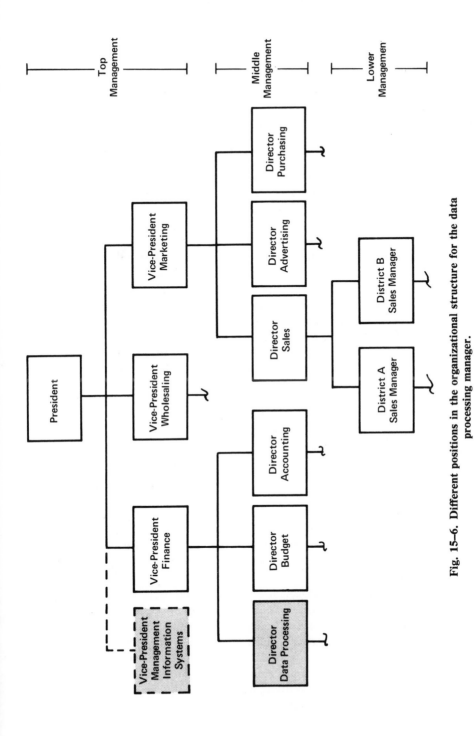

Fig. 15-6. Different positions in the organizational structure for the data processing manager.

331

ensued. It is easy to visualize the head of the purchasing department feeling that the data processing manager sided with his boss, especially if the two heads of purchasing and budget do not get along in the first place.

Pressures upon the elevated data processing manager are certainly less than when his position is several echelons down the line of authority. The data processing manager, for instance, is not compelled to pay attention to a financial officer in covering up a seemingly unbalanced account. Without positional independence, it would easy to yield innocently to the cloudy situation, given subtle hints that his job were in jeopardy.

To avoid situations similar to the examples discussed, larger companies with large-scale computer systems are increasingly placing the data processing department head at the top-management level. He gets a fancy title, something like vice-president of MIS (management information systems), and is expected to be more of a business manager actively participating in overall company operations and less in technical areas. In conclusion: We should pay attention to the fact that more profitable companies allocate almost twice as much toward the EDP budget as do less profitable companies. This goes far in justifying the EDP manager in the top-planning position.

20. DISSENT IN AN ORGANIZATION

The success of an organization lies to a great extent in the teamwork displayed and exercised by employees and management. The principle of teamwork implies that no one person can take full credit for a firm's well-being, nor can he bear the full brunt of failure. Of course business philosophy tells us that top-level management is ultimately responsible. This is true, but many people have contributed to that ultimate accountability whether it be good or bad, and thus the team itself is party to either success or failure.

In order that management can make sound decisions, lower echelons present their different beliefs, opinions, and even opposition. These views may be expressed in private meetings or in open discussions, depending upon the sensitivity of the problem. Once the person with total responsibility has made his decision, all supervisors who participated in providing the basis for that decision have an obligation to support it. The course of action may vary from policy governing neatness of work areas to the intricacies of programming a new system. Whether the decision is large or small has no bearing. A decision has been made and the team must work to assure its fulfillment.

If the decision is not supported, conflict arises within the group and trouble lies ahead in enforcing compliance with subsequent decisions because of questionable leadership. The outcome is clear. The door is left open for people affected by the decision to choose whether they follow it or not. Then disciplinary action must be taken and resulting resentments break down the organization's morale.

Whenever disputes between lower and higher management arise in the open and disturb work equilibrium, employees naturally feel that teamwork has been compromised. As we go up the line of authority, it may appear that either the manager who made the decision is not satisfied with the judgment of his subordinate supervisors or that the supervisors' confidence in the manager's decision is lacking. While the conflict gives employees a chance to choose sides, some are likely to decide that neither top or lower management have the right answer. Nevertheless, the situation is unhealthy because the best interest of the organization is promoted only when all levels of management are in agreement.

Although there are isolated cases where incompetent management should be challenged, the normal practice should be to express personal differences in private and uphold the final determination in the presence of those who must abide by the new decision. When one finds himself disagreeing with the boss more and more, he should *quit*—but only after failing to get the boss to conciliate on his own accord.

21. THE INSECURE MANAGER

Too often primary emphasis is placed by the boss on arrival and departure of employees for beginning and quitting work, coffee breaks, lunch breaks, and so on. Arriving a minute late may irritate him enough so that he never fails to mention the tardiness to the offender, even if that individual voluntarily worked late or arrived early the day before.

This form of petty reprimand does not encourage devotion to the job; rather, it encourages dissatisfaction among conscientious professionals whose output is highly valuable to the company's well-being. A conscientious employee might feel guilty and would resolve to correct his lateness, as much as possible. Reprimanding individuals who rarely repeat lateness can retard their productiveness as well as their efficiency. People normally are self-motivated* and take pride in doing an exceptional job; therefore, any manager would be foolish to jeopardize their positive attitudes toward

---

*According to McGregor's Theory X, management holds that people do not like to work —therefore must be directed and pushed. Theory Y holds that people drive themselves more effectively than they can be driven because they commit themselves to fulfilling objectives in order to satisfy their social and ego needs.

the job. In other words, the devoted programmer is less likely to contribute to company objectives according to his ability if reprimanded for something he is well aware of and attempting to correct himself.

On the other hand, the employee may have good intentions of reporting promptly next time, yet not be able to break the habit without encouragement. He is well aware that a reminder is in order and accepts it gracefully. The problem is usually solved, at least temporarily, and conflict or resentment is avoided.

Now that we have considered the employee's side, let us turn to the manager who does not know how to bring out the best in his people. A tyrant supervisor who places relatively unimportant events ahead of vital work may very well feel insecure and lack confidence in himself. By concentrating on nuisances that bother him, he is likely to take the position that accomplishment of the work will somehow get done. By avoiding involvement of projects in progress, he must therefore make his importance known to higher management in other ways. He does this by appearing to be busy with stacks of paperwork that he constantly shifts from place to place, and by holding too many meetings to discuss petty annoyances.

How can this type of boss effectively manage his people and the work? Above all, he should be concentrating on the quality and timeliness of the work in progress. By being close to the work, he has a better chance to stamp out small fires that get out of hand and create important problems. Also, he should be concerned with training weak programmers to increase their productivity, rather than assigning them to simple tasks and loading reliable programmers with big jobs. A possible explanation for some programmers who give the impression of not being capable of handling heavy tasks is that they have not been given the opportunity. This withholding of responsibility from the programmer is a significant indicator of an insecure supervisor. He continually assigns difficult work to his reliable programmers because he may look bad in the eyes of other managers if the program proves troublesome. After all, why risk having disgruntled customers because of billing errors caused by programming errors?

The insecure manager makes an unhealthy situation in any supervisory position. Nonetheless, such managers frequently exist. Although the problem may be recognized by the next level of management, it may well drag on until the most valuable professionals affected have resigned and the computer department becomes a shambles—all in hope that time will solve the problem. By then the entire organization has felt the impact, and top management must devote valuable time from pressing company objectives and planning in order to return the computer department to normalcy.

Unfortunately, management's responsibility to fire the inept supervisor may be exercised too late to save the department. Company management has much to lose by keeping EDP managers who are unable to cope with *people-handling,* and therefore it must reexamine its role in data processing supervision. Otherwise, the disintegration of an ongoing system will be a high price to pay.

22. THE DILEMMA OF PROMOTING GOOD TECHNICIANS

A data processing technician is a unique kind of expert. He may be a former teacher or a recent college graduate. He may enter data processing because the field appears exciting and marked by individual responsibility and self-expression. Indeed, he will find a challenge and his creativeness will be rewarded. Regardless of reason, computer professionals tend to be dedicated to the job from the beginning because their performance is the outgrowth of on-the-job training and their individual efforts, unfettered by the demands of formal schooling.

Many computer professionals may believe that they are exceptional because they have conquered the supposed mysteries of the computer and are therefore invincible. As a result, they overrate their importance and think they belong to a select breed of intellectuals. Actually, this kind of overrated self-esteem may inhibit their best performance and hinder their promotion. Although self-confidence is needed in handling many computer assignments, overt display of such confidence may encourage management to overcontrol their work. Even though they may retain enough freedom to express themselves, such stringent supervision may adversely affect assumption of greater responsibility.

Management will attest to the fact that programmers are hard to manage, with the best ones being even more difficult and temperamental. Consequently, managers tend to either oversupervise or undersupervise. Thus, on the one hand, we have *casual* supervision, resulting in loose and careless control. On the other hand, we have overdoses of supervision in trying to reshape the man to fit the job. Instead, managers ought to match the man's needs by allowing him to adjust to the needs of the job. In this manner, self-motivation commits the man toward higher quality work because he has higher self-imposed standards and more pride in the job than could be forced upon him.

Now having this image of the typical data processing technician, we are ready to discuss if successful data processors should, or even must, advance into management. There are two trains of thought concerning progression into technical management. One is that the manager must be technically competent in order to manage professionals. A newer but seldom practiced thought is that a manager need only have managerial know-how. Regardless, the former criterion is used predominately, whether selecting a new manager from outside the organization or promoting one from within. Even so, the manager's knowledge quickly becomes out of date as he spends more time in the day-to-day management activities and less time in technical matters.

When we elevate our best technicians to manager positions, the result is often to lose a good technician and gain a poor manager. The trend has been to promote a junior programmer to senior programmer because of his demonstrated ability to code instructions. Then a senior programmer easily becomes a systems analyst because of new experience gained from improving the program design handed over from a seasoned analyst. Eventually, he is shifted into a supervisory programming or systems position where he becomes so busy shuffling paperwork that he has little time to show others how to program more effectively. Unfortunately, this advancement is usually forthcoming to a programmer with little or no supervisory training. After getting some projects on the road through other people or perhaps accidentally, he is eligible as a competitor for a management position.

In light of so much dissatisfaction both up and down the line, the question is whether a technician reaches the *limit** of his capability and efficiency. The answer is an emphatic *yes* for many, especially those who advance from technician to manager. But how can management determine who should remain a technician and who should advance into a supervisory position? Who should handle the consequences if the promotion is premature? As we shall see, the latter can be the biggest problem and can have far-reaching implications.

For example: The programming manager has resigned and the vacancy must be filled immediately. Management has two choices: to promote from within or recruit from outside the organization. The choice of the outgoing programming manager is Bob, the senior programmer. Bob is an energetic programmer, likeable, a good teamworker, and keen thinker. Although he has been with the company only a short time, he has been highly successful in implementing new programs on time and in developing the skills of trainees.

The director of data processing has some reservations, since Bob has unproven managerial skills. Thinking ahead, he ponders *his* responsibilities in the event that Bob is unsuccessful in the higher position. On the other hand, Bob is certainly deserving, but his enjoyment and dedication appear to be centered in mastering the computer instead of supervising and making decisions. If the promotion does not work out, the director thinks, he is not

*The Peter Principle states that "in a hierarchy every employee tends to rise to his level of incompetence."

only stuck with an ineffective programming manager but has also lost a crackerjack programmer. After lengthy discussion with top management, the decision is made to advance Bob, primarily because of his proven ability to program and secondarily because of company policy to promote from within whenever possible.

Bob is anxious to accept the increased responsibility, which brings prestige and a pay increase. He feels satisfied that his past accomplishments have been recognized and rewarded. In moving to his private office, he brings along his reliable working tools, programming manuals, flowcharting template, and the like. In the weeks to come, the new programming manager asks that problems brought to him be left for solution. Instead of offering guidance to the programmers, Bob comes up with his own solution, thus frustrating his technicians. He has not only reduced his programmers to mechanical workers, but has also ignored their ideas. This is a sharp departure from the previous practice, which afforded them the opportunity to take part in determining how jobs should be done. The director notices that programming production has bogged down, and he is disturbed that Bob cannot readily give the progress of certain projects being undertaken by his programmers because *he* is tied up with detailed analysis work that his staff is getting paid for.

A frank talk with Bob concerning his supervisory responsibilities results in the work being returned to the proper place—with individual programmers. The new Bob has turned about-face, giving his attention to status charts, reports to update them, and countless memos. He sets and closely monitors unrealistic deadlines without taking into consideration individual levels of programmers. To protect himself, there is new paperwork to explain delays and the progress of work. As the real job of programming lags, Bob's mood changes accordingly.

The director of data processing turns his prime concern to the critical situation. It is now clear that Bob is not equipped to manage projects or people. To keep Bob as a programmer cannot be considered because a demotion would certainly humiliate a once proud technician. In addition, everyone would have to drop down a step in position even if it were possible to return Bob to the programming staff to fill his old position of senior programmer. The director must begin the unpleasant task of recruiting a programming manager from the outside who can raise the programmers' morale and return production to its original level. From the foregoing, it can be seen that professional technicians are misunderstood as much by management as by themselves.

MANAGEMENT OF
DATA BASES

23. DATA BASE—WHAT IS IT?

Data bases are discussed in two sections. This section defines the data base through illustrations, and Section 24 covers the advantages and disadvantages of concern to management. The idea behind a data base is to consolidate information stored on multiple tape or disk files into a single file in order to permit any program to have access to all company data from the same storage area (Fig. 15–7) and to eliminate duplication of information in different files (Fig. 15–8).

Therefore, a data base attempts to solve the problem of duplicated expense in maintaining multiple files while making all corporate information available from a common source. So, a data base is defined as a collection of data stored as a single file (usually disk) which satisfies the requirements of more than one application.

A data base consists of data elements or "key fields" that comprise the smallest addressable unit, such as a customer name or invoice number. Data elements belonging to the same key field make up a "record." A key field controls the access to particular records.

There are two parts (Fig. 15–9) to most records: the master record (also called "owner") and subordinate records (also called "members"). The subordinate records are detail records or transactions that affect the master record. These subordinate records are a simple means of extending the size of the master file. This permits a variable number of subordinate records for each master record.

Consider the relationship between the customer order (Fig. 3–12A), the shipping order (Fig. 3–12B), and the invoice (Fig. 3–13). The data processing steps involved, once an order is secured through requesting reimbursement from the buyer, are processed independently. This is the reason files have been traditionally organized independently. A new order is placed on the shipping-order tape, deleted from that file, and then placed on the accounts receivable file when the shipment is satisfied, and so on.

Under the data base concept, a new order is added to the master record as another subordinate record. Information is added to the same record as the processing progresses; for example, backorders, partial shipments, and amount-due calculations with discounts. In other words, the majority of

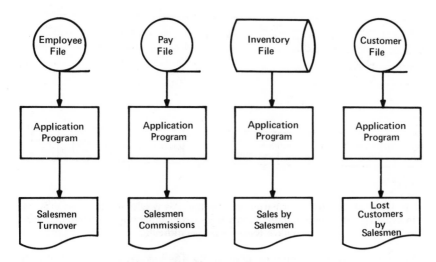

Traditional method where each application has its own file.

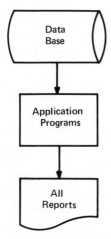

Fig. 15–7. Data base method makes all data available to any program from a single file.

information appears on the shipping order and the new information necessary for the invoice (item prices, their extensions, and discounts) is appended to existing data. The term "extending" denotes unit price times quantity minus discounts, to arrive at totals.

The master records are organized on disks in a sequential or random order. Records are located through a control field called a "key" data

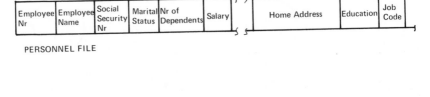

Employee Nr	Employee Name	Social Security Nr	Marital Status	Nr of Dependents	Salary		Home Address	Education	Job Code

PERSONNEL FILE

Employee Nr	Employee Name	Social Security Nr	Marital Status	Nr of Dependents	Salary		Check Mailing Address	Hours Worked	Gross Pay

PAYROLL FILE

Fig. 15–8. Duplicated information in multiple files results in increased expense in creating and updating data, causes inconsistency between file contents, and makes cross reference difficult.

element; this is the customer number in Fig. 15–9. Access to the subordinate records is provided by the disk address of each detail record. This tying together of related records is called "linkage."

Retrieving, adding, deleting, and changing records is a complex function. Each program having a need to use the data base would be proportionately larger if required to include this complex programming. To eliminate this duplicated effort, the application (or problem) program uses another program to provide linkage to the data base (Fig. 15–10) for communication. The application program can be modified or the data base can be reorganized or extended in size.

The development and operation of a data base is not so simple as this illustration would imply. In fact, many attempts have failed through not recognizing its complexity. Program packages to control the data base are available from computer manufacurers or software houses, which are companies that specialize in commonly used programs such as input and output functions. The linkage program between the application program and data base file has been called data base input-output control (DBIOC) because many packages are available under various names.

Section 24 deals with the factors of concern to management.

24. DATA BASE—CONCERN OF MANAGEMENT

The task of locating documents in manually kept files is simple when a small business starts. As the company grows, files become spread throughout the firm—personnel files in one department, payroll files in another

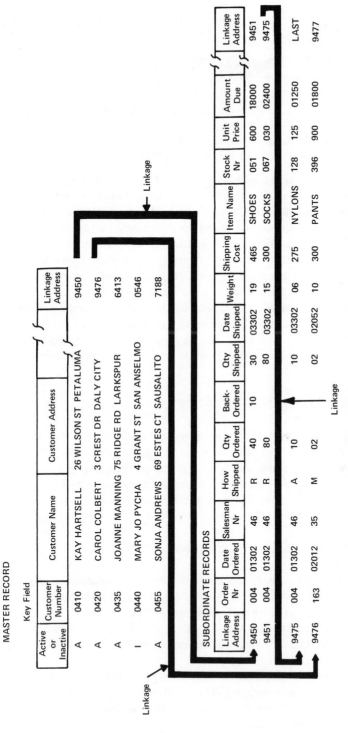

Fig. 15–9. Data base concept. Records may be linked to other records in the same file and files may be linked to other files.

341

Fig. 15–10. The problem program for different applications uses a special program to access information in the data base.

department, and so on. Finding records is time consuming as well as annoying. For example, the sales manager's time is spent pacifying a frustrated customer while his file is being located. The price paid for successful growth is unwieldy but necessary paperwork that slows down operations.

Manual handling and processing of the documents must eventually give way to mechanization in any growing company. Individual paper files are converted onto punched cards or magnetic tape for computer processing; this gives faster results as well as simplifying paperwork. Files are traditionally created and maintained separately according to application because the computer processes one application after another. In other words, there are personnel files, payroll files, inventory files, and the like. Organizing files by applications has advantages as well as drawbacks.

ADVANTAGES OF SEPARATE FILES

- If the payroll file, for instance, is destroyed or is in error, the processing of other applications can continue without interruption.
- Multiple files can be stored economically on tape.
- Separation of data processing assignments by applications is possible, therefore facilitating control and audit measures.

DISADVANTAGES OF SEPARATE FILES

- Much expense and effort is wasted in maintaining duplicate data stored on multiple files. By way of example: Redundant data items are entered for both personnel and payroll files as seen in Fig. 15–8.
- Inconsistencies are likely to exist between identical fields in different files. For example, an address change or deletion is made to one file and not to the other.
- Relationships are difficult to establish because of separate files. To cite one illustration: The number of laid-off employees is found in the personnel file, but their past overtime record must come from the payroll file.

- Management requests for special reports involving data from multiple files are expensive to satisfy.

Most of these disadvantages are resolved by consolidating all individual files into a single source, called a "data base." But the data base is not a panacea. There are arguments against as well as for data bases.

ADVANTAGES OF A DATA BASE

- There is less redundancy than in multiple files.
- Updating the data base is simpler and faster because there is only one file rather than multiple files.
- A single source of data is more valuable than data dispersed in multiple files.
- Inconsistencies are reduced or eliminated.
- Cross referencing is easy because data from different applications can be compared or combined.
- A consolidated file is potentially easier to control than multiple files.
- Savings should be evident in the long run because of the time reduced in updating a single file.

DISADVANTAGES OF A DATA BASE

- The programming needed to access and update the data base is complex, and the chance for error is increased accordingly.
- All corporate data is in the hands of fewer people; consequently, additional security measures to protect the information become vital.
- Accidental or deliberate change of data is easier with a data base, as opposed to multiple files where all files must be changed.
- The rebuilding of destroyed data can be an expensive undertaking.
- All work is at a standstill when the data base is unavailable because of program or hardware problems.
- Files previously maintained economically on tape are stored on more expensive direct-access devices, such as disk storage.

The decision to replace multiple files with a single data base is clearly not a straightforward solution. Furthermore, a data base could very well be the right road for one organization but the wrong one for another. Consequently, management must decide not only when the business can justify a data base, but also whether its organizational structure and operation would work better by using the data base.

Once the decision has been made to go the data-base route, management should become deeply involved before design is begun. The reason, of course, is because the stakes are high, and a large investment will be lost if the project fails. Even if the project is mildly successful, this means that major expectations were not reached; therefore, the cost involved may not have been worth the venture.

Beyond the investment lies the risk of computer disruption (see Section 26). For example, most companies do not have an alternate *backup* resource in case the computer operation is interrupted. If the computer operation halts for any number of reasons, the data base is unavailable for use and required information ceases to exist. How will the company survive? This bit of reality must be faced in the data-base decision and should be considered by weighing the consequences carefully mapped out; for instance:

- What would happen if customer orders had to be processed manually?
- How many additional people would be required in the manual backup system?
- Are manual procedures available? If not, how long would it take to develop them?
- Under a manual system, how much longer would the customer order be delayed than if handled by the present computerized methods?
- What results could be expected if customer orders were delayed?
- In a delayed fulfillment situation, what happens to the billing process, and how much money will be tied up in the extended period required to bill manually?

The foregoing considerations show that management has much to lose, as well as to gain, in going to a centralized data base. As might be expected, the data base is constructed essentially from the existing data stored in multiple files. However, the complexity of consolidating files should not be thought of as being an easy task. Design of the data base precedes any consolidation of files, and at least two things can lengthen the life of database usage. First, new areas that might be mechanized later can be anticipated if all portions of a company's operations are analyzed. If revisions to current applications are being considered, the long-run cost can be minimized by working them into the data base at the time of its development. Also, expansion and addition of new items to the data base will be less costly if considered in the initial design.

Much effort and time—a year or more in typical cases—go into constructing a data base. A common mistake is to place emphasis on the initial cost, for experience shows that the largest expenditure is in *maintaining* the data base once it is in use. It would not be unreasonable to estimate that the maintenance cost over the life of data base would exceed its original cost. This reason alone suggests that enthusiastic crash schedules be set aside in favor of a timetable that permits slow and extensive testing of the data base before completely relying on it.

In order to approach the data-base decision realistically, management must expand its knowledge of computer systems, since data-base techniques are different from former multiple-file processing. Managers should be more interested in the know-why and less in the know-how. It is common for management to wait until the project is in progress before questioning why something is designed in this particular way. By then it is too late to think about changing this and that in midstream. To avoid this trouble, managers can and should prepare before design is begun, by attending private executive seminars, computer vendor classes, and in-house training by staff members. In so doing, the "sell" pitch by vendors can be evaluated intelligently. Also, a wealth of information is found in articles written by people who have already been down the data-base trail. With this fund of knowledge, management can ask questions and weigh answers received, to determine if advice from staff and vendors is sound.

Some questions cannot be fully explored in the beginning. An ideal data base, for instance, would reflect both past and forecast information in addition to current operating data. Although ideal, the cost may very well prohibit the storage and processing of past and present data needed for prediction. On the other hand, managers must keep in mind that only data elements that are included in the data base can be retrieved, and it is they who set the requirements for information demands.

Data bases tend to grow and become cumbersome. Consequently, a large part of the data base investment will go for new storage devices, which vary widely in price and performance. To illustrate: The largest storage capacity, over 150 billion bytes, is available in data-cell storage (Fig. 13–7). Conversely, drum storage (Fig. 13–5) is faster, but its capacity is smaller than that of the data cell. On the other hand, disk storage (Fig. 12–5) gives the best combination of access time and mass storage. In other words, disk is faster than data cell storage and slower than drum storage, but it makes available more storage capacity than the drum and less than the data-cell device.

In determining the size of the data base, individual data items need examining and cross-referencing to each other to determine their dependency and interrelationship. Here is a sampling of such characteristics:

- What data elements should be stored? How much of each item is descriptive information, and how much is identification?
- What is the maximum size of the data elements, such as stock nomenclature? Should the description change, and if so, would the old one be saved for cross-referencing of orders that reflect the former nomenclature?
- What key fields will be used to locate data, and should individual data elements be retrieved or must the entire record be brought into internal memory?
- What is the expected rate of growth for the data base and how much will it cost to expand in order to keep up with the company's growth projections?

Other categories of considerations are of concern to management also. Some of those involving processing speeds and the security of data are:

- Will the present computer be adequate for retrieval and storage of the data base and at the same time be adequate to process current requirements?
- What are the alternatives if the data-base storage device becomes too crowded or too busy as a result of expansion? For instance, one alternative might be to transfer frequently accessed records onto the fast-access drum storage and leave less active records on the slower but less expensive disk, which also has a high storage capacity.
- What controls should be implemented to avoid unauthorized tampering with data? For example, false records can be easily recorded and subsequently eliminated to cover up an illegal transaction.
- What documentation and controls are necessary to keep track of changes to the data base and the programs needed to handle the data base?
- Is it economically feasible to include an audit trail in the data base? To illustrate: deleted records could be held in another area of the data base for historical reference. On the other hand, they might be recorded on less expensive magnetic tape and stored off line. When a change is made, the original record could be saved, but this is normally prohibited by excessive cost. Original data, such as former balances, usually has little value and therefore is destroyed.
- What management products are generated from the data base and, if they are necessary, should two or more reports be consolidated?

As you have seen, there are many arguments for and against constructing a data base. Therefore, management must weigh them against the cost to install and maintain the data base. The redundancy of data and the degree of relationships among multiple files are certainly key factors—but these alone should not be deciding factors. Before considering a data base, the performance of the present system should have been demonstrated to be inadequate or incapable of meeting demands. This section includes many of the positive as well as negative aspects of data bases. By investigating each, management is less likely to install an expensive system that does not do the job it was designed for.

25. THE IMPORTANCE OF CREATING TEST DATA

Too often, management's first order of business is started with the surprise greeting, "Morning Ed. Say, did you hear that the program-run the boss wanted for his ten o'clock meeting blew last night?" This embarrassment to the data processing operation can, in all likelihood, be traced to program instructions that worked correctly during testing but failed to give correct results under untried conditions. In other words, a type of input document that could not happen did in fact happen. Perhaps the program has been running successfully time after time, but one pitfall in programming is that a program fails when least expected and when needed most.

How can we tell if a program has been tested completely? One practice is to have the programmer perform extensive testing, either completely for a new program or only for the change if a modification is made. Then the program is passed to a testing section where it is tested for every possible condition in addition to its interaction with other programs in the system. This testing of all programs comprising a system is called "systems testing." To illustrate: The program that edits and formats input data for further processing is modified to put blanks in the required delivery date to signify a need for reassessment whenever the date is earlier than the current date. Before the modified program is activated, other programs must be geared to handle the required delivery-date field containing blanks. In other words, a change to one program may cause another program to blow—in this case a numeric field that suddenly contains blanks, which certainly is not numeric.

In discussing the importance and consequences of creating realistic test data, we shall concern ourselves with a single program rather than getting involved with multiple programs comprising a system. Let us cite a true example of how incompetent testing causes computer reruns, and then proceed to identify the characteristics of the accurate test data to be created.

An experienced programmer said that he had thoroughly tested a program to purge older-than-90-day transactions from a tape file. Upon closer questioning, the programmer indicated that his so-called conclusive test really consisted of an unchecked reel of output tape containing fewer transactions than the input reel. Which transactions were actually purged? He was not exactly sure, but he was confident that his program worked correctly because he seldom made mistakes. A conclusive test would include several transactions with dates less than 90 days old, dates more than 90 days old, one exactly 90 days, and another 91 days. A core dump or printout of the input and output tape would be manually compared and a final determination would be made as to the accuracy, after insuring that each transaction had been handled properly.

It is best to plan testing right from the start. This means that the art of creating acceptable test data begins with communication between the client or customer and the programmer or systems analyst. The customer has specified that there are to be no duplicate transactions.* Does this mean identical key fields (such as stock number) or records having the same information in all fields within the record? Does it mean that all records within the field are to be rejected as erroneous, or simply to keep one (which one?) and reject all others? Evidently there is much room for misinterpretation, and such instructions must be clearly defined before adequate test data is prepared so that the program will function as expected.

Other useful examples to demonstrate the creation of test data involve the use of arithmetic operations and editing of data. Let us assume that a statistical program is written to add "plus" numbers into one counter and "minus" numbers into another counter. The programmer punches -15 and $+15$ into two separate cards. The fact that the numbers print out as a negative 15 or positive 15 proves nothing conclusively. The program may be inadvertently adding minus numbers into the positive counter and plus numbers into the negative counter. A more accurate test would include, for example, the adding of $+22$ and $+33$ as well as adding -44 and -55. Because the values of these numbers are different, we could determine which test number entered which counter and whether the counter had added two or more numbers as intended. It is very easy to prove that a program can handle unintended conflicting data. If the user states that a certain field can never be negative, the programmer tries one or two records that will result in a negative total in order to see what happens. If the user states that the largest total in the inventory can be 675, then the programmer plans on at least one more position in anticipation, up to 9999, but in any case a larger number than 675.

*The "identical record" predicament is caused when a keypuncher makes an error, punches the record again, and forgets to destroy the incorrect record.

For every field edited for accuracy, a correct as well as incorrect field of data must be tried. For example: The Julian date should be 001 to 365, except for a leap year. Values on both sides must be tested; consequently, try 000, 367, a minus number, and several numbers within the range to definitely include 001 and 365.

Obviously, creating test data and evaluating the results needs only simple common sense. Nevertheless, getting people to do just that is an ever-present challenge to managers and an experience for those who must use computer-generated results that have not been adequately tested.

SECURITY
OF THE INSTALLATION

26. HOW SERIOUS IS THE THREAT OF COMPUTER DISASTERS?

The trend a decade ago was to set up the computer site as a showcase. Guided tours were happily arranged and proud companies displayed their computer status symbol to invite public attention. People were intrigued by this pleasant-looking room full of expensive machines with fascinating, flashing lights. Companies seemed to feel that this was the epitome of good customer relations.

Things changed almost overnight. The computer became a symbol of the "establishment" and big business—an image of poor repute today. Hiding the computer behind cement walls quickly became the trend of the future, prompted by lurid headlines in the news media.

News media are constantly reporting spectacular disasters to the data processing operation, sometimes intentional, sometimes by accident. Here are some of the incidents that cause widespread management concern.

Tours to See the Computer. A lady in a group being guided through a data processing installation took a punched card as a souvenir. The card could have represented $5 or $500, or even part of a program. A Boy Scout troop on tour ended with most of the firms magnetic tapes unintentionally erased. One Boy Scout had methodically raked a magnet along a tape storage rack.

Fire and Riots. Students destroyed $2 million worth of computer equipment at George Washington University. The machines can be replaced, but not the research data and the programs representing untold man-years to create. More damage is caused by accidental fires, however, than any other type of catastrophe.

Vandalism. It cost $100,000 to reconstruct a thousand tapes that were erased by magnets after an antiwar group ransacked Dow Chemical Corporation's research computer center. Millions of dollars are lost annually by other companies in similar ways.

Dissatisfied Employees. A bitter employee, when notified of being laid off, removed the identification labels from 1500 magnetic tape reels. It cost thousands of dollars to re-identify the data. Unhappy employees may very well be the greatest risk of all.

Unforeseeable Accidents. As many as 80,000 records were damaged when a repairman left his magnet-flashlight stuck to a magnetic data-storage drum.

Some managers feel incidents such as these were isolated and could not happen to them, and therefore do not take protection of the computer seriously. Others say that it is impossible to stop all disasters; besides, it is too expensive. The objective of security is, in reality, a measure to minimize errors at minimal cost. It is a business risk assumed by all ventures that pay off in the future, just like insurance or any other profit-making scheme. Thus it is management's responsibility to safeguard company assets, both data files and the computer installation.

The critical question is whether a firm can continue to transact its business if the computer operation is disrupted. This depends upon the company. To cite two examples: The primary product of a business that sells addresses of potential customers is its address file. Once the information is gone, can it be replaced? In a second example: The accounts receivable file is the item with largest value in some firms. Will the company go bankrupt if the data is lost? What impact would loss of data have upon a business if it were unable to prepare bills for several days or weeks?

Aside from spectacular disasters worthy of news stories, thousands of less costly damage and disruptions do happen in computer centers. They are caused by fire, dissatisfied employees, riots, sabotage, floods, earthquakes, hurricanes, and so on. Accordingly, management must balance the cost of preparation against the chances it is willing to take.

27. PROTECTION OF THE COMPUTER INSTALLATION

Only hindsight will reveal the impact of interrupted computer services and the value of data files. An ounce of prevention is worth . . . what? Here are some precautions that management should think about and which are generally worth their cost.

MINIMIZE FIRE THREATS

Lessons were learned from the famous Pentagon fire in 1959, the first major loss in a computer complex. Three large computers and over 5000 reels of tape were reduced to a charred heap. Investigation revealed considerable lack of planning, and the lessons learned have served to set protection standards in use today. A large light bulb left on beneath a combustible ceiling by an electrician started the blaze. The master power switch was located in a locked room, so the air conditioning fanned the fire. Also, smoke was vented through ducts everywhere. Firemen were forced to pour water on still running electrical gear. Other findings: wooden walls and doors, absence of emergency fire hoses, delay in notifying the fire department, and more.

Other major fires have revealed shortcomings equally disturbing. For example, one large and complex computer site had a power switch that turned off all power, including the power to the fire pumps. Other entirely noncombustible computer sites have survived damage while floors above blazed, only to be destroyed when these higher floors collapsed and dropped into the fail-safe computer room.

A few thought-provoking topics of major concern are listed below. While reading these, you will undoubtedly think of other safety planning.

1. The computer installation will be safer in a separate, single-story building constructed of reinforced concrete. Walls, doors, ceilings, and furniture should be noncombustible. Fire and smoke detectors will be more effective if placed also in false ceilings and floors housing electrical wiring.

2. If two or more computers are in the installation, they should be in separate rooms.

3. Tapes and disk packs are kept in fireproof vaults. Backup information (see Section 28) is stored at another location.

4. Fire-fighting procedures should be practiced regularly by computer operators. Fire alarms can be hooked directly to the fire department. Power shut-off switches for the computer and air-conditioning equipment are best located near the computer (recall the Pentagon fiasco mentioned above).

5. Plastic covers have saved many computers from water damage, especially in minor fires. Computers otherwise undamaged by fires and explosions have been put out of commission by fire sprinklers or fire fighting, and even water seepage from pipe breakage in floors above.

6. Water drains should be installed below false floors (Fig. 12–2), covering a maze of hopefully fireproof electrical cables, thus preventing flooding of the computer.

MINIMIZE SABOTAGE

Threats of physical violence at the computer site are difficult to prevent these days. Underground newspapers from antiwar groups publish directions on how to wreck computers. Saboteurs have even trained as programmers and joined the company to create disaster from within.

Elaborate security measures can be costly, ranging from magnetic sensors to closed-circuit television (around $25,000) used for surveillance. Many companies place guards at data processing entrances to control access. To illustrate the striking security sensitivity of many businesses: A complete security system was installed by a California bank for $200,000. In addition, it spends a whopping $35,000 every month to operate the system. In another illustration: An airline spent $100,000 for backup generators to prevent electrical failures from disrupting its flight reservations system. Power failures do happen—recall the New York area blackout in 1965 that brought nine states to a halt.

Here are some less costly prevention measures:

1. Computers are no longer safe as a display item. Fragile showcases are being replaced with reinforced concrete. Buildings that house computers are no longer tempting when obvious identification signs are removed.
2. Tours should be eliminated. If necessary to enhance customer relations, the number in the party should be escorted in small groups of four to six by a data processing representative. Programs, data input, and printouts should be kept out of reach from the tourist.
3. Access to the computer room must be restricted. Intrusion comes most often after normal operating hours, so tamper-resistant doors are a "must." Entrance to the computer room by unauthorized persons can be prevented by double doors that are separated by a small waiting room. An individual is held between both locked doors until a computer operator verifies his identification tag. Otherwise, the intruder is confined until he can be questioned or apprehended.
4. Visits to office buildings are now being controlled by guards. Employees have permanent identification badges with their photographs. Visitors wear a temporary badge and the person they are visiting is responsible for the visitors' whereabouts and activities. Access to the computer room is limited to special-colored badges for those with a need to be there, such as computer operators. Even programmers or vice-presidents cannot enter the computer site in some firms. After all, when security steps are taken, why compromise the system?
5. Internal malice is impossible to stop. In one case the computer gave incorrect results for days before it was suspected that the troubles went deeper than normal malfunction. It was discovered

that someone knew how to switch a particular wire in a circuit card, one that was difficult to trace and isolate as a hardware malfunction. This incident might have been avoided had management policy prohibited an employee's access to the computer room once he had been given notice that his services were no longer required.

Threats toward computer security come from outside sources *and* from within. Fire and weather also pose a threat not to be taken lightly. The design, location, and layout of the EDP site can reduce the possibility of external and internal sabotage, riot or fire damage, and weather hazards. The most difficult problem to control is the spiteful employee who was not promoted or is laid off. Instinct and questionable circumstances play perhaps the largest role. For example, sabotage can come in small doses, posing the question, "Is it accidental or intentional?" (Section 28 discusses this further.) Background checks may reveal radical activities in a potential employee's life, but they seldom pinpoint the more frequent threat, an employee who feels a firm has treated him unfairly. Background investigations are expensive and are subject to the invasion of privacy question.

Management awareness that hazards do exist in the computer complex, which could cripple the organization, is a vital step in holding down disasters. The degree of security varies with each firm. To cite an example of loose security: I know of one computer system that is visible through huge glass walls facing a very busy street in a major city. Users are sometimes on the second floor while no one is on the first floor where the computer is located. Yet, entrance to the impressive showcase is free to anyone through unlocked doors. It has been this way for years—day, night, weekends. Although no misfortunes have happened in the cited case, there is no assurance that they might not occur. The lesson is plain: The greater the preparation against hostile acts, the less the risk of disaster.

28. SECURITY OF PROGRAMS AND DATA FILES

Full protection against losses from fraud, accidental destruction of data or programs, and other hazards is near impossible. So, why bother with preventive measures? Every new case that comes to light seems to be a clever attempt that security planners did not contemplate. Just as management is caught off guard with a lack of controls, people should be aware that hidden controls exist throughout the system. New controls are being devised daily, which increase the risk of a saboteur's being caught.

On the other hand, if management is reluctant to press security seriously, it can expect ever-increasing attempts to upset the installation. It takes very little manipulation to alter the profit picture, whether it be by accident or intentional. What motivates employees to behave in a way detrimental to the company's well-being?

First, an employee may feel that companies make too much money. So, why not share the wealth? Second, almost any person can be *bought*, regardless of his background or position. Third is the desire to "get even" with the company because management has treated him unfairly. Fourth, we have the unintentional errors. As a start, management ought to make its employees aware of the real value of information they handle and what its loss means to the company, in terms of profits that must be realized in order to pay salaries and bonus awards.

Disasters by accident do not publically surface easily. In many cases, the employee is simply reprimanded or is quietly fired. In other cases, intentional disasters are sometimes revealed if the company's image does not suffer. There are many times that companies will not prosecute cases of theft because of adverse publicity. For example, to admit that a bank employee stole funds is admitting that public funds are not safe in that bank. Here are some diverse cases that can and do happen. They illustrate why security should be of day-to-day concern at all levels of management.

- A programmer can alter a bank's programs so that his checking account is bypassed during the processing of bad checks. He is therefore free to write checks in excess of his balance.
- Stock exchange prices can be raised or lowered by inserting a special subroutine that adjusts a particular stock each time it is quoted. This creates selling or buying pressure, allowing purchase at the desired price and unloading at an inflated price.
- A customer account can be opened under an assumed name. Merchandise can then be shipped to the fictitious company. Afterward, the program modification is eliminated, thus returning the program to its original state.
- An employee's pay record can be set up under a fictitious name, allowing a check to be made out to this assumed person.
- A file containing valuable information—for example, the names and addresses of companies' customers—can be copied and sold to a competitive firm.

Controls making accidental or intentional hazards more difficult to carry out is a *must*. For example, procedures should be inserted throughout a system to show that people and the hardware are acting according to the wishes of management. Three basic categories involved in a processing cycle need protective measures: the programs, the data files, and the computer operation. Each is discussed separately in Sections 29, 30, and 31.

29. PROTECTING THE PROGRAMS

Programs are more susceptible to misuse and unauthorized changes than any other area. Their size and complexity offer the best comfort of safety to anyone wanting to embezzle badly enough. Even vice-presidents have been caught altering programs in order to cover up theft of company funds. To make matters worse, the possibility of anyone discovering the misuse of production programs is small if the person is both an expert in programming and clever at scheming. How do we protect programs?

Off-site storage of a firm's programs is the easiest of all security controls. Yet, many computer installations, both private and government, do not take this precaution. Programs represent many man-years of work. So, keeping duplicate backup decks of programs at another location is cheap insurance against theft or catastrophe. Moreover, programs are preserved in case of disaster and operations can be resumed quickly. Of course duplicate programs must be kept up to date, which means replacing out-of-date programs with the new versions.

Monitoring of program changes offers the best control against unauthorized routines being inserted for personal gain. Program changes should be numbered and approved after they are written up. The control number can be inserted along with the source COBOL statement stored on disk (Fig. 15–11). Records are thus kept of added, deleted, and changed source statements. These are printed periodically so that they can be analyzed for identification of illegal program changes. Documentation is a "must" if program modification is to be effectively controlled.

While it is common for all programmers to have access to all programs, access to sensitive data should be limited to those programmers having a need in their areas of responsibility. For example, responsibility for one programmer may involve computation of pay, whereas another programmer formats the data names and addresses, and a third programmer prints the checks. Access to these three segments of a whole program, referred to as "modules," is regulated through keywords furnished to the computer by control cards (explained in Chapter 14). The keyword is checked against a table of information, which identifies each module. When the check verifies the keyword, access to the program is granted. The keywords, of course, should be changed frequently for tighter control.

Unannounced production programs should be run periodically according to a random rotating schedule. Using test data that gives known results

```
04391   COMPUTE-GROSS-PAY-ROUTINE.
04392   MULTIPLY REGULAR-HOURS BY PAYRATE GIVING REGULAR-PAY.        73-001 365
04393   MULTIPLY OVERTIME-HOURS BY PAYRATE GIVING PARTIAL-OT.
04394   MULTIPLY PARTIAL-OT BY 1.5 GIVING OVERTIME-PAY.              72-434 031
04395   ADD REGULAR-PAY OVERTIME-PAY GIVING GROSS-PAY.
04396   MOVE GROSS-PAY TO GROSS-PAY-PRINTOUT.
04397   COMPUTE-NET-PAY-ROUTINE.
04398   SUBTRACT TOTAL-DEDUCTIONS FROM GROSS-PAY
04399        GIVING NET-PAY.                                         72-434 031
04400   MOVE NET-PAY TO NET-PAY-PRINTOUT.
```

COBOL statements

Statement number

Year

Change Nr.

Julian day
of compile

Fig. 15–11. Control of changes to the payroll program.

357

is reasonable assurance that unauthorized changes have not been programmed. Additional accuracy is insured by having auditors verify the printed output. In this technique, the output can be compared against the known results to insure that unauthorized program changes are not present.

30. PROTECTING THE DATA FILES

The value of computer-stored information is often underestimated. Once it is lost, it may be too late to think how and if it can be replaced. The circumstances causing data loss, or who was responsible, are of little importance at this stage. Management should be concerned *beforehand* as to how much it will cost if the company has to reconstruct the data files and what the company will do in the meantime.

Protection of data from the point of collection through distribution of the results is of vital concern. Controls are sometimes so inadequate that they are nonsensical. For example, consider two vice-presidents who are present in the computer room when the financial statement for the firm is being listed. When finished, they grab the printed output and quickly depart. The tapes containing the financial health of the company are left mounted on the tape units. Consequently, security effectiveness lies more in the hands of honest operators than it does in effective controls. It would have been simple for an employee to rerun the financial tape and hand over confidential information to a rival company interested perhaps in negotiating a merger.

As with programs, backup data in case recovery procedures are needed is a must. Three cycles of complete processing are normally kept for safety insurance. This concept is referred to as the "grandfather-father-son" backup scheme (Fig. 15–12). The most recently updated cycle, called the "son" files, are backed up by the two preceding generations of processing. It is possible to fall back on the "father" cycle, or if this had errors, an additional backup exists in the "grandfather" file.

It is important that files of the very last cycle be used in the current update processing. To prevent using an older file, labels (see Chapter 11) containing identification, such as job number and date, are written at the beginning of tape and disk files. These identification labels, which are handled by the computer software, also serve as a control to prevent erasing an active file. No processing takes place until the labels have been checked. A tape or disk file label not agreeing with information the program is attempting to access causes processing to halt.

Unauthorized access to data files can be prevented in two basic ways, external and internal controls. First, a person is usually made responsible

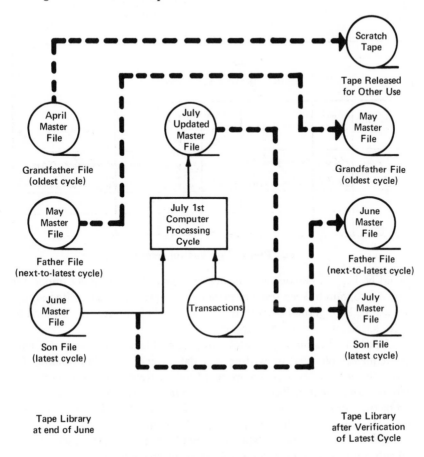

Fig. 15–12. Grandfather-father-son concept.

for issuing tapes and disk packs stored in the library vault. The librarian maintains a list of employees who have permission to sign out individual data files. A tape-control record (Fig. 15–13) is kept on files leaving the library; thus, accountability is stressed.

Second, a program must identify a file before accessing is permitted on that file. Labels recorded on disk or tape, as previously mentioned, perform this function. Keyword is another field included in labels (Fig. 15–14). The security keyword is used to prevent unauthorized entry into files containing sensitive data, such as payroll files. Before access is granted, the user must know the keyword. The operating system looks for the keyword, which is furnished usually through job control cards. If unavailable, or if the comparison is unsuccessful, the file cannot be accessed.

Besides the keyword control, which should be changed often, a record

			TAPE LIBRARY			
			RECORD OF REEL LOCATION			
Serial Nr. of Reel	Job Nr.	File Name	Loaned and Returned			Intended Use
			To	Out	In	
046	P640	Earnings to date	Kay	1015 JULY 6	1100 JULY 6	Production run
125	C177	Customer Names	Barb	1030 JULY 6		Purge old accounts

Fig. 15–13. Tape control record.

should be kept of persons attempting to access files containing important data. A program to keep track of persons attempting to read limited-access files can be kept permanently in the computer. This control can be used to detect suspicious usage or tampering.

Updating files on disk creates a unique problem in that data elements are frequently changed by writing new data over the old information. Of course this action destroys the original version. Recovery of programming errors or equipment malfunctioning that might erase both old and new data can be overcome by recording the data before and after changes. An audit trail is thus left, providing a history of file changes.

Controls over original data entry should be monitored closely. It is a difficult job to distinguish, for example, if an unwanted entry is really an accident or intentional. To cite an example: Loss of revenue can occur in processing accounts receivables simply by misspelling a name, say, Freidman instead of Freeman. Or an account number can be transcribed in error. Controls can be established to insure accuracy throughout data processing operations by using batch control totals, credit limit checking, hash totals, consistency checks, and other validation techniques. These terms are explained in the Glossary at the end of the book.

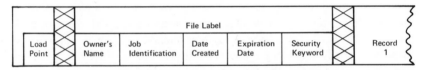

Fig. 15–14. File identification label at the beginning of disk and tape files.

31. PROTECTING THE COMPUTER OPERATION

Factors that cause concern in the computer room range from the equipment's not being operational to problems that result in accidental or intentional processing with damaging effects.

To emphasize the magnitude of problems with an illustration on the lighter side: A pretty girl wearing a nylon miniskirt and strutting past the blinking computer may be a pleasant sight for the eye, but it is bad news for the hardware. Dropped bits in memory, which cause parity errors (see Chapter 7), have been reported. The phenomenon is caused by static electricity built up by the nylon as she walks.

Limited access to the computer room naturally reduces the possibility of outside tampering with data files and programs. Accountability is consequently where it should be—with the operations' supervisor and his operators. A bonus from this control is reduction of chance operator errors through less interruptions.

Rotating duties lessens the chance of too much control being in the hands of a single operator. Overspecialization can result in an ingenious operator manipulating data for personal gain, or a clever operator can bypass controls built to circumvent illegal activities.

Programs and internal data can, and have been, altered through the console. By knowing where to look and what to change in the operating system (see Chapter 14), any program or data file wanted by the operator can be called from disk. He can also bypass disk and label checks designed to limit access to data files.

Separating duties is a *must*. Most installations do not permit programmers to operate the computer nor do they allow operators to have access to programs. A step toward removing temptation is not to leave source programs listings and documentation lying around. It is a very common sight in computer installations to see program listings and documentation on open shelves or on a programmer's desk.

Procedures can be implemented to handle *sensitive* processing, such as the company's financial condition, or to verify important processing with value, such as the payroll. As checks are written, another tape can be written, containing the same information. A different operator (better still, on another shift) then has the responsibility for running a program to compare the checks written on the tape with a tape file that contains a record of legal check recipients.

Equipment backup agreements with similar firms is a precaution so that essential computer operations can continue in case of maintenance problems, fire, unexpected work loads, and so on. Trial runs should be practiced regularly by each installation to make sure both computers are compatible. Unless both computers have identical software, auxiliary input-output devices, memory size, etc., the backup may be meaningless. In other words, it is unwise to make a backup agreement, and then forget about it. The installation being depended upon may increase its workload to the point where support is impossible; worse still, it may change its hardware.

TECHNOLOGY
AND FUTURE
DEVELOPMENTS

32. FUTURE TRENDS IN COMPUTER ARCHITECTURE

Two supercomputers hold promise of influencing new architecture in the fourth generation of commercial computers. Both the STAR-80 (STring ARray) and ILLIAC (ILLInois Array Computer) are radically different in *design* from conventional computers (Fig. 15–15), and in fact are different from each other. Whereas conventional computers perform only one operation at a time, the new concepts permit millions of computations simultaneously. In this fashion, the supercomputers act like many small computers, all operating at the same time. The notion is that two computers work twice as fast and, to overcome the double cost, more than one arithmetic unit should be driven by only one control unit.

Several speed kings of the third-generation stereotype computers belong to the MIPS (million instructions per second) club. For a short time the Control Data CDC–6600 held the world's speed record at 2 to 5 MIPS. Soon it would be performing I/O operations for its faster sister, the CDC–7600, capable of executing from 10 to 25 MIPS. Computers as powerful as these were designed to solve difficult problems where faster speeds and large memory capacity were of prime importance.

Just what uses do these mammoth machines serve? Primarily, they are used for controlling air traffic, predicting weather, large-scale agriculture planning, allocation of natural resources, and similar wide-range projects. However, they have commercial uses also. For example: The S360/195 delivered to the Mellon National Bank in Pittsburgh replaced 22 computers, including two 7074 and six 1401 second-generation computers, two S360/65, and several S360/30 third-generation computers. The S360/195 has some impressive characteristics: It has four million bytes of main memory, enough to handle all instructions for a space mission; it executes an instruction in 54 billionths of a second, or the time it takes light to travel 53 feet; and it controls 500 remote data terminals. All this capability can be purchased for the modest sum of $7 to $12 million or rented for $165,000 to $300,000 a month.

The $10 million CDC STAR computer is in the 100 MIPS class (from 15

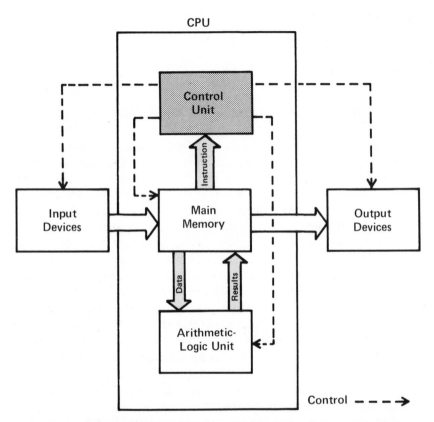

Fig. 15–15. Computer design includes four components under the supervision of
a fifth unit—the control unit. Steps in computing are: (1) The control unit
fetches an arithmetic instruction from memory and determines what has to be
done; (2) the control unit moves the data into the arithmetic unit; (3) the
arithmetic unit computes the data under directions from the control unit; (4) the
control unit returns the results to memory.

to 700) and operates ten times faster than the S360/195. The STAR is
capable of handling tens of thousands of remote data terminals. Massive
on-line data bases in excess of ten billion bytes are available to users such
as banks or insurance companies. To give an idea of the size of such memory
requirements, the STAR could store and access the combined names and
telephone numbers in all United States cities. The first of four planned STAR
systems was built for the Lawrence Radiation Laboratory at Livermore,
California, near San Francisco.

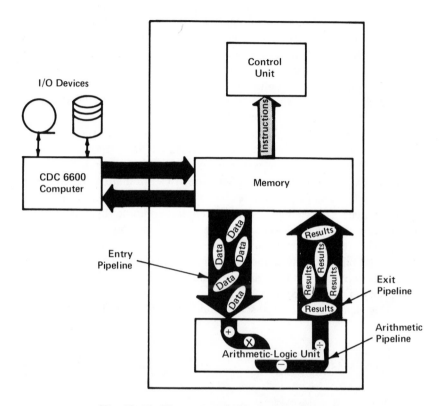

Fig. 15–16. The CDC STAR-80 pipeline computer.

The technology of STAR centers around a concept referred to as "pipeline processing." The pipeline technique means that an array of numbers arranged in a string (hence the acronym STAR for STring ARray) are constantly streaming through a pipeline between memory and the arithmetic units (Fig. 15–16). This implies that many different arithmetic operations are being calculated at one time in a production-line atmosphere. That is, one part of a lengthy instruction, consisting of many parts, is executed in a specialized unit and then passed to another unit that performs still another type of processing in assembly-line fashion. Present-day computers execute an instruction in its entirety (fetch the instruction, decode it, retrieve the data from memory, compute in the arithmetic unit, and return the results to memory) before starting another. Contrariwise, the STAR retrieves a string of numbers from memory and sends the data through the pipeline for processing. Before processing is completed on the first set of data, the next set is sent on its way through the pipeline. Thus, maximum speed and efficiency are achieved when the exit pipeline is returning results to memory at the same time that new sets of data are entering the arithmetic unit. The arithmetic unit is also built in a pipeline fashion so that many pairs of numbers in a stream can be calculated in an assembly-line manner. Thus, the pipeline between memory and processing is filled with instructions and data in various stages of completion.

Not since the experimental Mark I and ENIAC has there been a computer that came close to the physical size of the mammoth ILLIAC IV (Fig. 15–17). This 80-foot giant was jointly built by Burroughs Corporation and the University of Illinois for NASA at a cost of $24 million. Upon completion at Paoli, Illinois, ILLIAC IV was moved to NASA's Research Center at Mountain View, California, not far from the STAR installation. Whereas the STAR is a pipeline computer, the ILLIAC is a parallel computer. That is, the computer steps—retrieving data from memory, compute the data, and return the result to memory—are performed at one time, but on many operations in different subcomputers—hence the term "parallel processing." Speed of one billion computations a second is achieved by additional control units, each having 64 independent arithmetic-logic units. The one-trillion bit memory is partitioned into 256 memory banks, one for each of the 256 processing elements. The large-scale Model B–6500 computer (Fig. 15–18)

Fig. 15–17. The ILLIAC IV parallel computer. (Courtesy of Burroughs Corporation.)

performs all input and output for the ILLIAC IV and sends data to one of the four control units. Each processing element (PE) can access data in another PE memory bank.

The control unit of the ILLIAC, which works much like third-generation computer control units, decodes the instruction but relies upon one of the 64 PEs to carry out the execution. The ILLIAC is a marked departure from conventional architecture in that many instructions are executed together, rather than one at a time. This potential speed of one billion computations a second means that 24-hour weather forecasting can be made more accurately because simulation of weather models that takes 25 days on present computers can be done in a few hours. The ILLIAC relies upon another computer, the Burroughs B6500, for I/O operations. No small computer itself, the B6500 is five times faster than the next largest B5500. The B6500 not only decides which of the four control units in the ILLIAC is free to accept data, but also does program compiling for ILLIAC.

At first glance, the STAR and ILLIAC appear only slightly faster than other third-generation speed kings, but the speeds are misleading because of the difference in processing methods brought about by the pipeline and parallel techniques. Although CDC 6600, CDC 7600, and IBM S360/195 perform some operations faster than the two supercomputers, the STAR at maximum performance can outperform over one-hundred CDC 6600s because of its many subcomputers.

The STAR offers advances over the serial processing design of present computers through its pipeline approach. The ILLIAC offers still different advances through its parallel method of processing. The STAR, because of its capability to handle hundreds of 64-bit operands in a single instruction, has an advantage over the ILLIAC because it has to execute fewer instructions in problem solving. On the other hand, ILLIAC's parallel processing allows faster processing on certain operations. For example, the ILLIAC multiplies faster than the STAR, but the STAR can divide faster. Comparable performance is difficult to assess because it all depends on the kind of problem one is talking about. The speed, therefore, appears to be a standoff.

Designs of both the ILLIAC and STAR developmental computers will likely be featured in future fourth-generation models. Although both have limited uses at present, it remains to be seen whether their sophisticated design and innovations are suitable for the relatively simple commercial market. Their future hinges to a large extent upon the nature of their programming, which differs radically from present approaches.

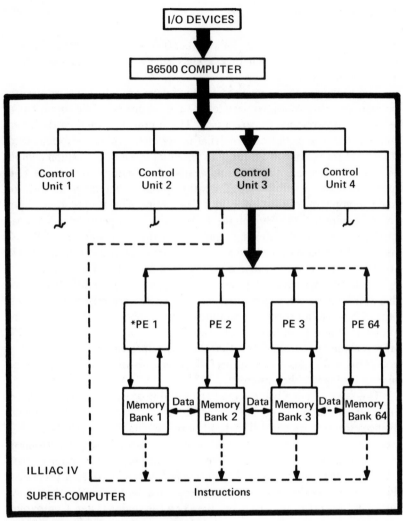

*PE (PROCESSING ELEMENT) USED FOR
ARITHMETIC LOGICAL OPERATIONS.

Fig. 15–18. The B6500 computer performs all input and output and sends data to one of the four control units of the ILLIAC IV supercomputer for processing. Each processing element (PE) can access data in other PE memory banks.

33. WHAT MANAGEMENT SHOULD KNOW ABOUT VIRTUAL STORAGE

Virtual memory (see Chapter 13) is a term applied to an arrangement in which the amount of main high-speed memory appears to be unlimited. This permits programs to be written and run on the computer as if main memory were larger than it actually is. The technique entails bringing in parts of programs and the data needed by those program segments from the external storage of the lower-speed, on-line drum or disk and placing them in the internal memory of the computer. The concept was first used in the Atlas computer at Manchester University, England. Burroughs Corporation borrowed the technique for use in its B5000 series computers in the 1960s, and others, such as RCA, have used it since then. Now IBM appears headed in the virtual storage direction for all of their improved S/370 line.

Aside from the fact that virtual storage has been effectively used for some time, management should seek an answer to the question, "Why now?" Virtual storage provides a new dimension for programming, but at a cost. First, virtual storage is a solution for certain problems, but not for all. For example, large programs having big segments that are used infrequently will find it advantageous because the occasionally used chunks can be kept on lower-cost disk and brought into main memory as needed. Managing the task of transferring data or program segments between disk (referred to as "virtual" storage) and the central processor's internal memory (referred to as "real" storage) is the responsibility of the operating system; therefore, the programmer is relatively detached from the process. However, the swapping process, or "paging," as it is called, is made possible by a combination of new hardware and software features, thus incurring a higher cost for the user. In addition, its efficiency is not so great as it might seem because the newer operating systems required by virtual storage are larger than for a system without virtual storage.

But there is good news also for virtual storage users! The earlier IBM DOS (disk operating system) partitioned main memory into three areas. The newer DOS/VS has been enlarged to five partitions. Whether IBM will continue to support DOS, thus forcing users into DOS/VS, remains to be seen. The more powerful operating system has two versions, called OS/VS1 and OS/VS2; the OS/VS1 has 15 fixed-size partitions, and OS/VS2 can run up to 63 jobs at the same time in variable-size regions.

Virtual storage permits running large jobs that could not be run previously without stepping up to bigger memory. However, program efficiency is not improved. Programmers can now experiment with techniques that eat up storage, and this increase in program size will cause the job to run proportionately longer and hence is more costly. In addition, sloppy programming habits that formerly increased program size, and accordingly decreased computer run times, will still exist. Lazy or inefficient programmers will simply have more memory to juggle. Therefore, managers must exercise closer supervision of programs because larger programs made possible by virtual storage take longer processing time, increasing operating cost considerably.

One of the biggest drawbacks to virtual storage is that swapping parts of programs and data back and forth between main memory and disk results in unproductive computer usage, also increasing operating cost. It is imperative that controls be implemented to keep program sizes within the real memory whenever possible.

In summary: Virtual storage offers business the advantages of using more powerful operating systems and designing larger programs without investing in added hardware. On the other hand, management must anticipate and prevent problems that accompany virtual storage, such as the longer run times caused by the scheme that makes virtual storage possible.

34. IMPACT OF MINICOMPUTERS

Imagine an attorney, a secretary, or a vice-president writing a program to get exactly what he wants instead of having to translate and communicate his needs to a programmer! This sounds much like a salesman's pitch, but it is the thinking of many newly indoctrinated minicomputer users. Businessmen are reporting that they can spend an hour a day getting the most out of the computer themselves, leaving the remainder of the day to running their business. Contrast this to teaching your company's affairs to a new programmer each time a well-trained person moves on. Then the programmer has to try producing what you want.

The minicomputer mainframe, without input and output devices, costs as little as $5000 and as much as $60,000, excluding I/O peripherals. As more peripherals (card reader, disk, etc.) are added, cost rises to maximum. However, the general classification of minicomputers puts the top price at $25,000, so that most models are available well under the maximum range. The physical size of the "mini," as they are called, varies from models that fit on desk tops to models as large as a refrigerator. The mini's popularity can, to a great degree, be attributed to the steady downtrend in cost, which is now one-third less than it was five years ago (Fig. 15–19). Another attraction, following close behind price, is its simplicity, which permits office personnel to use the mini after only a few days of training, rather than requiring computer-skilled people.

Today, minicomputers are finding their way into businesses that never

Fig. 15–19. The General Automation 18/30 minicomputer systems come in small and large versions, giving small businessmen computing power. (Courtesy of General Automation.)

dreamed of being able to afford computer assistance, such as real estate and law offices. The mini aids realtors in keeping track of tenants' rent payments, vacancies, and revenue. Law practices reduce operating cost by storing the contents of repetitive letters and having the mini print them as needed. Even the date of the letter is computer-generated, and the legal secretary can enter data variables. Instead of personal dictation, an attorney selects relevant, preformatted paragraphs stored in the mini's memory, and nonstandard material is inserted wherever necessary. In addition, the mini performs the bookkeeping chores. The result is that one bookkeeper is able to do the accounting work of three people and one typist turns out the work of three or four typists with the assistance of the mini. Turnover of personnel is of less concern because a new person can be trained in about two days.

In still other uses, the desk-top mini has found its way into individual classrooms because of the low cost and the fact that the mini can be used without previous computer exposure. Now students can see what they are doing as they do it. If a mistake is made, the mini notifies the student and either shows him the right way or displays an easier problem.

The expandable mini configuration has upward mobility to small-scale computer systems when the business outgrows the mini. A case in point is the IBM System 3 (Fig. 15–20), announced in 1969 to fulfill the data processing needs of small companies. A typical first-time candidate for the small computer is a current user of accounting machines or the mini, or a growing

Fig. 15–20. The IBM System 3 small-scale computer. (By permission of IBM.)

business that rents computer time through the timesharing technique explained in Chapter 14. The System 3 *card-oriented* computer (Fig. 15–20) starts at about $1000 a month and rental ranges upward, depending upon optional features such as increased memory capacity or addition of disk-storage capability.

Operating expenses are held to a minimum, since one person can serve both as programmer and operator. Little programming experience is necessary because programs are written normally in the Report Program Generator language (RPG) rather than more sophisticated languages that require additional skill and computer knowledge. A program is created in RPG by coding the job specifications of the processing desired onto RPG coding forms. The specifications consist of defining the fields to be printed and totals to be tabulated. Then the specifications are keypunched into cards and the RPG compiler creates a program from the punched specifications. Then it is a simple task to feed the program along with the data to be processed into the System 3. Improvements have expanded input and output capabilities from the new type of card (Fig. 15–21) to the CRT (cathode-ray tube), disk and tape storage, and forms of direct data entry such as optical and magnetic character readers. The IBM 96–column card contains 32 punch positions. The coding scheme is the same as the binary coded decimal (BCD) described in Chapter 7.

Management of small companies is turning to minicomputers in growing numbers because the low-cost and simple-to-operate mini can be used

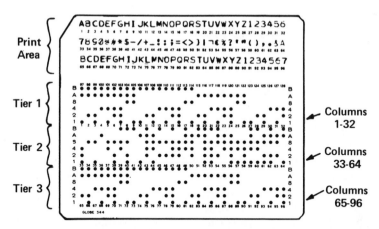

Fig. 15–21. The IBM 96-column card, successor to the Hollerith 80-column card. (By permission of IBM.)

without incurring the heavy cost of an EDP staff. Current computer users have centralized their computers in many instances, to meet rising EDP operations. It is quite obvious, therefore, that the minicomputer is likely to effect reversal of this trend because numerous minis cost much less than a larger computer of equivalent computing power. Although mini prices have fallen by one-third in the past five years and are expected to come down by at least another 50 percent in this decade, a mini-system price can be deceiving. One reason is that input and output peripherals often cost more than the mini mainframe itself. Nevertheless, the minicomputer will remain a logical stepping stone from a manual system to the first computer system.

SOCIETY
AND THE COMPUTER

35. FINDING HAPPINESS IN DATA BANKS

A data bank is a collection of all known information about people in a single location. There is great concern these days that centralized information puts excessive power in the hands of a few people, thus creating the danger of deliberate abuse. This is true to a certain extent, but the advantages of data banks far outweigh the threat of invasion of privacy and citizens' fear of their misuse. Instead of thinking in terms of government snooping and how our private lives are being invaded, we should give serious thought to the worth of data banks and how their presence aids, rather than hinders, mankind.

Let us start by removing some of the mystery that surrounds computerized data collection. People leave a trail of records behind them from birth until death—birth and school records showing places, dates, discipline problems, academic history, fingerprints, data on parents, and so on; licenses such as marriage, dog, and business; tax records showing income and how it is spent; military records reflecting security investigations and the family tree, job performance; insurance applications showing the medical histories of applicant and his family; and much more personal information on employment and credit applications, court and credit records; and on and on.

All these records display a wealth of personal data that includes psychiatric care, drinking problems, health of relatives, voter registration, past salary history, former employment and reasons for quitting, credit ratings, school grades, and even extramarital affairs. So, if we really think about it, we can conclude that all this fearsome information is already available and known to hundreds of people.

The concern really lies in keeping the facts secret, not public. But what do we generally mean by "concern" and why is privacy essential? The concern diminishes if we reveal our profiles when it is to our advantage. For example, we reveal whatever is necessary for credit ratings, in order to drive that car we cannot afford to buy with cash. But we scream "invasion of privacy" if we are fired from a job because the truth is discovered about covered-up facts in the job application. In other words, privacy is essential only when we want to keep the past from interfering with the future.

Californians voted in the 1972 election to amend the state constitution to include the right of privacy as an inalienable right. However, the right of privacy is not completely guaranteed. Would the public rather pay the cost of other peoples' bad checks through higher consumer prices than suffer surveillance by computerized credit checks? Or should working citizens be forced to pay welfare payments to undeserving people who use the right of privacy to conceal their wealth and earnings? Both examples may very well be unconvincing if we believe that the right to protect our privacy outweighs the penalties imposed by dishonest people. So, let us examine different arguments in support of the data bases that summarize our private lives.

Data bases can bring together employers and job hunters. If all available jobs could be channeled through one agency, more of the unemployed would be able to find work. The unemployment rate is too high, we say; yet jobs go unfilled because an employer fails to find qualified people, and because many unemployed people with the desired qualifications are unaware of that employer's needs. Most job hunters would welcome the computer's ability to store their data on a single job application and to automatically send it to five employers who might need their skills. Instead of laboriously filling out 50 job application forms, all containing the same repetitive data, the applicant could expand his coverage of prospective employers.

Information stored in data banks can serve very useful purposes in our day-to-day lives, and as the following case illustrates, could be expanded enormously! Migrant families move from harvest to harvest, from state to state. There was no way to keep track of the children's school progress until the computerized Migrant Student Record Transfer System was set up. Now teachers get records of each child's previous performance, health, and other pertinent data stored in a centrally maintained computer data bank.

One migrant student received a routine tuberculosis test at school and the test showed that she had a bad case of TB, needing immediate attention. In the meantime, the family had moved on. No one knew where. Unless the girl was found soon, her condition would prove fatal as well as exposing others to the contagious disease. A search of the computer data bank at Little Rock, Arkansas, revealed that the family had settled in another state. She was located and treated within a few hours of elapsed time.

Although data bases tend to hold information of a private nature, they can be beneficial if administered right. In other words, as long as citizens have a right to review the data and challenge erroneous entries, as long as the security of the information is not compromised and does not interfere with a person's future, data bases have a rightful place in our society.

As you have seen, the right of personal privacy should not subordinate a balance between the needs of people and the ability of local and federal governments to protect an individual's interests. More dangerous than the sacrifice of privacy is the lack of a person's control over the accuracy of government and business records of his personal data. A person should be aware of his record in the data base. To insure this, Congress enacted legislation on April 25, 1971, allowing any person the right to review data collected by agencies and giving him the right to challenge and correct any facts detrimental to him.

On the minus side, we have information in data bases that tends to say that a person is guilty until proved innocent, rather than the opposite. For example, Baltimore has created a data bank for entry of data when someone is arrested. In still another case, about 700 life insurance companies have access through remote terminals to the Medical Information Bureau's data bank at Greenwich, Connecticut, containing millions of medical reports about people who thought such records were known only to themselves and their physicians. When a person signs up for insurance, his application is checked against the medical data, enabling insurance companies to reject persons who lie about their health problems. Included in the file also are nonmedical facts, such as credit ratings. All checking of this information is done without the knowledge of the applicant. Are the rights of privacy being abused, or are the rights of individuals to cheaper rates being protected? Do insurance companies have the right to check on cheaters?

On the unquestionable plus side, President Kennedy might still be alive had the data on Lee Harvey Oswald in the CIA files and FBI files been consolidated into a centralized data base, thus tying together the picture of a potential criminal. Data bases are controversial, to say the least, but the worthwhile benefits are unlimited.

36. A COMPUTERIZED, CHECKLESS SOCIETY

There is much talk these days about having the computer electronically transfer funds for consumers and businesses rather than using the conventional bank draft or check. Everyone is supposed to benefit, but the day of rejoicing may be a long time off, for reasons other than the computer's ability. Theoretically, the customer could benefit from the resultant lower prices because the cost of handling business transactions would be cut drastically and these savings might be passed on to the consumer. Businesses would reap higher profits with the decrease in paperwork and from automatic inventory updating resulting from information fed into the computer at the point of sale.

For those who question whether this prediction will come about, some hindsight may be in order. The elimination of coins and script as media of exchange began in the seventeenth century when the check was first introduced. Now there are more than 65 million checks written in the United States every day. At a cost of fifteen cents for processing a check from start to finish, a sizable chunk of $3.5 billion yearly could be trimmed off retail prices by cutting down on the number of checks written.

Credit cards have conditioned people to live without money in their wallets, and most folks prefer it this way. They can travel from one coast to the other and charge gasoline, car repairs, hotels, food, clothing, entertainment, and everything needed to keep happy. Even their pay checks can be deposited into their bank account directly by their employers' computers. So why not a checkless society where there is an electronic transfer of funds instead of transfer by paper and checks?

Some people like the idea; others do not. Of the latter, many simply do not want to yield control of their checkbooks to a computerized system. One reason can be attributed to the public's distrust of computers. People have formed angry opinions from reading about, or having personally experienced, the anguish of trying to convince an unsympathetic computer that an unpaid bill has in fact been paid. These adverse effects are corporate management's fault, not the computer. Why? Simply because some employee failed to let the computer know that the payment had been made. Most businesses have not geared their operations to stop false billing and threats after customers write or phone about the error.

Whenever management gets the latter nuisance solved, the checkless society will be upon us. Capitalism has a way of selling the public and forcing those who object into going along with the new way. For example, a check could be drafted on anything in the 1960s, even a watermelon. Now, a $2.00 or more fee is charged the depositor unless he writes on bank-issued checks that have pertinent information printed in magnetic ink for computer recognition. Before MICR check-handling machines, there were no standards; therefore, the size and format of checks varied from business to business. For example, checks were bulky and had to be folded into a wallet. We now take for granted the use of a standard sized check that is computer identifiable by the account number and bank where the deposits are held.

Elements of the electronic fund-transfer system consist of a credit ID card used to identify the consumer, a data terminal at the point of sale to record the transaction, and a powerful computer at the bank. The checkless and almost cashless era will work something like this: Coin transactions involving small sales will still exist. Other purchase transactions will be made by presenting an optical character recognition (OCR) imprinted identification card, similar to the plastic gasoline credit card. The sales clerk will insert the ID card into a data terminal connected by telephone communication lines to a giant centralized computer network (Fig. 15–22). The clerk then keys in the stock number identifying the item and the quantity. The merchant's computer looks up the unit price stored in memory, extends the sale amount, and then transmits the figures back for printing on the customer's receipt. The computerized sale is automatically recorded in the bank by decreasing the buyer's bank account and increasing the store's account, all stored methodically in the computer's memory. At the same time, state and federal taxes are kept track of. More important, the keyed stock number is used to update the store's physical inventory.

If the customer has insufficient funds to cover the purchase, the bank computer notifies the sales clerk, thus solving the problem of "insufficient funds" checks. This alone will put an estimated $4 billion back into the pocket of honest consumers who must make up the bad checks of others through higher prices. Undoubtedly, a system will be devised whereby customers may prearrange a limited bank loan which will automatically take care of overdrafts on cash balances. In keeping with our charge-all times, credit will still be available for our borrowing society. But the loss from fraudulent sales* due to unverified credit and poor credit risks will be reduced considerably.

The chain of events begins when the centralized bank computer credits each employee's account by the amount of net earnings and decreases the employer's bank account. This transfer of funds is transacted in the form of a company payroll recorded on reels of magnetic tape prepared by the firm's computer. A copy of the earnings statement is sent to each employee by the employer. These tapes, representing money in physical form, translate into an innovative type of electronic transaction involving transfer of money from the employer's bank account to each employee's account. Immediately, recurring payments such as rent or mortgage payments, utility bills, car payments, insurance premiums, and furniture payments will be paid automatically by debiting the customer's account and crediting the vendor's account. Who would object to this worrisome chore being taken over by computer?

What are the implications and advantages of a checkless and near-moneyless society? First, the budget deficit of families constantly in financial trouble will certainly continue to be a problem, but less than at present. Credit limitations will be easier to control because an individual's financial status will be consolidated. Therefore, quick-spenders of borrowed money can be identified and constrained. Missing identification cards will plague

---

*Lost credit cards will be controlled more rapidly by issuing a replacement card with the same number, but with an appended control digit signifying a lost card. The old number is stored in the centralized bank computer for use in apprehending criminals trying to use the lost card.

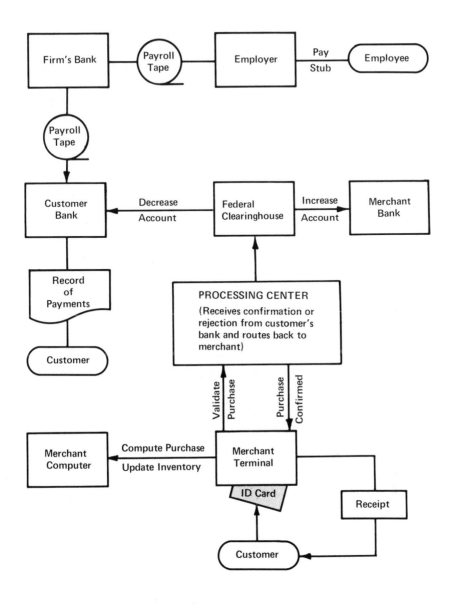

Fig. 15–22. Electronic transfer of funds in the checkless society.

the new checkless era, but this is less a problem than the present fraudulent check problem and the danger of lost credit cards. To recognize questionable card holders, photographs will be an integral part of the ID card.

On the plus side, businesses will profit through more economical and efficient accounting, inventory control, and payroll recording. These savings will be passed on to the customer, thus benefiting both business and consumer through increased commodity purchases. Elimination or reduction of the 24 billion checks annually will no longer threaten to clog the banking system. Government, as well as the public sector, should welcome the checkless society because more revenue will be produced through fairer taxation and elimination of beat-the-system techniques that are prevalent today.

In summary: The computerized transfer of money from one account to another is near and in fact has already made its trial debut in California and a few other states. In this revolutionary and bold system of exchange, many problems of today's credit and check-writing society will certainly become a thing of the past. But unforeseen problems will inevitably creep into the system, such as the difficult-to-discover fraud by brilliant computer embezzlers. By and large, the improvement will be welcomed generally. The troublesome "No cashing of personal checks" sign will no longer be around to irritate honest citizens, whose leisure time will be increased, since the computer will have taken over the burden of record keeping, tax return preparation, and check writing.

37. AUTOMATION, COMPUTERS, AND PROGRESS

We hear less nowadays about computers and other progress moving society toward ruin and despair. On the contrary, the computer industry has become the third largest employer in a few short years, and the public has become accustomed to newly created jobs replacing obsolete jobs. A classic example is the jet airliner, which carries more passengers at cheaper rates than the less efficient propeller-driven craft. Speed has not been the only benefit from the jet age. More sky lounges are required to move people to visit relatives and to play areas such as ski resorts. New planes mean additional people to build and maintain them. But more important, related employment is affected and new jobs are created or added in the suitcase, rent-a-car, motel, and other industries.

Automation, including computers, is apparent in any of the mentioned industries. Automation is thought of as any method in which the processing or producing of a product is controlled by self-operating machines. While management calls them labor-saving devices, critics and unions have other less complimentary names for them and seem to ignore that three jobs are being created for every two lost. The fact that an automated industry uses fewer people does not necessarily mean that fewer jobs will be available. The product of the automated industry sells at a lower price than one produced otherwise. More people can now buy the product at the lower price, providing more jobs. In addition, those spending less for the product than they formerly did will use the leftover income to purchase other products. The increase in sales of other products will provide job openings that will absorb people released from the automated industry.

More recently, criticism is pointed toward electronic computers as being the evil of all automation. The fear springs from the misconception that automated machines controlled by computers do not simply augment muscle power as previous machines did, but replace and outperform human intelligence. Therefore, computers in the future will not only run other machines but will also repair themselves and run businesses—and people will be outdated. Such conceptions are ill-founded. Business leaders know that computers are still not the ultimate in decision making and that every computer is dependent on man's judgment, knowledge, and guidance.

In answer to critics who cling to the cry that computers replace people, there are an estimated one million Americans directly employed in the EDP business. Specifically, there are over 175,000 programmers, 150,000 analysts, and 175,000 operators, according to statistics given by the Department of Labor. In addition, many more people are indirectly involved in manufacturing mountains of paper and cards for computer consumption. Contributing to the support of the economy were the EDP expenditures of $35 billion (including foreign computer shipments), which accounted for nearly 3 percent of the gross national product.

While it is true that some people employed in clerical and mathematical jobs were displaced by the computer, a better than balanced effect has been obtained in the higher demanding (thus, higher paying) positions. The computer zips out mounds of paper facts, and this management information must be analyzed by people more qualified than those in the simple manual days. In support of this, more people are employed in city jobs than ever before and the trend is rapidly moving toward professional occupations. A comparative survey, shows that of 100 workers,

1947		*1967*
35	were white-collar workers	45
10	were engaged in service jobs	13
41	were blue-collar workers	37
14	were farmers	5

Because of automation we now need less people on the farm, even though more food is needed to feed the growing population. In fact, the employees in the infant computer industry, which had practically zero employment two decades ago, now *outnumber* those in agriculture employment. Obviously, these professional and white collar careers demand higher education and better qualified credentials than did the jobs of yesterday. Naturally, many of the unemployed are the result of technological development. The skills formerly required are not necessarily adequate for today or tomorrow. In order to participate in progress and the resulting higher living scale, workers must prepare for future advancement. Otherwise, progress, and not automation, will increase the total of jobless people.

To say it another way, workers who fail to prepare themselves will be victims of technological unemployment. What, then, is there to fear from automation? While the controversy over automation is debated, the number of people in new and higher-paying jobs continues to multiply.

Chapter 16

A COMPUTER MANAGEMENT PRIMER

The managerial ideas set forth below focus upon the data processing manager's role and his responsibilities in successfully establishing and maintaining an effective computer operation. The discussion concentrates upon overall management, but particularizes problems that are peculiar to computer environments.

TRAITS OF A SUCCESSFUL MANAGER

What kind of person might one expect to deal with in data processing? Let us begin by looking at the character traits of a successful departmental head. He first earned recognition as a technician and then later as a supervisor of one or more data processing functions such as programming or computer operation. A typical manager, therefore, is one who has worked his way into a responsible position by demonstrating ability in getting things done. He usually handles people well, is technically competent himself, and expects expertise from those who work with him. Being knowledgeable in most aspects of the company's job requirements, he possesses the know-how to produce unquestionable results. Above all, he keeps abreast of work in progress, and thus is able to provide on-the-spot information about his team members, the computer schedule, and the programming work load.

In turn, he demands these same principles from his section supervisors. Although he is cool when under pressure, the chances are that an employee's haphazard working habits during production upset him. This manager, having accepted these qualities as professionally necessary, has little patience with mediocrity and evaluates his technician's performance accordingly when considering personnel for advancement.

MANAGEMENT DEFINED

Let us now establish a management definition. Management is the process of getting things done in the most efficient manner within a given time limit. Although management can be defined in a number of other ways, none states specifically everything that management should include. So, what does a manager do? By knowing what established goals should be achieved, he assigns individual tasks so that desired results are produced through other people. In general, we have defined management a second time, except that we have added the key supervision element—that of reaching objectives through other people by using the talents and skills of his section supervisors, such as the programming supervisor and project leaders involved in designing, say, data bases. This seems simple enough, but this important step is a big order. Much thought and work must have preceded this delegation of work. For instance, who will do the work in light of their qualifications and other responsibilities, and—very important—pass on what must be done without misunderstanding.

Throughout our discussion, we shall use the terms "goals" and "objectives," which are synonymous. Goals, or objectives, are the ends toward which effort is directed. Accordingly, goals comprise all work that has to be done through the total effort of the manager and people he has hired or inherited. In other words, goals are individual projects that are transformed from an idea to a useful end product.

The manager's display of technical competence and sense of responsibility is not enough to influence full effectiveness in reaching goals. He must apply other skills when considering the many factors that affect the operation as a whole, including the impact upon other departments within the company. Too, projects cannot be adequately completed by rushing into technical construction without realistic planning. Otherwise, the trial-and-error approach prevails; thus, the reason for the planning phase of management.

PLANNING IN DATA PROCESSING

Planning, which is the first step toward completing the project, is the process of considering the alternate routes, selecting the best, and mapping the course of action. It is especially important during planning that we try to prevent problems, not just solve problems. We should also point out emphatically that related computer processing must be considered during modifications or creation of solutions to new requirements. Data processing procedures should be designed as a system rather than "piecemeal."

Proper planning, therefore, entails studying an inventory system as a whole before writing individual programs to give computer output. This output would consist of items on hand, shipments scheduled, items reordered, sales analysis, financial products, and the like. It is critically important that programs and procedures be initially written to give the required output with the least amount of computer processing and human effort. Modifications to programs naturally ensue to conform with business transformations. Consequently, the entire system must be analyzed in order to accommodate modifications that affect other operations so that continuity and smooth processing are assured.

One of the first and most important considerations in planning is to understand the needs of the customer or of higher management. We often mention the term "customer" because data processing essentially provides service to the many departments of a business, such as marketing and accounting departments. Too often, customers do not know exactly what they want. Confusing? Not at all. It is quite normal. Although he knows his problem, he may not necessarily be familiar with the characteristics of data on file, how the data is organized, and the computer's capabilities. As a result, the systems analyst may suggest ways to give a more useful product, and perhaps at less cost. For example, by talking to the customer about his problem in depth, the systems analyst finds that modification of existing computer reports will satisfy the customer's requirement.

Whenever a thorough discussion and study of the problem reveals that a new computer product is justified, it may prove beneficial to eliminate other products or incorporate them, in whole or part, into the new project. Here is where knowledge of the company's operation and computer techniques proves its worth. By having a sound concept of what the customer needs, more useful information can be provided after giving careful consideration to information that is already available, and computer know-how can be applied to produce new information. Planning, consequently, is the never-ending process of understanding what must be done, defining the problem in relation to other business aspects, and selecting the best method to give desired results.

ORGANIZING DATA PROCESSING ACTIVITIES

The planning phase, which is essentially a mental process of deciding how to obtain better end results, is followed by the organizing phase of management. Organizing is the task of blueprinting the technique by which the project will be accomplished. Specifically, people are selected to get the project rolling, their responsibilities are clearly defined, and then they are given freedom to create a system that uses the resources available (humans, hardware, and software) in order to transform data into management information.

Let us consider an illustration involving a new computer application. The installation manager, or his representative, is usually approached first about the requirement. The feasibility of the proposal is discussed between him and the requesting department manager. Unless insufficient computer time or cost restrictions prevent further consideration, the two managers agree in principle to explore the feasibility of the proposed project. They call in knowledgeable experts from both agencies to discuss the project in more detail. In the case of data processing, the experts are usually the systems and programming supervisor, and perhaps his project leader, who offers technical guidance and estimated time tables.

We should point out, however, that those directly involved in the organizing phase do not spend considerable time in the planning phase, although they may be called upon to some extent. In other words, we cannot establish a hard rule as to which people are included in each phase because it is impossible to say when planning ends and organizing begins, since all management phases overlap. Consequently, we shall say that people are called upon as the need arises.

It is quite evident that some systems people, those who develop the processing procedures, should be deeply involved from the time that the project is planned until its completion. The programming people, on the other hand, usually enter the project after the systems analyst designs the system. Although the computer operations supervisor is concerned to a lesser degree during construction of system flowcharts and programs, he is consulted about the additional workload in relation to the present work schedule. As a result, all people that the new project will affect have been kept informed.

DELEGATION OF RESPONSIBILITY

Since the detailed groundwork is laid during the organizing phase of implementing the new or revised project, the handling of several factors by the installation manager can mean the difference between success and failure. Responsibility in any organization varies at different levels, but, as always, the responsibility and means of accomplishing the total goal ultimately rests with the manager. Accordingly, the success of the project is based upon the concept of total management and the confidence subordinate supervisors have in management leadership.

The reason that so many people are consulted during the early stages of discussion is that the manager who tries to do everything himself does so at the expense of more vital issues. There is no surer sign of a bogged-down department than one having a manager who neglects to delegate work. The reason for failure to delegate responsibility can be weak managerial traits or undependable subordinates. Either case demands immediate relief because no department within an organization stands alone; thus, ineffectiveness is widespread. Management responsibility, therefore, includes the unfortunate task of weeding out misfits who counteract efforts to build a stable work force.

Consequently, management must assign the responsibility for fulfillment of the assignment. By this, we mean that the responsibility is handed down, not given away. For example, responsibility for development of new or revised procedures lies with the systems supervisor or, in a small installation, with the systems and programming supervisor. The right to act, as dictated by the requirement and experience of the person accepting the assignment, must accompany this responsibility. The management concept is centered around the fact that responsibility for what the subordinate does lies with the manager, whether the results be good or bad. Therefore, the power to make decisions is delegated, and the manager holds the ultimate responsibility. To say it another way, any supervisor constantly passing the buck to protect himself is not doing the job correctly.

Selecting supervisors from technicians has always been a problem because the ability to program, for example, does not guarantee success as a manager. While the technician does not necessarily have to have supervisory ability, the manager does. The systems supervisor, for example, must act upon his own conclusions and draw from his technical background. In addition, he uses discretion as to what constitutes a need for higher decision. In general, guidance from customer-liaison and data processing practices is sufficient as long as common sense is exercised within company policy and fiscal limitations. Nevertheless, agreements and matters that may be questioned at a later time should be documented in writing.

The systems supervisor has the responsibility to keep his boss informed. On the other hand, the supervisor must have the freedom to act without having the manager look over his shoulder. (We should point out that delegation of work does not relieve the manager of his responsibility to follow the work.)

SPAN OF CONTROL

Another characteristic affecting successful management is span of control. As the term implies, this involves the amount of work that can be done, the number of people a supervisor can handle, and the number of supervisors that can be managed by one individual. There are other factors that can affect the span of control. Some are: qualifications and experience of the technicians; the type of work; and the distance between the supervisor and those he supervises.

Since work varies in simplicity and complexity, span of control is not fixed. To illustrate: A keypunch supervisor may control 20 or more operators doing relatively the same work. In contrast, a programming supervisor usually has responsibility for a considerably smaller number of programmers. The span of control also depends upon whether the supervisor is expected to do programming, and upon the number of on-the-job trainees. If a programming branch consists of highly skilled technicians, then the span of control is greater because the individual supervision is less. Other considerations involve the complexity that exists between different kinds of programming, such as systems programming, applications programming, business programming, and scientific programming. Obviously, the control is governed by what a manager is able to accomplish by giving guidance, talking over problems, and improving people's skills. Needless to say, the span of control greatly affects the management process and thus the quality of the end result.

In summary: Organizing is the orderly process of developing the ways and means to accomplish the objective that was decided upon in the planning stage. Personnel are selected for the project, and the authority is delegated to get the job done. Of prime importance in selection of technicians and their supervisor is the span of control, which means the amount of work that can be done effectively. When the objective or goal is clear, data processing professionals are provided with guidelines that govern what is expected, and work begins. Systems analysts study and evaluate the problem in order to create computer solutions, and programmers reduce these solutions to instructions that the computer uses in processing the data.

COORDINATING DATA PROCESSING MATTERS

The third phase of management is called "coordinating." As the system is designed and programs are written in the organizing phase, difficulties and unforeseen problems come to light. This is the way it normally happens, since the planning phase is used mainly to establish objectives and select the way to get there. Obviously, more meetings are held with the customer and between sections within data processing to talk things out. This process, involving communication in verbal or written form, is the art of coordinating.

We communicate in order to exchange ideas and information so that the project will proceed according to plan. Most coordination, or communication, takes place in a less formal atmosphere, such as conversations over the telephone or in office visits. More formal communication occurs at meetings where the important decisions made are based upon problems encountered. These meetings can and do vary as to the level of those attending. Top-management executives are usually present when there is a chance of misunderstandings that would hamper the outcome of the project. It is not unusual to uncover new evidence which indicates that original estimates must be exceeded by additional man-hours. Management must weigh the facts presented at these meetings, and decide whether to scrap the project or continue. Although many people would prefer to operate without meetings, they do perform a useful purpose in the phase of coordination, especially to discuss progress during the life of the project.

Technical problems, such as gathering additional information to satisfy a programming requirement, are usually handled without involving the upper management level. However, the lowest level of management should be aware of most coordination. This is how bypassing the boss could be handled: With knowledge of the programming supervisor, the programmer makes contact with the accounting supervisor who will eventually use the computerized product. Either he answers the question or turns it over to one of his accountants.

In summary: Coordination means exchanging conversation in order to overcome obstacles that would otherwise prevent reaching the objective. We do not want to overlook the fact that coordination is not limited to problems but includes suggestions that enhance or improve the project. Consequently, coordination is applicable at all levels, but from an informational standpoint it is usually carried out on a lower level than that which involves business operational aspects at higher management levels. We should point out that coordination directly influences the success of the project; thus, frequent contact during the developmental stages reduces the chance of major problems in the final testing and implementation of the programs.

DIRECTING PEOPLE AND MACHINES

Directing is the fourth phase of management. It is here that management exercises its responsibility to insure that all work is continuing on course and that implementation of the new or revised system actually achieves the established objective from an operational standpoint. In so doing, managers direct both people and the progress of work performed by computers. Here we deal with the overall system that will produce the end product. This involves bringing together the four major resources of data processing: humans, who design and program the system, the software, the hardware, and the input data needed for processing.

In directing the overall system, the manager deals with the two interacting resources of people and machines. To separate the two is impossible because both are necessary to get the job done. Yet we must deal with both quite differently. Hardware is *mechanical* and therefore should be approached mechanically. This impersonal approach cannot be applied to humans because attitudes, motivation, and other psychological factors enter the picture. Although human relations is an integral part of management study, we shall cover only aspects having a direct bearing.

We should first accept that the primary job of a manager is producing, not making people happy. Even though the latter is attempted, it is impossible to keep everyone happy all the time. As a result, there are times when the work must come first. So, in directing, managers reach their objectives through people who must master machines, and each is handled quite differently.

BYPASSING THE LINE OF AUTHORITY

The line-of-authority concept lies in the organizational structure, which dictates that each worker has a boss and each boss has someone over him. Although there are modern-day arguments against this time-tried theory, it plays an important part in the phase of directing and can create a dilemma for all employees, from the top of the organization chart to the bottom. Let us illustrate with a typical situation involving programming priorities:

The data processing manager drops into the programming shop to talk to the supervisor, but finds him absent. He proceeds to chat with individual programmers, as is his normal practice. In this way he keeps in touch with problems and gains a feel of their thoughts and impressions. For example, he asks Joe how his work is coming along. Joe gives the manager a quick rundown and hints that progress is slow this morning because the turnaround for program compiles is slow. Since Joe appears to have more spare time than the other programmers, the data processing manager asks Joe to do a small but important job. Joe is pleased to tackle the task because the boss seldom goes directly to a worker to assign projects.

In this scene, we have two important aspects that affect the phase of directing. First, the programming supervisor was not available and the data processing manager bypassed the line of authority, which in this case involves the programming supervisor. Theoretically, the manager should not bypass the middleman in assigning programming tasks. However, bypassing the line of authority is justified at times because something important may be delayed otherwise. If the manager can wait for the information he needs, he should leave word for the supervisor to contact him upon returning.

How should the bypass be carried out effectively when time is of essence? Simple enough—the boss goes directly to whoever can help, which in our illustration is Joe the programmer, and the bypass is justified by necessity. Assuming that the request is reasonable, the only answer acceptable to the manager is, "Yes sir, right away." Consequently, any future disagreement that the programming supervisor might have is with the manager, not with the subordinate who simply followed orders as he should have.

We have made an exception to management policy in relation to the line of authority. The rationale behind this exception lies in the fact that policy must be flexible, as long as confusion does not result. In other words, policy must not be so rigid that the line of authority blocks the process of getting the job done correctly. If management is not practiced with discretion, the organization inevitably suffers and someone gets hurt. What harm can result and how should it be handled? The programming supervisor is responsible for the actions in his shop and must be aware of all that goes on in order to run it efficiently.

Coordinating the Bypass

To satisfy the requirement of keeping the programming supervisor informed, the data processing manager should tell him what transpired while he was absent. Should the manager fail to coordinate this bypass, the responsible supervisor could be left in the dark. As compensation for this possibility, the programmer assigned the task should know that it is *his* responsibility to inform his supervisor of the request made by the data processing manager. Now we have the bypass of authority satisfied in a second manner.

What effect does the bypass have on the organizational setup if carried out properly? Two interesting attitudes should prevail: The manager gets what he wants and at the same time the programming supervisor feels that he still has control, since he has been kept informed of what goes on within his shop. The chances are that even had the supervisor been present, the situation would have been handled in essentially the same manner.

Nevertheless, coordination is more difficult to enforce when going up the line of authority than going down. This means that while the programming supervisor may insist upon his subordinates complying with given instructions, he will be far more flexible with *his* boss, for it is a human trait to concede the authority of a superior. In the end, therefore, the programming manager holds Joe responsible for keeping him informed, even though he was doing what he had been instructed to do.

The second factor of importance in our example is the direct contact of Joe by the big boss, which boosted morale through management's recognition of the worker. To put it another way, higher management has recognized and made contact with the lowest level of management—the worker. We generally do not think of workers as managers, but in a sense they are. Programmers make important decisions when writing programs, and use discretion in gaining approval of questionable things that they feel should be included. As an example, a programmer may make the decision as to when a particular program should be initially tested in order to meet the completion deadline, and pace himself accordingly. Consequently, his decisions involve some degree of management. Accordingly, the degree of management involvement really depends upon how high in the organization one has risen. Now we have an important criterion used in selecting people for advancement: If a man cannot manage his own work, then he obviously cannot manage the work of others.

MOTIVATING THE PROFESSIONAL

The last criterion is a far-reaching statement and leads us to motivation, which largely determines the pride in one's work. Motivation is essentially the responsibility of the individual, but he must feel that management has an interest in him. When the data processing manager asked Joe about his work, an interest in Joe was established. This is just one informal way of showing that management is concerned about each individual. When the manager requested Joe to do a rush job, he felt important. As a result, Joe has been motivated by the fact that the data processing manager had confidence in Joe's ability to perform. And Joe knows that it his responsibility to keep his supervisor informed. After all, Joe is aware that his boss is still responsible even though he may be tied up on something else.

Another point illustrated is that the data processing manager is familiar with the detailed work that accomplishes the goals for which he is held accountable. Maintaining this knowledge is one of the many ways to assure himself that everything is under control. His main means of control, however, is exerted through his supervisors. During meetings between section supervisors, he brings up his findings resulting from conversations with technicians. For example, he asks: What is causing the slow turnaround of program compiles that Joe mentioned in the informal chat? The supervisor answers the question at the managerial level and consequently does not feel left out of the management process. By the fact that the manager does ask questions at the programmer level, each supervisor knows that he must be able to discuss whatever goes on within his area of responsibility.

In overseeing the operations the data processing manager does not give orders directly to the worker when he discovers something amiss. Instead, he brings it to the attention of the responsible supervisor, who in turn directs someone in correcting the problem. As programs and procedures are completed for a specific job, the data processing manager's responsibility is to direct their implementation. In this role, he directs the individual supervisors of the systems, programming, computer operations, and data entry sections. Each section should know what the other is doing, and this is brought about by directing them as a team. If this way of bringing things together were to fail, you could be assured of chaos.

For example: New programs may not be ready when the computer is scheduled for the initial processing, or vice versa, and the input data may not be ready in machine-readable form. Surprisingly enough, these interdependent sections of systems, programming, computer operations, and data entry do not always complete their parts of a project on time. Due to unforeseen complications, this unfortunate setback will happen occasionally, regardless of how well the activities are directed. Therefore, section supervisors must be flexible in order to compensate for delays by setting up schedules for other work.

To summarize: Directing is the management phase of overseeing operations so that projects proceed according to plan. In so doing, the manager directs people who develop and implement programmed systems that satisfy company goals. He must approach directing from two angles: machines from a mechanical standpoint, and people from a human standpoint. He directs through observing, talking to people, making decisions that send supervisors directing, and in general seeing that things go right. When all is not going right, he tightens control. When satisfied that performance of the data processing operation has risen to his expectations, the manager slacks off on the reins. In turn, section supervisors direct more vigorously when things are off course, and then permit technicians to continue under their self-imposed discipline when improvement is apparent.

CONTROLLING THE RESOURCES

The last phase of management is *controlling,* which consists essentially of applying the checks and balances established to verify the extent to which operations contribute to overall effectiveness. The manager controls when he determines what has gone wrong, takes corrective action, and brings back into line whatever has fallen below given standards. In directing, the manager monitors the work in progress and intervenes when the project runs into trouble. This is not the same as controlling, the purpose of which is to evaluate potential problem areas and regulate those that are discovered *after* they occur. Once a project is operational, however, the manager should take a somewhat detached attitude in order to interfere as little as possible with whoever has the responsibility of executing the work. His actual controls are imposed through various means such as company policy, staff meetings, and other managerial techniques peculiar to the organization. These tools of management are discussed in subsequent paragraphs.

MANAGING THROUGH POLICY

As stated, a manager who handles everything that comes across his desk does not have time to consider vital issues that involve decision making. Neither will he have time for creative thinking. So—to give guidance to his first-line supervisors so that they can practice technical supervision and make decisions at a lower level—he establishes policy.

Policy, therefore, allows others to carry out the wishes of the manager as if he were doing it himself. This policy may be stated in writing, or may be established by repetitive actions. If the regular working hours are from 8:00 A.M. to 5:00 P.M., for example, then this is policy, even though it is unwritten. Other informal policies are adhered to by the simple fact of knowing what the manager likes and dislikes. But if a policy is complex or of an operational nature, it ought to be in written form.

Infrequent job requirements are an example of tasks that are best handled in written form. Special processing requirements of a one-time nature may disrupt normal production and endanger management control unless the request is written and the job is handled in an orderly sequence. The one-time job requirement is usually written on a special form (Fig. 15–5) that includes blocks for identification information (name of requesting agency and job, etc.), the date needed, the processing desired, validation of the need, and a signature block for approval. As such, the one-time job form serves to coordinate the data processing sections involved in coding and keypunching the input data, programming the requirement, and machine processing the data.

Whatever the manager deems necessary to maintain effective control over these special jobs is written up in a statement that becomes policy. If he includes in the policy that a particular subordinate has the approving authority for processing cost up to $100, then he has freed himself by getting the job done through delegation. In this manner, policy can impose limits on the authority of lower management as well as furnish the guidelines for carrying out the task.

STAFF MEETINGS

Another aspect of controlling has to do with meetings. Most managers have informal staff meetings on a regular basis and as the need arises. Meetings serve many purposes, such as exchange of information between the manager and his supervisors. Thus, the manager knows what is going on and each supervisor can keep abreast of what others are doing which might affect his work. Decisions may very well originate in these meetings. If the programming supervisor agrees that certain programs will be ready for running on the computer supervisor's night shift, and the keypunch supervisor states that punching of all input data will also be finished, a decision and commitment have been made.

SUMMARY

Effective management is determined by results, and a manager must accept the consequences regardless of the outcome. Good results depend upon how well the planning, organizing, coordinating, directing, and controlling phases of management have been applied. There are no shortcuts, and sometimes success is made possible by "playing it by ear." But more often than not, success is achieved by doing the right things at the right time. Regardless of the technique, the manager must never lose sight of the end result. He establishes priorities and pays particular attention to his main resources—people and machines. The manager identifies and corrects problem areas by knowing when and what changes to introduce. In so doing, he obtains the best from his people by making them feel a part of the organization, regardless of their faults and abilities.

Management is never perfect. Therefore, improvement is always possible. A manager should introduce changes gradually and adjust operations accordingly, while keeping in mind that new ideas and their objectives must be understood in order to be accepted. However, if the choice of always making people happy compromises the objective, the inevitable result is good morale but an unproductive organization. Effective management means keeping in touch with problems as they arise and accepting the fact that errors do happen. The important thing is that a manager must be able to recognize problems and know what corrective action is needed. The frequency of these errors, however, may indicate underlying operational or human deficiencies, which, of course, must be corrected.

In conclusion, perfect management has never existed, but effective performance is possible through hard work and technical competence, a working knowledge of the company, sound judgment, and above all, an appreciation of human relations.

GLOSSARY

Absolute. Refers to actual machine language. For example, an absolute address indicates the actual location in memory where the data is stored.

Access Time. The elapsed time between the instant at which data is called for and the instant at which the data is available at the desired location.

Accounting Machine. The most important machine in a unit record or punched card system. Capable of detail or group printing, accumulating totals, and summary punching when connected to a reproducing punch. Also called a *tabulator.*

Address. A designation in either symbolic or machine language, a location in storage, or a device where data is stored. Also called the *operand* of an instruction.

Address, Absolute. A machine-language designation that indicates the true location of data or an instruction in storage.

Address, Symbolic. A name assigned by the programmer, which represents a storage location. The symbolic address is translated into an absolute address by an assembler or compiler program.

Alphabetic Characters. A set of symbols arranged to express the letters A to Z, which is designed for communicating between people and machines and is intelligible to both.

Alphameric. Data that may consist of alphabetic characters A to Z, numeric characters 0 to 9, or special characters used, for example, as punctuation, such as $ and % symbols.

Application. A kind of data processing operation such as inventory-control application or customer-billing application.

Arithmetic Unit. A hardware component in the central processor unit of the computer system where addition, subtraction, multiplication, and division are performed. Also where logic operations, such as comparison of two sets of data, are performed in order to make decisions.

Assembler Program. A program usually provided by the computer manufacturer which converts low-level nonmachine-language source programs written by the programmer into machine language (assembly language). An assembler assigns absolute addresses to symbolic names assigned by the programmer and converts mnemonic operation codes to a language the computer can act upon.

Automation. A method by which processing of a product is controlled by self-operating machines.

Batch-Control Totals. Used to ascertain overall accuracy on quantitative data by entering totals of each batch of transactions derived from adding machines into the computer where processed results are checked with the batch totals.

Batch Processing. Periodic processing in one computer run of accumulated groups of similar data, such as payroll time-attendance records. Also referred to as sequential processing because the saved transactions for a specific period are often arranged in a particular sequence, such as employee number, in order to process. Used in applications when the current status of information is not critical, therefore transactions can be saved and processed randomly or sequentially as the need arises.

Binary. A numbering system using a base of 2 as opposed to the base of 10 in the decimal system. Used by computers because of its two-state (zero or one) characteristic.

BCD (binary-coded decimal). A system of binary notation in which each decimal digit or alphabetic character is represented by the binary digits 0 and 1; BCD was predominate in second-generation computers.

Bit. The smallest element in a binary character. Each bit has two states, either "off" or "on," representing "0" or "1," respectively.

Blew. A universal data processing term referring to programs that have bugs (errors) resulting in program failure.

Blocking. A technique whereby two or more data records are grouped on tape or disk storage and the physical block of records is read or written as a unit in order to speed the input or output operation.

Buffer. A small hardware memory device located between the central processor and all input-output devices; used to temporarily hold two or more records being input to the computer or output from the computer. Also refers to segments of internal memory set aside by the programmer to store blocks of records awaiting input or output.

Card Column. One of 80 vertical divisions of a card normally accommodating one numeral or letter. Each column, consisting of 12 rows, is divided into two parts. The bottom 10 rows contain punching positions for decimal digits 0 to 9; three top rows, 0, 11, and 12, are combined with a digit punch to represent an alphabetic character.

CRT (cathode-ray tube). A TV-like screen that permits a visual link by telephone cables to data stored inside the computer.

Centralized EDP Facility. Installation where computers are consolidated at corporate headquarters and input data from lower levels is sent by mail or entered via data terminals, such as the CRT.

CPU (central processing unit). The computer without the input and output units. The CPU houses the control, internal storage, and arithmetic-logic sections. Also called the *central processor.*

Channel. Hardware element that provides a path for the movement of data between input-output units and the central processor; acts as a small computer to relieve the CPU of having to stop processing in order to execute I/O operations.

Character. A set of symbols specially arranged to express the decimal digits 0 to 9, the letters A to Z, and special characters.

Coding. Changing data to an abbreviated form before punching in cards or keying onto tape or disk by assigning letters and numbers in order to facilitate machine processing. Also refers to writing a series of *computer instructions* that make up a program.

Collator. A machine that has two card feeds and four or five stackers; used in comparing two or more fields in a card to perform sequence checking, matching, merging, and selection of desired cards.

Comparing. Examining two or more fields to establish if one field is equal to, lower than, or higher than the other field.

Compiler program. A special program that converts a high-level nonmachine-language source program written by a programmer into an object program that the computer can use to process information or solve a problem.

Computer. A group of machines interconnected to function as a unit under the control of a stored program. Once the program is stored in the computer's memory, processing of data, such as reading, computing, comparing, and punching or printing of the results, is controlled and accomplished without human intervention. Also called a *system.* (*See* digital computer)

Computer, General-Purpose. A machine designed to perform a variety of jobs, as most commercial computers are classified.

Computer, Special-Purpose. A machine designed for the sole purpose of performing one specific task, such as the small special-purpose computer aboard space crafts.

Console. A display panel mounted on the central processor or a separate table; consists of lights, buttons, and switches for manual control and observation of the system.

Control Panel. A removable device in the machine into which wires are plugged to complete electric circuits, thus controlling machine operations.

Control Character. Any character used to distinguish one record from another; for example, master records are recorded with an X in position 80 while detail records have no X in position 80.

Control Field. See Key Field.

Control Unit. A component of the computer which controls the entire system by decoding each instruction in the program and carrying out the action called for by the instruction.

Controller. Hardware equipment that responds to channel commands in overseeing the operation of input or output units such as disk drives.

Consistency Check. Checking to see that two or more fields of data are consistent. A customer order is usually checked to see if it is consistent with credit terms coded in the record. For example, determining if the order is eligible for discount calculation involves comparing the total of the merchandise to see if the minimum-discount amount is exceeded. In another example, the total of the order cannot exceed the credit limit established in the record. Also, fields may be checked individually for inconsistency, such as: Gross pay over $500 is erroneous.

Conversion. See Data Conversion.

Cycle. An interval of time that a machine requires to complete a given series of operations such as a storage cycle, which refers to the time needed to store or retrieve data.

Cylinder. All tracks in a stack of disks that can be accessed at one time without movement of the read-write heads.

Data. A collection of elements made up of numeric, alphabetic, or special characters denoting facts; in particular that information to be *input* into the computer for processing. The opposite of information that comprises the results of processed data.

Data Base. A collection of data files stored in a single storage unit such as disk storage.

Data Cell. The largest storage medium, consisting of strips of magnetic tape on which data is recorded.

Data Communication. A means of transmitting data over electrical transmission lines in order to eliminate delays caused by mail or courier.

Data Conversion. Changing one form of input or output medium to another; for instance, a card-to-tape operation.

Data Manipulation. The movement of data from one place to another within the computer, such as transferring completed results to the output area for recording, or the alteration of data to meet the requirements of processing, such as changing 0203 (Feb. 3) to Julian 034 in order to compute interest rates for a given number of days.

Data Processing. The input of raw data, processing inside the computer, and output of the results in meaningful form.

Data Processing System. The combined effort of people and machines organized to process the data requirements of a company in order to produce management information. Such a system minimizes the need for manual handling of data, with primary emphasis on elimination of retranscription of data and duplication of effort.

Debugging. Data processing terminology that refers to locating and correcting errors in computer programs.

Decentralized EDP Facility. An installation where computers are located at levels below the head office in order to be close to the work source, usually in a different locality.

Desk Checking. The act of manually examining a program in order to determine that every path the computer takes in processing variable data is working and so that errors are detected and corrected with a minimum of computer test runs.

Detail File. A collection of data records, individually representing business transactions, that is used in current processing and then filled as historical backup data.

Detail Printing. Printing all or a portion of the data from each record passed through the machine.

Digital Computer. A computer that operates on digits represented in a binary form of ones and zeroes, as opposed to an analog computer that performs calculations on physical measurements.

Direct Access. Retrieval of data directly from any location in a random-access device without having to examine records one by one in order to get to the needed record; the converse of sequential processing, where each record is processed one after another in turn.

Direct-Access Storage. A device, such as disk, drum, or data cell, designed to hold mass data at a cost lower than the faster internal memory of the central processor and in such a way that one record can be randomly accessed from the middle of the file or any other position without reading the preceding records in the file.

Disk Pack. A stack of disks enclosed in a protective container; inserted in a disk drive whenever needed or stored off-line in a library whenever not in use.

Document. A typed or handwritten representation of source information, such as an invoice form that must be converted to an input medium acceptable to the machine.

Documentation. A collection of paperwork that describes all facets of a job, including computer processing instructions, flowcharts, program listings, the reason and authorization for modifications to the program, input formats, output sample listings, test data, and so on.

Drum Storage. A cylinder-shaped on-line device similar in concept to the disk storage device; usually employed to augment internal memory.

EBCDIC (extended binary coded decimal interchange code). A computer coding scheme made up of eight bits that represent letters, special characters, and one or two numbers. Used predominately in third-generation computers.

Editing. Checking of data for impossible elements to insure accuracy. In *programming,* refers to the rearrangement, deletion, or addition of data to improve the appearance and meaning, such as punctuation of money-amount fields.

EDPS (electronic data processing system). *See* Computer.

Emulator. A special program that enables one computer to execute machine-language programs written for another computer. Emulator programs are often used until programs can be rewritten in the different language of the new computer; thus the reason to acquire equipment compatible with other equipment types and models.

Exception Reporting. The production of limited management information that requires management action, thereby omitting the bulk of information available.

Execute. To carry out a machine operation based upon given instructions in the program stored within the computer.

Field. A predetermined number of columns set aside in a record for similar data; for example, a field containing customer name.

File. A collection of facts or data about related items recorded in a machine medium such as a card file, tape file, or disk file. A master file contains semipermanent data, whereas a detail file contains transient data for recent transactions.

Fixed Word Length. Refers to a computer where the number of characters in a machine word is constant (determined by the design of the equipment).

Flowchart. A graphic representation using symbols to show step-by-step machine operations. A system flowchart shows the flow of processing between machine runs or job steps, whereas a program flowchart shows the detailed processing to be performed within the machine.

Gang Punching. Punching repetitive data in all cards of a file.

Garbage. Data processing jargon for unwanted and meaningless data recorded in input media or produced by a machine. May consist of mispunched cards, reports with overprinting, or an inaccurate product produced by the machine.

Group Printing. Printing a single line with accumulated totals for a group of records having identical key fields. Also called *tabulating.*

Hardware. The electronic and mechanical devices or components of which a machine is constructed.

Hash Total. A means of detecting errors in data elements such as account number. The digits in the identification number are calculated according to a predetermined technique, and therefore can be recalculated during other processing stages to determine accuracy. The total, in itself, has no meaning except as a means of detecting errors in recording or transmission.

Hexadecimal. A numbering system using a base of 16 as opposed to the base of 10 in the decimal system. Used predominately by third-generation computers. Commonly referred to as *hex.*

High-Level Language. A problem-oriented program that resembles the problem being solved, such as FORTRAN or COBOL. *See* Low-Level Language.

High Order. Leftmost position of a data field, storage location, or machine word. Also referred to as *left-justified.*

Housekeeping. Pertaining to instructions, usually at the beginning of a program, which are necessary but do not directly contribute to the solution of a problem and which are normally executed only once.

Information. Knowledge derived from processed data representing business facts that have been reduced to numeric and alphabetic equivalents. Decisions are made from information plus judgment.

Input. Any form of input medium containing data that is used to provide the computer with data for processing.

Input Device. A unit that reads cards, tape, or other input media and moves the data to the computer where processing is being accomplished.

Instruction. Precise directions in the form of a stored program, which is an element of a program and which causes the computer to perform a specific operation. An instruction consists of two parts, the operation code and one or more addresses that cause the computer to perform the indicated operation upon the data located at the address(s).

IDP (integrated data processing). A data processing concept that includes capturing input data in machine-readable language at the point of data origin, thus eliminating manual retranscription such as keypunching source documents into card form.

Intermediate. Of three fields or totals, the one of middle importance. *See* Minor and Major.

Interpreter. A machine used for printing information on cards.

Intersperse Gang Punching. Punching the same data in individual groups of cards.

I-O-Bound. The speed at which the computer executes the program is limited by the speed of the slowest input or output device; therefore the amount of I/O processing exceeds the calculation and other processing time.

IOCS (input-output control system). A part of the operating system that facilitates programming of I/O operations and controls the I/O operation. For example, the programmer writes I/O instructions by specifying general characteristics about the operation and IOCS causes the necessary detailed instructions to be generated.

Iteration. A set of instructions in a program which are repeated until certain conditions are satisfied; may contain modifications to instructions within the iteration between successive repetitions.

Jargon. A technical vocabulary peculiar to data processing.

JCL (job control language). A set of job control statements that contains job-to-job-transition information needed by the operation system in stacked-job processing.

Job. A total processing application that involves execution of one or more programs required to complete the application.

K (kilo). Refers to approximate storage capacity in thousands. Although K = 1024 positions of memory, a 1K, 8K, or 64K computer would be said to contain a capacity of 1000, 8000, or 64,000 positions, respectively.

Key Field. Data element in a record used to distinguish one record from all others; for example, social security number. Also called *control field.*

Keypunch. Machine with a keyboard similar to a typewriter; used for punching data from source documents onto cards. Sometimes called a *card punch.*

Label. Identification information written in BCD or EBCDIC and appended to the beginning of a tape or disk file by programmed information in order that the program can test whether the correct input file is being used.

Language. The program or communication media between man and machines. People write programs in low- or high-level languages, called "source" programs, which are translated into object programs, the language of the computer.

Location. *See* Address.

Loop. A set of instructions in a routine or program in which the last instruction can cause the previous instructions just executed to be repeated if certain conditions exist.

Low-Level Language. So-called machine-oriented programs because the language written closely parallels the machine language used by the computer in executing programs. *See* High-Level Language.

Low-Order. The units or rightmost position of a storage location or field. Also called *right-justified.*

Machine Language. The vocabulary that engineers have designed into the machine. To simplify communication between man and machine, non-machine programming languages were developed; these are convertible by assembler or compiler programs to a language the machine understands.

Machine Word. See Word.

Magnetic Core. A form of high-speed storage capable of storing one binary bit. The core is magnetized in one direction or the other; thus the binary 1 or 0 representation.

Magnetic-Core Plane. Screen strung with several thousand magnetic cores. A stack of planes comprises a storage unit or module in which each column of cores represents a storage location that can store a BCD or EBCDIC character.

Magnetic Disk. An auxiliary memory device for mass storage, consisting of a stack of disks. On each disk surface the data is recorded in binary, BCD, or EBCDIC on tracks similar to a phonograph record, permitting random access processing.

Magnetic Tape. A reel of tape, usually a half-inch wide and 2400 feet long, on which several hundred characters are recorded per inch in the form of seven or nine binary bits. Two characteristics of tape are compact storage and fast reading or writing capability.

Mainframe. See CPU (Central Processing Unit).

Major. The most important field or total. *See* Minor and Intermediate.

Mark Sense. Refers to data handwritten on specially designed cards or documents which can be automatically converted to punches, other input media, or read directly into the computer memory for processing.

Master File. A collection of semipermanent data that is used time after time in preparation of reports, checks, invoices, and so forth.

Matching. Operation of examining two or more fields to see if there are corresponding records or a group of records.

Memory. See Storage.

Merging. Filing or combining two files into a single file. Certain records can be omitted during the same operation.

Microsecond. One millionth of a second; 0.000001 second; abbreviated as μs.

Millisecond. One thousandth of a second; 0.001 second; abbreviated as ms.

Miniaturized Circuits. Microscopic circuits used in third-generation computers; designed to reduce the distance that electronic impulses have to flow.

Minicomputer. A class of small computer that ranges in price from $5,000 to $60,000.

Minor. The least important field or total. *See* Intermediate and Major.

MIS (management information system). Business data transformed into meaningful information to enable management at all levels to control the firm's activities. Needed information that reflects progress, or lack of progress, made in achieving company goals and which aids in making operating decisions.

Mnemonic Operation Code. That part of an instruction designating the operation to be performed, which is written in an easy-to-remember symbolic notation. For example, the mnemonic operation code of A is much easier to remember than the absolute operation code of 5A, which the computer recognizes for the ADD operation.

Monolithic Storage. Microscopic transistors, a likely replacement of internal core storage.

Multiprogramming. The process of executing concurrently two or more programs that reside in memory at the same time.

Nanosecond. One-billionth of a second; 0.000000001 sec. Abbreviated ns.

Numeric Characters. A set of symbols arranged to express the decimal digits 0 to 9, and which are designed for communication between people and machines and which are intelligible to both.

Object Program. A machine-language program ready for execution by the computer.

Octal. A numbering system with a base of 8.

Off Line. Processing operations performed by auxiliary machines that operate independent of the main computer. Used mainly to relieve the main computer of slow input and output operations. Also refers to equipment; for example, a slave computer or communications machines operate off line from the main computer in a supporting role.

On Line. The updating of business data files as transactions occur, as opposed to batch processing in which transactions are accumulated and files are updated periodically. Processing operations performed by various machines under direct control of the primary computer. Commonly used to describe random-access processing. Equipment attached to the computer or files that are directly accessible by the computer are said to be "on line."

Operand. See Address.

Operating System. A set of special software programs that are designed to increase computer efficiency and relieve the programmer and computer operator of certain tasks.

Operation Code. That portion of an instruction designating the operation to be performed.

Optical Character Recognition (OCR) Machines. Means of reading source documents having magnetized characters directly into the computer without transcribing the data into other forms of input media.

Optical Mark Reader. A machine that reads special pencil marks, thereby permitting bypassing keying of input data.

Overlapped Processing. Ability to input, process, and output data concurrently by turning I/O operations over to the channel and controller units while the central processor returns to handle other records awaiting processing.

Packed. Storing two numbers in the basic unit of storage, the byte. Converse of *unpacked,* where only one number is stored in each byte.

Parity Check. A system in which the total number of binary "1" bits in a character determines its accuracy. Accuracy can be checked by either odd parity or even parity, depending upon the hardware design of the computer.

Partition. A subdivision of main storage set aside for each program residing in the computer memory.

Printing. See Detail Printing and Group Printing.

Procedure. Written narrative instruction, usually accompanied by flowcharts, giving step-by-step directions how a job is processed on the computer.

Process-Bound. The speed at which the computer executes the program is limited by the speed of the central processor; for example, the amount of processing and calculating is greater than input or output time.

Processing. The handling of data from the point where source documents are converted to input media to the point where the final product is completed. This includes reading and storing of data, handling that data by checking for accuracy, and classifying it in preparation for calculation, performing decision-making operations, and summarizing the results for recording as output in such forms as bank statements. *See* Batch, Random, Real-time, Off Line, and On Line.

Program. A series of steps in the form of instructions that are arranged and automatically executed in a prescribed sequence to accomplish reading and storing of data, calculating, and decision-making operations necessary to give the desired results, and providing the solution in the desired format.

Program Listing. A printout of the source program written by the programmer, including (if the translator performs this task) the machine language resulting from assembling or compiling.

Programmer. A person who defines and solves a problem, draws a flowchart of the solution, and writes a program from the flowchart. In larger installations, the problem solving and drawing of systems flowcharts is done by a *systems analyst.*

Punched Card. A card, usually consisting of 80 vertical columns, used to record data by punching characters in each column. The input data then can be read and processed by other machines.

Punched-Card Data Processing System. A set of conventional machines consisting of sorters, interpreters, collators, reproducers, calculators, and accounting machines.

Random Access. Refers to accessing data in a nonsequential manner as opposed to sequential processing required by card and tape operations. Data files randomly accessed are stored on disk, drum, or data-cell storage devices.

Random Processing. Processing transactions without regard to the sequence of the data. Because of the way direct-access devices are designed, one record is available as quickly as another; thus, it is suitable for applications where files must be updated as transactions occur. *See* On-Line and Real-Time Processing.

Real-Time Processing. Immediate processing of current data in time to use the results while the action is still going on and in time to influence the final outcome. For example, an airline reservation is processed fast enough to confirm the ticket while the customer waits, rather than notifying him later. Generally, input data or inquiries are received via data terminals, such as the CRT, processed by the computer, and the results are returned to the user the same way as received.

Record. A group of characters and fields relative to a specific item that is processed as a unit.

Record Density. The number of bytes that are written per inch on magnetic tape.

Register. A hardware component of the central processor used to temporarily store and act upon data or instructions.

Reproducer. A machine capable of punching data from an original deck of cards onto a new deck of cards.

Routine. A set of instructions that solve a problem when executed in sequence by the computer. A program is often referred to as a "routine." *See also* Subroutine.

RPG (report program generator). A relatively easy-to-learn programming language in which specifications of the job are coded on special forms, keypunched, and the computer generates a program that will process the data as desired. Used for simple jobs, generally speaking.

Sequential Processing. Accumulating transactions or documents and sorting them into a predetermined sequence before processing. Converse of random processing.

Simulation. A trial-and-error approach in order to determine what happens to business conditions when certain elements are provided. For example, the reorder level is determined by simulating inventory amounts, consumption, and shipping time for restockage.

Software. Programs associated with a computer, such as assemblers, compilers, and certain subroutines, including programs such as card-to-tape utility. Although all programs are classified as software, the term is usually reserved for those provided by the manufacturer, and user written programs are called "application programs."

Software House. A firm that specializes in writing programs for others, especially computer performance software such as programs that efficiently update data-base files.

Solid State. Refers to computer circuitry, such as semiconductor devices like transistors, made of solid materials that replace the vacuum tube, and mounted on circuit boards with resistors and diodes. Gives higher reliability and lower power consumption than vacuum tubes.

Sorting. The function of arranging records into numeric, alphabetic, or alphameric sequence, either ascending or descending.

Source Program. A program written in a nonmachine language that must be converted to machine language by a compiler or assembler before execution by the computer.

Stacked-Job Processing. The termination of one job and automatic starting of the next job without human intervention. *See* JCL (Job Control Language) and Operating System.

Statistical Machine. A sophisticated sorter that compiles facts and prints or punches the derived statistics. Also called a "card proving" machine because of its editing capability.

Storage. A device such as magnetic core or magnetic disk in which information can be kept for current or later use. Internal storage holds the operating system, the program being executed, and the data being processed. External storage can be on-line, as is the case of disk, or off-line, as is the case of data stored on punched cards or magnetic tape not available to the computer.

Stored Program. A program executed from instructions stored inside the computer.

Subroutine. Part of a program consisting of a set of instructions that deviates from the main program to accomplish alternate processing. Usually, a subroutine is used repetitively to solve part of a problem and is programmed so that it can be repeated as often as necessary, with program control being returned to the main routine after the last instruction in the subroutine is executed.

Summarize. Accumulating totals along with identifying information from a group of records in order to reflect a single record.

Supercomputer. A mammoth computer that acts similar to many small computers functioning together. Such supercomputers as the ILLIAC IV and STAR process instructions measured in millions per second.

Supervisor. Part of the operating system that supervises the overall computer system by handling the switching of control between programs during multiprogramming, handling input or output interrupts, and so forth.

System. A family of applications or subsystems. An accounting system is made up of subsystems such as accounts receivables, accounts payable, and so on. Also an assembly of people, machines, procedures, and methods by which a business is run.

System, Computer. A group of machines united to process the requirements of a business.

Systems Analyst. A person who translates business problems into data processing solutions, skilled in initiating or improving machine solutions to problems.

Table. A collection of values such as interest or tax data in the form of a matrix consisting of rows and columns. Data elements are found and retrieved by their relative positions within the table; for example, row 4 and column 2. A simple table would, for instance, consist of purchase price (row) and the corresponding sales tax (column). As an example, row 4, column 2 might identify $0.06 sales tax for a $1.00 purchase.

Telecommunication. See Data Communication.

Test Data. Dummy transaction data prepared according to specifications written in the program and requirements in the documentation. Also, test data can be created by selecting representative data from existing files, or entire files may be used to test the program (called live test data).

Testing. Attempting to get a program to work using all types of input data or, once working, trying to get the program to fail under given conditions to prevent unexpected failures during the production cycle.

Throughput. The time taken to enter input data into the computer, process the data, and record the results on the output device.

Timesharing. A method of using a computer system that allows a number of users to share execution of programs concurrently by entering or receiving data via data terminals, such as a Teletype. The term often refers to the rental of spare time from other users.

Unit Record. *See* Punched Card.

Variable Word Length. Refers to a computer in which the number of characters or storage positions comprising a machine word is set by the programmer in the program.

Verifier. A machine similar to a keypunch which verifies the data previously punched into cards.

Virtual Storage. A technique that allows programs and data not needed at a particular instant to be retained on external direct-access storage devices until necessary; it thereby permits running programs larger than the actual size of internal memory.

Voice Communication. A means of transmitting or getting up-to-date information to and from the computer by a portable audio terminal connected to the computer via the common telephone.

Wired Program. A set of step-by-step instructions provided to (usually) unit record machines by a wired control panel.

Word. A predetermined set of characters that occupies one area of storage and is treated by the computer as a unit. Word lengths may be fixed, variable, or a combination of both.

Zero Suppression. Eliminating unwanted zeroes in a numerical field, such as left-justified zeroes (that is, leading zeroes to the left of the first digit 1 to 9).

Zone. One of the three top punching rows in a card: 0, 11, 12 punches. Also, zone bits that comprise a letter or special character on tape, disk, and other magnetic storage devices.

BIBLIOGRAPHY

History of Computers and Data Processing Machines

Goldstine, Herman H., *The Computer from Pascal to Von Neumann,* Princeton University Press, 1972.

Introduction to Data Processing

Awad, Elias M., *Business Data Processing,* Prentice-Hall, Inc., 1971.

Davis, Gordon B., *Computer Data Processing,* McGraw-Hill Book Company, 1969.

Feingold, Carl, *Introduction to Data Processing,* William C. Brown Company, Publishers, 1971.

Murach, Mike, *Principles of Business Data Processing,* Science Research Associates, Inc., 1970.

Price, Wilson T., *Introduction to Data Processing,* Rinehart Press, 1972.

Sanders, Donald H., *Computers in Business,* McGraw-Hill Book Company, 1972.

Assembly Language Programming

Chapin, Ned, *360/370 Programming in Assembly Language,* McGraw-Hill Book Company, 1973.

Colbert, Douglas A., *Data Processing Concepts,* McGraw-Hill Book Company, 1968.

Laurie, Ed., *Modern Computer Concepts,* South-Western Publishing Company, 1970.

High-Level Language Programming

Murach, Mike, *Standard COBOL,* Science Research Associates, Inc., 1971.
Stern, Nancy B., and Robert A., *COBOL Programming,* John Wiley & Sons, Inc., 1970.

Flowcharting

Bohl, Marilyn, *Flowcharting Techniques,* Science Research Associates, Inc., 1971.

Job Control Language

Shelly, Gary B., and Cashman, Thomas J., *OS Job Control Language,* Anaheim Publishing Co., 1972.
Shelly, Gary B., and Cashman, Thomas J., *DOS Job Control for COBOL Programmers,* Anaheim Publishing Co., 1971.

Punched Card Data Processing

Colbert, Douglas A., *Data Processing Concepts,* McGraw-Hill Book Company, 1968.

Periodicals

Computer Decisions, Hayden Publishing Co.
Data Management, Data Processing Management Association
Datamation, Technical Publishing Co.
Infosystems, Hitchcock Publishing Co.

INDEX

Abacus 14
Access time 103, 225
Address 105, 108, 176, 219
Aiken, Howard H. 13, 15, 17, 19, 24
Airlines reservations 7–8, 34, 249, 323
ALC 159–160, 321
Alphabetical data: *see* Data, alphabetic
ANSI 151
Analog computer 132–133
ANSCII 117
Arithmetic-logic unit 138–140, 180–181
Application 75
    see also Computer uses
Assembler language 159–160, 321
Auxiliary storage 144–146
Arithmetic operation 38, 99–101, 107, 144,
    183–184
Array 114
ASCII 117
Audio terminal: *see* Voice communication
Automation 380–382
Babbage, Charles 14
Batch processing 52–53, 205, 213
Batch total 398
BCD 95–97
    representation of alphabetic data 113
    representation of numeric data 112
    stored in memory 112
    stored on tape 195
    see also EBCDIC

Billings, John S. 15
Binary 23, 91–93
    arithmetic 99–101
    storage of 116–117
Bit 111, 194
    numeric 120, 194
    stored in memory 109–111, 361
    stored on disk 216, 221
    stored on tape 194–196
    zone 120, 194
    see also Byte
Blocked data
    advantages 199
    illustrated on disk 218
    illustrated on tape 194, 196–199
    see also Record, Physical and logical
BPI 193
Buffer
    hardware 82, 223–228, 249
    programmed 198, 226, 274, 275–276, 325
Bug 168
Burks, A. W. 24
Byte 116–117
    see also Bit; Data, Numeric; Data, Alpha-
        betic
Calculation 38, 99–101, 107, 144, 183–184
Card column 73
Card reader 27, 131, 145
Centralization 57, 277, 296–300, 373
Central processor 137, 138

415

Channels 136–137, 144, 201, 227, 266, 324, 364
Character 76, 193
Checkless society 376–380
COBOL 157, 159, 161, 320–321
Coding 36, 83–85, 164
Communication 42, 67, 95–97, 141, 149–150, 157, 385, 389
Compile 164, 325
Computer
    accuracy 6, 132, 133, 149, 194, 196, 285
    aid or hinderance 300–301
    architecture 27–28, 136–137, 364
    architecture in future 28–29, 363–368
    business need 2–4, 31
    centralization 57, 277, 296–300, 373
    communication with 67, 95–97, 141, 149–150, 157
    components 136–137, 364
    criticism 285, 374–376
    cycle 326
    electronic brain 42
    history 13–29
    master 59–60, 207
    milestones 18
    off-line 59–60, 207–208
    on-line 59–60, 207–208, 248
    optimization 215, 222, 226, 323, 324, 325
    performance 28, 134, 138, 200–201, 221–228, 236–237, 258, 262
    scientific need 4–8, 31
    slave 59–60, 207
    system 137
    see also Computer classification; Computer hardware; Computer models; Computer operator; Computer speed; Computer system; Programmer; and under Management concern
Computer circuits
    electromechanical 17, 132, 137
    electronic 20–22, 132
    electronic signal 67–68
    integrated 27–28, 232
    LSI 28
    MOSFET 232
    transitor 17, 25, 28, 231
    tube 24, 25, 231
Computer classifications
    analog 132–133
    business 135, 327
    digital 133
    first generation 24–25, 270, 327
    general-purpose 17, 21, 135
    minicomputer 370–373
    scientific 28–29, 135, 327

    second-generation 25–26, 95, 231, 236, 270, 327
    special purpose 17, 133–134
    supercomputer 363–368
    third-generation 26–27, 95, 205, 231–232, 302, 327, 363
Computer cost: see under Management concern (cost considerations)
Computer hardware 136, 141
    arithmetic-logic unit 138–140, 180–181
    central processor 137, 138
    channel 227, 266, 324
    channel block multiplexer 201
    channel function 144, 201
    channel multiplexer 201
    channel selector 201
    computer components 136–137, 364
    control unit, function 140, 144, 174
    control unit, operation 143, 176
    controller 203–205, 227
    I/O bound 138, 189, 226, 265
    interaction with software 142–144
    malfunction 115
    peripheral devices 201
    process bound 265
    —DASD
    data cell 239–241
    defined 211
    drum 237–239
    —Input-output
    card reader 27, 131, 145
    conversion 59
    CRT 41, 249
    console typewriter or CRT 27, 98
    MICR 67, 69
    on-line I/O devices 248
    paper tape 15, 22, 67
    printer 27, 131, 145
    types of 137–139
    visual display 249–251
    see also Computer; Computer circuits; Punched-card machines; Storage
Computer installation 163
    access to 353–354
    backup agreement 344, 361, 362
    centralized 57, 277, 296–300
    decentralized 297–298
    organization 297, 298
    protection 351–354
    threat to 350–351
    see also Data processing
Computer manager: see Data processing manager
Computer-management relationship 287–293
Computer maintenance 301–303

Computer manufacturers
  Burroughs 27, 29, 163, 221–222, 258, 369
  CDC 27, 28, 163, 258
  Honneywell 27, 163, 258
  IBM 17, 25, 163, 221–222, 258
  NCR 27, 163, 222, 258
  UNIVAC 17, 25, 27, 163, 222, 258
Computer models 18
  ABC 21, 22, 89
  analytical engine 14
  Atlas 369
  Burroughs series 218, 265, 232, 366–367, 369
  CDC 6600 28, 363, 367
  CDC 3000 series 105, 264, 325–326
  CDC 7600 28, 363, 367
  Complex calculator 19
  Difference engine 14
  EDSAC 22, 89
  EDVAC 23, 89
  ENIAC 6, 20–22, 325
  IBM S/360 26–28, 98, 106, 232, 265, 325–327, 363, 364, 369
  IBM S/370 26–28, 106, 137, 203, 212, 232, 264, 265, 325–327, 369
  IBM 700 Series 25, 109
  IBM 1400 series 25, 105, 363
  IBM 7000 Series 25–26, 105, 257, 327
  IBM S/3 371–372
  IAS 29
  ILLIAC 7, 29, 363–368
  Mark I 15, 17, 19–20, 22, 325
  Mohawk 2400 60
  SSEC 23
  UNIVAC I 22–23, 25, 129
  UNIVAC II 29
  UNIVAC 9700 27
  Whirlwind I 108
  Zuze 17–19
Computer numbering systems: *see* Numbering systems
Computer operator
  duties 200, 259, 271, 274, 361
  loyalty 361
  O/S aid 259, 268–270
Computer pioneers
  Aiken, Howard 13, 15, 17, 19, 24
  Atasanoff 22, 24
  Babbage, Charles 14
  Billings, John S. 15
  Burks, A.W. 24
  Bush, Vannevar 132
  Eckert, J. Presper 21–22, 24
  Forrester, Jaw W. 109
  Goldstine, H. H. 24
  Hollerith, Herman 15, 16, 73

  Jacquard, Joseph Marie 14
  Leibnitz, Gottfried 14
  Mauchly, John W. 21–22, 24
  Pascal, Blaise 14
  Powers, James 15, 17
  von Neumann, John 24, 29, 89, 92
  Stibitz, George R. 17
  Zuze, Konrad 19
Computer speed
  access time 103, 225
  comparisons 26, 28, 104, 133, 224, 325–327, 363–364
  compute 104, 326
  considerations 326–327
  CPU 104, 326
  data entry 79
  determinant 200–201, 219–221, 322–328
  illustration 5, 28, 232, 264
  magnetic disk 216, 219–222, 224, 225
  magnetic tape 189, 191, 193
  microsecond 26
  nanosecond 27, 99
  processing 104, 107
  transfer rates 190–191, 201, 203, 224, 227
Computer system 103, 131–132, 136
Computer uses
  airlines reservations 7–8, 34, 249, 323
  banking 32, 68–69, 249, 300
  billing 33, 42–44
  car repairs 8
  census bureau 15
  child abuse detection 8
  colleges 32, 243
  credit 249, 252, 378
  engineering 6
  gas stations 69–71
  highway traffic 8
  hospitals 249
  insurance 249
  invoice preparation 44–49
  inventory 38–39, 48, 146, 215–216, 243, 309, 378
  law enforcement 249
  mankind 7
  manufacturing 249
  merchandising 32, 377–380
  military 5, 19, 20, 23
  motel reservations 249
  payroll 378
  prediction 25
  purchase order 42–44
  research 7
  retailing 245, 249
  scheduling 61
  scientific problem solving 5, 6

space achievements 5, 133–134
stock exchange 249
transit system 7, 8
weather forecasting 367
Computers and society
checkless society 376–380
data banks 374–376
invasion of privacy 374–376
Consistency check 400
Control punch 74, 77
Control unit 140, 143, 144, 174, 176
Controller 203–205, 227
Conversion of data 27, 34, 59–60, 80, 207–
  208
Conversion of numbers 92, 98–99
Cost considerations: see under Management
  concern
CPU 137, 138
Cross referencing 48–49, 85, 343
CRT 41, 249
Cylinder 218, 223
DASD:—DASD
Data 31–33, 76, 135, 150
backup 358–360
coding 36, 83–85
collection 34
consistency check 400
constant 180
conversion 27, 34, 59–60, 80, 207–208
creation of test 312–315
editing 35–36, 347–349
element 47
hierarchy 77
levels of importance 42
maintenance 36
manipulation 36–37, 180
movement 36–37, 107
organization 75, 77
packed 117
program testing using 312–315
recording 34
retrieval 34–35
security 343, 346
sorting 36
source 31–32, 75, 374
storage 34–35, 67–68
stored in tables 47, 221
summarization 38–40
symbols 67–68
test 314–315, 347–349, 356–358
see also Blocked data; Data communication; Information
Data, Alphabetic
stored in cards 74
stored in memory 113–114, 120, 122
stored on tape 195

Data, Numeric
computing 38
packed 117, 119, 121
stored in cards 74
stored in memory 114, 118
stored on tape 195
unpacked 120
Data bank 374–376
Data base 338
advantages 8–9, 343, 375
concept 338–340
disadvantages 343, 376
society, implications to 374–376
Data cell 239–241
Data communication 57, 245, 299
Data entry
controls 360
cost considerations 65–66, 81, 85–86, 240
direct entry 240–245
key to card 15, 72
key to disk 82–83
key to tape 79–82
problems 68–71, 245
steps 34
see also Data communication; Optical
  Character reader; Optical mark reader
Data management 262
Data processing
bottleneck 68
centralization 57, 277, 296–300, 373
commercial 327
controls 236, 306, 360
customers 385
decentralization 297–298
defined 2, 3, 31
functions 385
history 13–29
misconceptions 42, 285
need for 2–4, 31–32, 132, 135, 249, 377–
  380, 381
responsibilities 385
see also Computer installation; Management concern
Data processing manager
awareness of business 293, 294
controlling 236, 258, 304, 306, 355–360,
  369–370
coordinating 388–389, 391–392
higher management 330
motivating professionals 392–393
organization hierarchy 330–332
responsibilities 334, 390
staff agencies 330–332
staffing 328–329
traits 383–384
see also Management

Data terminal 57, 59, 363–364, 377
Decision making 42, 330, 332
Desk checking 314
Digital computer 133
Disk: *see* Magnetic disk
Document 68
Documentation 79, 303–305
E phase 176
EBCDIC 115–117, 124–125
  relationship to hexadecimal 120–125
  stored in memory 117–118
  stored on tape 195–196
  see also Data, Alphabetic; Data, Numeric
Eckert, J. Presper 21–22, 24
Editing 35–36, 347–349
EDP 3
Electromechanical 17, 132, 137
End of reel 199
Execute 143–144
Facilities management 279
Field 76, 105
  control 77
  key 77, 348
  see also File; Record
File 200, 205–206, 342, 358–360
  control 358, 359
  detail 76, 152
  master 76, 152
  see also Field; Record
Flowchart 151
  development 150–154, 314
  program 151, 156
  program symbols 153
  systems 151, 152
  system symbols 153
  writing the program from a 154–157
FORTRAN 159, 162, 320
General-purpose computer 17, 21, 135
GIGO 184
Goals 286, 306, 316–317, 319, 384
Goldstine, H. H. 24
Hardware: *see* Computer hardware
Hash total 403
Hexadecimal 97
  alphabetic representation 123
  numeric representation 97, 120–125
  relationship to EBCDIC 120–125
High-level language 159–163, 171, 320
Hollerith, Herman 15, 16, 73
IBG 196–197
ILLIAC computer 7, 29, 363–368
Information 31–33
  retrieval 35
  use to management 33, 38, 41, 374–376

Instruction
  address 105, 108, 176, 219; (absolute) 157; (symbolic) 143–144, 159, 169
  branch 180–181
  compare 140, 149–150, 176
  compute 107, 183–184
  defined 143–144, 150
  E phase 176
  execution 140
  format 143–144, 176
  I phase 176
  macro 165
  move 180, 182
  operation code 143–144, 159, 176
  print 184
  read 176, 178
  translation 163–165
  see also Program
Integrated circuit 27–28, 232
Interrupt 263–264, 268, 272–274
Invoice 44–49
I/O: *see* Computer hardware—*Input-output*
I/O bound 138, 189, 226, 265
IOCS: *see* O/S
I phase 176
Inventory 38–39, 48, 146, 215–216, 243, 309, 378
Jacquard, Joseph Marie 14
JCL 270–274
  see also O/S
Job accounting 258, 268
Job control 261–262, 270
Job recovery 259
Job scheduling 258, 267
K 105, 235
Keypunch 72, 164
Keyword 359, 360
Label 200, 262, 358, 359
Languages
  ALC (assembler) 159–160, 321
  choice 322
  COBOL 157, 159, 161, 320–321
  FORTRAN 159, 162, 320
  high-level 159–163, 171, 320
  low-level 165, 320
  machine 157
  RPG 372
Leibnitz, Gottfried 14
Load point 199
Logical record 197, 274
Loop 154, 184
Low-level language 165, 320
LSI 28
Magnetic core storage
  access time 103, 225
  array 114

magnetism 109–111
  plane 109
  see also Parity check; Storage
Magnetic disk
  access time 103, 225
  advantages 213–215
  blocked data 222
  characteristics 218–221
  comparison to magnetic tape 213
  cylinder 218, 223
  disk pack 27, 216–219
  evaluation 213, 224
  examples using 214–216
  read-write head 216, 220, 222
  recording on 216–222
  surface 216
  track 216–218, 220
  see also BCD; Binary; Buffer; EBCDIC;
    Labels; On-line processing; Parity check;
    Random processing; Virtual storage
Magnetic drum 237–239
Magnetic tape
  advantages 190–191
  blocked data 194, 196–199
  BPI 193
  characteristics 193
  comparison to magnetic disk 213
  cost considerations 190–191
  density 193
  end of reel 199
  error detection 194–196
  evaluation of 189–190
  examples using 205–206
  file protection ring 200
  IBG 196–197
  library 192, 359–360
  limitations 191–193
  load point 199
  protection of 350, 352, 358–360
  read-write head 190, 196
  recording on 194, 200
  sequential processing 205–206
  7-channel and 9-channel 194–196
  tape mark 199–200
Management 384
  by exception 308–309
  bypassing line of authority 390–391
  communication 42, 385, 389
  computer effect upon 288
  control of computer facility 236, 304, 355–360, 369–370
  control of reruns 310–312
  controlling 287, 393–395, 306
  coordinating 388–389, 391–392
  directing people and machines 173, 332–335, 389–390

decision making 42, 330, 332
delegation of responsibility 330, 334, 386–387
drawbacks caused by the computer 300–301
education for 286, 319, 320–322
functions 286–287, 385, 386, 388–394
goals 286, 306, 316–317, 319, 384
handling employee dissent 332–334
handling of meetings 395
incompetent 333–335
involvement 187, 286–288, 306–308, 344
knowledge of computer 51, 173, 184–187, 318–319, 345
motivating the professional 333–335
negative approach 285–286
nonparticipation 306, 334
of minicomputers 370–373
organizing 287, 386
planning 286, 384–385
policy making 391, 394–395
relationship to the computer 287–293
responsibility 318, 390, 395–396
span of control 388
support 332–333
traits 383–384
types 333–335
see also Data processing manager; Management concern; Management goals; Middle management; MIS; Organization chart; Top management
Management concern
  business survival 344, 351, 354
  computer facility 173
  computer language, choice of 322
  computer maintenance 301–303
  computer selection 63, 307–308, 325
  computer utilization 307, 323
  customer relations 300–301, 322
  data base design 338–347
  data communications 254
  data entry considerations 65–67, 80, 240–245, 360
  documentation 79, 303–305
  embezzlement 308, 355
  employee loyalty 350, 356
  errors 191, 194, 299, 301, 312–315, 360
  facilities management 279
  lost business 211, 213–214
  new equipment 323–328
  operating systems 142, 258, 327
  processing 41–42, 63, 214
  programming guidelines 313
  promoting professionals 335–337
  reruns 307, 309, 310–312
  safety of the computer 351–354

software 146, 166
technology nuisance 236
testing 169, 312–315
timeliness 49, 246, 300, 301
—Cost Considerations
computer budget 146, 189–190, 287, 310, 316–318
data base 345
data entry 65–66, 81, 85–86, 240
equipment investment 207, 232, 287, 316–317, 381
equipment selection 325
hardware purchase/rental 146, 303, 326
magnetic disk 59, 213
magnetic tape 190–191
minicomputer 370, 373
O/S 144–146, 262 276
processing 51–52, 63, 211, 236–237
program design 315
reruns 310
software 146
storage 213
see also Savings of time and money
Mark I 15, 17, 19–20, 22, 325
Memory: *see* Storage
Microsecond 26
Middle management 288–293, 300
Minicomputer 370–373
MIS 33, 346
Module 356
MOSFET memory 232
Multiprogramming 138, 227
defined 258, 262
example 262–264
storage protection 259
see also Timesharing
Nanosecond 27, 99
Numbering systems
BCD 95–97
binary 91–94, 99–101
decimal 90–91
EBCDIC 115–125
hexadecimal 97–99, 120–125
Numeric data: *see* Data, Numeric
Object program 163–165
Off-line computer 59–60, 207–208
Off-line processing 207, 245
On-line computer 59–60, 207–208, 248
On-line processing 52, 54–55, 213
Operation code 143–144, 159, 176
Operator: *see* Computer operator
Optical character reader 242–243
Optical mark reader 243–245
Optical tape reader 245–246
Organization chart 290, 297, 298

O/S 142, 176
characteristics 258–259
control programs 260–262
data management 262
defined 142, 257
interaction with application program 272–273
interaction with JCL 271–273
interrupt 263–264, 268, 272–274
IOCS 196, 200, (aid to programmer) 262, 274–276
IPL 271–273
job accounting 258, 268
job card 271
job control 261–262, 270
job management 262
job recovery 259
job scheduling 258, 267
levels 260, 369
management concern 258, 325
modularity 259
parts 260
processing programs 260–261
stacked job concept 268–270
storage size 142, 260
supervisor 261, 265–268
task management 261
see also JCL; Multiprogramming
Overlap processing 144, 203–205, 226
Pack 117, 119, 121
Page 233, 369
Paper tape 15, 22, 67
Parity check 23, 115
core storage 115
tape storage 194
Partition 265
Pascal, Blaise 14
Performance 28, 134, 138, 200–201, 221–228, 236–237, 258, 262
Personnel, recruitment 318, 328–329
Physical record 197–198, 274
Plane 109
Polarity 110
POWER 324
Printer 27, 131, 145
Printing
detail 41
group 41
—Illustrations
bank statement 33
forms printing 66, 244
inventory transaction report 39
invoice 45
payroll 155
purchase order 43
sales report 41

shipping order 43
stock status report 40
Problem definition 42, 150–152
Process bound 265
Processing 32
  batch 52–53, 205, 213
  calculation 38, 99–101, 107, 144, 183–184
  considerations 53, 55
  editing 35–36
  management concern 41–42
  methods 213
  off-line 207, 245
  OLRT 52, 55–58
  on-line 52, 54–55, 213
  overlap 144, 203–205, 226
  random 52, 54–55, 216–217
  random versus batch 57
  real time 34, 55–58, 214, 322–323
  recovery 358–360
  reruns 310–312
  sequential 52, 54, 192, 205–206, 237
  sorting 36–37, 42, 141, 205
  steps 33–41
  tables 47, 221
  see also Computer Uses; Printing
Program
  application 141
  assembly 158, 165
  assembly versus compiling 165
  blowup 312–313
  bug 168
  coding 164
  compile 164, 325
  control changes 356–357
  debugging 249, 314, 347
  defined 104–105, 150
  desk checking 314
  execution described 143–144
  execution illustrated 174–184
  interaction with O/S 262–264
  listing 160–162, 164, 167–168
  loading 176
  loop 154, 184
  module 356
  object 163–165
  relocatability 258–259
  security 308, 354–360
  source 163
  stored 22, 24, 141
  systems 141
  testing 169, 312–315
  see also Instruction; Languages; O/S; Pro-
    gramming; Software
Programming
  coding 304
  CPM 61–62

defined 150
desk checking 314
linear 60
PERT 61
simulation 63, 289
unforeseen problems 315, 343
see also Flowchart; Languages; Program
Programmer
  application 260
  debugging 249, 314, 347
  desk checking 314
  documentation 304
  embezzlement by 308, 355
  incompetence/errors 194–195, 285, 312,
    347, 348, 369–370
  IOCS aid 274, 276
  logic errors 140, 169, 348
  management 335–337
  motivation 392–393
  O/S 257, 259, 274
  promotion 335–337
  responsibilities 141–142, 312–315
  rotation 324, 356, 361
  systems 260, 321
  training 324
  virtual storage 233
Punched card
  control punch 74, 77
  how to read 73
  96-column card 372–373
  unit record 73
  see also Data entry
Punched-card machines 17, 24, 129–131
  support of computers 130
Random processing 52, 54–55, 216–217
Read-write head 190, 196, 216, 220, 222
Real-time processing 34, 55–58, 214, 322–
  323
Record 76–77
  blocked 194, 196–199, 218
  control character 77
  logical 197, 274
  master 74, 205
  physical 197–198, 274
  transaction 75, 152, 205
RPG 372
Savings of time and money 2–4, 16, 19, 22,
  61, 81, 191, 276, 307
Self-checking number 46
Sequential processing 52, 54, 192, 205–206,
  237
Simulation 63, 289
Society and computers: *see* Computers and
  society
Software 141, 260
  interaction with hardware 142–144

packages 340
POWER 324
Sorting 36–37, 42, 141, 205
Source data 31–32, 75, 374
Source program 163
Space achievements 5, 133–134
Special-purpose computer 17, 133–134
Speed: *see* Computer speed
Storage protection 259, 265
Stored program 22, 24, 141
Subsystem 75
Supervisor 261, 265–268
System 75
  see also Computer system; MIS
Systems programmer 260, 321
Storage 109–111
  address 105, 108, 143–144, 157, 159, 169,
    176, 219
  auxiliary 144–146
  buffer hardware 82, 223–228, 249
  buffer programmed 198, 226, 274, 275–
    276, 325
  core 108–126
  external 103, 213
  internal 103–105, 138, 213
  I/O area 104, 105, 198, 325
  memory-to-memory 183
  partition 265
  protection 259, 265
  read-in and read-out 115, 180, 183, 193,
    200
  selection 138, 254
  word, fixed 105
  word, variable 105–107
  working storage 104, 105
—*Capacity*
  CPU 138, 218, 363, 366
  data cell 239–240, 345
  disk 218, 224, 364
  drum 237–239
  tape 191, 193

  see also Computer circuits; Magnetic core
    storage
Systems analysis and design
  incomplete results 304
  management concern 287, 288, 292–293,
    306, 324, 344
  proposals 294–295, 385
  unforeseen problems 315, 343
Systems analyst 381
Table 47, 221
Tape: *see* Magnetic tape; Paper tape
Tape mark 199–200
Task management 261
Teleprocessing: *see* Data communication
Terminal 57, 59, 363–364, 377
Test data 314–315, 347–349, 356–358
Throughput 137, 190
  increase 196, 203, 221–228, 257
  optimization 222, 307, 324–325
Timesharing 277–279
  see also Multiprogramming
Top management 289, 293
Track 216–218, 220
Transistor 17, 25, 28, 231
Unit record 73
UNIVAC 17, 25, 27, 163, 222, 258
Virtual storage 233–236, 369
  concern to management 236
  evaluation 236, 369–370
  page 233, 369
Visual display 249–251
Voice communication 251, 253
Weather forecasting 367
Word 105–107
Working storage 104, 105
Zone
  memory 113, 116, 120
  punched card 73, 74
  tape 195
Zuze, Konrad 19